D0944902

DISCARDED
JENKS LRC
GORDON COLLEGE

BOLD ENDEAVORS

BOLD ENDEAVORS

Lessons from Polar and Space Exploration

JACK STUSTER

JENKS L.R.C.
GORDON COLLEGE
255 GRAPEVINE RD.
WENHAM, MA 01984-1895

Naval Institute Press
Annapolis, Maryland

Q
180.55
.P75
S78
1996

© 1996 by Jack Stuster

All rights reserved. No part of this book may be reproduced without written permission from the publisher.

Library of Congress Cataloging-in-Publication Data

Stuster, Jack, 1947–
    Bold endeavors : lessons from polar and space exploration / Jack Stuster.
        p.   cm.
    Includes bibliographical references (p.   ) and index.
    ISBN 1-55750-749-X (alk. paper)
    1. Research —Psychological aspects. 2. Space flight—Psychological aspects. 3. Antarctica—Research—Psychological aspects. 4. Social isolation—Psychological aspects. I. Title.
Q180.55.P75S78 1996
155.9'6—dc20   96-8131

Printed in the United States of America on acid-free paper ⊗

03 02 01 00 99 98 97 96   9   8   7   6   5   4   3   2

First printing

CONTENTS

ILLUSTRATIONS

TABLES

PREFACE

The purpose of this book is to present recommendations to facilitate human adjustment and performance within isolated and confined environments. The recommendations focus on the design of spacecraft and space habitats and on the operation of long-duration space expeditions, but they also apply to shorter missions and to a variety of Earth-bound conditions. The research documented in these pages involves the study of conditions on Earth that are comparable in important ways to what might be reasonably expected for future long-duration space missions. The approach is a continuation of my previous study concerning space-station design and operation (Stuster 1986). The research approach derives from the understanding that valuable lessons can be learned about human behavior in space by studying groups living and working in isolated and confined conditions on Earth, both currently and in the past.[1]

Although the recommendations and habitability principles presented here can be particularly useful to spacecraft designers and planners of future space expeditions, they are relevant to a broad range of other pursuits. The most obvious of these are the design and operation of Earth-bound remote-duty environments. Indeed, recommendations from the earlier space station study have been incorporated into the designs of underwater habitats, remote-duty military systems, and command and control centers intended for long-term autonomous operation. Ironically, some of my recommendations for space stations were also adopted at small Antarctic facilities that were among my sources of inspiration for the recommendations. The habitability recommendations presented in this book are likewise applicable to the operation of future special habitats, but they are not limited to remote duty or even to isolated and confined living. Rather, these recommendations and behavioral principles can apply to nearly all forms of human relationships, ranging from the relationship between the staff of a corporate or governmental field office and its headquarters personnel to the relationships among members of a sequestered jury or even a family. In a very real sense, we are all crew members onboard a spaceship. Perhaps we might learn how to adapt better to our condition and get along with each other by studying examples of groups that have succeeded and failed in their relationships under circumstances far more difficult than our own. In important ways, studying small groups in isolation and confinement is like viewing society through a microscope. There is much of general value to be learned from this approach.

Three main themes emerge from this study:

1. Attention to behavioral issues is important under conditions of isolation and confinement, but interpersonal and psychological problems are not inevitable if appropriate precautions are taken.
2. Future space expeditions will resemble sea voyages much more than test flights, which have served as the models for all previous space missions.
3. Many lessons can be learned from the experiences of military and scientific remote-duty personnel and from previous explorers that are extremely relevant to the planners of future expeditions and to others, as well.

REASONS FOR STUDYING ISOLATION AND CONFINEMENT

Critics of exploration have always postulated insurmountable obstacles to bold endeavors. Columbus, for example, had great difficulty obtaining funding for his first voyage of discovery, largely because of the popular belief that it was unsafe to sail for many days outside the sight of land.[2] Much later, some people criticized Thomas Jefferson for sponsoring the Lewis and Clark Expedition across North America because they could foresee no possible commercial value resulting from it. Similarly, the polar explorers were attacked for risking their lives and precious resources on impossible expeditions to the Arctic and, later, to the Antarctic. Fridtjof Nansen's response in 1892 to critics of his plans to reach the farthest point north seems strangely appropriate to the present debate regarding the future of space exploration:[3]

> People, perhaps, still exist who believe that it is of no importance to explore the unknown polar regions. This, of course, shows ignorance. It is hardly necessary to mention here of what

scientific importance it is that these regions should be thoroughly explored. The history of the human race is a continual struggle from darkness towards light. It is, therefore, to no purpose to discuss the use of knowledge; man wants to know, and when he ceases to do so, he is no longer man. (Quoted in Cherry-Garrard, 1930, 348)

Nansen's compatriot, Roald Amundsen, was even more blunt two decades later when confronted with a question about the value of Antarctic exploration. Amundsen responded: "Little minds have only room for thoughts of bread and butter." A few years later, Apsley Cherry-Garrard, a member of Robert Falcon Scott's last expedition to Antarctica, produced a book accurately titled *The Worst Journey in the World*. He notes:

It is really not desirable for [those] who do not believe that knowledge is of value for its own sake to take up this kind of life. The question constantly put to us in civilization was and still is: "What is the use? Is there gold? Is there coal?" The commercial spirit of the present day can see no good in pure science. The English manufacturer is not interested in research which will not give him a financial return within one year. The city man sees in it only so much energy wasted on unproductive work.... The members of this expedition believed that it was worth while to discover new land and new life, to reach the South Pole of the Earth, to make elaborate meteorological and magnetic observations and extended geological surveys with all the other branches of research for which we were equipped. They were prepared to suffer great hardship; and some of them died for their beliefs. (Cherry-Garrard, 1930, 226–27)

More recently, awful consequences were predicted for anyone foolish enough to be propelled to a velocity faster than the speed of sound. Chuck Yaeger proved the predictions to be false in 1947; ever since, pilots and passengers have been breaking the sound barrier with no ill effects. Responsible scientists warned the managers of the Mercury Program that humans could not long survive in the absence of gravity; others advised against even brief orbital missions because of the high probability of bizarre behavior resulting from the isolation, confinement, and sensory deprivation that astronauts would experience in a space capsule. These concerns about bizarre behavior had diminished by the time the astronauts of *Apollo 11* reached the moon, and criticism had shifted to questions about the value and the cost of further exploration.

Current plans for an international space station, lunar base, and mission to Mars are receiving the same criticism as that directed toward previous exploration. In particular, some observers believe that humans would have great difficulty enduring the isolation and confinement of long-duration space expeditions, and some predict serious behavioral problems similar to those described by Capt. Brian Shoemaker in the introduction that follows. Others criticize the plans for space exploration with the claim that society receives only minimal returns on the "investment" or that the expenditures are not affordable. These same two arguments, essentially, have confronted explorers and the pioneers of science throughout the ages: (1) something terrible will happen as a consequence of the endeavor and (2) the cost is too high in relation to the benefit that might be received.

Much of the criticism of exploration, including the criticism of space exploration, is a manifestation of the conservative tendencies of culture; that is, it is natural for systems to resist change and for some individuals to expect the worst possible outcome. Some of the criticism, however, is clearly antiscience and antitechnology, although attempts are usually made to cloak it in other terms, such as the relative priority of addressing social problems on Earth. Do the specific arguments against conducting long-duration space missions have merit, or are they merely the current expressions of human tendencies, ancient fears, and modern superstitions?

Many of the individuals quoted in this book testify eloquently about the value of knowledge and a seemingly innate human desire to discover answers to questions, explore new territories, and ultimately expand the range of the species. If a practical reason were required for space exploration, there could be none more compelling than to expand the range of the human species as a means for survival. The comet that struck Jupiter during July 1994 would have obliterated a smaller planet and, accordingly, provides evidence of our extreme vulnerability, limited as we are to a single world. A fundamental biological imperative to survive, rather than a quest for knowledge, might be the factor that best encourages space exploration, but the justification for sponsoring human space exploration is beyond the scope of this book.

The question of whether something terrible will happen, however, is the focus of the guidelines presented in these pages. Are behavioral and interpersonal problems inevitable, or even likely, among the crews of long-duration space expeditions? Or, have these possibilities been overstated, either out of genuine concern or as an expression of some other belief or motivation?

This book provides evidence that humans are fully capable of enduring the isolation and confinement of long-duration space missions and other remote-duty environments when proper preparations have been made. Indeed, many examples of psychological problems, conflict, and disaster attributable to the stresses of isolation and confinement exist; some, described in Part II, can offer a guide for learning from the mistakes of others. The research conducted for this book has uncovered details of many additional examples of highly successful missions and expeditions during which the participants lived and worked under conditions far more arduous and dangerous, and for longer durations, than those to be expected in future space missions. In providing examples of successful expeditions, I suggest that as much or more can be learned from these examples as from the disasters that have been the traditional focus of studies of conditions analogous to future space missions.

ORGANIZATION

This book consists of three parts:

Part I provides a detailed description of the research tasks conducted as part of the study. It also includes a summary of scientific interest in the behavioral issues associated with isolation and confinement and a discussion of the relevance of analogue studies to the design and operation of space systems.

Part II presents the results of the research. The results are organized and discussed in terms of a set of behavioral issues identified in Part I; the discussion of each issue concludes with specific recommendations for the design and operation of space facilities, such as a lunar base and interplanetary spacecraft, pertinent to that particular issue.

Part III discusses some of the implications of the study results and provides a summary of the relevant principles of habitability. Research requirements to answer unresolved questions are also identified in the final chapter.

Sequentially numbered notes cited throughout the text further explain or amplify various points so as to avoid disruption of continuity.

ACKNOWLEDGMENTS

Many debts of gratitude are incurred during research of the type and duration that supported the preparation of this book. I am indebted to so many individuals for the information reported here that I hesitate even to begin to express appreciation. It would be impossible to acknowledge all who contributed to this effort, but I will mention those most responsible. First, the research on which the following pages are based was made possible by the Life Sciences Division of the National Aeronautics and Space Administration (NASA). I am grateful to Drs. Janis Stoklosa and Frank Sulzman of NASA Life Sciences Division for recognizing merit in the suggestion to review relevant examples of previous human performance in isolation and confinement as a means to identify lessons that might be applicable to the design of spacecraft, space habitats, and associated procedures for future long-duration expeditions. I also greatly appreciate the contributions of NASA Contracting Officer's Technical Representative Barbara Woolford at the Johnson Space Center.

Many individuals contributed to this volume by subjecting themselves to open-ended interviews concerning the issues associated with isolation and confinement. I interviewed a wide range of subject-matter experts, including behavioral scientists, psychologists, psychiatrists, physicians, and the crews and managers of remote-duty stations. The individuals whose scientific work contributed most to this research are Dr. Ben Weybrew, the principal submarine psychologist of the nuclear age, and Dr. E. K. Eric Gunderson, whose studies of behavior conducted more than three decades ago at U.S. Antarctic stations are as relevant today as they were then. I personally interviewed many individuals about their experiences with isolation and confinement; I am particularly grateful for the information and observations provided by Drs. Fred Glogower, Sidney Blair, Ker Boyce, and Anthony Sebbio of Operation Deep Freeze; Dr. Claude Bachelard of the French Institute of

Polar Research and Technology; Dr. Desmond Lugg of the Australian Antarctic Division; and Captains Brian Shoemaker and Joe Mazza, commanders of the U.S. Naval Support Force Antarctica, and Master Chief of the Command Arthur Violanti. I am especially grateful to Dr. William K. Douglas, who reviewed the first draft and contributed technical guidance and encouragement, to Terry Belanger for her expert editorial advice, and to Barbara Gates for preparing the manuscript. Finally, I appreciate the patience and indulgence of my family, Joan, Dana, and Juliet, during the months when my thoughts were thousands of miles away.

The information and recommendations contained in this book are the author's and do not necessarily represent the opinions or positions of any organization, company, or government agency. Further, although many individuals have contributed to the book, the author is ultimately responsible for any errors or omissions.

This book is the most recent in a series of efforts to address the behavioral issues that would be confronted by the designers of and participants in future long-duration space expeditions. During the last half of the twentieth century, many thoughtful scientists and engineers have devoted major portions of their careers to the issues addressed in these pages. I have reviewed dozens of books, scholarly papers, and technical reports prepared by individuals who had every reason to assume that the missions about which they wrote and recommended were imminent. But, the pace of space exploration is exceedingly slow; sometimes, it seems unlikely to advance at all. For this reason, this book is dedicated to the countless individuals who have worked on the designs of spacecraft, most of which were never developed, and to those who are currently working on plans in hopeful anticipation of future space expeditions. An optimistic vision of the future is the fuel of exploration.

INTRODUCTION

The outgoing crew experienced the normal feelings of intrusion when the "newcomers" arrived at the remote Antarctic station on the scheduled relief flight. The relief flight also brought mail, supplies, the first fresh fruits and vegetables seen at the facility in months, and a few visitors. There might have been some friction during the few days that the two crews shared the small facility, but that is to be expected when a well-established routine is interrupted. Crews are warned about this reaction, but it happens anyway. If there was an incident, it did not seem to affect the new eight-man crew fresh from the real world. New routines would be established as soon as the old crew and visitors departed.

The new crew functioned smoothly at first during the Antarctic summer. A few months after the sun disappeared, however, the medical corpsman visited the engineering building to borrow a tool from the diesel mechanic, but the mechanic was not at his station. This was extremely unusual because the diesel-powered generator was the sole source of energy for the entire facility. It was a critical system; a failure could be catastrophic because the station could not be resupplied or evacuated for several more months. The corpsman searched for the mechanic and found him nearly catatonic, curled up in a fetal position in his bunk. The corpsman had sufficient training to recognize the seriousness of the condition, and he spent many hours applying all of his technical knowledge and personal skills in an attempt to bring the man out of his depression. He told him that he was important to the crew, that he was a key component in the system, and that the others could

---

The introduction is based on information supplied by Capt. Brian Shoemaker, former commander of Naval Support Force Antarctica and now secretary of the American Polar Society, Reedsport, Oregon. Captain Shoemaker has wintered over in both the Arctic and the Antarctic.

not survive the winter without him. The corpsman told the mechanic that he must endure, regardless of how difficult it might be for him. After days of relentless attention by the corpsman, the mechanic reluctantly agreed to return to his duties.

Within a week of the mechanic's return to work, the corpsman noticed that neither of the scientists was in the laboratory during their shifts. He found them drinking heavily and grumbling about the way they had been treated by their employers, who only visited the station for a few days at a time under optimal conditions during the brief summer. How could the principal investigators, located in their comfortable labs thousands of miles away, possibly understand the constraints imposed by the limited equipment at the station or what must be endured to accomplish the work? The scientists were depressed and angry, a dangerous combination. Again, the corpsman worked with the men to bring them from the depths of their despondency and, eventually, to a mental state that permitted them to return to their work.

The cook was next. His precipitous decline was apparent to all members of the winter-over party: an unhappy comment by one of the scientists about the quality of dinner sent him into a fury. Storming out of the galley, he informed all hands that he would cook no more for such an ungrateful group. He isolated himself in his quarters and refused to come out. Only through persistence and sensitivity did the corpsman finally talk him into returning to his duties a few days later. He remained withdrawn and uncommunicative for several weeks, but the corpsman finally convinced him of his important role in the isolated community. The cook gradually regained the motivation to continue, and even his sense of humor returned. The loss of the cook would have been disastrous.

Following the discovery of the initial cases, the corpsman found a similar condition afflicting each member of the crew; the phenomenon developed rapidly during the course of a four-week period. The corpsman worked heroically at first to defuse the deep depressions, and continuously throughout the remaining months of the long, dark winter he attempted to buoy the spirits of his comrades. Visiting all members of the crew each day, he injected them with doses of humor, recognition, and hope. Individual productivity eventually returned to an acceptable level, and nearly all objectives for the winter were ultimately achieved.

The effect of the long winter night on men who were not fully screened for the experience has been suggested as the cause, but to this day it is unknown how the problem started. Maybe it was triggered by unpleasant personal news from home or the absence of an expected communication. Perhaps a tardy response to an administrative matter by distant support personnel or some other perceived slight set the phenomenon in motion. It is well known that trivial issues are magnified out of proportion under conditions of isolation and confinement. Later, for others among the crew, the problem could have resulted from the message that they received from their principal investigator. The message had reminded them of the importance of remaining on schedule so all of the data would be collected by the end of the winter. To the scientists working twelve-hour shifts in a remote station, the message was interpreted in the worst possible manner; they felt rejected and knew they would fail to live up to the high expectations established by others. The cook's decline was clearly linked to the negative attitudes of the others in the group, which he interpreted as a lack of appreciation for his role in the mission.

Whatever the cause or causes, personal problems grew like a malignancy among the small crew. One by one, seven of the eight men were "infected" by the malaise and fell into deep, clinical depressions, resulting in a cascading series of negative consequences to performance, productivity, and interpersonal relations. Oddly, the medical corpsman remained immune and, at first, unaware of the growing despondence among his comrades. Medical personnel often suffer the worst during isolation and confinement because they usually have very little to do in their area of expertise. For this reason, a wise decision had been made to assign the corpsman a series of small construction projects that would occupy him for much of the winter. He was busy and happy with his progress in achieving these interim goals: a set of shelves in the infirmary, a partition in the equipment room, and a new storage shed; the work kept him apart from the others during most of his shift. Fortunately, he discovered the problem before the consequences became fatal to the station.

No one in the outside world was aware of the problem. The commander of Naval Support Force Antarctica discovered the near psychological collapse of the station at the conclusion of the winter when he interviewed the crew. He brought what he had learned to the attention of psychologists who examine winter-over personnel about their experiences. The psychologists were shocked by the interviews and horrified by what might have happened. Each member of the crew related a different story of how the corpsman had saved him during the winter. Without the corpsman's persistent and skillful intervention, each believed that he would not have survived.

ABBREVIATIONS

CRM	crew (cockpit) resource management
ESA	European Space Agency
EVA	extravehicular activity
IBEA	International Biomedical Expedition to the Antarctic
IES	Illuminating Engineering Society
IGY	International Geophysical Year
MARS	Military Affiliate Radio System
MMPI	Minnesota Multiphasic Personality Inventory
MWR	morale, welfare, and recreation
NASA	National Aeronautics and Space Administration
NHRC	Naval Health Research Center
NISARP	NASA–International Space Analogue Research Program
NRC	National Research Council
NSF	National Science Foundation
NUTEC	Norwegian Underwater Technology Center
OIC	officer in charge
SEAL	Sea-Air-Land (team)
VDT	video display terminal

BOLD ENDEAVORS

PART I

THE RESEARCH

The Earth is the cradle of mankind, but one cannot remain in the cradle forever.

—Konstantin Tsiolkovsky

Every age has its dreams, its symbols of romance. Past generations were moved by the graceful power of the great windjammers, by the distant whistle of locomotives pounding through the night, by the caravans leaving on the Golden Road to Samarkand, by quinqueremes of Nineveh from distant Ophir. . . . Our grandchildren will likewise have their inspiration—among the equatorial stars. They will be able to look up at the night sky and watch the stately procession of the Ports of Earth—the strange new harbors where the ships of space make their planetfalls and their departures.

—Arthur C. Clarke

Inevitably, members of the human species will again walk on the face of the moon and ultimately establish a permanently occupied lunar base. Also, inevitably, humans will venture to the planets within the solar system, most likely beginning with Mars or the martian satel-·lite, Phobos. These missions will take place because the species that contemplates them is driven by an insatiable desire for knowledge and understanding and because the technical means to accomplish these objectives are possible. There is no question that humans will establish outposts on Earth's moon and make interplanetary journeys. The only uncertainties concern *when* and *how* these expeditions are to be made. This book offers specific guidance to those who seek answers to the latter question. Although the recommendations presented here pertain specifically to future space expeditions, most of the recommendations and all of the general principles discussed also apply, in varying degrees, to missions of shorter durations and, in many cases, to the full range of human experiences.

Just as a 90- or 120-day tour onboard an international space station will be fundamentally different from a brief space shuttle mission, a one-year lunar base tour or a two- or three-year mission to Mars will be unique. Despite superficial similarities to other space missions and analogues, the extended durations and astronomical distances involved in lunar and martian missions will make these activities far more difficult and dangerous. Crowded conditions, language and cultural differences, logistics problems, radiation concerns, communications lag times, workloads, and a variety of additional issues will conspire to impair the performance and affect the behavior of long-duration crew personnel. Above all stressors, however, the durations of the missions will impose the greatest burdens and extract the most severe tolls on the humans involved. On long-duration space missions, time will be the factor that can compound all issues, however trivial, into serious problems.

Anecdotal accounts and previous research have indicated that behavioral and performance problems are relatively common among the personnel involved in long-duration isolation and confinement. Although most of the problems reported are relatively minor, the need for optimal human performance and the potential for disaster resulting from behavioral problems on long-duration space missions are too important to relegate to peripheral concerns. How will people adapt to long-duration isolation and confinement? Will they experience psychological disorders or amotivation, and, if so, what might be the effects on others or on the mission? Will there be interpersonal conflict; if there is, how might it be resolved? What are the acceptable minimum standards of privacy, personal space, and food? What kind of social organization and leadership style are best? Essentially, what must be understood are the factors characteristic of long-term isolation and confinement that contribute to the degradation of human performance and impair successful adjustment. If these factors are identified, they can be avoided, mitigated, or, at least, anticipated. If isolation is, as the philosopher Carlyle has described it, "the sum total of wretchedness to man," how can we render it less wretched?

How can these potentially serious, perhaps mission-threatening behavioral issues be identified in advance so that problems can be avoided or mitigated? One approach is to conduct high-fidelity simulations of the proposed missions. That is, a crew composed of personnel similar to those expected on long-duration missions could occupy an Earth-bound spacecraft simulator for one to three years and perform tasks similar to those expected of the actual missions; contact with the "outside world" would be limited to voice and perhaps video communications. During this period, behavioral scientists would closely monitor and study the crew's technical performance and adjustment to the confined and isolated conditions of the simulator.

The first human explorers on Mars, as envisioned by artist Paul Hudson. Undoubtedly, they will experience many of the same problems encountered by explorers of previous eras. The details will differ, but the types of problems will be essentially the same. (Courtesy of Paul Hudson)

Possible modular lunar facility to support the extraction of oxygen from surface material. Living off the land has been a feature of many successful expeditions in the past. (Courtesy of NASA)

Controlled experiments and high-fidelity simulations would provide valuable information for the design of facilities and procedures. Also, they would be extremely useful as components of a personnel selection program if actual mission candidates were to participate as crew, and they would provide valuable training experiences for both crew and mission support personnel. Ultimately, full-mission simulations will be necessary prior to the actual implementation of long-duration space missions. But, at this early stage of program development, there is an approach available that is likely to be instructive and certainly far more cost-effective than a high-fidelity simulation of a long-duration space mission. That approach is the study of Earth-bound conditions that are similar in important ways to proposed lunar and interplanetary missions.

CHAPTER 1

SCIENTIFIC CONCERN ABOUT BEHAVIORAL EFFECTS OF ISOLATION AND CONFINEMENT

Although people have lived and worked under conditions of isolation and confinement for countless generations, only since the 1950s has there been a scientific interest in understanding the problems associated with human adjustment to those conditions.[1] For the most part, this interest can be traced to two events: (1) the recognition that isolation and confinement played integral roles in the "brainwashing" of prisoners of war during the Korean War and (2) the development of a highly disruptive schizophrenia by a member of the team that was sent to Antarctica to prepare for the 1957–58 International Geophysical Year (IGY) program.

SENSORY DEPRIVATION

Interest in brainwashing led to a series of studies during the 1950s that involved individual isolation and sensory deprivation. Work by Hebb, Vernon, Zubek, and other experimental psychologists resulted in limited agreement concerning the effects of perceptual or sensory deprivation. Early studies report a variety of unusual subjective phenomena, such as vivid and highly structured hallucinations, delusions, and gross alterations in perception upon emerging from isolation. In addition to these introspective accounts, objective evidence was obtained that indicated increased susceptibility to persuasion, impairment in cognitive and perceptual functioning, and a progressive slowing of alpha frequencies with increasing duration of isolation and sensory deprivation (Zubek 1973). It was later learned that two persons isolated together, where some social exchange was possible, did not exhibit the serious perceptual distortions characteristic of individual isolation. Apparently, the stimulation provided by just one additional person is sufficient to mitigate most of the perceptual effects of isolation and sensory deprivation.

Sensory deprivation is not considered to be a central concern for long-duration space missions because it is anticipated that they will be conducted by crews composed of at least four individuals; that is, the stimulation provided by interactions with other crew should eliminate concern about sensory deprivation effects under normal operations. Problems could occur, however, if an individual were to become isolated, for example, as a result of equipment failure.

ANTARCTIC RESEARCH STATIONS

The Antarctic incident involved the emergence of psychotically paranoid behavior by a member of the crew sent to Antarctica in 1955 to establish the main U.S. base on the continent. The only psychological intervention possible by on-site medical personnel could not help the individual recover a rational state of mind; he slipped into increasingly disruptive behavior that negatively affected others in the group. A special room, lined with mattresses, was built adjacent to the infirmary to contain the sounds of psychotic ravings and to protect the seriously disturbed comrade. This intervention failed, however, and the individual spent most of the remainder of the winter under sedation.

The incident shocked the managers of the Antarctic program and led to an area of study directly relevant to the problems associated with long-duration space missions. Psychological studies, sponsored by the Navy's Bureau of Medicine and Surgery, were immediately initiated at U.S. Antarctic stations during the IGY. Mullin, Connery, and Wouters (1958), Mullin and Connery (1959), and Mullin (1960) interviewed and tested eighty-five members of wintering-over parties. The researchers found that more than one third of the men experienced "absentmindedness and wandering of attention"; a few individuals reported an extreme degradation of vigilance that is described by Mullin as "mild fugue states" (1960). An individual might remember leaving his quarters but then found himself somewhere else several moments later and wondered how he got there and why he was there. Reports of these mild dissociative states later inspired a program of research concerning hypnotic phenomena (Barabaz 1984).

Also, during the IGY, Rohrer (1961) conducted interviews and made observations concerning individual and group adjustment problems. Smith (1961) and Smith and Jones (1962) evaluated selection procedures for Antarctic scientists, and Smith (1966) studied group structure and social relations during a dangerous seven-man Antarctic traverse of four months' duration. Based on the results of psychological tests, diary observations, and medical records, McGuire and Tolekin (1961) evaluated individual and group adjustment at South Pole Station in 1959. Nardini, Herrmann, and Rasmussen (1962) studied the psychiatric screening program during and immediately following the IGY; they concluded that psychiatric evaluations had been relatively successful in predicting the performance of individuals as determined by leaders' ratings.

Since 1961, E. K. Eric Gunderson of the Naval Health Research Center (NHRC) has conducted the bulk of research involving the behavior and selection of Antarctic personnel. The objectives of Dr. Gunderson's research have been to study the nature and degree of stress experienced in the Antarctic environment, to construct improved selection methods, and to develop effective performance measures. Gunderson studied groups, ranging in size from eight to thirty-six men, composed of approximately 60 percent Navy personnel and 40 percent civilian scientists and technicians. Gunderson found that, although cases of psychosis or severe neurosis were extremely rare at the early Antarctic stations, minor emotional disturbances were very common (Gunderson 1963). He also found a significant decline in morale among the military personnel during the winter but little or no decline among the civilians; he concluded that occupational role can be a factor in adjustment to isolation and confinement (1966a). Perhaps most important, Gunderson identified three behavioral components of effective performance: (1) emotional stability, (2) task motivation, and (3) social compatibility. Earlier, Gunderson and Nelson (1963) had found that the best single measure of effective individual performance was a standard score derived from the choices of peers and supervisors regarding whom they would prefer to have in their groups if they were to return to Antarctica.

Capt. Paul D. Nelson, a Navy social psychologist, focused on the attributes of successful leaders at U.S. Antarctic stations (Nelson 1962, 1964a, 1964c; Nelson and Gunderson 1963a). Nelson found that esteemed leadership was correlated with a relatively democratic approach, in which the leader participated in group activities, developed personal relationships with each member of the group, and sought individual opinions of the members in matters that directly concerned them. Popular leaders were more self-confident and alert, but the characteristics in which they most differed from unpopular leaders were emotional control, adaptability, and the ability and motivation to maintain harmony within the group. The sources of data for the extensive series of NHRC studies were clinical examinations, military records, questionnaires, station leaders' logs and diaries, debriefing interviews, and observations made during site visits.

Later, anthropologist Lawrence Palinkas, working for Eric Gunderson, conducted a longitudinal study, in which he examined the health and service records of more than three hundred enlisted Navy personnel who wintered over at small, isolated Antarctic stations between 1963 and 1974. He found that their winter-over experiences did not place them at any greater risk for first hospitalization subsequent to their return from Antarctic duty than those who applied for Antarctic duty but did not serve. In addition, he observed no significant differences on any of the long-term performance indicators that he reviewed. Further, he found that individuals with high needs for achievement and control over others were likely to experience a reduced risk for long-term disease incidence (Palinkas 1987b). Also, Palinkas (1987a) discusses the relevance of Antarctic stations as models for the human exploration of Mars.

In other research programs, Palmai (1963) studied a small Australian contingent that wintered on Macquarie Island. He reports a decline in morale and increases in interpersonal conflict and psychosomatic complaints. Owens (1966, 1968) studied four winter-over groups of the Australian National Antarctic Research Expedition. He makes the important distinction between living at a permanent station and participating in more dangerous work in the field. He also reports evidence that single men adapted better to the isolation and confinement of Antarctica than their married comrades, who were separated from their wives. A few years later, Desmond Lugg wrote a medical thesis titled *Anatomy of a Group in Antarctica* (1973); his subsequent research concerning Australian Antarctic personnel indicates a relatively low incidence of mental disorders, on the order of 4–5 percent of total morbidity. He reports:

> Many nations and Antarctic operators deny the existence of psychiatric and psychological problems. Some nations do vast batteries of preselection tests; others do nothing. In private discussions with doctors and researchers from a number of nations currently working in Antarctica, the figures given here

that 4 to 5% of the total morbidity is related to mental health probably represent the average findings for groups in Antarctica. With insomnia and other (minor) conditions being included in the classification, it is obvious that severe psychotic and neurotic illness occurs at a frequency much lower than 4%. (Lugg, 1991, 39)

Taylor writes with considerable insight about the New Zealand Antarctic Program (1978, n.d.). He finds no significant differences between baseline and postmission personality measures, despite the subjective reports by personnel (e.g., slowing down, impaired memory, apprehension). Taylor suggests that crews be selected on the basis of optimum compatibility; his notion of selecting crews, rather than individuals, is a good one and predates the introduction of the concept in the field of aviation personnel selection.

In a more recent work, Rivolier and colleagues describe the International Biomedical Expedition to the Antarctic (IBEA), an overland excursion performed during a six-month period in 1980–81. The IBEA was conducted, in part, to demonstrate the relevance of Antarctic conditions to space programs:

> While it is important to ensure that in future development of Antarctica humans are not the weakest link, it is possible to envisage the isolation, uniquely available there, as a model for long term space travel. (Rivolier et al. 1988, xxv)

The authors discuss and explain physiological and psychological responses to expedition conditions, including serious individual and interpersonal problems that occurred among the twelve men from five countries. They report, "Some developed physical problems, others withdrew into themselves and one withdrew from the scene entirely" (Rivolier et al. 1988). Rivolier and Bachelard (1988) elaborate on the similarities between living at an Antarctic scientific base and on a space station. They draw on their IBEA experiences and many years of support to French Antarctic and other remote-duty programs to develop recommendations concerning the design and operation of remote-duty stations, such as space facilities.

OTHER REMOTE DUTY

Several additional conditions characterized by long-duration isolation and confinement, including remote military outposts, submarines, and underwater habitats, have been the objects of behavioral analysis.

For example, Sells (1962) finds that men who adjusted well to remote Arctic military bases were those who also adjusted well to their military assignments elsewhere. Wright and associates (1967) investigated the adjustment to Arctic isolation of nearly two hundred civilian electronic technicians employed by the Bell Telephone Company to staff the radar stations of the Mid-Canada Defense Line. The technicians lived in remote groups of two to eight men each. The authors suggest that the factors differentiating well-adjusted and poorly adjusted groups appear to be relatively independent of Arctic conditions.

The advent of nuclear-powered submarines and their extended endurance capabilities stimulated interest in the behavioral and psychological feasibility of long-duration submerged patrols. In an early study, Weybrew (1957) identifies some of the symptoms of stress resulting from submerged isolation and confinement onboard the USS *Nautilus*: fatigue, dizziness, headaches, muscular tension, and amotivation. In a later study onboard a Polaris-class submarine, Serxner (1968) identifies the primary causes of stress among crewmen during sixty-day submerged patrols. These included the inability to communicate with persons in the outside world, insufficient personal territory, monotony, and concern for the conduct and welfare of family members ashore. Serxner, as well as other investigators since the Polaris study, find depression to be the common mode of adjustment to the confined and isolated conditions onboard submarines. A continuing Navy program of behavioral research aimed at maximizing the productivity and readiness of nuclear submarine crews has resulted in the incorporation of many design and operational features and motivational techniques in both ballistic missile and attack submarines.

The vast depths of the world's oceans frequently have been compared, by scientists and novelists alike, to the isolation of outer space. In many ways, the preparations necessary to sustain human life in these radically dissimilar environments are the same (e.g., a relatively small, pressurized habitat; complex life-support systems; communications difficulties; hostile outside environment). The similarities of undersea habitats (e.g., *Tektite I* and *II*) to space vehicles have been recognized and made a focus of research concern. The similarity is apparent from Radloff's (1973) description of *Sealab II*:

> Saturation divers are under severe stress; furthermore, those stresses have not been imposed or contrived by psychologists. While their spatial separation from a normal environment may

seem slight, they are separated by many hours or even days . . . from a return to the normal world, because of decompression requirements. Saturation divers live in constant danger from equipment failure or human error which could result in fatal or disabling accidents. They live in close confinement and are highly dependent on each other and on surface support personnel. (p. 197)

The results of several undersea habitat experiments are reviewed in previous research for the National Aeronautics and Space Administration (NASA) (Stuster 1983, 1984, 1986). They include *Conshelf, Ben Franklin* submersible, *Tektites I* and *II*, and *Sealab II*. In addition, interviews with saturation divers working in the offshore oil industry offered an operational perspective on life in the isolation and confinement of a deck-mounted saturation chamber. The experiences of saturation divers who live and work in a commercial, rather than a research, environment are considered to be particularly relevant to the more mature stages of space habitation.

Laboratory and field experiments simulating confinement and isolation are also relevant. The physical conditions of the isolation studies range from French cave experiments to high-fidelity simulations of technical environments. Recent examples include a full-mission simulation of a military system designed for remote, sustained, and autonomous operation (conducted for the U.S. Strategic Air Command in 1989 by a group of military and civilian researchers) and Ragnar Værnes's multidisciplinary human isolation studies conducted for the European Space Agency (ESA) (1991, 1993). The military simulation involved specially designed railcars; the ESA simulations used chambers at the Norwegian Underwater Technology Centre (NUTEC) in Bergen, Norway, to simulate spacecraft.

Another area of analysis concerns circumstances involving involuntary isolation, such as shipwrecks, disasters, and prisons. Although the risks and motivational factors associated with those conditions differ greatly from what might be expected of a space expedition, useful information might be obtained from experimental studies and accounts of involuntary isolation and confinement for long durations.

CHAPTER 2

DESCRIPTION OF THE RESEARCH

The objective of the book's research, as described in this chapter, is to develop procedural and design recommendations concerning biological, psychological, and sociological issues associated with long-duration space missions. The fundamental assumption, on which the technical approach to the research is based, is that a potentially useful source of behavioral data exists in the forms of "naturally" occurring groups living and working under conditions of isolation and confinement. Further, I believe that this approach is assisted, rather than impaired, by the naturally occurring conditions; that is, field conditions are imposed with greater force and fidelity than a researcher could possibly produce in a laboratory or simulation. It is my intention to capitalize on this fidelity through exploration of the enormous reservoir of human experience analogous to space missions.[1]

DEFINING THE LIKELY CONDITIONS OF SPACE MISSIONS

Before beginning the study of conditions on Earth that might be analogues to space missions, it is first necessary to learn more about what lunar and interplanetary missions might be like. Developing an understanding of possible long-duration space missions is necessary to determine if the assumptions about the similarity of those missions to Antarctic research stations and expeditions are correct. I defined probable space mission parameters by reviewing published sources and planning documents provided by NASA.

Many published sources contain detailed plans for both lunar and interplanetary missions.[2] The moon is always within a few days of Earth by spacecraft; consequently, the major differences among the various lunar scenarios are determined by time spent on the surface and the size of the crew. There are several options for getting to Mars;

however, they involve different trajectories and different transit and surface durations. Oberg (1982) provides a summary of thirty years of plans for missions to Mars, beginning with Wernher von Braun's 1952 proposal titled *Das Marsprojekt*. In this early plan, ten large spacecraft would travel in convoy to Mars; they would carry three "landing boats" to transport fifty people and supplies from martian orbit to the surface for a stay of four hundred days. In a later plan, the fleet was reduced to two ships, each with a crew of twelve. By the mid-1960s, several engineering studies had been completed regarding a mission to Mars under the reasonable assumption that a successful Apollo Program would lead to this next logical step. Most of the mission scenarios of this period involved crews of four to six and mission durations of two to three years.

Oberg (1982) and O'Leary (1987) describe the physics of getting to Mars in understandable terms. A key factor that will determine the expense of a Mars mission is the number of launches required to lift the components of the interplanetary spacecraft out of the gravity well of Earth to be assembled in low Earth orbit; fuel for the voyage will be among the heaviest components. The trajectory to Mars that requires the least fuel, called a Hohmann transfer, begins with a departure from Earth orbit when the Earth is at its closest to the sun (perihelion) and ends with arrival at Mars at its farthest point from the sun (aphelion). This outward-bound leg of a Mars mission would take about nine months with the use of conventional chemical propulsion. The planets are properly aligned for this trajectory every two years (i.e., one martian year); however, an eighteen-month stay on the surface would be required to wait for the planets to move into position for the second Hohmann transfer for a return to Earth. O'Leary suggests a "Venus swing-by" as a means to reduce the mission duration from three years to somewhat less than two years; the Venus swing-by option would provide astronauts with about sixty days on the surface of Mars. He also suggests a high-speed flyby of Mars without making a landing; in this plan, the planet's gravity is used to swing the spacecraft promptly back to Earth within a total mission duration of twelve months, the quickest Mars mission scenario that has been identified. A variation of the Hohmann transfer with Venus swing-by is the option selected by former Apollo astronaut Michael Collins (1990) in his description of a mission to Mars. Collins borrows liberally from many sources to describe his "vision" of a Mars mission, including the behavioral problems that the four-person crew might encounter during their twenty-two months together.

Among the more recent proposals for a mission to Mars is a variation of the Hohmann transfer with a Venus swing-by that requires only seven-month transits in each direction, with a sixteen-month stay on the martian surface (Zubrin and Baker 1990). In this plan, only one robotic staging mission would be needed to establish an automatic processing plant to produce the fuel required for the four-person crew's return to Earth. A modified version of this approach, involving six-month transits and eighteen-month surface stays, is also possible (Foley 1995). Also, Mark and Smith (1991) propose a "fast track" approach to Mars, using an ion rocket vehicle, that would reduce the mission duration to about fourteen months: five months to Mars, one month on the surface, and seven and one-half months to return to Earth. This plan calls for the three-person crew to be preceded by two automatic staging missions, powered by conventional rockets, that would each require three years to reach Mars.

Table 1 summarizes several plans for missions to the moon and Mars developed by NASA and the aerospace industry. Important trade-offs must be made between mission duration and energy expenditure when determining which option to select for either a lunar or a Mars mission. For a lunar mission, the trade-off is primarily between longer surface stays and fewer launches required to rotate crew personnel. The equation is more complicated for a mission to Mars, in which more energy means a faster transit to and from the destination. More energy, however, means more launches to haul more fuel into Earth orbit and construction of faster spacecraft. Thus, more launches equal higher costs.

What makes these trade-offs complicated are the unknown factors. Will the physiological effects of space travel, such as bone demineralization, muscle atrophy, and radiation loading, limit mission duration for the human crew? Is there a reason to limit mission duration out of concern for the crew's mental health and performance or because of other psychological factors? Or, would the additional cost of developing systems to support a human crew on a longer, more energy-efficient mission negate the savings in fuel and staging launches?

The cost of developing systems to support the crew during extremely long voyages probably would be much greater than that needed for support systems in shorter missions. The typical approach to achieve the increased reliability necessary for longer missions has been to add backup systems; triple redundancy is NASA's traditional approach. Triple redundancy is not a bad idea, but it increases costs significantly (both system costs and the weight penalty of the additional hardware). One way to reduce the costs of long-duration reliability is to provide a single backup to on-board systems but design the systems for maintenance by the crew. Alternatively, no backup system would be necessary if the system were designed to degrade gracefully and if sufficient spare parts were provided for repairs by the crew. Mission cost is outside the scope of this book except to the extent that the results of my research provide information about one of the important unknown factors, namely, the ability of human crews to endure long-duration isolation and confinement.

Table 1. Summary of Possible Missions to the Moon and Mars

Possible Missions	Approximate Mission Duration	Outbound Trip	Surface Stay	Inbound Trip	Crew Size
MOON					
Exploration emphasis	2 months	<10 days	14–45 days	<10 days	4
Modified reference	12 months	<10 days	6–12 months	<10 days	4
Pre-Mars test	12 months	<10 days	6–12 months	<10 days	8
Energy enterprise	25 months	<10 days	2+ years	<10 days	12-30
Expanding human presence	25 months	<10 days	2+ years	<10 days	30+
MARS					
Sprint	12 months	180 days	0	180 days	4
Fast track	14 months	150 days	30 days	225 days	3
Exploration emphasis	14 months	100-200 days	14–45 days	100-200 days	8
Energy enterprise	14 months	100–200 days	14–45 days	100-200 days	4
Aggressive Mars	18 months	100–200 days	14–45 days	200-300 days	8
Venus swing-by	24 months	330 days	60 days	330 days	4
Refuel on surface	30 months	210 days	500 days	210 days	4
Modified reference	44 months	200–300 days	1–2 years	200-300 days	4
Expanding human presence	48 months	300+ days	2+ years	300+ days	30+

The results of the review summarized above indicate that crew tour durations for lunar bases might exceed two years and the durations of missions to Mars might exceed four years (i.e., two-plus years on the surface of Mars and approximately one year in transit each way). The most likely mission scenarios, however, involve stays at a lunar base of about twelve months and a mission to Mars of two to three years' duration.

Crew size might range from as few as four personnel during initial missions to more than thirty individuals in a fully mature lunar or martian outpost. Crew tasks would include facility construction and assembly, operation of automated and robotic equipment, maintenance of equipment, geological and biogeological fieldwork, Earth observation and astronomy, life sciences experiments, housekeeping functions, and administrative tasks. The anticipated crew sizes and the work likely to be required of crews on long-duration space missions are comparable to these factors at smaller and earlier Antarctic research stations and on many previous expeditions. Further, the outside environments in Antarctica and in space are similar in their hostility to human life. Although Mars is colder than Antarctica, the average annual temperature at South Pole Station is –60°F. Under normal wind conditions at this temperature, exposed flesh freezes in fewer than thirty seconds. Temperatures drop to –112°F during the winter.

The similarity of life at Antarctic research stations to life onboard spacecraft and at future lunar or planetary bases has prompted many observers to make behavioral inferences about life in space from life in Antarctica. With the exception of Sells's (1973) efforts to develop a taxonomy of isolation and confinement, however, little attention has been devoted to evaluating the appropriateness of the comparisons or the likely utility of the inferences. In a previous study, I made systematic evaluations of relevance by comparing thirteen conditions characterized by isolation and confinement to a low–Earth-orbit space station; comparisons were made in terms of fourteen dimensions, including size of group, duration of tour, amount of free time, and hostility of outside environment (Stuster 1986). That evaluation found the twenty-person South Pole Station to be only sixth of the thirteen analogues in similarity to a space station; the only expedition on the list was rated eleventh. The leading analogues were *Skylab 4* (naturally), three undersea habitat experiments (*Sealab II* and *Tektites I* and *II*), and ballistic missile submarines, but those comparisons were made to a ninety-day space station tour, not to a twelve-month lunar surface stay or a three-year mission to Mars. I believe that a systematic evaluation of the type performed for a space station would result in high ratings of similarity for both small Antarctic research stations and certain expeditions from the recent and historical past.

Scientists, engineers, and other professionals apparently agree. Officials of the National Science Foundation (NSF) and NASA discussed the possibility of building prototype lunar and Mars outposts in Antarctica to evaluate life-support hardware, science equipment, and telerobotic operations, as well as to investigate human adaptation to isolated and confined conditions (David 1990). NASA/NSF (1990) developed a formal plan and progress has been made toward achieving the ultimate goal. In the meantime, researchers from Australia, the European Space Agency, and the French Polar Program approached NASA Life Sciences managers with offers of cooperation and assistance. The NASA–International Space Analogue Research Program (NISARP), implemented in 1993, involves the conduct of interdisciplinary research at the Dumont d'Urville station in Antarctica and at several remote-duty stations located in the South Indian Ocean. Currently, plans are being developed to conduct high-fidelity simulations of lunar base operations at a specially built, internationally staffed Antarctic facility to be called DOME-C.

It is important to understand that all interest in life at Antarctic research stations as a model, or testbed, for life in space derives from two factors: (1) the clear similarities of the conditions, in terms of the isolation and confinement, hostility of outside environment, types of tasks performed, composition of group, and so forth, and (2) the recognition that the important conditions are imposed with greater force and fidelity under actual isolation and confinement than possibly could be imposed in a more controlled laboratory simulation. Tierney (1984) writes:

> Antarctica has been heralded as a laboratory for the space program ever since the 1959 Antarctic Treaty, which dedicated the continent's five million square miles to "freedom of scientific investigation" and foreshadowed the outer-space treaty of 1967. Planners of the Mariner missions to Mars used Antarctic valleys as test models, and legend has it that Wernher von Braun's observation of Antarctic scientists at work convinced him that manned flights were superior to automated ones. (P. 118)

Also, reportedly, the Soviet space program, during the late 1960s, utilized the Soviet Vostok Station high on the South Polar Plateau as a behavioral testbed in preparation for the Salyut Program. More recently, Antarctica has been the site of U.S. experiments involving the remote operation of robotic devices similar to those anticipated for future space missions.

As mentioned previously, the guiding hypothesis of this study is that the duration of a space mission is likely to be a principal factor affecting individual adjustment, performance, and productivity. Also, mission duration and crew size are principal factors in issues involving group interaction. For these reasons, I determined that previous assumptions about Antarctic stations and the experiences of explorers probably were correct. In other words, twelve months at a small Antarctic research station is about as close to what life at a lunar base might be like as can be achieved here on Earth; multiyear expeditions to the polar regions and other remote areas are perhaps comparable to what might be expected for a mission to Mars. As a result, my interview and archival research focused on Antarctic research stations and exploratory and scientific expeditions as the most relevant conditions analogous to the long-duration space missions defined earlier.

Artist Robert S. Murray's concept of a Mars analogue habitat located next to an ice-covered lake in the dry valleys of Southern Victoria Land, Antarctica. With a facility such as the one depicted in the illustration, space expedition planners could test and evaluate operational procedures, habitat design, and other equipment and conduct studies of human performance and behavior under conditions similar to those expected at a future planetary outpost. (Courtesy of Robert S. Murray and Martin Marietta)

IDENTIFYING BEHAVIORAL ISSUES

The next research step was to identify the behavioral issues that have design and procedural implications for long-duration isolation and confinement. I identified several key behavioral issues by reviewing the relevant literature and interviewing NASA space human factors specialists. There is considerable overlap between the issues that I had identified previously for space stations and those identified as relevant to long-duration space missions, but there are also significant differences. My previous study addresses design implications only, whereas this work encompasses a range of behavioral issues, including leadership, personnel selection, and the remote monitoring of performance. Despite the overlap of issues, there will be fundamental behavioral differences between relatively brief and routine tours of duty on a low–Earth-orbit space station and a long-duration space mission of a more expeditionary nature.

A preliminary list of issues guided my open-ended interviews with Antarctic winter-over personnel and others experienced in living and working under conditions of isolation and confinement. I added issues to the list as they emerged from the interviews and review of archival data.

Fifteen behavioral issues are used to organize and present the results of the research discussed in Part II:

1. sleep
2. clothing
3. exercise
4. workload
5. leadership
6. medical support
7. personal hygiene
8. food preparation
9. group interaction
10. habitat aesthetics
11. outside communications
12. recreational opportunities
13. personnel selection criteria
14. privacy and personal space
15. remote monitoring of human performance and adjustment

IDENTIFYING SOURCES OF INFORMATION

During previous research for NASA (Stuster 1986) and ESA (Stuster 1990a, 1990b), I had found additional sources of potentially valuable behavioral data in the forms of personal journals, logs, diaries, other archival records, and published accounts of scientific expeditions and voyages of discovery. The personal and operational experiences of explorers and remote duty personnel, represented in materials of this type, are an untapped and potentially valuable source of information concerning the design of equipment and procedures for future explorers of the moon and Mars.

Four categories of sources, as illustrated in Figure 1, provide information about the behavioral issues associated with isolation and confinement at Antarctic stations and during multiyear expeditions:

1. personal interviews
2. diaries, logs, and journals
3. debriefing reports
4. accounts of expeditions

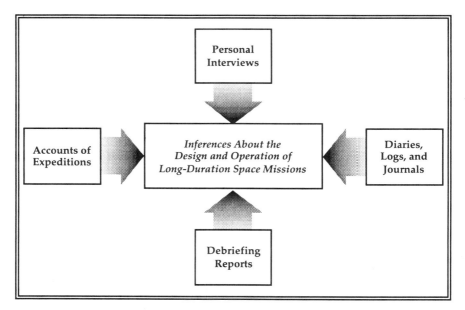

Figure 1. The four primary sources of information for the study

The research activities concerning each of the sources are described above.

Personal Interviews

I conducted open-ended interviews with Antarctic winter-over personnel regarding the full range of previously identified behavioral issues. Many of the people interviewed were members of U.S. Naval Construction Battalions (nicknamed Seabees); the Seabees have had the primary responsibility for construction and maintenance at all U.S. Antarctic stations, both before and since the IGY in 1957–58. The Navy Seabees have developed unique capabilities to design and build facilities, from airfields to entire military installations, rapidly and under the most hostile environmental conditions. They are also accustomed to the special requirements of limited space and life-support systems. In fact, many of the techniques used by Seabees to design special-purpose military facilities might be useful to the designers of space facilities. For example, Seabees designed an extremely compact field hospital housed within a shipping container. The container can be transported in the cargo compartment of an aircraft, then deployed on site by folding down the sides of the box; each subsystem within the hospital is hinged to fold out and snap into place. Design techniques such as these might be useful to the planners of future lunar and martian bases. In many ways, the remote-duty and special construction experiences of Navy Seabees are relevant to the development of space facilities. Interviews with Seabees and other Antarctic personnel provided valuable information about life in isolation and confinement from the perspectives of both management and operations.

The interviews with Antarctic personnel also offered considerable insight into the forms of behavior that might be useful for remote monitoring of individual adjustment to isolated and confined conditions. Most of the interview data concerning this particular topic came from former medical officers of the Seabees' Naval Support Force Antarctica, also known as Operation Deep Freeze. The medical officers' responsibilities included the remote monitoring of the physical and mental health of personnel at Antarctic stations. Although the force medical officers visit Antarctica each year, the remote monitoring is conducted from offices in Port Hueneme, California, nearly 10,000 miles away. A list of potential performance and adjustment indicators compiled from the interviews is discussed in chapter 17.

I interviewed former commanding officers of the Naval Support Force Antarctica, many Seabee technicians and chiefs, Navy psychologists and psychiatrists who have been responsible for screening and selecting personnel for Antarctic duty, and civilian contractors who have wintered over at Antarctic research stations. Also, I interviewed members of the French Antarctic program and other experts in the field of human performance during sustained and continuous operations.

Diaries, Logs, and Journals

Unobtrusive Measures: Nonreactive Research in the Social Sciences (Webb et al. 1966) has influenced a generation of behavioral scientists. The authors caution researchers about the influence that the research process can have on the results of a study; that is, people who know they are subjects in a study might be inclined to act differently than they would if they were not participating in a research project. Similarly, for a variety of reasons, subjects might respond with less than complete candor to questions on a survey instrument (e.g., to please, impress, deceive, or mislead the researchers), with inaccurate results as the outcome regardless of the subjects' motivation. Caution regarding the methods used applies to all behavioral science research, but it is particularly important when socially sensitive issues are involved or when participants' responses might be perceived as having possible negative consequences, despite the researchers' assurances of confidentiality or anonymity.

Webb and colleagues encourage the use of unobtrusive measures, research techniques in which subjects are unaware that they are participating in a study, as a means to avoid the intentional and unintentional biases of subjects. Pursuing this approach in behavioral research sometimes requires considerable creativity and patience, but it eliminates the need to make the dubious assumption that subjects are not influenced by their participation in a study. For example, self-reported data by participants in a recent military simulation were questioned when the sleep logs and mood inventories of the officer in charge (OIC) appeared to be too consistent. A review of videotapes made to monitor the simulation unobtrusively proved that the OIC's responses were inaccurate, probably to conceal the sleep deprivation that he was experiencing as a result of his leadership style and the fast tempo of the simulated operation. In this case, the unobtrusive monitoring of behavior was more reliable than the traditional questionnaire approach. Capturing behavior on videotape can be an effective unobtrusive technique, even when the participants know the cameras are present; participants eventually become desensitized to the cameras and behave normally, which is the basis for the best *cinema verité* documentaries. Subjects rarely become desensitized to questionnaires.

Nelson concludes his chapter on the indirect observation of isolated and confined groups with the same quotation from a statistics text that Webb and colleagues use in the conclusion of their work. It was appropriate more than two decades ago, and it is particularly appropriate in the current context:

> We must use all available weapons of attack, face our problems realistically and not retreat to the land of fashionable sterility, learn to sweat over our data with an admixture of judgment and intuitive rumination, and accept the usefulness of particular data even when the level of analysis available for them is markedly below that available for other data in the empirical area. (Binder 1964, 294; quoted in Nelson 1973, 190)

In 1969, the NATO Symposium on Man in Isolation and/or Enclosed Space essentially defined the field of study described by the title of the edited collection of papers that emanated from that symposium, *Man in Isolation and Confinement* (Rasmussen 1973). In that important collection, Nelson (1973) suggests the use of several indirect methods for the study of isolated and confined groups; these include interviews, questionnaires, site visits (i.e., observation), organizational records, and diaries or logs.[3]

Self-initiated diaries and official logs usually provide descriptive accounts of events in a chronological sequence; whether nautical, meteorological, logistic, or personal, they are always responding to the question, "And then what happened?" (Labov and Waletzky 1967). This is precisely the question that behavioral scientists would ask if they had access to the isolated and confined group described in the text; instead, the answer is provided in the form of a narrative account, or record. The level of detail provided in a well-written narrative can be considerable and sometimes overwhelming. It must be understood that many of the accounts in this book were written in simpler times, before electronic communications had reduced the arts of letter writing and journal keeping. In particular, before the advent of the telephone, most literate people wrote long and thoughtful letters about the important issues in their lives. Further, when people traveled, they typically maintained journals of their experiences that were often rich in detail and usually illustrated by pencil or charcoal sketches. The ubiquitous camera replaced the diary or journal, as the telephone eliminated the need to compose one's personal thoughts and observations to another on paper. A common response of (even) modern folks to isolation and confinement, however, is to become avid letter writers and journal keepers. Even the most unlikely candidates, such as oil field saturation divers, have been known to develop latent writing skills and conduct lengthy correspondence during their weeks of confinement to a pressurized deck chamber. Some members of expeditions use their diaries as outlets for the feelings that they dare not permit themselves to expose or act upon. In this way, maintaining a diary serves a therapeutic purpose for some individuals.

Riessman (1993) maintains that traditional research methods are limited in their abilities to provide an understanding of social life; she suggests that the analysis of narratives, such as found in letters and diaries, can transcend those limitations, thus revealing the organizing principle for human action. Further, reviewing diaries, logs, journals, and other archival sources is a less obtrusive method of obtaining information about individuals and groups than either interviews or questionnaires. Perhaps more important, archival materials can be the only sources of information about previous experiences, such as the expeditions and voyages of discovery conducted in the historical past. I identified several relevant diaries during the current study, and reviewed them with references to the behavioral issues that have design and procedural implications. The diaries included both unpublished and published materials. Examination of a broad range of materials was important to this study; as a consequence, the documents reviewed range from a recent translation of Columbus's log of his first voyage of discovery (Fuson 1987) to the diary of a Russian cosmonaut (Lebedev [1983] 1988).

People who are unfamiliar with nautical matters often fail to comprehend the nature of a ship's log. The log is a record maintained for the vessel's aid and safety; it is a running account of the daily progress that is made and a repository for the information that would be necessary to replicate the voyage or retrace the course to safety. The dead-reckoning navigator must systematically record many details, including heading, speed, sea state, winds, leeway, and all other factors that might affect the ship's course. Before the relatively recent development of extraordinary technologies, navigators were forced to be scrupulous and systematic in their recording because that was all they had to determine their location. Similarly, the logs of military and other remote duty stations are maintained not for posterity or to prove a point, but to record events as they occur.[4]

One of the most interesting unpublished documents that I reviewed is the Commanding Officer's Log for the Williams Air Operating Facility on Ross Island, McMurdo Sound, Antarctica. Lt. Comdr. David Canham, Jr., maintained the log from 20 December 1955 through 24 March 1957, the period during which the Navy was preparing for the IGY. In 374 pages of single-spaced type on legal-size onionskin paper, the young officer described the complete sequence of events regarding the first establishment of a permanent human presence in Antarctica. The log begins with the anchoring and unloading of the ship that brought the Navy Mobile Construction Battalion and associated civilians to Ross Island. The log continues with daily descriptions of the progress made and the problems encountered as the men established a temporary base camp, then struggled to build an airfield and a permanent facility to protect them from the hostile Antarctic environment. Canham describes the reaction of the men to the accidental death of a young equipment operator in their third week on the ice. He portrays several additional crises, including the highly disruptive psychosis, mentioned earlier, that emerged only three months into the fifteen month mission. Many less dramatic problems are documented in the log, as well; personal communications with loved ones and relations with command personnel located elsewhere were constant sources of aggravation to the winter-over party.

The structural similarities between the pioneering experience described in the commanding officer's diary and what might be expected of lunar and planetary exploration are clear. This unique source of information describes many of the problems that are likely to confront the astronauts selected to establish the first lunar base or martian outpost. Perhaps more important, the log also details the responses and attempted solutions to the problems. The responses are sometimes successful in their outcome; in other instances, they fail. Many important lessons relevant to space mission planners can be learned from both the successes and failures, as well as the other experiences, of the men who established the first permanently occupied facility in Antarctica. Among the many additional diaries and journals that I reviewed, none was so clearly relevant to future lunar and planetary expeditions as this unpublished document.

Debriefing Reports

Each year, a specially configured C-130 cargo plane arrives at South Pole Station in late October, which marks the end of the Antarctic winter for the twenty station inhabitants. On the plane are food and other supplies, crew replacements for the next winter, and some temporary visitors, including a Navy psychologist. During the next three or four days, the psychologist interviews each of the winter-over personnel about their experiences. Formal psychological tests are often administered by the psychologist, in addition to the personal interviews, or debriefings. The objectives of these debriefing sessions might include any of the following:

- Assess the functioning of each individual at the end of the winter-over period.
- Make recommendations regarding reentry of the individual into society.
- Assess the functioning of the group as a working unit.
- Make recommendations regarding group effectiveness in the future.
- Obtain feedback regarding the prewinter psychiatric screening.
- Obtain information to assist future screening.

A similar interview protocol is followed by all of the debriefing psychologists, but the format, style, and behavioral focus of the debriefing reports vary with each psychologist. Some of the reports are extremely long and detailed, whereas others are more to the point. The reports always include the psychologists' evaluations of the winter-over personnel. In particular, individuals who are identified to have adapted badly or to have been disruptive during the winter are not recommended for a return to the ice, if they should apply. Psychological intervention measures or treatments for alcoholism are specified for others. Members of the party who appear to the psychologist to have performed well are also identified. All recommendations are supported by information obtained by the psychologists during the interviews that include self-ratings and ratings of other crew performance during the winter-over period.

The psychologists frequently note that the debriefing interview appears to serve a psychological need of those interviewed. For troubled individuals, the debrief is often an opportunity to convince the psychologist that they are really all right and that any stories that might be circulating about them are untrue or, at least, exaggerations. For most of the participants, the debriefing interview appears to be an opportunity to bring closure to an important experience in their lives.

The debriefing reports are considered to be confidential in the medical sense. For this reason, Navy psychologists removed the names of station personnel from the documents before providing them to me for review. Throughout this book, further steps are taken to protect confidentiality during discussion of any debriefing reports so as to prevent the attribution of particular behaviors to specific facilities or individuals.

A well-prepared debriefing report provides an excellent "case study" of life in isolation and confinement. By extrapolation (and with a few assumptions), these examples suggest what might be experienced in future remote duty outposts, such as onboard spacecraft and at lunar and planetary bases. Following is a summary of a representative debriefing report for a relatively small Antarctic station:

- Personal jealousies and animosity among three individuals, including the station leader, were disruptive to the group throughout the winter.

- Four of the male crew members persisted in bothering the few female personnel with requests for dates and sexual favors, despite having received firm negative responses from the women.

- Three of the crew members suffered breakups of relationships with wives at home; two men experienced the deaths of loved ones. One unfortunate man who suffered two deaths and a "Dear John" letter developed a major depression, which responded to medication.

- The power plant operator was poisoned by carbon monoxide and received medical treatment for five weeks.

- Some of the crew insisted on "free cycling" (staying up late and sleeping during the mornings) and were frequently unavailable for cooperative tasks.

- Station leaders reported that the station was "completely and totally ignored" by the Navy, civilian support contractor, and the entire outside world during the winter months.

- Four clearly distinguishable subgroups formed, but all personnel reported that they felt comfortable and welcome with any individual or group (with the exception of the group labeled as the "party animals").

- Two of the crew became extremely isolated from the others by withdrawing from group interaction. Two people missed the group photograph.

- None of the crew believed alcohol consumption to be a serious problem for the group; only three alcohol-related injuries were reported.

Accounts of Expeditions

Many who have written about space exploration have compared the endeavor to previous expeditions and voyages of discovery. The similarities between traveling to a remote area of the world and traveling to a distant planet are clear. Apparently, Wernher von Braun recognized the similarities and was fond of comparing future space missions to expeditions of the past. Oberg (1982) reports that, in his early Mars mission proposal, von Braun recommended that two identical spacecraft be launched together to provide mutual assistance, if necessary. Von Braun wrote with historical accuracy in support of the plan:

> Columbus... chose not to sail with a flotilla of less than three ships, and history tends to prove that he might never have returned to Spanish shores with his report of discoveries had he entrusted his fate to a single bottom. So it is with interplanetary exploration. (Quoted in Oberg, 1982, 51–52)

Von Braun was also fond of comparing the actions of fifteenth-century Chinese Mandarins to their counterparts in modern government who attempt to minimize or eliminate space exploration. Oberg (1982) summarizes this poignant story, which has been retold many times and even included in the advertising copy of an aerospace firm, the management of which apparently recognizes the importance of learning from history:

> Early in the fifteenth century, great Chinese "treasure ships" with crews of 500 sailors were crisscrossing the Indian Ocean, visiting Bengal, Ceylon, and the East Coast of Africa. This naval power enhanced Chinese overseas influence and enriched the Chinese economy. It also invigorated the technological progress and cultural life of the nation. But the social instabilities that such activities were bound to unleash displeased the traditionalist Confucian imperial bureaucracy, which tried to eliminate such ferment by cutting off the expeditions of the great fleets. In 1436, the Cheng-t'ung Emperor came to the throne and an edict was issued that forebade the building of high seas ships ... within half a century there were imperial regulations making it a capital offense to build seagoing ships with more than two masts. (P. 175)

As the result of the Mandarins' antiexploration policies, China lost its leadership in technology and trade and isolated itself from Western civilization's Age of Discovery. Metaphor is a powerful technique for conveying important lessons, and the lessons contained in this metaphor are clear.

Anecdotal comparisons are frequently made between expeditions of the past and future space missions, but few attempts have been made to study formally the accounts of expeditions for other than historical purposes. Anthropologists Jeffrey Johnson and Ben Finney (1986) analyze Huntford's (1984) account of Roald Amundsen's and Robert Falcon Scott's race to the South Pole. They focus on the relationship between prescribed or formal hierarchical structure and informal, emergent structure; they also identify and discuss the implications of the emergent structure to group effectiveness. In addition, they analyze the contributions of different status positions within the parties to group cohesiveness.

More recently, Mocellin and Suedfeld (1991) performed content analyses of thirteen original diaries maintained by members of British polar expeditions from the mid-nineteenth to the early twentieth centuries. They categorize journal entries into five areas and rate individual words in terms of pleasantness and arousal. Results of the content analysis indicate that Antarctic expedition members were more negative about their experiences than were their colleagues who ventured to the Arctic, but both polar regions generated many positive and negative reactions. The researchers conclude that the experiences of the expeditioners were not generally aversive or stressful. They further suggest that the popular conceptions about the difficult living conditions of explorers in polar regions are, at least partially, the result of overgeneralization and dramatization. Finally, Nicholas and Penwell (1995) review information about mountain-climbing teams and Huntford's (1984) account of the Scott–Amundsen race to the South Pole in their analysis of leadership traits. The analysis also includes information from aviation, polar bases, and submersibles and identifies the common themes of effective leadership.

From an engineering perspective, the differences between future and past expeditions are considerable. Spacecraft are far more complex than sailing ships, and one of the factors that drives spacecraft complexity is the requirement to support the crew in the hostile environment of space. The technological differences are significant, but from a behavioral perspective, are the differences really that great between confinement in a small wooden ship locked in the polar icecap and confinement in a small high-technology ship hurtling through interplanetary space? The psychological differences are probably few. For this reason, there is considerable merit in studying the accounts of previous expeditions in order to derive behavioral inferences about the conduct of future expeditions in space.

Perhaps the best encouragement for studying accounts of expeditions as analogues to space missions is provided by Scott (1905) in the introduction to his account, *Voyage of the* Discovery:[5]

> The first objective of writing an account of a Polar voyage is the guidance of future voyagers: the first duty of the writer is to his successors. (P. vii)

Consistent with Scott's advice, I identified expeditions that had been particularly well documented by personal diaries, published accounts, and historical reconstruction. I attempted to include a broad range of expeditions and eras, but the primary criterion for selecting a document for review was the comparability of some aspect of the expedition to what might be expected of a long-duration space mission. As a consequence of this approach, my review began, chronologically, in 1492 with accounts of Columbus's first voyage to the New World. Although the outward-bound trip for Columbus's three small ships took only thirty-three days and the total duration of the voyage was about seven months, there is considerable relevance to the future in the accounts of this expedition. Columbus faced many of the same problems, including strong-willed and independent subordinates, that will confront the leaders of future expeditions. Additional examples of the materials reviewed include accounts of Charles Darwin's famous voyage on-board the *Beagle*; a collection of letters from Midshipman William Reynolds, a particularly observant young officer who traveled around the world as part of the U.S. Exploring Expedition of 1838–42; descriptions of commercial whaling and sealing voyages; and accounts of more recent adventures, such as Thor Heyerdahl's *Kon-Tiki* (1950) and *The* Ra *Expedition* (1971).

Although I reviewed a broad range of expeditions, most of the materials are accounts of polar expeditions of the nineteenth and early twentieth centuries. Notable among these are Fridtjof Nansen's Norwegian Polar Expedition (1893–97); the Belgian Antarctic Expedition (1898–99); the Amundsen and Scott race to the South Pole (1910–12); and Adm. Richard E. Byrd's two expeditions to Antarctica.

Summary

During the course of this research, I identified as many relevant sources of information as possible about life in isolation and confinement. These sources include personal interviews; diaries, logs, and journals; psychological debriefing notes; and accounts of previous expeditions and other conditions characterized by long-duration isolation and confinement. A review of the scientific literature concerning human adaptation to extreme and austere environments supplemented the information obtained from the primary sources. In this respect, my research efforts were consistent with the following advice quoted by Nelson (1973):

> The investigator should use as many methods in combination as the situation permits to increase breadth of understanding as well as reliability of observation. As Webb and his colleagues (1966) have it, "So long as we maintain, as social scientists, an approach to comparisons that considers compensating error and converging corroboration from individually contaminated outcroppings, there is no cause for concern. It is only when we naively place faith in a single measure that the massive problems of social research vitiate the validity of our comparisons." (Pp. 181–82)

The methods used in my research result in an alternative to the traditional behavioral science perspective on life in isolation and confinement. This alternative perspective places new emphasis on the many examples in which humans have operated successfully for long durations despite their austere, isolated, and confined conditions. The well-known disasters are instructive because they remind us of the need to be careful in the design of habitats, equipment, and procedures and in the selection of personnel for special duty. The successes, however, are equally instructive. Perhaps more important, the many examples of humans who have successfully adapted to austere and confined environments can provide considerable encouragement to those who will endure the inevitable stressors at future lunar bases, onboard interplanetary spacecraft, and during other expeditions involving long-duration isolation and confinement.

PART II
THE STUDY RESULTS

In all aspects, particularly the psychological, the risks sur-rounding the project were very real. Whosoever should elect to inhabit such a spot must reconcile themselves to enduring the bitterest temperatures in nature, a long night as black as that on the dark side of the moon, and an isolation which no power on earth could lift.... Now, against the cold the explorer has simple but ample defenses. Against the accidents which are the most serious risks of isolation he has inbred resourcefulness and ingenuity. But against darkness, nothing much but his own dignity.

In the kind of station we had in mind the normal risks of a polar base would be intensified a thousand fold. The difficulties would be great. The amount of supplies that could be advanced would be small, and, therefore, only very few men could occupy it. The men would be jammed together at arm's length in a tiny shack buried in the snow. Wind and cold would keep them from ever leaving it for more than a few hours a day. Change in the sense that we know it, without which life is scarcely tolerable, would be nonexistent. The party would be dedicated to an iron routine. The day would be the repeated pattern of the hour; the week, the repeated pattern of the day; and one would scarcely be distinguishable from the other, even as an interval in time. Where there is no growth or change outside, men are driven deeper and deeper inside themselves for materials of replen-ishment. And on these hidden levels of self-replenishment ... would depend the ability of any group of men to outlast such an ordeal and not come to hate each other.

—Richard E. Byrd, *Alone*

Adm. Richard E. Byrd decided to experience the isolation in his small Antarctic hut alone, rather than subject any others in his party to the austere conditions and "psychological risks" of Advance Base. That was a mistake. He injured his shoulder before the logistics team departed, which impaired his ability to perform routine tasks. Later, he locked himself out of his 9-by-13-foot hut and nearly froze to death while attempting to break in. Most important, he was continuously exposed to toxic fumes from his stove and collapsed with acute carbon monoxide poisoning when he attempted to inspect a gasoline-powered generator on the 64th day of his planned 180-day mission.

The year was 1934; radio technology was primitive and unreliable. For two months, Byrd successfully concealed his distress to prevent a dangerous rescue attempt. Fortunately, his deteriorating condition was reflected in his Morse code messages to Little America—he missed scheduled transmissions because of equipment problems; when he did communicate, his messages were increasingly difficult to understand. Severe Antarctic storms turned back several rescue attempts before a relief party was finally able to reach Advance Base 130 days after leaving Byrd alone. Admiral Byrd eventually recovered from the

Adm. Richard E. Byrd at Advance Base, 1934, prepares a meal at the beginning of his four months of isolation and confinement in a 9-by-13-foot hut located one hundred miles from the main base at Little America, Antarctica. (Courtesy of The Byrd Polar Research Center Archival Program, The Ohio State University)

physical and psychological stresses of his experience and later provided posterity with an introspective account of life, at its worst, in isolation and confinement. Byrd's experiment was plagued with problems and the mind-numbing sameness of routine. In the admiral's words, "Time was no longer like a river running, but a deep still pool."

Much about Byrd's unique experience is relevant and instructive to the planners of future space expeditions and other remote-duty missions. Although most of the specific problems Byrd experienced have been eliminated by modern technologies, the *types* of problems he experienced are fundamental and unchanging. For example, it is unlikely that a petroleum-fueled stove would be used at a lunar base, but a malfunction or other unplanned event could cause some piece of equipment in a space habitat to produce or emit toxic fumes as, or more, insidious than the fumes that poisoned Byrd in 1934. The injury that impaired his physical performance, equipment design flaws that contributed to human error (such as the hatch that froze shut behind him), ambiguous communications, and the inability to repair the radio were the specific problems encountered by Byrd. Even though technology has changed immeasurably since that winter more than six decades ago, the same types of problems will confront future space explorers: there will be injuries, errors will be made as the result of inadequate equipment or software designs or unclear procedures, communications will be misunderstood, and equipment will malfunction that cannot be repaired. Only the details of the problems will differ.

There were serious, preventable flaws in Byrd's equipment, procedures, and mission planning. Preparedness for medical emergencies, application of the principles of human factors to the design of equipment and habitats, effective procedures to guide outside communications, remote monitoring of performance and psychological adjustment, and designing for maintainability are solutions to some of the types of problems that, in combination, nearly resulted in the death of Admiral Byrd at Advance Base. This brief example, of course, contains only a few of the many threats to isolated and confined living.

DEFINITIONS

Many of the behavioral issues associated with long-duration isolation and confinement are called "habitability" issues, especially those that have clear design implications (e.g., food preparation, privacy and personal space). Much has been written about spacecraft habitability during the past forty years, but there is little agreement among authors regarding concepts, terms, and the key habitability issues. For example, Fraser (1968a) defines habitability as the equilibrium state resulting from the interaction of components of a crew-machine-mission environment complex, which permits physiological homeostasis, performance, and social relationships. In an earlier work, Kubis (1965) defines habitability as the sum of interactions between operators and environment. The interactions include physical, physiological, psychological, and social. To Kubis, habitability can be viewed as a series of layers: "a bedrock of sheer survivability, a segment of tolerable discomfort with a possible but tolerable reduction in efficiency, and a relatively comfortable condition characterized by effective performance."

Fraser, however, maintains that "comfort per se is not a critical attribute of habitability, nor is it likely to influence crew effectiveness to any significant extent." To Fraser, and to most observers, there is no ultimate standard for determining habitability. It must be considered and defined relative to the duration of the tour or occupancy and to the purpose of the occupancy. Further, the standards will vary substantially according to the previously established customs (a principal component of Webster's definition) and practices of the occupants.

Along these relativistic lines, Celentano et al. (1963) define habitability as the presence of desirable qualities to which the tenant is accustomed, and to ensure habitability one provides an environment as close to the natural environment as engineering resources permit. White and Reed (1963), when considering these issues, define habitability as "the resultant of the interplay of all the factors relating to the man, his machine, his environment, and the mission to be accomplished."

Fraser (1968a) interprets White and Reed to mean that a particular crew-machine-environment system defines its own habitability in terms of the assigned mission. That is, habitability is defined by other factors in addition to the acceptability of an environment. Consequently, habitability can be manipulated by altering any of the components of the total system—crew, machine, environment, or mission. According to Fraser, "Man has a dual role within such a system. He is an interactive component of the system, contributing to the habitability, and at the same time he provides the criteria by which the habitability is judged." Though Webster defines habitable in terms of the "class of tenant" (expectations), the interactive model of Fraser and others suggests that habitability requirements can be altered by modifying the habits, needs, and tolerances of the occupants. Modifications of these types might be effected through personnel selection, training, and enculturation. Human capacity for modification, however, is limited. Also, durations of missions are somewhat fixed by mission, technical, and economic factors. That leaves the environment to be modified as a principal means of improving habitability.

Discovery Expedition campsite at McMurdo Sound, 1901–4. Expeditions and Antarctic winter-over experiences resemble in many ways the conditions of isolation and confinement that will be experienced by future space travelers and those who will live and work at lunar and martian outposts. (Courtesy of The Royal Geographical Society, London)

Essentially, appropriate habitability design includes all of the features of a built environment that people need to remain content and productive. Accordingly, habitability may be defined as those aspects of an environment that affect human performance and adjustment, either immediately or eventually. This definition acknowledges both the immediate and cumulative effects of environmental stressors, and recognizes that isolated and confined environments present both positive and negative features to the occupants. The question remains: What are the habitability features and other behavioral issues that affect human adjustment and performance in isolation and confinement?

CATEGORIES

A list of fifteen habitability and other behavioral issues, or categories, emerged from my reviews of archival sources and interviews with Antarctic winter-over personnel. Some of the issues have clear implications regarding the design of habitats, equipment, and software. Others involve the design of procedures to be followed by mission managers or the crew members of an expedition, rather than hardware or software. Two of the most important issues, personnel selection and leadership, do not involve design at all.

I devoted considerable attention to identifying and naming the behavioral issues, with the objective of developing a comprehensive list composed of the fewest reasonable number of issues. Any effort of this type requires that decisions be made somewhat arbitrarily. For example, the label of *outside communications* is assigned to the category of issues related to communications between the remote-duty station and other locations, usually a distant headquarters (analogous to mission control). Issues related to intracrew communications, however, are encompassed in this taxonomy by the relatively broad category of issues labeled *group interaction*. Assigning labels to the issues implies that each issue represents a discrete category; in fact, there is considerable overlap among the issues. In particular, the label of *food preparation* refers to the design of equipment and systems that provide certain desirable features related to mealtimes and nutrition, but this issue also includes important elements related to group interaction, recreational opportunities, and the remote monitoring of human adjustment. In other words, the individual issues are not mutually exclusive, but I made every effort to ensure that the list, as a whole, is comprehensive of the behavioral issues associated with long-duration isolation and confinement.

The inferences derived from the study of conditions analogous to long-duration space missions are presented in the following chapters in terms of the fifteen behavioral issues. Personal interviews and research materials offered considerable information about some of the issues; for others, relevant material is meager. The following discussions reflect the relative availability of information on which to base behavioral inferences about specific issues.

CHAPTER 3

SLEEP

Sleeping like a log . . .
Out like a light . . .
Bagging some Z's . . .

The universality of sleep is reflected in the many words and clichés that describe the phenomenon; but sleep remains a mystery despite an abundance of common knowledge and a century of scientific investigation. We know many important things about sleep: we have named the phases of sleep cycles and measured corresponding brain activity, there is general agreement on the neurological and biochemical mechanisms of sleep, and we understand the effects of sleep disturbances and sleep deprivation on human performance. We simply lack an answer to the most important question: Why do we sleep? Informed speculation suggests that the need for sleep evolved in early species because of some fundamental, adaptive advantage that sleeping provided in the phylogenetic past, probably with regard to food availability and predators (Moore-Ede, Sulzman, and Fuller 1982). Science has not provided any convincing argument, however, to explain why we must spend nearly a third of our lives "dead to the world."

Although the neurophysiology and certainly the evolutionary origins of sleep are beyond the scope of this book, three important topics relevant to long-duration space missions are within the general behavioral issue of sleep: sleep management, noise control, and safety. These topics, addressed below, are followed by design and procedural recommendations.

SLEEP MANAGEMENT

The daily rhythms of behavior, such as activity and sleep, envelop us and appear to be clearly linked to the cycle of day and night. The apparent effects of external factors, however, are only part of a complex process. Since the 1950s, the presence of internal, self-regulating physiological "clocks" in organisms has been generally accepted. Internal clocks with daily, self-sustained periods of about 24 hours are called circadian rhythms (Halberg 1959), coined from the Latin *circa* (about) and *dies* (a day). Almost all physiological, psychological, and behavioral parameters, including body temperature, production of serum and urinary corticosteroids and electrolytes, cardiovascular functions, muscle strength, alertness, mood, and memory, follow circadian rhythms. Although circadian rhythms are generated internal to an organism, they are regulated by external cues, primarily the cycle of light and darkness. For example, when a human lives under normal conditions, with exposure to the night/day cycle and other temporal cues, sleep/wake and body temperature rhythms are expressed in periods of 24 hours and they maintain stable phase relationships to the day/night cycle. If the individual is isolated without access to any time cues, however, the sleep/wake cycle and body temperature rhythms drift toward later times each day and are expressed in free-running periods of 25.4 hours; at this rate an individual's sleep/wake cycle could drift nearly 10 hours per week in the absence of diurnal cues. Internal rhythms become again synchronized to external cues when the individual is returned to normal conditions. (See Scott 1994 for an excellent review.)

The imposition of period and phase control by environmental cues is called entrainment. The daily rhythms observed in organisms result from the entraining action of external factors on the organism's internal oscillators (Takahashi and Zatz 1982). In other words, the activities and autonomic functions of each human (and other species) are regulated by an internal physiological clock, but the clock must be reset each day by exposure to entraining diurnal cues.[1] The cues, known as "zeitgebers" (from the German for "time givers") include the light/dark cycle, social factors, mealtimes, and other regular external stimuli. The time shifts experienced by transmeridian jet travelers and by shift workers result in desynchronization between the internal circadian rhythms and external zeitgebers. The behavioral manifestation of this desynchronization is the constellation of symptoms known as jet lag and shift lag; symptoms include daytime sleepiness or fatigue, diffi-culty in sleeping at night, impaired concentration, slowed physical reflexes, and irritability (Toby 1988).

The crews of polar research stations and spacecraft share the experi-ence of living in the absence of the normal diurnal cues necessary to reset the physiological clock. The inhabitants of Earth's polar regions must live in almost total sunlight or total darkness for much of the year, whereas space travelers receive conflicting cues. The latter expe-rience more than a dozen sunrises and sunsets each day in low Earth orbit; lunar days and nights are each twenty-eight Earth days long; and the body clocks of future voyagers to Mars might receive equally con-fusing signals as the spacecraft gently rotates to prevent overheating in the constant glare of the sun. On the surface of Mars, however, the explorers' internal clocks will regain an Earth-like synchrony with outside cues because Earth and Mars have nearly identical rotation rates (twenty-four hours and thirty-seven minutes for Mars). Earth and Mars also share a similar sequence of seasons because their polar axes are tipped almost identically.

Essentially, the occupants of spacecraft and the residents of lunar bases and the Earth's polar regions live in the absence of the normal diurnal cues of daylight and darkness. Under these conditions, physio-logical clocks tend to drift with resulting sleep disturbances and other individual behavioral consequences, including increased irritability and an increased propensity for inadvertent acts and other errors. For example, cosmonaut Valentin Lebedev ([1983] 1988) reported in his diary that he had a tendency to make mistakes on days following an unusually late bedtime; on one occasion he took fifty Earth-observation photographs through a closed porthole before realizing his error. The mistake negatively affected task schedules and upset the mission con-trollers and other cosmonauts involved in the mission.

Reports of a particularly virulent form of insomnia among early U.S. Antarctic personnel precipitated an extensive program of sleep re-search at Antarctic stations. The condition, known as "polar big eye" (Mullin 1960) was reported in about 60 percent of the early debriefings (Strange and Klein 1973). The researchers found the sleep of Antarctic personnel to be affected somewhat by conditions (e.g., hypoxia due to altitude), but no evidence of the polar big eye phenomenon existed among the research subjects (Shurley 1974).[2]

As operational experience in Antarctica accumulated, an explanation of insomnia and some cases of hypersomnia at remote polar stations became apparent. For more than half of the year, the Antarctic continent is shrouded in either twilight or complete darkness. Lacking the normal circadian cues of daylight and darkness, individuals, when permitted, tend to become desynchronized; that is, they retire to bed at a later hour and remain awake longer each night. Although the actual sleep periods might remain at approximately the same duration, they gradually encroach on subsequent 24-hour periods. In extreme cases, an individual can cycle completely around the clock. The pattern, known as "free cycling," is the behavioral manifestation of the characteristic drift in the physiological clock described previously.

Dr. Ker Boyce, a former medical officer for Naval Support Force Antarctica, described two informal free-cycling experiments conducted by personnel at two smaller Antarctic stations. At both stations, all personnel, except those with cooking and communications responsibilities, ignored clocks to the extent possible and permitted themselves to free cycle. The average advance was estimated to be about two hours per day, which offers the welcome illusion of a longer workday when there is much to be accomplished. The system was found to work tolerably well during the period of the experiment at the smaller of the two stations; there were fewer than ten people in the crew, and, for the most part, they worked autonomously on large individual projects. Free cycling caused problems at the larger of the two stations, however, where the performance of several cooperative tasks was impaired by the conflicting sleep schedules of crew members.

Eric Gunderson has studied adaptation to Antarctic conditions for more than thirty years. He reports that free cycling typically results in irregular work habits and schedules, which in turn negatively affect task performance and overall productivity. Desynchronized individuals can also affect interpersonal relations and group morale. For example, if one is asleep or not fully awake when needed to assist with a task, both performance of the task and interpersonal relations might be negatively affected. Gunderson also found that Antarctic personnel who free cycled tended to suffer more physiological symptoms than those who did not.

In the absence of normal diurnal cues, or zeitgebers, operations-level leaders and other experts have found that adherence to a schedule of sleep and activity is critical to maintaining sustained human productivity. Most Antarctic station managers now insist that schedules be followed. During the early 1980s, for example, the commanding officer of Naval Support Force Antarctica implemented a requirement for an 0800 muster each morning as a means to encourage adherence to a sleep schedule. With the waning influence of the Navy in station management in recent years, it is more difficult to impose sleep schedules on civilian personnel. The Navy, however, is still responsible for screening both civilian and military personnel for Antarctic duty. During the process, Navy psychologists, such as Capt. Fred Glogower, strongly suggest that all personnel be required to arise at 0700 each day. Whether an 0800 muster or an 0700 wake-up call, this approach offers sufficient latitude to accommodate individual differences and requirements, yet it accomplishes the objective of discouraging free cycling. It is instructive to note that remote-duty leaders have been aware of the importance of sleep schedules for many years. In 1882, for example, Lt. Aldophus Washington Greely required that all in his party of twenty-five arise at 0700 each day of their first winter in the Arctic; he also ordered that no naps be taken between breakfast and dinner so as to avoid free cycling, despite the inactivity imposed by the conditions (Todd 1961).[3]

Sleep disturbances still occur at modern Antarctic research stations, primarily during the winter, even when the crew follows an established sleep schedule. During the brief austral summers when much physical work must be accomplished at Antarctic stations, the personnel work according to a fixed schedule and tend to become fatigued; most sleep well at night during this busy period. Fewer fatiguing tasks are performed during the long winters, however, and the personnel are largely confined to the station buildings by weather and darkness, with resulting inactivity and boredom. As a consequence, some individuals experience difficulty in getting to sleep. Other sleep problems also occur; for example, a Navy master chief, with many years of Antarctic experience, blames the lack of diurnal cues for a general disorientation regarding time:

> You might wake up, look around for your clock and find that it is 9:00. So, you hop out of bed believing that you overslept and are late for work—only to find that its 9:00 at night. People adapt pretty fast to the conditions, unless there are disruptions to your schedule, such as having an extra long work shift, partying too hard, or receiving bad news from home. (Arthur Violanti, personal communication)

A recent commander of Naval Support Force Antarctica reports that all parties involved understand that special conditions exist at polar stations because of the absence of diurnal cues and uneven workloads, and no stigma is attached to most sleep problems in Antarctica. Most personnel adapt to the conditions without experiencing serious or persistent sleep disorders.

The problem involving sleep that presents the greatest cause for concern is excessive sleeping, that is, when an individual withdraws from normal interpersonal contact and retreats increasingly into sleep. Although withdrawal from interpersonal contact is a reasonable and healthy coping mechanism, excessive withdrawal often indicates a serious adjustment problem. This issue is addressed in chapter 11; in the current context, it is important to note that it is possible that a situation might occur in which excessive sleeping by spacecraft crew would be acceptable, even encouraged. For example, inactivity and boredom would probably result if equipment or system failures greatly reduced the workload (i.e., the work opportunities) of the crew on a long-duration mission. Under emergency conditions, there might be little meaningful work to divide among the crew and few recreation opportunities. Possibly, as a result of serious equipment failure or other emergency, future space crews might be forced to retreat to extremely austere conditions, similar to those endured by Fridtjof Nansen and Hjalmar Johansen one hundred years ago.

Nansen and Johansen departed the *Fram*, which had been locked in the Arctic ice cap for more than a year, and made a dash toward the pole on dogsleds. They spent a total of four months on sleds and in kayaks before coming ashore on the large Arctic island known as Franz Josef Land, where they built a 10- by 6-foot hut from stones and walrus hides. There, they spent the next nine months in inactivity and darkness, their world illuminated only by the pale glow of a blubber lamp. It was too cold to venture outside for more than a few minutes at a time. They had nothing to occupy their days in the hut except conversation, but nearly all topics of conversation had been long exhausted. So, they slept. Nansen (1897) describes the experience:

> Many days would sometimes pass almost without our putting our heads out of the passage, and it was only bare necessity that drove us out to fetch ice for drinking water, or a leg or carcass of a bear for food, or some blubber [from a cache they had made just outside the hut].... We had to prepare supper, eat until we were satisfied, and then get into our bags and

> sleep as long as possible to pass the time.... The brain worked
> dully, and I never felt inclined to write anything.... The entries
> in my journal for this time are exceedingly meagre; there are
> sometimes weeks when there is nothing but the most necessary
> meteorological observations and remarks. The chief reason for
> this is that our life was so monotonous that there was nothing
> to write about. The same thoughts came and went day after
> day; there was no more variety in them than in our conversa-
> tion. The very emptiness of the journal really gives the best
> representation of our life during the nine months we lived
> there.... Thus did our time pass. We did our best to sleep away
> as much as possible of it. We carried this out to a high pitch of
> perfection, and could sometimes put in as much as 20 hours'
> sleep in the 24. (Vol. 2, pp. 435, 439, 464)

Nansen's Norwegian Polar Expedition is mentioned many times throughout this book and even suggested as a model to be emulated by the planners of future space expeditions. In the current context, it is sufficient to note that Nansen and Johansen survived their unplanned confinement, despite the austere, brain-numbing conditions that required them to sleep away their time. Nansen's (1897) words might comfort the fears of future space explorers and those concerned about human capabilities to endure a worst-case condition of isolation and confinement:

> It was a strange life, and in many ways it put our patience to a
> severe test; but it was not so unendurable as one might sup-
> pose. We at any rate thought that, all things considered, we
> were fairly well off. Our spirits were good the whole time; we
> looked serenely towards the future, and rejoiced in the thought
> of all the delights it had in store for us. We did not even have
> the recourse to quarreling to while away the time. (Vol. 2, p.
> 464)

NOISE CONTROL

Anyone who has lived with a nocturnal pet or an infant child knows what it is to have one's sleep disturbed, on a regular basis, by noises in the night. Owning a cat or having a small child often results in sleep deprivation as a way of life. Although some individuals can occasionally "sleep through a storm," it is a folklore belief that all people adapt to regular sounds and are not affected by noises perceived during their sleep. In fact, the sleep of most people is disturbed by even the most regular sounds; for some individuals, the quality of sleep can be reduced without conscious recognition or complete awakening. Apparently, throughout most of human evolution, those individuals who are roused from their slumber by noises in sufficient time to avoid danger in the night have had an advantage. Having our sleep disturbed by normal noises is the price we pay for nocturnal vigilance and safety.

Evidence of sleep disturbances resulting from inadequate noise control is abundant. For example, *Skylab* astronauts were repeatedly awakened by the noises made by other crew members during nighttime visits to the waste management facility (i.e., the toilet), by the sounds of a weightless elbow or knee striking a thin wall or bulkhead, and by a symphony of clicks and hums associated with the normal, automatic functioning of the space station. *Skylab*'s hull expanded and contracted with the changing temperatures as the station's orbit carried it from sunlight into darkness and back again. Falling asleep and remaining asleep were sometimes difficult because of the resulting bangs and pops, combined with the sounds of automatic thruster jets and nearby crew mates.

Astronaut Joe Kerwin in his sleep chamber onboard *Skylab*. (Courtesy of NASA)

Further, the crews of Project Tektite in an underwater habitat, similar in size and configuration to what might be expected of a lunar or planetary base, also complained that noise affected their sleep. In particular, conversations and use of the communications channel were impossible without disturbing those in the crew quarters. A similar condition emerged during a recent high-fidelity simulation of the deployment of a military system designed for autonomous operations; the crew worked in twelve-hour shifts and sleeping crew members were regularly disturbed, even though all personnel attempted to be considerate when others were sleeping. The worst offender was the "beep" of the microwave ovens in the galley, which was located adjacent to the sleeping compartments. Similarly, onboard submarines and in the deck chambers of saturation divers, sleeping crews are frequently disturbed by the changing of watches or shifts during twenty-four-hour operations. The relatively larger size of modern Antarctic stations provides greater insulation from sound than the other habitats studied, but the earlier Antarctic explorers endured frequent interruptions of their sleep by watch changes and the constant sound of diesel-powered generators.

At a meeting in Paris in 1990, French spationaute Gen. Jean-Loup Chretien, who worked onboard both *Salyut 7* (in 1982) and *Mir* (in 1988), described his preparations for sleep each night on the space stations. He attached a hammocklike sling to fixtures in an unoccupied place in the space station, then climbed in and went to sleep; his comrades were similarly slung and snoring. This is about what space shuttle astronauts do at bedtime during their brief orbital missions (probably complete with the snoring). General Chretien and others believe that nothing else is really necessary to accommodate sleeping on a spacecraft; private quarters, or sleep chambers, are viewed in this Spartan approach as unnecessary luxuries. My ten-year research on analogue environments, however, strongly suggests that "camping-out" conditions might be acceptable for relatively brief periods and under emergency circumstances, but the associated stress is cumulative and threatens individual adjustment and performance during long-duration missions.

Although the Soviet/Russian space program has accomplished much and currently sets the pace for long-duration space experience, certain aspects of the program seem to be seriously lacking. In particular, a glaring inconsistency exists between providing extensive psychological support services for an on-orbit crew and ignoring the details of habitability for the spacecraft, such as providing private quarters for crew personnel. There are indications that, near the end of long missions, Russian mission managers get only about three hours of productive work from a cosmonaut out of each twenty-four-hour cycle (Col. Gerald Carr, commander of *Skylab III*, quoted in Reichhardt 1990). Following the *Mir* mission, Craig Covault reported in *Aviation Week and Space Technology* that the Soviets had acknowledged the degraded condition of cosmonauts Yuri Romanenko and Alexander Alexandrov during the final days of their mission onboard *Mir*. Romanenko had set a new record of 326 days in space; Alexandrov arrived later and spent twenty-three weeks in orbit.

> "The crew is not concealing that they feel the monotony of the flight," the Soviets said just before reentry. "Their fatigue is building up and even two days off no longer refreshes them." The flight was difficult physically and hard on morale, according to the Soviets. Soviet mission personnel said the crew had its work day reduced to only 4.5 hours in the weeks before reentry, and were being given several hours of leisure time and 9-hour sleep periods. (Covault 1988)

SAFETY

The crew of a ship locked in the polar ice during the days of sail were exposed to the sporadic creaks and groans caused by the formation of pressure ridges and by the pressure of the ice against the ship's hull. The onset of the pressure was unpredictable, and the booming of pressure ridges and groaning of the ship's timbers could last for hours at a time. No one could or dared sleep through these periods because the pressure could easily crush the ship and send her to the bottom before all hands and supplies could be evacuated. The crew stowed small boats and survival supplies in several locations on the deck and ice in preparation for a quick evacuation and also memorized the locations of compartments and passageways to permit escape in complete darkness. Dozens of wooden ships were "pinched" and lost in this manner in polar pack ice during the nineteenth century.

Fire is the greatest threat to polar stations. For this reason, since the earliest sojourns in Antarctica, expedition planners have designed their huts and larger complexes with fire control and evacuation of personnel and equipment in mind. The same principle should be applied to the design of spacecraft, planetary bases, and other remote-duty habitats. This safety design principle was not followed, or could not be followed, when *Skylab* was pieced together from leftover Saturn rocket components. Before retiring each evening, the commander of each *Skylab* mission made a final inspection of the station. With checklist in hand, he ensured that the flare alarm on the solar console was activated, that the ground control alarm was functioning, that the fire alarm was operational, and finally that the air pressure alarm was in the "on" position. The air pressure alarm would sound in the event the station was punctured by a meteoroid. No meteorite emergency occurred, but the *Skylab* astronauts urged that the sleep chambers on future spacecraft not be so far from the exit.

An equipment malfunction, fire, or micrometeoroid collision could be as catastrophic to future space travelers as the pack ice was to Arctic explorers, sealers, and whalers. The crews of spacecraft and planetary habitats, however, will not need to remain as vigilant during sleep periods as polar sailors because they will be alerted by automatic sensor systems to any emergency.

RECOMMENDATIONS

Following are specific recommendations regarding sleep during long-duration space missions:

- Adhere to regular schedules of sleep and activity on all future long-duration space missions. Maintaining a sleep schedule will contribute to individual adjustment and performance and facilitate group harmony.

- Avoid scheduling tasks to be performed within one hour of the scheduled sleep period so that crew personnel can relax before attempting to go to sleep.[4]

- Provide zeitgebers to help regulate the physiological clocks of crew personnel and facilitate adherence to the sleep schedule. For example, automatically dim or alter the color of internal spacecraft illumination in common areas for eight to twelve hours each mission "night" to correspond with the day/night cycle at the site of the principal mission control facility. Living and working on "Houston time," supported by a set of appropriate diurnal cues to facilitate maintenance of normal circadian rhythms, would contribute to individual abilities to adhere to a sleep schedule and, ultimately, to adjustment, performance, and mission success. Also, this procedure would make life easier for the crew at mission control.

- Develop or adapt a program of "sleep hygiene" that can assist space crew personnel to maintain the sleep/activity schedule. The program would include autogenic routines, such as sensory relaxation, to hasten the onset of sleep.

- Design and provide individual, well-insulated sleep chambers for crew personnel. The chambers should be fitted with hatches or sound-absorbing coverings to shield the occupants from noise and light.

- Locate the sleep chambers near the fire exit for safety and peace of mind, and away from the waste management facility and the galley to minimize noise.

- Avoid or minimize shift work that would disturb sleeping crew members; if shift work is necessary, prevent personnel from drifting (i.e., retiring and arising later than usual) on days off.

- Equip the sleep chambers with communications devices. A simple annunciator is sufficient to alert sleeping crew members to danger, but a two-way voice capability is better because it would have other than emergency applications. A combination of Klaxon, visual display, and intercom is ideal.

CHAPTER 4

CLOTHING

I have had to change my shirt again. This is the last clean side that I have got. I have been wearing two shirts and each side will now have done duty next to the skin, as I have changed round each month, and I have certainly found the benefit of it, and on the point we all three agree.

—From Lashly's diary, in *The Worst Journey in the World*

There is a tendency to consider certain items, such as changes of clothing, to be luxuries when all supplies must be carried or dragged for long distances overland. The three members of Scott's first support party were forced by the failure of their tractors and ponies to pull, or "man-haul," heavy sledges loaded with food and equipment as they established caches of supplies for later use by the polar party. Each pound of personal equipment had to be hauled for miles over the rough, icy terrain every day for nearly four months during the austral summer of 1911–12. To minimize weight, most members of Scott's expedition carried only one change of clothes with them in the field, regardless of the duration of the trek. Thus, Lashly and the others could change their shirts only once, but each shirt offered two sides— one for each month of the four-month journey.

Nansen's experience with clothes was far worse. Neither he nor Johansen had a change of clothes during the nine months they spent together in their small hut on Franz Josef Land. They attempted to wash their garments periodically, but the best they could do was to scrape the polar bear and walrus fat off them while the clothes were still wet and warm. The amount of oil extracted in this manner produced a measurable quantity of fuel for their blubber lamps.

Nansen's and Johansen's dreams were filled that winter with images of Turkish baths and shops well stocked with clean clothes.

It is unlikely that future space explorers will need to endure long periods without changes of clothing as did their predecessors who explored the remote regions of Earth. These examples, however, indicate that human tolerance concerning this issue is extremely elastic.

Lessons learned from *Skylab* missions provide considerable guidance regarding clothing for a "shirt-sleeve" working environment in space. For example, two-piece outfits (i.e., pants and shirts) were considered convenient by *Skylab* astronauts for the same reasons as on Earth: better fit than coveralls, more adjustable, and more convenient for personal hygiene. *Skylab* crews, however, disliked the fabric of their outer garments. Besides the color (a brownish gold considered by some to be boring), the fireproof fabric did not breathe well and developed a peculiar odor, especially following exercise. Conventional cotton undergarments were also provided. The crews of space shuttles have benefited greatly from the *Skylab* experience. Shuttle crews often wear colorful and seemingly comfortable polo shirts and color-coordinated

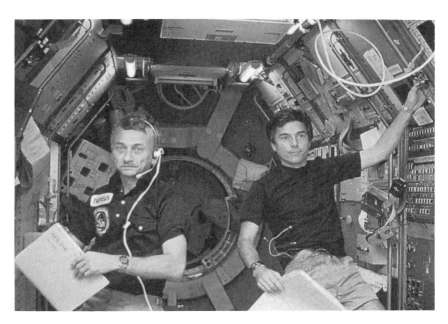

Crew personnel working in the "shirt-sleeve" environment of the space shuttle. (Courtesy of NASA)

shorts or trousers.

Three factors with design and procedural implications that relate to clothing for long-duration space missions are hygienic functions, psychological effects, and fugitive lint.

HYGIENIC FUNCTIONS

Separating the issues of clothing and personal hygiene is difficult; in particular, it is important to recognize that clothing can appear clean on the outside yet be contaminated by excessive wearing. Although it is unlikely that this condition would have physiologic implications for space crews, certain characteristics of soiled clothing could result in health problems. Fraser (1968a) suggests that the attributes of concern are those associated with mechanical and chemical irritation, hypersensitivity, and media that encourage microbiological growth on the skin or in body niches; the latter presents the most serious concern.

Skylab astronauts believed that their clothes rarely became soiled and suggested one to two weeks' wear for outer garments and daily changes of underwear (NASA 1974). In a previous report, I suggest at least one change of outer garments each week, daily change of underclothes, and special athletic gear (shorts and shirt) for daily physical exercise as the minimum requirements for space station crew personnel (Stuster 1986). Based on the results of my current research, however, it seems reasonable that less frequent changes of clothing might be acceptable on long-duration missions if appropriate personal hygiene facilities are provided; two weeks or more might be possible. Actual clothing requirements could be further specified during premission simulations.

Storage space for clothing will be extremely limited on interplanetary spacecraft and at lunar and martian bases. The penalty for "extra baggage" will be fewer items in other categories competing for weight allowances and scarce storage space. Weekly changes of a two-garment ensemble on a mission to Mars would total more than three hundred items and require nearly 20 cubic feet of storage space. Cutting those numbers in half by changing outer garments every two weeks would significantly increase space for other supplies and probably not affect crew performance. Just as previous explorers tolerated grubby conditions for long periods when necessary, it is probable that future space explorers will understand the unique nature of their endeavors and accept less in all amenities than their colleagues who routinely staff a low–Earth-orbit space station. The crews of missions to Mars and those who staff lunar bases will probably make only one such tour during their careers because of safety limits for radiation exposure. For this reason, they will likely share the perspective of former explorers regarding tolerance of conditions, including fewer changes of clothing. Space station crews, however, will probably spend several 90- to 120-day tours in orbit, on a rotational basis, during their careers. The work of space station crews will be more routine than expeditionary, and they will not receive the same level of personal notoriety and other rewards, as will long-duration crews, that might serve to offset the negative effects of austere conditions.

PSYCHOLOGICAL EFFECTS

There is a tendency among some people in isolated and confined conditions to allow standards of personal hygiene and appearance to slip. Capt. Noel Howard, a Navy psychiatrist, described this phenomenon as a common form of regressive adaptation to a captive situation (one may be held captive by others or by an environment). Usually at each small Antarctic station there is at least one individual, typically among the scientific rather than the military staff, who seems to take some pleasure in becoming offensive to others (i.e., dirty and slovenly). This phenomenon, also occasionally reported among the crews of nuclear submarines, is cause for concern. It must be understood that, in isolation and confinement, issues that would be insignificant elsewhere are typically magnified beyond all reasonable proportions. The seemingly trivial issue of wearing dirty clothing and being otherwise offensive might be overlooked elsewhere, but it can cause serious interpersonal problems in isolation and confinement.

There are at least two separate psychological effects of a clean set of clothes: (1) on the individual and (2) on the group. The refreshing effect of a shower is generally recognized in our culture; part of that effect is attributed to the additionally invigorating effect of clean clothes associated with the shower. Similarly, the subjective feelings of group cohesion and morale are affected by the appearance of others within the group. To this end, military managers have encouraged adherence to standards characterized by a crisp and clean appearance. The psychological value of clothing is believed by military psychologists to be a definite factor in morale and productivity.

Famous English explorer James Cook recognized the physical and psychological benefits of good hygiene and clean clothes. Captain Cook insisted on weekly bathing for his crew (including the time spent in Antarctic waters during 1773) and frequent changes of clothing. The powerful psychological influence of clothing has been used in the reverse, as well. Dressing prisoners poorly is frequently an initial step in the process commonly known as "brainwashing," in which attempts are made consciously to manipulate a prisoner's self-image. Crew leaders should attend to this issue and encourage individual crew members to change clothing according to a predetermined schedule, if necessary. This will facilitate positive individual and group perceptions and minimize a potential source of social conflict.

The final psychological aspect of clothing concerns the wearing of idiosyncratic dress, rather than, or in addition to, a uniform (required for previous and current astronauts). Two important reasons support the wearing of personal items of clothing, provided they meet safety and outgassing standards: (1) wearing idiosyncratic dress contributes to variety in the visual field (lack of variability is one of the principal stressors in confined and isolated conditions), and (2) wearing personal items of clothing permits crew members occasionally to express individuality, usually without jeopardizing group solidarity.

At modern U.S. Antarctic stations, military personnel are required to wear uniforms when on duty, but off-duty personnel and civilians are permitted to wear anything they want, as long as they remain warm— the primary concern. Even military dress standards are relaxed under the special conditions of isolation and confinement. A career Navy Seabee, for instance, might wear a uniform, but with a bright yellow scarf, florescent shoelaces, or some other nongovernment issue item (usually in a bright color), when in Antarctica. These expressions of individuality are tolerated, even encouraged at some stations, as a means to add variety to a relatively monotonous environment.

Personal clothing can be useful in other ways, as well. During a recent military simulation, for example, group leaders required on-duty personnel to wear uniforms and off-duty personnel to wear civilian clothing. This "clothing code" permitted the leaders to determine instantly who among the eighteen crew members were on duty (and available for work) at any given time in the crowded habitat. This practice probably would be unnecessary in the small crews planned for interplanetary voyages and the initial lunar missions. The practice of coding shifts by color or type of clothing, however, will be useful to group leaders when planetary and lunar bases are staffed by more than a few individuals and even more important when shift work is imposed.

FUGITIVE LINT

A few years ago, the principal design concern of the habitability group at the Johnson Space Center was fugitive lint, that is, the fine ravelings and short fibers that are generated by fabrics and escape into the weightless atmosphere of a habitat (analogous to "fugitive dust" caused by construction projects). Several problems can be caused by lint in the absence of gravity; they include fouling of ventilation systems, inhalation by crew, and contamination of food and equipment. Fugitive lint from astronauts' and workers' uniforms caused a computer to overheat during a shuttle mission in 1990, and the possibility of lint contamination remains a concern for the planned space station and future spacecraft. In this regard, as the number of crew members increases, more clothing and towels will be required and more lint will be produced.

Lint was never mentioned as a problem in any of the documents reviewed concerning expeditions and Antarctic experiences. Lint is a major problem onboard submarines, however, with some of the same consequences as those onboard spacecraft. On submarines, lint is countered by the use of a lint-free material in garment construction and the installation of high-capacity air filters. Similarly, suggestions for lint prevention during long-duration space missions, as well as on board space stations, include using prewashed, lint-free clothing and towels to reduce on-orbit lint generation; encouraging the wearing of rugby or "safari" shorts rather than long pants (less material to generate lint); and locating an intake fan and air filtration system near the primary clothing and towel dispensary to trap fugitive lint at its source.

RECOMMENDATIONS

The hygienic and psychological advantages of changing clothes frequently on long-duration space missions must be weighed against the architectural requirements for storing clothing, fuel, and all of the other equipment and supplies needed for the trip. For this reason, it is important to note that, according to the experiences of previous explorers, human tolerance regarding clothing can be considerable when conditions demand it.

Following are specific recommendations regarding clothing on long-duration space expeditions:

- Provide sufficient supplies to permit crew members to change outer garments every two weeks.

- Provide sufficient supplies to permit crew members to change undergarments every other day.

- Provide special clothing (shorts and shirts) for physical exercise; one set per week should be sufficient.

- Encourage crew leaders to establish a schedule of uniform or clothing changes if individual crew members begin to slip in their hygiene standards.

- Permit the wearing of idiosyncratic dress during off-duty periods and personal items with crew uniform at any time. Encourage the wearing of colorful items.

- Provide prewashed clothing and towels to reduce lint.

- Provide and encourage the wearing of short pants as an alternative to trousers to minimize lint.

- Locate an air filtration fan and filter near the clothing and towel dispensary.

- Consider designing the hygiene facility to permit handwashing of garments. This feature can greatly decrease the number of garments and amount of storage space for clothing needed on long-duration expeditions.

CHAPTER 5

EXERCISE

[I h]ave determined that, beginning from to-morrow, every man is to go out snowshoeing two hours daily, from 11 to 1, so long as the daylight lasts. It is necessary. If anything happened that obliged us to make our way home over the ice, I am afraid some of the company would be a terrible hindrance to us, unpracticed as they are now ... if they had to go out on a long course, and without snowshoes, it would be all over with us.

—From Nansen's diary, in *Farthest North*

What Nansen called snowshoes, we now call skis. The thirteen-man crew of the *Fram* skied as a group, and their outings on the ice were so successful that Nansen later wrote that they did it regularly: "Besides being good exercise, it is also a great pleasure; everyone seemed to thrive on it." Nansen had a firm grasp on one of the key principles of human behavior regarding exercise: if you want people to do it, make it enjoyable in some way. After Nansen departed the *Fram* with Johansen on their dash north, the captain of the vessel, Otto Sverdrup, ordered every man to take two hours of exercise each day, despite the subzero temperatures. Sverdrup was very fond of these walks, which, he wrote, "freshened up both soul and body." He often wandered on the ice in the vicinity of the *Fram* for four hours a day, two hours in the morning and two in the afternoon.

Nansen was fortunate to have access to such a pleasant form of exercise as skiing, and his crew of Norwegians were accustomed to the extreme cold. (There is no such thing as bad weather, just bad clothes, according to an old Norwegian saying.) Many explorers before Nansen had recognized the physical and psychological benefits of exercise when crews were isolated and confined. In 1819, for example, Lt. Edward Parry established the first intentional Arctic winter-over camp at Winter Harbor on Melville Island. Parry had planned well for the experience in both equipment and procedures. The morale of the crew that winter was excellent, buoyed by many planned activities, including a regular schedule of exercise. When it became too cold to exercise on shore, the men jogged around the decks of their ship and sang songs taught to them by the older whalers in the crew. At age twenty-eight, Parry was the oldest member of the Arctic expedition. The physical condition and morale of his men were such that Parry wrote:

> I verily believe there never was a more merry and cheerful set of men than ours, and I must in justice add that they seem fully sensible of attending to the precautions adopted for the preservation of their health. (Quoted in Mountfield 1974, 75)

Later, in an 1879 American attempt for the North Pole, Lt. George De Long ordered regular exercise and organized games for his crew on the ice; several footballs are listed among the USS *Jeannette*'s recreation equipment (Guttridge 1986).

Two decades after the *Jeannette* steamed north out of San Francisco Bay, an American, Dr. Frederick A. Cook, was onboard the *Belgica* as

Snowshoe practice during the Norwegian Polar Expedition, 28 September 1894. (From Nansen, 1897)

the medical officer for the Belgian Antarctic Expedition, the first intentional winter-over in Antarctica. The *Belgica* Expedition, as it is usually called, was nearly a complete disaster because of a mysterious malaise that afflicted the crew during their long, dark Antarctic night. Other members of the crew later credited Cook with saving the expedition from physical and psychological collapse (see chapter 8). To help his own state of mind, Cook chose to exercise, in a manner similar to Sverdrup a few years earlier at the opposite end of the Earth. Cook notes in his journal:

> I have selected [midday] to take a daily walk over the pack [ice] to neighboring floes, and to distant icebergs, to study the ice and life, and to obtain sufficient physical exercise, as well as mental recreation, to retard the spell of indifference which is falling over me. (Cook [1900] 1980, 289)

As evidenced by the preceding examples, exercise has been used therapeutically by explorers for generations to help counter the negative effects of isolation and confinement. Exercise, however, is a critical concern for the crews of long-duration space missions as a countermeasure for the negative effects of zero gravity. Muscle strength is lost from lack of use in the absence of gravity; the muscle strength needed to stand erect and walk about on Earth is unnecessary in space, so the muscles atrophy from disuse. Even more insidious is the bone demineralization (i.e., loss of calcium, nitrogen, and phosphorus) that occurs under zero gravity. Demineralization is accompanied by decreased bone diameter and the formation of urinary stones. Bone tissue is in a constant state of "remodeling" in response to external stimuli, in particular, the jarring impact conveyed to bones by regular use in the gravity of Earth. Essentially, under normal Earth-bound conditions, the osteoblasts make bone cells about as fast as the osteoclasts can break them down. In the absence of gravity, there are fewer impacts to the bones to stimulate the generation of bone cells; the balance is tipped in favor of the osteoclasts and the result is brittle bones. If permitted to demineralize, the bones of spacecraft crew members could become so weak as to break under martian gravity or on return to Earth. (See Connors, Harrison, and Akins 1985 for a review of physiological effects of zero gravity.)

Exercise techniques will be developed to help counter the negative effects of zero gravity on human muscles and bones. The results of bed rest studies that simulate a weightless condition, however, suggest that exercise alone is an insufficient countermeasure (Vernikos-Danellis et al. 1974). Many of the required data are already available from previous U.S. space missions, in particular *Skylab* (NAS 1972; Gibson 1975; Kerwin 1975). Also, valuable information and innovative procedures should result from cooperative missions to the Russian *Mir* space station and, ultimately, from research to be conducted onboard the international space station, but it is apparent that much additional work will be required to define the types and amounts of exercise and other procedures needed to counter the negative effects of zero gravity on muscles and bones during long-duration space missions. What does seem certain, however, is that interplanetary explorers will be required to perform considerable exercise, perhaps two hours each mission day en route to and from their destinations, to maintain acceptable levels of cardiovascular capacity, muscle strength, and bone chemistry.

Evidence from previous space missions suggests that some astronauts and cosmonauts have resisted performing the prescribed amount of vigorous exercise. While physiologists work to define the types of exercise that might slow the negative effects of zero gravity, behavioral scientists need to address the psychological aspects of routine exercise, that is, the development of methods and strategies of exercise that are less boring and more motivating than those employed in space or elsewhere in the past. In other words, a "motivational framework" is necessary to increase the probability that crews of long-duration space missions will perform the exercise needed to maintain individual health, fitness, and performance.

Clearly, the same factors will not motivate all members of any particular group to exercise. Research on this subject led to the identification of a set of principles regarding human motivation to exercise. The three main principles, discussed in the following sections, appear to be tangible results, recreational exercise, and the integration of activities.

THE PRINCIPLE OF TANGIBLE RESULTS

Many individuals who exercise regularly under conditions of isolation and confinement do so for one of two reasons: either for the recreational value or for the achievement of some tangible result. The latter category includes building up muscle tissue, reducing excess body fat, and/or attaining a performance goal (established by the individual or others, or competitively). Until the relatively recent physical fitness phenomenon, only rare individuals engaged in daily exercise simply for health maintenance, at least to the extent that will be required to counter the effects of zero gravity. In almost all remote-duty conditions studied, either recreation or some tangible result of the activity has been the objective of most regular, vigorous exercise.

There are many ways that tangible results of exercise can be offered to confined crews. For example, the U.S. Navy found that, by appealing to vanity and concerns for health, naval personnel can be successfully encouraged in the regular use of compact weight machines (i.e., machines that use friction rather than heavy weights) installed onboard ships and submarines. Similarly, recent experience indicates a pronounced preference among confined and isolated U.S. Air Force personnel for weights and weight machines, rather than bicycle ergometers or similar aerobic devices. The preference exhibited among these military personnel is consistent with the personal motivation of some individuals to build up body tissue.

Some people, however, respond better to competition, either against others or themselves, as a means of achieving tangible results of their exercise efforts. To induce these people to exercise, individual physical ability and performance records can be maintained and competitions (ongoing or periodic) held to provide a motivational framework that encourages crew personnel to exercise regularly. For example, many of the *Skylab* astronauts kept their exercise performance records on the bulkhead of the experiments room and reviewed them on a daily basis.

Former Master Chief of the Command for Naval Support Force Antarctica Arthur Violanti also has used competition to encourage his personnel to exercise (e.g., 5K and 10K runs to Scott Hut, weight lifting, and even golf on the ice).[1] Violanti hastens to add, however, that it is important to keep the competition friendly by avoiding big awards; a handshake and a two-cent ribbon are customary. He also recommends doing all that is possible to avoid deflating human egos, which are made even more fragile than usual by the special conditions of isolation and confinement. In this regard, it is important to recognize that not all people are motivated by competing with others. For this reason, participation must be voluntary in any motivational framework based on competition that is implemented to encourage the crew to exercise. Competitions must be selected by individuals and initiated by mutual agreement of the competitors. Procedures for contest termination also must be developed as a contingency against the possibility of deteriorating interpersonal relations resulting from the competition. Some crew members will respond well to competitions involving physical exercise, and well-designed competitions of this sort do not present serious threats to social harmony among isolated and confined crew.

Another technique that can show tangible results when a crew exercises regularly is the installation onboard the spacecraft of a bicycle ergometer, or other exercise device, connected to an electrical generator that contributes to the spacecraft's power requirements. With this type of device, crew members can monitor their individual contributions to the overall energy requirements of the spacecraft as they exercise. This technique was suggested for space stations more than a decade ago; I still believe that this approach could be helpful for individuals who are motivated to exercise by cooperation rather than competition.

It is important to emphasize that not all individuals will respond to the same motivational framework or incentives. Accordingly, it will be necessary to provide a range of exercise options and motivational frameworks to ensure that all crew members are sufficiently motivated to maintain the rigorous daily exercise schedule necessary to counter the negative effects of the zero-gravity environment during long-duration space missions.

THE PRINCIPLE OF RECREATIONAL EXERCISE

Crew members who are not motivated to exercise by the promise of tangible results or by competition might be more inclined to exercise if the activities are recreational (i.e., fun). The *Skylab* astronauts were pleased to have access to their bicycle ergometer, and some complained bitterly when their time on the device was cut short by mission controllers. There was a problem, however, in maintaining interest in pedaling a stationary bicycle while looking at a bulkhead. The astronauts reported that they needed mental diversion after about fifteen minutes on the ergometer. Some listened to recorded music and found that sufficiently stimulating to allow them to continue, but what they *really* wanted to do was to look out the window while exercising. Charles Conrad, commander of the first *Skylab* mission, once pedaled continuously for ninety minutes, or approximately one revolution of Earth; this allowed him to claim that he had bicycled around the globe (Cooper 1976). Placing the bicycle ergometer near a window might motivate future space personnel to do the same. A window in front of the exercise device is perhaps the most frequently recalled habitability recommendation of the *Skylab* astronauts. Their judgment cannot be disputed; if at all possible, a viewing port should be within sight of the exercise equipment included onboard all future long-duration spacecraft.

At first, the only exercise equipment onboard *Skylab* was the bicycle ergometer, but a Thornton treadmill was added for the final mission. The treadmill was a sheet of slippery Teflon, attached to the floor, on which the astronaut walked in stocking feet. Bungee cords formed a harness to substitute for gravity (Compton and Benson 1983). The treadmill offered effective exercise for the calf muscles, but the astronauts preferred the bicycle for overall conditioning. Edward Gibson (1975) reports that he always felt good after using it, and Joe Kerwin felt that "strong glow of health" associated with a good workout on Earth (NASA 1974). A bicycle ergometer was also preferred to an exercise device that simulated cross-country skiing during a recent military simulation involving isolation and confinement. None of the participating personnel had skied before, so they found the necessary coordination of upper and lower body movements to be difficult, despite the many exercise advantages of the skiing simulator.

It is estimated that only one exercise device would be necessary for a crew of six on an interplanetary mission, but at two hours per crew member the device would be in use for twelve hours during every twenty-four-hour cycle. At this rate of use, the device would probably wear out before the mission was over. For this reason, and to ensure that at least one device is always operational for health maintenance, a supply of replacement parts and at least one complete backup device would be necessary. Preferably, the backup device, or devices, should not be the same type as the primary exercise device. Some crew members might prefer a bicycle ergometer to a treadmill; others might want a rowing machine or a device that simulates the body movements of cross-country skiing. It is also quite likely that, despite their original preferences, the crew would appreciate an occasional change in exercise mode, if for no other reason than to break the monotony of the routine. In addition, individual preferences can change during the course of a long mission. For these reasons, I strongly recommend that at least two different types of exercise device be included onboard future long-duration spacecraft. If storage capacity is available, it would be advisable to take as many types as reasonably possible to ensure maximum variety of exercise opportunities. For example, a cross-country skiing machine could replace a treadmill when the crew becomes bored with simulated walking or to correspond with the winter season at mission control.

Research conducted during high-fidelity mission simulations should explore the acceptability of various exercise devices and optional motivational frameworks. Possible motivating strategies include competition (among crew members or among crews), personal goal setting, cooperation/contribution (e.g., generating electrical power for station use), and recreation, to name a few. Several exercise devices should be evaluated during simulations either by the actual crew of a spacecraft or by personnel similar to those who might be selected for space missions (e.g., scientists, aerospace engineers, civilian or military pilots).

It is probably safe to specify that one of the devices included onboard a spacecraft should be a bicycle ergometer because of its general acceptability and the quality of the workout it offers. As mentioned in *Skylab* reports, motivation to remain on the device for the prescribed periods might be increased by placing it in front of a window or television screen. A television and videotape player would probably provide sufficient entertainment to encourage most crew members to endure the otherwise monotonous exercise for the required periods.[2] In addition, a more important value might be derived from this arrangement. To the extent that recreation is embedded in exercise, the amount of separate recreation time needed to maintain individual adjustment and productivity could be decreased. Because productivity is a primary objective of habitability, any time that is freed from other requirements, such as recreation, can be redirected to productive activity. Although productivity will be a central concern onboard future space stations and at lunar bases, a primary concern on interplanetary missions will be the reduction of boredom resulting from the scarcity of meaningful tasks to perform en route to the destination planet and during the return trip to Earth.

THE PRINCIPLE OF INTEGRATION OF ACTIVITIES

The final principle presented here in regard to exercise motivation is related to the discussion in the previous paragraph. Where practical, it might be a good idea to incorporate physical exercise into routine operations, as well as to incorporate routine operations into periods of physical exercise. The latter can be accomplished by linking leisure to exercise, for instance, by viewing entertainment or news programming while performing the required exercise. The application of this principle could be extended, as a matter of individual preference, to include mission-related reading or task preparation.

The first principle, that of tangible results, however, offers a truly creative opportunity for collaboration among engineers, physiologists, and ergonomists: to design equipment and devices for which the power is provided by the physical exertion of the crew. As an example, a trash compactor that is capable of processing the volumes of paper and plastic waste generated by the crew during normal operations will be required on board the spacecraft. An average of one pound of trash (mostly bulky food packaging) per person was generated during a recent military simulation involving isolation and confinement. Trash storage became an acute problem for the crew when their normal method of disposal was unavailable. An automatic trash compactor requires a fairly sophisticated design, complex machinery, and electrical power for operation. A simpler solution, involving a far less complex design, could be operated manually by a crew member; manual, rather than electromechanical, operation would also contribute to reliability and maintainability. To the extent that the exercise involved in operating the device counters the effects of muscle atrophy, the astronaut-operators would be well served. This suggestion was originally made more than a decade ago for space stations; within a few years, NASA personnel developed a small, manually operated trash compactor for use on space shuttles.

If the principle of integration of activities were to be applied systematically in other contexts (e.g., hatches, pumps, etc.), the time prescribed for actual physical exercise conceivably could be reduced and free the crew for more productive pursuits. Perhaps more important, it would provide meaningful work for crew members to perform during their months of inactivity on a long-duration expedition.

OTHER TOPICS RELATED TO EXERCISE

There is evidence that physical activity can also contribute to the maintenance of crew morale, in addition to countering the negative effects of zero gravity. Because many of the potential crew personnel for future expeditions are physically active in their lives on Earth, it is likely that exercise opportunities while living in space will be appreciated; this was clearly the case onboard *Skylab*. Also, there is evidence to support the notion that structured exercise improves task performance and cognitive functions as well (Zubeck 1963). In this regard, it is likely that physical exercise on long-duration space missions will have value beyond its efficacy in countering the negative effects of the weightless environment.

A final consideration is the physical layout of the exercise area. Body heat generated by exercise tends to remain near its source because convection is absent in a weightless environment. Consequently, a small fan was mounted on the wall near the ergometer during the third *Skylab* mission to provide some relief. Also, the space allocated to the ergometer onboard *Skylab* was too small to allow other task-oriented work in the vicinity. Designers of future spacecraft should address these issues by providing a well-ventilated area dedicated, perhaps exclusively, to physical exercise.

RECOMMENDATIONS

Future space explorers will lack Nansen's access to skiing as a form of exercise, but many options are available to provide crew members of long-duration spacecraft sufficient motivation to engage in regular and vigorous physical exercise. More research is required, perhaps, onboard the international space station and at space habitat simulations to define further the necessary types of exercise and motivational frameworks. In the meantime, the following specific recommendations relate to exercise during long-duration space expeditions:

- Apply the principle of tangible results.
    - Develop compact zero-gravity isotonic and isometric devices.
    - Maintain personal physical ability and performance records.
    - Design ergometer-driven power generator with readout.

- Apply the principle of recreational exercise.
    - Design the exercise system to allow placement of the ergometer near a window for outside viewing during exercise.
    - Place television with variable programming near the ergometer.
    - Encourage the development of zero gravity physical games.

- Apply the principle of integration of activities.

- – Incorporate physical exercise into routine operations (e.g., manual trash compactor, trash ejector, waste pumps, etc.).
- – Incorporate routine operations into physical exercise periods (e.g., task preparation while exercising).

- Design the exercise area and equipment as a dedicated "mini-gym."

- Provide adequate ventilation.

- Provide backup exercise equipment and spare parts for maintenance.

- Provide more than one type of exercise device to be used on a rotational basis to offer variety. Consider rotating devices to correspond with seasonal changes at mission control.

CHAPTER 6

WORKLOAD

From his reading of Arctic literature the commander [Lieutenant Greely] knew that man's greatest winter enemy is boredom; he sought by every possible means to postpone the shutdown of outdoor work, which would force the men into idleness. Sledge parties stayed out on the trail well into November in the deep twilight of half-day, and frequently under the bright moon, which permitted a view of hills twenty miles away. From this night work the men gained self-confidence to venture forth whatever the hour. The instruments were purposely placed some distance from the house so that the routine of visiting them for readings offered relief from monotony.

—A. L. Todd, *Abandoned*

Work keeps at bay three great evils: boredom, vice, and need.
—Voltaire, *Candide*

Workload assessment, a traditional activity of the human factors specialist, has applications to the design of equipment and procedures, the development of personnel selection criteria, and the identification of the number of human operators required for a system. Workload has been defined in many ways: the requirements of task performance (Klein 1970); demands and effort, or intensity, needed to satisfy task requirements (Cooper and Harper 1969); effort and accomplishment (Cantrell and Hartman 1967); and actions required of an operator under specific conditions (Chiles 1982). The last definition is distinguished from the others by its recognition that workload, task, and situational factors are highly interrelated. This is an important distinction. Neither the general concept nor a specific instance of workload can be fully understood without reference to the number, characteristics, and sequence of tasks that comprise a job, as well as the procedural and environmental conditions under which the tasks are performed. For example, in a recent analysis of the most physically demanding activities performed by U.S. Navy SEALs (members of Sea-Air-Land [teams]), it quickly became apparent that individual tasks performed by the operators are not what make the work particularly difficult (Stuster et al. 1994). Rather, the sequence of tasks, their durations, and the conditions under which the tasks are performed render the work performed by SEAL personnel uniquely difficult. A special operations task described out of context conveys nothing about the many difficult tasks immediately preceding it nor indicates that the task was performed during the course of several days of similar work under extreme environmental conditions and that the operators probably had insufficient water, food, and rest. The same considerations are appropriate when assessing the work to be performed onboard future spacecraft.

The lack of agreement among workload experts is attributable to the practice of using the term *workload* to refer to more than one phenomenon: the demands imposed on an individual; the effort exerted to accomplish those demands; and the physiological, subjective, and performance consequences of an individual's actions. Workload is a complex subject; the term must be defined for each specific application.

Most research concerning workload and the associated definitions has focused on high workload. This is due to the many advantages derived from obtaining as much work as possible from the fewest number of human operators (from assemblyline workers to airline pilots). As a consequence, most definitions and workload assessment techniques tend to be inappropriate when a job is characterized by low workload or fluctuations between high- and low-workload conditions. Connors, Harrison, and Akins (1985), however, provide a definition of workload that is relevant to future space missions:

> Workload will be defined broadly as the total work demand placed on the operator, including the amount and intensity of operator effort required to accomplish the task. If we think of a continuum of workload, we can assume that some optimal workload exists for a given individual at a given level of skill. Thus, the optimal load varies within certain limits according to individual differences in capacity, skill, and reactions to situa-

tional factors. The extremes of this continuum have adverse implications for performance. (P. 125)

It is important to include situational factors in a general definition of workload and in techniques developed to measure specific workloads. A task or task sequence that is described or the performance of an activity that is measured without reference to situational factors conveys nothing about the many difficult tasks or the days of mind-numbing inactivity that might have preceded it. Further, viewing workload as a continuum, from too low to too high, is essential for understanding certain jobs, such as that of explorer, both past and future.

HIGH-WORKLOAD CONDITIONS

Because of the high cost of launching humans and maintaining them in Earth orbit or on the surface of the moon or Mars, it is essential that these efforts be performed as efficiently as possible (i.e., to achieve the desired results at the lowest possible cost). To this end, it will be necessary to define the optimal and maximal sustainable workloads or workload cycles for the personnel under the specific environmental conditions of their missions. For example, the work onboard orbital space stations of the future probably will be performed in twelve-hour shifts, similar to blue and gold teams onboard nuclear submarines and blue and red teams on the more recent space shuttle missions. Shift work is necessary when a facility must be operated continuously to achieve production quotas or additional efficiency. Shift work is an effective approach in an isolated and confined habitat if habitability features have received sufficient attention. Important habitability features include private sleeping quarters that are insulated from the sounds generated by the shift on duty and procedures designed to facilitate task-related communication between the shifts.

The early lunar missions of the twenty-first century will probably resemble the Apollo missions in that crews will be relatively small, with well-defined objectives and high workloads; it is unlikely that shift work will be necessary during the early return missions because all members of the small crews will be required to work cooperatively. The need to implement shift work, however, almost certainly will develop as the lunar base evolves with added capabilities and personnel. Human occupation of Mars is likely to follow the same pattern as lunar development: small "pathfinder" missions, characterized by small crews, short surface stays, high workloads, and no shift work, to be succeeded by larger crews, longer surface stays, and high workloads facilitated by the implementation of shift work. Again, the added efficiency and productivity of shift work are purchased at the cost of sleep disruptions and degraded human performance if appropriate attention is not devoted to habitability features and procedures.

Fatigue is generally the word used to describe the condition that occurs in human operators as a consequence of performing mental and physical work for sustained periods or with insufficient rest. There is no generally accepted definition of fatigue, but most human performance specialists probably agree that fatigue involves lowered sensitivity, responsiveness, and capacity for work and a decrease in the volume of information that can be processed by a human operator. The effects of fatigue resulting from high workloads are relatively well understood. Fatigue slows complex task performance, results in irregular and disordered performance, and contributes to human errors and inadvertent actions.

Another important consequence of high workloads can be the stress (or strain, to be more precise) associated with attempting to "keep up" or maintain a tight schedule. For example, individual workers feel additional pressure when the speed of an assembly line increases. The workers might be unable to maintain the pace, then fall behind. Fueled by the desire to perform well but constrained by personal capabilities, situational limitations, and the stress of falling behind, an individual's efforts to catch up might result in an increased propensity for error, which contributes to falling farther behind. A consequence of many jobs is the creation of time-related stress for the incumbents, from assembly-line workers to corporate and government engineers, scientists, and managers. Workload-related stress of this type is tolerable when experienced only occasionally, but it can quickly become intolerable when a job involves a relentless stream of scheduled deadlines and serious consequences if they are not met. This must have been what the crew of *Skylab* 4 experienced in 1973. Col. Gerald Carr, commander of the eighty-four-day mission, describes the condition onboard *Skylab*:

> Everything was done sequentially on a very tight schedule. We were all so success-oriented and job-oriented that "following the carrot" got us in trouble, because when you are busy "following the carrot" and "running on the treadmill," if you make a mistake it is hard to go back and do the task over again.

If you do you get farther behind, the work keeps piling up behind you, and you finish the day frustrated because you didn't accomplish all that had been scheduled. There is going to be a morale effect because of all that pressure and the fact that you are not doing what you set out to do. We even had some experiments on our mission that were added at the last minute for which we had not trained. There was no time in our schedule for additional training so they put the experiments on and we were expected to ad lib it. But there was no slack in the schedule; it only made the situation worse. (Carr 1986, 18)

The plan during *Skylab 4* was to provide a rest day for the crew every tenth day of the mission. The crew members agreed to give up their first three rest days because they were painfully aware that they had fallen behind in the schedule and that they needed to work through their assigned rest days to catch up. When mission controllers suggested that they work through their fourth scheduled rest day, however, Colonel Carr's response was, "No, we had better not work today; we had better get some rest." The crew took their scheduled day off; this has been widely but erroneously described as the first mutiny in space. On the following day the crew resumed their scheduled tasks but continued to fall farther and farther behind. Carr reports:

We just couldn't keep up, so we had what I like to call the first sensitivity session in space. I sent a recorded message to the flight director as part of our daily health report to the flight surgeon, "We've got a problem. We don't feel that we are doing our job well; we are making too many mistakes, and our morale is getting low. We would like to know from you where we stand relative to where we should be [in the schedule] at this time," which was about the mid-point of the mission. I said, "We need to talk about these things and find a way to get some things squared away so that we can be more productive." Two days later they scheduled a meeting with us as we were flying over the U.S. It was about a 14-minute pass. We had about seven minutes to tell them all the things they were doing to make life miserable for us, then we listened as they told us all the things we were doing to their schedule and planning. That was really a catharsis for us; we managed to air our problems and people began to understand the constraints under which both sides operated. (Carr 1986, 19)

One day later, mission control presented the *Skylab* crew with a new plan. Its key element was to remove from the schedule all of the tasks that were not time dependent with regard to the trajectory (course) of the space station. Tasks that had to be performed at specific times, because of the location of the station, remained on the schedule as firm requirements, but all other tasks were removed from the rigid schedule and placed on what was called the "shopping list." Colonel Carr continues:

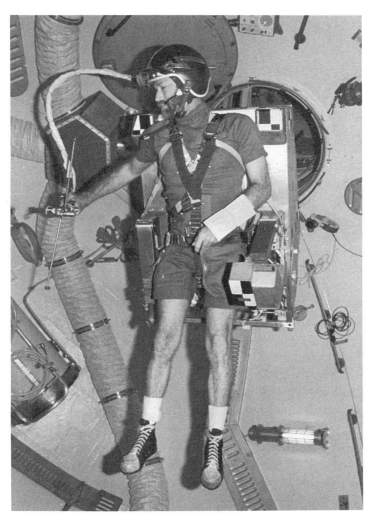

Astronaut Gerald Carr working onboard *Skylab*. (Courtesy of NASA)

> We literally pinned the shopping list up on the wall of the space craft and when we had a free minute we'd go down and pick a job that we felt like doing on the shopping list, draw a line through it, then go do it. Surprise of all surprises, our productivity went way up. We should have done it earlier—it certainly did a lot to help make our life easier, and we ended up the mission completing all of our scheduled experiments. We even managed to make up about a dozen more and perform them ad hoc. (Carr 1986, 19–20)

Clearly, the manner in which tasks are scheduled can contribute to subjective perceptions of workload. In particular, performing daily sequences of tasks according to a rigid schedule can result in perceived stress when task performance begins to lag behind the schedule (e.g., as the result of equipment problems or human error) and frequent reminders that the schedule is slipping can contribute to the problem. In other words, factors that influence workload include the work itself, the scheduling of tasks, and the conditions under which the tasks are performed. All of these factors must be addressed when designing a high-workload job or task sequence. In this regard, it is understood that humans, when fatigued, can perform simple tasks better than complex tasks; many individuals recognize this human limitation and attempt to perform their most difficult tasks early in the workday. Similarly, under high-workload conditions, it would be appropriate for space mission planners to schedule complex tasks to be performed by crew members soon after sleep or rest periods. Less complex tasks can be scheduled for later in the workday when fatigue is greatest. The following specific recommendations for the scheduling of work are among those offered by Connors, Harrison, and Akins (1985):

- A maximum duty period of four hours is the most effective when a passive task is combined with one or more active tasks, the workload is not too great, and a high level of performance must be maintained.

- Attention cannot be adequately sustained to ensure satisfactory performance for periods longer than two hours when a passive task is performed by itself.

- The duty period can be extended to ten hours if there is a considerable variety of primary tasks, with active participation by the operator, or if passive tasks have readily detectable signals to which the operator must respond.

LOW-WORKLOAD CONDITIONS

Performance is degraded when a human operator is overloaded with task requirements: behavior and judgments become confused, and signals are missed while the operator is attending to other demands. Errors and inadvertent actions are the usual consequences of exceeding an individual's capacity for workload. In contrast, when the operator has insufficient work, the individual's attention tends to drift with corresponding degradation of vigilance and he or she becomes lethargic in responses and overall task performance. Although the behavioral effects of overloading and underloading are quite different, the ultimate consequences are about the same: vigilance is impaired, signals (displays, messages, cues) are missed, and errors in judgment and action are made. In addition, underloaded operators might even fall asleep at their workstations; astronauts have dozed off while strapped in their spacecraft as they wait for a countdown to resume. Underloaded crew personnel can fall asleep in the strangest circumstances. For example, the two-person crews of small Navy submersibles have vastly different workloads. The pilot must maintain the craft on the proscribed course by constant attention to controls and displays, while the navigator's tasks are performed far less frequently. Experienced navigators have been known to fall asleep between way points, despite the fact that they are wearing diving gear and an underwater breathing apparatus and are immersed in frigid water.

As described previously, low workloads probably will not be a factor for the crews of space stations and lunar and planetary bases. Time will be a precious commodity in these conditions, and work will fill the days of those selected to perform this special duty, as it did for the crews of *Skylab*. Most observers, however, believe that the crews of interplanetary missions will experience prolonged periods of low workload. They also assume that interplanetary missions will consist of a flurry of activity following launch or departure from orbit and another flurry in preparation for arrival at the destination planet. Between these flurries, however, more than a year might pass with the crew performing relatively few meaningful tasks. Boredom probably will become a significant stressor, and competition likely will exist among the crew to perform the limited number of mission-related tasks. For these reasons, interplanetary missions will be fundamentally different from low–Earth-orbit missions and the time spent on the surface of the moon or Mars, in terms of both workload and the requirement to fill crew time with meaningful activity.

Oberg (1982) disagrees; he predicts a much busier crew during the long voyage to Mars than most other observers:

> If recent spaceflight experience is any evidence, the Mars-bound crew will be overworked and constantly challenged. Far from brooding over the view of an unchanging field of stars, the voyagers might not have time to look out the window for days on end. Far from sitting by the radio hungry for voices from Earth, the astronauts will probably come to see radio communications as an unwanted interruption of their busy schedules. There will be plenty of things to do in those eight to ten months en route. (Pp. 85–87)

According to Oberg, the crew will perform system checks, rehearse programmed abort procedures, and prepare for their stay on the martian surface by studying and practicing. These important high-tempo activities will consume crew time, especially just following departure from Earth orbit and during the weeks preceding the spacecraft's arrival at Mars. But, despite Oberg's prediction, it is believed that most of the outbound journey to Mars, the cruise phase, will be characterized by relatively low workloads for members of the crew.

This chapter begins with a passage from Todd (1961) about the famous Greely Expedition to the Arctic in 1881: "From his reading of Arctic literature the commander knew that man's greatest winter enemy is boredom." Perhaps a few additional passages are appropriate to describe how common it was on previous expeditions for crew members to experience low-workload conditions and to illustrate further the consequences of low workloads during long-duration isolation and confinement. The following examples also describe some of the measures implemented to occupy a crew's time.

In 1845, the British Admiralty dispatched Sir John Franklin to locate and navigate the Northwest Passage. The Admiralty accepted as a certainty that Franklin and his carefully selected party of officers and men, reportedly the pick of the Royal Navy, would succeed where others had failed. Two ships, the *Erebus* and *Terror*, were loaded with sufficient supplies to support the 129 men for four years. After departing England, they hailed a group of whalers off Greenland on their course north, then vanished without a trace.

For most of the next two decades, polar exploration was dedicated to finding, and perhaps rescuing, any survivors of the Franklin

Expedition. Most of the diaries from those expeditions were written in the dry and pompous style of that era and contain little about the actual behavior of individual members of the crew. An exception is the diary of Royal Navy Lt. Sherard Osborn, who commanded the HMS *Pioneer*, one of the search vessels sent to the Arctic by the Admiralty in 1850. The young lieutenant's diary provides detailed descriptions of the many activities conducted to maintain the mental health of his crew during the Arctic winter. But, at the heart of the matter, he wrote:

> Monotony was our enemy, and to kill time our endeavour; hardship there was none; for all we underwent in winter quarters in the shape of cold, hunger, or danger, was voluntary. Monotony, as I again repeat, was the only disagreeable part of our wintering at Griffith's Island. (Quoted in Mowat 1977, 272)

German Lt. Julius Payer's steamer, the *Tegetthoff*, was crushed by the pack ice north of Novaya Zemlya in 1874. The crew escaped the ship with sledges and three small boats, but they made little progress over the ice and decided to wait for warmer weather to clear a passage for the boats. Weeks of extreme tedium followed, during which Lieutenant Payer wrote, pathetically, "It was a happy event to find a hole in one's clothing because the task of darning it occupied one's attention for a time" (quoted in Mountfield 1974).

Although Fridtjof Nansen might have been the most prepared and capable of the polar explorers, he was not immune to the inactivity and boredom that are characteristic of polar winters. Writing in his journal was his primary outlet for pent-up energy, anxiety, and loneliness. Many of his entries, written while locked in the ice onboard the *Fram*, are quite sad and reflect the burden of long-duration isolation and confinement, compounded by the boredom of routine and longing for loved ones left behind. For example, he writes:

> Oh! At times this inactivity crushes one's very soul; one's life seems as dark as the winter night outside.... I feel I must break through this deadness, this inertia, and find some outlet for my energies. Can't something happen? (Nansen 1897, vol. 1, 397)

About one month later, Nansen notes:

> I know this is all a morbid mood; but still this inactive, lifeless monotony, without any change, wrings one's very soul. No struggle, no possibility of struggle! All is so still and dead, so stiff and shrunken, under the mantle of ice. Ah!... the very soul freezes. What I would not give for a single day of struggle—for even a moment of danger. (Nansen 1897, 423)

Nansen created work for his crew to keep them busy throughout the long winter and to supplement the normal routine of scientific observation, vessel maintenance, and housekeeping chores (e.g., melting ice for water). The engineer disassembled the *Fram's* engine and meticulously oiled, inspected, and stored each part for later reassembly; he worked on the engine daily, winter and summer, for the three years of the *Fram's* voyage. Each of the others in the thirteen-man crew were assigned specific maintenance, housekeeping, and scientific responsibilities. In addition, the crew established several shops on board, including sail making, blacksmithing, tin work, shoe repair, and even bookbinding in order to repair books in the well-used library. Everyone had a specialty and made a significant contribution. The crew even made items that they would never use, simply to occupy their time. Nansen writes:

> And all these occupations were carried on with interest and activity during the rest of the expedition. There was nothing, from the most delicate instruments down to wooden shoes and ax handles that could not be made on board the *Fram*. (Nansen 1897, vol. 1, 238)

After a year in the frozen grip of the polar ice cap, Nansen discovered a box of cigars among his scientific supplies. The joy of being surprised, and pleasantly so, moved a bored Nansen to record in his journal:

> Great rejoicing! It will help to while away a few more months, and where shall we be then? Poor fellow, you are really at a low ebb! To while away time—that is an idea that has scarcely even entered your head before. It has always been your great trouble that time flew away so fast, and now it cannot go fast enough to please you.... Sometimes I seem almost to be longing for a defeat—a decisive one—so that we might have a chance of showing what is in us, and putting an end to this irksome inactivity. (Nansen 1897, vol. 1, 494)

The depression evident in Nansen's journal entries during this period changes abruptly a few weeks later when he begins a program of research and observation with a microscope. He becomes cheerful in his work and increasingly philosophical:

> [The concern about the weather and our progress] occupies my thoughts no longer. I know well enough there will be a change some time or other, and the way to the stars leads through adversity. I have found a new world; and it is the world of

animal and plant life that exists in almost every fresh-water pool on the ice-floes. From morning till evening and till late in the night I am absorbed with the microscope, and see nothing around me. I live with these tiny beings in their separate universe, where they are born and die, generation after generation; where they pursue each other in the struggle for life, and carry on their love affairs with the same feelings, the same sufferings, and the same joys that permeate every living being from these microscopic animalcules up to man—self preservation and propagation—that is the whole story. Fiercely as we human beings struggle to push our way on through the labyrinth of life, their struggles are assuredly no less fierce than ours—one incessant, restless hurrying to and fro, pushing all others aside, to burrow out for themselves what is needful to them.... With all our brain cells, we do not feel more strongly than they, never live so entirely for a sensation. But what is life? What matters the individual's suffering so long as the struggle goes on? (Nansen 1897, vol. 1, 513–14)

Dr. Frederick Cook, medical officer of the Belgian Antarctic Expedition of 1898–99, described in eloquent detail the condition of lethargy that afflicted the international crew of the *Belgica* during their terrible Antarctic winter-over experience:

All have an abundance of work, but our ambition for regular occupation, particularly anything which requires prolonged mental concentration, is wanting; even the task of keeping up the log is too much. There is nothing new to write about, nothing to excite.... The regular routine of our work is tiresome in the extreme, not because it is difficult of execution or requires great physical exertion, but because of its monotony. Day after day, week after week, and month after month we rise at the same hour, eat the same things, talk on the same subjects, make a pretense of doing the same work, and look out upon the same icy wilderness. We try hard to introduce new topics for thought and new concoctions for the weary stomach. We strain the truth to introduce stories of home and of flowery future prospects, hoping to infuse a new cheer; but it all fails miserably. We are under the spell of the black Antarctic night, and like the world which it darkens, we are cold, cheerless, and inactive. We have aged ten years in thirty days. (Cook [1900] 1980, 294–301)

Later in the winter, Cook commented in his diary about the differential effects of their conditions on the crew of the *Belgica*. But, after a few months, even those members of the crew who enjoyed the luxury of daily physical work succumbed to the malaise that had previously afflicted the officers and scientific staff of the expedition.

> The men forward [crew in the forecastle] are kept busy with the usual work of the ship, cleaning, restowing, repairing sails, ropes, and woodwork, etc. One man is constantly occupied in keeping the fires going. Another man keeps up the supply of snow, which is melted for water. The work of sounding, taking deep sea temperatures, and fishing, keeps many busy.... Thus the sailors are evenly occupied in easy work which keeps them from feeling the melancholy of our isolation from the world, and also helps them to forget the prolonged darkness of this dayless night. (Cook [1900] 1980, 305)

The Norwegian explorer, Roald Amundsen, was among the crew of the *Belgica* during the austral winter of 1898–99. He and other members of the crew credited Cook with saving the expedition from madness. The near disaster onboard the *Belgica* did not deter Amundsen from further winter-over experiences; rather, it served as his education.[1] During his Northwest Passage Expedition of 1903, Amundsen wrote that he was pleased to have Anton Lund, an experienced sealer captain, as the first mate of the *Gjøa*. Lund knew the importance of keeping a crew occupied during long, dark winters, so he helped Amundsen to devise methods of employment. In particular, they had the crew make lightweight trade goods, such as knives and arrowheads, to exchange later with the native Alaskans for artifacts during their sledge journey to the Magnetic Pole. They deliberately arranged for the work to be performed during the expedition, rather than bringing ready-made items, to occupy the time of the small crew of the *Gjøa* during the winter. According to Amundsen:

> On a polar expedition idleness can be quite demoralizing. For that reason alone, it is inadvisable to have too many people... to find work for a huge crowd would be virtually impossible.... One might be affected by the [winter] darkness. But no—we are cheerful.... We are always busy and that is the main thing in wintering. (Quoted in Huntford 1987, 21–107)

In 1914, Sir Ernest Shackleton set sail in the *Endurance* for the South Atlantic Ocean; the objective of the well-planned Imperial Trans-Antarctic Expedition was an overland crossing of the Antarctic continent. Still hundreds of miles from the intended base, however, the ship was trapped and later crushed by the pack ice. The crew abandoned the *Endurance* before she sank. Then, in a heroic story of endurance and survival, they lived for months as castaways, first on ice floes and later on a desolate island. The fact that the entire party was kept busy at organizing itself, packing rescued supplies, and practicing escape procedures contributed much to the men's feelings of well-being. A crew member wrote in his journal, despite the dismal conditions: "One of the finest days we have ever had... a pleasure to be alive." After months of preparation and practice, however, the castaways simply ran out of things to do:

> The boats were completed and ready to go. A test launching had been held, and they had been found entirely satisfactory. The stores for the trip had been repacked and consolidated. Charts of the area had been studied, and probable winds and currents had been plotted. [Frank] Hurley had finished the boat pump and gone on to make a small portable blubber stove for the journey. They had completed their part of the bargain. Now all that remained was for the ice to open. But it didn't open. One day wore into the next.... Time, indeed, was beginning to weigh a little heavily. Each day blurred anonymously into the one before. Though they invariably tried to see the good side of things, they were unable to fight off a growing sense of disappointment. (Lansing [1959] 1994, 88)

The ice floe on which Shackleton and his party were encamped broke up gradually over a period of months from solid ice for miles, to a mile in diameter, to 200 yards. Shackleton gave the order to launch the boats when the floe, measuring only 50 yards across, began to break up beneath them. He wrote in his journal that they made a pitiable sight: three small, open boats, packed with the odd remnants of a once proud and well-equipped expedition, carrying twenty-eight suffering men in a final, desperate attempt at survival. He recalled the lines of Coleridge:

> Alone, alone, all, all alone,
> Alone on a wide wide sea.

Finally, after 497 days at sea and on ice, the three small craft landed on a desolate rock called Elephant Island. There, the men established a camp and made plans to launch a boat and crew to seek help. Shackleton and five others then made a harrowing voyage of nearly 1,000 miles through the roughest seas on Earth to reach South Georgia Island and ultimate rescue for the crew of the *Endurance*. The danger of the voyage was matched by the exceedingly difficult conditions endured by the twenty-two crew members waiting for rescue on Elephant Island. With little to occupy their time, they talked. Any and all topics were suitable for conversation, but their rescue was the primary subject, followed by food as a close second. After more than four months on the island, Frank Hurley, the expedition photographer, wrote in his journal:

> Today seems to be particularly monotonous.... If there were only some duties, useful or otherwise, to be performed, the burden of time would be more pleasant. (Quoted in Lansing [1959] 1994, 213)

The theme that emerges from these and other examples of low-workload conditions is that crew members must be engaged in meaningful, nonrepetitious work to effectively pass the time effectively during isolation and confinement for long durations. Boredom and lethargy are the inevitable behavioral consequences when individuals are required to perform monotonous tasks or to endure long periods of mental and physical inactivity; the conditions can also result in more extreme effects on mental state and behavior. For centuries, ships' captains and explorers have known the wisdom of providing work to keep their crews occupied. The managers of modern Antarctic programs apply this lesson and regularly validate its efficacy by individual experience. Fred Glogower, the Navy psychologist who is responsible for screening all U.S. Antarctic personnel, made the point clearly: "The key to a successful winter-over at a station is to keep the people busy" (personal interview). To this end, station managers encourage activities that occupy the abundance of free time characteristic of the winter months at Antarctic stations. Recreation and independent study activities are addressed in chapter 14; relevant to workload is the practice of saving tasks and projects to keep people busy during the winter, just as Nansen and Amundsen did a century ago.

Experienced Antarctic managers strive to identify and assign worthwhile projects to crew members that can be completed within the period of isolation and confinement. Dr. Ker Boyce (personal interview) observed that working toward an established goal, such as constructing a new building or reading the requirements for a medical residence, eases boredom during the twelve-month tour of confinement and provides a sense of accomplishment when the goal is achieved. Clearly defined interim goals make a goal-oriented approach even more effective.

There will be many ways for crews to occupy their time meaningfully during interplanetary voyages. System checks, emergency abort rehearsals, and preparations for landing and surface activities will clearly keep a crew busy for much of the time during a mission to Mars. But, even with those important activities, the crew will have an abundance of free time if all goes well. In addition, there might be more free time than they can easily endure if serious malfunctions prevent the performance of planned mission phases or otherwise constrain their activities. For these reasons, it is essential to consider the consequences of low workloads and prepare effective countermeasures.

TRANSITION FROM LOW-WORKLOAD TO HIGH-WORKLOAD CONDITIONS

How would the crew respond if a Mars-bound spacecraft were to experience a serious emergency several months into the cruise phase of the expedition? Would they be numbed by boredom and the sameness of their daily routine? Would their responses be lethargic and misdirected, or would they respond immediately and appropriately to rapidly changing and dangerous circumstances, despite a long, preceding period of relative inactivity? Military planners asked similar questions of the National Research Council (NRC) concerning the performance of future Army tank crews. There are plans to reduce the size of M1A main battle tank crews by automating some functions and distributing the remaining tasks to other crew members; the result would be a higher workload for the smaller crew during battle. Army planners were concerned that crew performance at the higher workloads might be negatively affected by the hours or days of waiting that a crew typically experiences prior to a tank engagement. Very little relevant information was available.

The NRC Committee on Human Factors' Panel on Workload Transition recognized that, in the absence of empirical data about the transition from low- to high-workload conditions, it would be possible to obtain valuable insights by reviewing systems and teams similar to the tank crews that were under study. The committee adopted an analogue, or comparative approach similar to my research by studying a variety of crews and teams that are called on, at least occasionally, to make a rapid transition from low workloads to extremely high workloads; it focused on team transition conditions that were also characterized by personal risk, either to members of the team or to others. The committee's report describes activities of the crews of commercial air-liners, freight trains, merchant and military ships, nuclear power plant control rooms, emergency medical facilities, and disaster relief organizations. It identifies generalizations derived from the common themes among the various conditions and the application of human factors principles and data (Huey and Wickens 1993).

The researchers learned from many anecdotal accounts and case studies that high workloads and abrupt shifts from low to high workload can, at times, seriously and dangerously degrade human performance. The abrupt shifts in workload in the circumstances studied are the results of emergency situations, which are accompanied by the arousal, anxiety, and sometimes, fear associated with the possibility of failing to perform required tasks or to make necessary decisions correctly and quickly. Whether a trauma team responding to the victims of a traffic collision, a tank crew suddenly thrust into battle, or a space-craft crew awakened by equipment malfunction alarms, the personnel involved are likely to experience the indirect effects of their increased workload (i.e., arousal, anxiety, and possibly fear) in similar ways. In particular, attentional tunneling, degradation of short- and long-term memory, communications problems, impaired decision making, and shifts in performance strategies all tend to occur in humans under emergency response conditions.

Attentional tunneling is probably an adaptive response that permits an individual to focus attention exclusively on the problem at hand; this response in the extreme, however, has been responsible for many aircraft disasters, for example, when an overloaded pilot is unable to contend adequately and simultaneously with multiple problems. There is a tendency to address multiple problems in order of priority, which can be an appropriate strategy. But, if the judgments regarding priority are faulty, an individual or crew can waste valuable time focusing on an unimportant issue. Attentional tunneling occurred during the Three Mile Island incident, when control room personnel focused their attention on a single faulty indicator that supported an incorrect hypothesis concerning the problem. In that case, tunneling of focus prevented the crew from attending to more reliable indicators that supported an opposite, and correct, hypothesis about the cause of the event.

Degradation of short-term, or working, memory has been established as a result of a variety of stressors (Mandler 1979; Hockey 1986). It also appears that the combined effects of noise and anxiety are particularly disruptive of memory tasks involving spatial representations (Stokes, Belger, and Zhang 1990) and of decision-making processes that rely on spatial visualization (Wickens et al. 1988). Communications are also impaired by the degradation of short-term memory (as an operator is unable to recall what has just been communicated); this effect is compounded by the attentional tunneling that prevents a stressed individual from attending to multiple tasks and sources of information. Long-term memory is less affected by stress than short-term memory, but consistent findings indicate that stress often leads to a regression to earlier learned response patterns, even when those patterns are inappropriate for the current circumstances.

There is also evidence that stress caused by risk and time pressure leads to consistent shifts in processing and decision-making strategies. Hockey (1986) found that noise and/or anxiety stress results in a shift in the speed-accuracy trade-off of human operators; that is, performance becomes less accurate, without a corresponding decline in speed. Under real-world circumstances, there appears to be a natural tendency to want to do something quickly regarding an emergency, but this approach can be counterproductive if the nature of the problem is not understood. For example, the response of the operators in the Three Mile Island incident was to shut down an automated device that had been performing properly; this action substantially exacerbated the crisis. Decision making appears to be degraded in specific ways by direct and indirect stress; most important, the stress generates a premature closure to the process, which results in a decision prior to an evaluation of all of the issues and available options.

The NRC committee discovered that several research domains are directly related to the transition from low to high workloads, including workload, stress, sleep problems, circadian rhythmicity, vigilance, geographic orientation, cognitive task management, decision making, communications, leadership, team coordination, and training. Also, regardless of the source of the workload, the committee found that appropriate interface design, adequate training, adoption of strategies appropriate to the circumstances, effective leadership, and fluid crew coordination can mitigate many of the detrimental effects of imposed task demands, abrupt transition from low to high workloads, environmental stressors, and fatigue.

In summary, the crews of interplanetary spacecraft probably will experience long periods with few work-related demands, punctuated by periods of high, but tolerable, workload. Emergency conditions might also occur that would require crew members, probably under extremely stressful conditions, to make rapid transitions from relative inactivity to very high workloads. Laboratory research and the analogous experiences reviewed in this chapter indicate that low- and high-workload conditions can have negative behavioral consequences. The information obtained from these sources, however, also suggests that appropriate training, procedures, and equipment design features can substantially mitigate the performance-degrading effects of workload extremes and the abrupt shifting from low to high workloads.

RECOMMENDATIONS

The following recommendations for long-duration space expeditions are based on the preceding discussion of high, low and transitional workloads.

- Consider situational factors when planning and evaluating workloads. In particular, consider task sequence, sequence duration, environmental conditions, and temporal factors in designing activities and evaluating performance.

- When shift work is practiced:
  - Ensure that sleeping crew are not disturbed.
  - Establish "hand-off" procedures to facilitate transitions between shifts.

- Schedule time-dependent tasks as hard requirements.

- Permit more flexible scheduling of tasks that are not time dependent (e.g., a checklist of activities, rather than a time line). Caution is advised, however, regarding the group "shopping list" approach implemented during *Skylab 4*. The approach would not work with all crews because it is believed that some individuals probably would be penalized by a system based on voluntary actions. This was the case during Scott's last expedition; Cherry-Garrard claims that "we wasted our manpower" by allocating tasks to volunteers and not having a routine schedule of work, which resulted in some men becoming overworked.

"They should not have been allowed to do too much," Cherry-Garrard writes. Perhaps individual checklists of activities, rather than a group shopping list, would be more appropriate.

- Under high workload conditions, schedule complex tasks to be performed early in the shift and less complex tasks later, when crew members are more likely to be fatigued.

- Cross-train crew personnel to assume multiple responsibilities, where possible. In addition to their primary responsibilities, all crew members should have major responsibilities in areas outside their primary fields of expertise. Cross-training is most important for the medical officer, who is particularly vulnerable to underloading in isolated and confined environments, but it should extend to each member of the crew. This approach facilitates an equitable distribution of work and insulates individuals from excessively low workloads if a major responsibility is eliminated by equipment malfunction or another unforeseen factor.

- Rotate housekeeping chores; include crew leaders in the rotation. Rotate other task responsibilities when practical.[2]

- Expect errors during periods of extremely high and extremely low crew workloads.

- Include information in premission training for interplanetary missions concerning the need for crew personnel to learn to be idle without feeling guilty. Dr. Glogower tries to prepare prospective winter-over personnel by informing them that each individual's sense of self-worth is defined by what he or she does. As a consequence, most people who are motivated to perform exciting and unusual work, such as special Antarctic duty, find it uncomfortable to experience long periods of forced, or induced, inactivity. Glogower encourages winter-over personnel to learn how to waste time without feeling guilty about it when they get to Antarctica.

- Consider the amount of meaningful work to be performed during the slow phases of a mission when defining crew size.

- Design activities, not directly related to the primary mission, to assign during low-workload periods. It is important to keep the crew occupied with meaningful work. For example, experiments that require frequent tending over long durations (e.g., biological and botanical experiments, gardens) would provide activity and an enjoyable diversion for some crew members. Earth and celestial observation, acceleration and zero gravity research programs, and news reporting are among activities that can supplement mission preparation and operations tasks, if necessary. In short, the accumulated wisdom regarding workload, from the days of sail to the present, is to keep the isolated and confined personnel relatively busy with meaningful work, but not so busy that scheduling or performance pressures contribute to additional stress.

- Plan, rehearse, and anticipate all actions required for emergency conditions. This approach is already firmly in place at NASA, but the importance of training to human performance and decision-making under extreme stress cannot be overstated. All possible emergencies should be identified, appropriate contingency procedures developed, and training conducted (repeatedly) in the performance of the procedures under high-fidelity conditions. Crews will revert to well-trained patterns under conditions of task and information overload.

- Design equipment so as to facilitate crew performance under high-workload and transitional workload conditions:
  - Display information that is required and eliminate nonessential information.
  - Highlight critical information.
  - Use familiar elements, metaphors, and qualitative methods to display information.
  - Integrate displays, where possible.
  - Make on-line emergency procedures brief and clear and phrase them as actions to be taken (e.g., "Close hatch now!").

CHAPTER 7

LEADERSHIP

Be swift to hear, slow to speak, and slow to wrath.

—James, 1:19

...reason and calm judgment, the qualities specially belonging to a leader.

—Tacitus, 55–117 AD, *History*

Nothing gives one person an advantage over another as to remain always cool and unruffled under all circumstances.

—Thomas Jefferson, 1743–1826

There are no bad regiments; there are only bad colonels.

—Napoleon, 1769–1821

No matter what may be the ability of the officer, if he loses the confidence of his troops, disaster must sooner or later ensue.

—Robert E. Lee, 1863

A leader is a person who has the ability to get other people to do what they don't want to do, and like it.

—Harry Truman, *Memoirs*, 1955

The qualities of effective leadership have been important topics of discussion for millennia, certainly predating the ability to record those thoughts in writing. Human beings are social animals that, through coordinated group activity, achieve the species' most uplifting accomplishments or commit its most despicable acts. Leadership is a fundamentally human social skill that has been characterized and analyzed by scholars, leaders, and the led. We all become experts during our lives in defining leadership and, in particular, what makes an ineffectual or undesirable leader; we learn about bad leadership from personal experiences, but the elements of good leadership are more difficult to identify and articulate. With the amount of attention devoted to leadership qualities throughout the ages, is there anything of relevance or utility that the study of expeditions and Antarctic winter-over experiences can possibly contribute to the discussion of leadership?

LEADERSHIP CONDITIONS UNIQUE TO ISOLATION AND CONFINEMENT

Although much that has been written about the personal qualities and skills of effective leaders is applicable in all contexts, including politics, military campaigns, and small-group activities, the features unique to isolated and confined conditions place special demands on leaders. Capt. Sidney Blair, a Navy psychiatrist who was responsible for Antarctic personnel screening for many years, developed considerable sympathy for the leaders of remote-duty stations. He recognized that the job of remote-duty leader is particularly difficult for two reasons: (1) the people attracted to special duty, although not abnormal, are certainly not typical of the general population; and (2) remote-duty leaders are deprived of many of the tools on which most leaders rely for assistance in their leadership tasks.

Concerning Dr. Blair's first reason, the people attracted to special duty, such as Antarctic research stations, space missions, and other expeditionary endeavors, tend to have relatively strong personalities and are confident in their technical abilities. These are valuable traits, but they can propel an individual into conflict with a command structure. With regard to the second reason, remote-duty leaders are deprived of normal leadership assets, such as the power of punishment. What can a leader do under austere conditions to punish a crew member? What can be taken away? In isolated and confined environments, crew members believe that almost everything that they have is absolutely necessary to survival; this includes recreational opportunities and any other available amenities. Privileges that would be considered trivial, if withheld as punishment in a normal environment, are perceived as unacceptable deprivations in the context of a remote-duty station, such as an Antarctic research facility. As a result, the leader is limited in what he or she can implement in the way of punishment.

The leader of an isolated and confined group is also denied the customary status conveyed by the role in a normal setting. The usual interpersonal distance that can be instrumental to a leader erodes as the length of time in isolation and confinement increases and as conditions result in other status-leveling forces. Living together in close proximity amid the associated shared experiences typical of a small group renders informal even the most formal of hierarchies. A leader who relies on the power or status of the leadership role in dealings with subordinates is significantly impaired, and probably an inappropriate choice, for isolated and confined duty.

Perhaps most important, the remote-duty leader must operate in the absence of the normal matrix of other leaders who can provide support and validation for specific decisions and general courses of action. This is one of the reasons why some Antarctic station leaders spend considerable time on the radio; they must frequently seek support from others within the management structure at locations thousands of miles away. In Dr. Blair's words: "Those people who are in leadership positions down on the ice are very lonely leaders. It's awfully difficult to be a leader under those conditions" (Blair 1986). The leaders of future long-duration expeditions will experience similar conditions and constraints. The same observation might be made of all remote-duty leaders, including managers of corporate and governmental field offices.

THE STUDY OF LEADERSHIP TRAITS

Because of the ubiquity of leadership roles in society and the complexity of organizational phenomena, it should not be surprising that many paradigms have been applied in attempts to understand better the qualities of effective leaders. Theories of social cognition, models of social interchange, and the concept of behavioral styles are a few of the most recent approaches to the study of leadership. The most intuitively appropriate approach relative to isolation and confinement, however, focuses on the specific leadership traits of successful and unsuccessful leaders. Trait, or "great man," theories were largely discredited during the 1940s and 1950s for producing weak correlations and poor predictive validities regarding leader performance. The criticism of trait-based studies of leadership during that era impeded the full development of the approach; however, a recent analysis of those critical studies finds substantial errors and limitations in the techniques used (Mumford et al. 1994). Focusing on the traits and previous experiences of successful leaders is again acceptable, and the use of background or biographical information to predict leadership and other specialist performance has been increasing for the past decade. This approach is firmly founded on the fundamental principle of the behavioral sciences: the best predictor of future performance is past performance. Accordingly, some indication of an individual's leadership potential can be discernible from responses on a psychological test, but better indicators might be found in the person's resumé or brief autobiography.

The way individual traits are translated into differential leadership performance is best described by a functional model: a leader has performed well if he or she manages, by whatever means, to ensure that all functions critical to both task accomplishment and group maintenance are adequately addressed (Hackman and Walton 1986). To achieve a successful outcome, a leader must also influence the behavior of others in the group to achieve the group's goals; it is important to note that this activity occurs within the context of a dynamic social and technical environment. In this regard, an effective leader must possess the ability to identify problems and develop solutions, which clearly requires intelligence and technical competence. At the individual level, however, leadership involves discretion regarding when, where, and how actions should be taken to influence others in the group toward the common goal. This discretionary behavior also involves intelligence, but more important, it requires inter-personal skills and the motivation to apply them. In other words, a leader must be relatively intelligent in order to identify problems and develop solutions, but intelligence is not sufficient to be a good leader. To be an effective leader, the individual must also know how to influence other people in the group to modify their behavior or to do something that is not in accord with their inclinations (and "to like it," in the words of Harry Truman, quoted at the beginning of this chapter). The manner in which the leader influences the others tends to be the key difference between successful and unsuccessful leaders. This is the step in the process that makes us all experts in what we consider to be negative leadership traits. The question remains—what are the traits that permit an individual to be an effective leader?

RESEARCH ON LEADERSHIP AT SMALL ANTARCTIC STATIONS

During the early 1960s, the Navy Medical Neuropsychiatric Research Unit (now the Naval Health Research Center) conducted a series of studies concerning leadership at small Antarctic stations. In that research program, Nelson (1962) found that esteemed leaders tended to possess a relatively democratic leadership orientation and a leadership style characterized by greater participation in activities than traditional for a military organization. Further, the esteemed leaders developed individual relationships with each of their crew members and reportedly sought the opinions of individual crew members about issues directly concerning them. Nelson offers a two-part explanation of the esteemed leaders' effectiveness in the small, isolated groups: (1) their traits facilitated a psychological distance between leader and crew member that was compatible with the physical and status distances under these special conditions, and (2) the esteemed leadership approach was likely to result in decisions that were based on the best information available and supported personally by the crew members.

Later, Nelson (1964a, 1964c) reports that popular and unpopular leaders both possessed traits characterized by aggressiveness and industriousness, but the popular and unpopular leaders were distinguished in important ways. Popular leaders tended to be more self-confident and alert, but they differed most from unpopular leaders by exhibiting greater emotional control and adaptability and maintaining harmony within the group. The latter trait again emphasizes the motivational component of effective leadership; that is, the esteemed leader takes the time to speak personally with crew members and do whatever is necessary to preserve group solidarity. Many ineffectual leaders probably know that they should make these efforts, but they refrain because of insufficient motivation.

Nelson (1964b) also compares the traits of a large number of leaders and followers at four Antarctic stations. All personnel were evaluated on the basis of several personal characteristics, including likability. Nelson found that both liked and lesser-liked leaders were more self-confident, alert, job motivated, and aggressive than the follower groups of comparable likability. The liked leaders and liked followers, however, were more satisfied with their assignments, emotionally controlled, accepting of authority, and motivated to be effective group members than the lesser-liked leaders and followers. Overall, the attitudes of the liked leaders and liked followers were found to be the most similar, compared with those of the liked leaders and lesser-liked leaders, the liked followers and lesser-liked followers, and the lesser-liked leaders and lesser-liked followers. Nelson suggests that the underlying trait common to the liked leaders and liked followers was an attitude characterized by teamwork and respect for various forms and sources of authority.

In general, Nelson found that a specific leader's status and esteem in a small Antarctic group were determined by the manner in which three types of decisions were made. First, crew members expected technical or task specific decisions to be based on consultations with the appropriate specialists and individuals involved. Second, crew members expected decisions about general or routine station policy matters that would affect all personnel, such as scheduling of housekeeping and recreational activities, to be made by the leader following consultation with the entire group. Third, crew members expected leaders to make decisions regarding emergency matters as quickly and autocratically as necessary under the circumstances. Further, they expected the leader not to abdicate the leadership role; that is, the leader would fulfill the decision-making obligation regardless of the type of decision to be made (Nelson 1973). This final point again refers to the motivational requirement of effective leadership; leaders must attend to their responsibilities and remain actively involved in their roles to be perceived as effective by subordinates. Leaders risk losing the respect of their crew when they avoid decisions or fail to deal with persistent issues, such as an interpersonal problem in the group.

In studies of adaptation to Antarctic duty, Gunderson (1966a) found that a leader's effectiveness at small stations was positively correlated with the amount of the leader's Navy experience, or, more precisely, with the leader's age. Presumably, the quality of a leader's decisions and interpersonal skills increase as he or she accumulates experience over time, but there is probably a subjective component involved in the correlations as well; that is, the perceived credibility of a leader is influenced by several factors, including age and experience. The credibility of leadership personnel remains an important issue for those individuals who are responsible for selecting remote-duty crews.

Dr. Glogower (personal communication) described a case in which a young person was suggested for a position of considerable responsibility at a small Antarctic station. Those who made the suggestion said that if the others in the group were uncomfortable with the leader's age, it would be their problem. Dr. Glogower hastened to point out that when the leader's age is an issue for the crew, it quickly becomes a problem for the leader and then a problem for the program managers located thousands of miles away. It is far better to assign leadership roles to individuals who have credibility and the confidence of their personnel from the start, rather than require leaders to prove themselves to obtain the necessary credibility for effective leadership. Age and experience are factors that contribute to credibility.

The issue of personnel selection is addressed in chapter 15, but of particular relevance here are Gunderson's observations on personal qualities that he found to be important in the people called on to assume leadership roles in remote-duty environments. Gunderson (1966b) reports that there is a tendency to equate self-confidence, assertiveness, and achievement motivation with leadership, but, although these traits are desirable, they are insufficient for effective leadership. A leader's effectiveness at small Antarctic stations should be evaluated not only by his or her ability to motivate individual accomplishments, but also by the ability to generate and maintain morale and group solidarity ("group spirit" in Gunderson's words). In particular, data from the Navy's program of leadership research, involving many small groups over the years, indicate that the effective leaders (as judged by station managers and crew personnel) exhibit greater emotional control, greater flexibility, and greater interest and concern for the problems of individual crew members than do the less effective leaders; more effective leaders also tend to remain neutral concerning controversial issues. Gunderson concludes that individuals who are overly demanding, inflexible, and explosive in temperament will probably encounter difficulty under conditions of isolation and confinement, especially if placed in a leadership role.

To the list of important traits for remote-duty leaders, Strange (n.d.) adds the following two characteristics based on debriefing interviews with Antarctic winter-over personnel: (1) leaders must possess the ability to tolerate intimacy and status leveling without loss of authority and respect of the group, and (2) they must be self-reliant in the lonely responsibilities of command.

TRAITS OF EFFECTIVE LEADERS IN ISOLATED AND CONFINED ENVIRONMENTS

The research described in the previous section identifies several personal attitudes, abilities, and behaviors that correlate with effective and esteemed leadership at small Antarctic stations. These individual leadership traits are described below with reference to additional conditions of isolation and confinement.

Problem-Solving Ability and Alertness

An individual must be alert and possess well-developed problem solving abilities to be an effective leader under most conditions. The leader must be vigilant to be able to perceive that a problem or potential problem exists and sufficiently intelligent to be able to identify appropriate courses of action to correct or contain the problem.

Interpersonal Skills and Motivation to Apply Them

To be an effective leader of a small group, an individual must know when, where, and how to take leadership actions within the social context of the group. An effective leader must be able to influence the behavior of others in the closed society without being abrasive or dictatorial. Also, the leader must be motivated to perform those leadership tasks, even if they are considered unpleasant. For example, a leader who prefers to ignore a persistent interpersonal problem among the crew, rather than address the issue, will suffer an erosion of the crew's confidence in his or her leadership abilities.

Democratic Orientation

Isolated and confined personnel come to expect a more democratic orientation from their leaders. This expectation is a consequence of the environmental conditions that require the leader and members of the crew to live and work in close proximity and to endure the same deprivations. Proximity, frequent interpersonal exchange, shared experiences, and other status-leveling factors contribute to crew members' expectations of a more egalitarian social organization. In this regard, remote-duty crews expect their leaders to make decisions involving specific individuals after consultation with the parties involved; they expect leaders to make decisions affecting the group as a whole on the basis of consensus, to the extent possible; and they expect leaders to make emergency decisions as quickly and autocratically as required by the conditions.

Concern for Well-Being of the Crew

Exceptional leaders have always exhibited greater than normal concern for the well-being of crew personnel. For example, Columbus displayed considerable affection for his crew, despite the fact that many under his command were insubordinate and attempted to undermine him in other ways. Columbus was a remarkably tolerant captain for his era, and he was prepared to do everything in his power to obtain his crew's confidence and to maintain morale. With regard to concern for his crew, however, Capt. James Cook set the early standard for expedition leaders. Cook was arguably the greatest maritime explorer of any century. The results of his exploration in terms of lands discovered and seas charted placed him far above any previous explorer; but what really distinguished Cook from all others of his era was his concern for the health and well-being of his crew. This was evidenced by the fact that only four fatalities occurred among Cook's complement of 112 during an arduous three-year voyage of discovery (1772–75). He was aware of the importance of cleanliness, hygiene, and proper diet, and he rigorously enforced policies to maintain his crew's well-being.

Adm. Richard E. Byrd possessed considerable leadership skill and routinely exhibited many of the traits of exceptional leaders described in these paragraphs. For example, he believed in a relatively democratic and egalitarian approach, despite his formal separation from the group. He was called "Commander," and he was the only one during his first expedition to Antarctica to have his own room. He practiced the Navy tradition of a leader maintaining distance from his men to ensure that his decisions would be made objectively. Although he was insulated from the group, he made a conscious effort to remain personally in touch with every member of the expedition. Rodgers (1990) describes Byrd's technique:

> Every day he would invite one or two of them for a walk. He asked them what they were doing, answered questions, inquired about problems, counseled each one on work or personal difficulties, determined how particular men felt about the expedition's happenings, and when appropriate offered reassurances. (P. 125)

Byrd's concern for the well-being of his men generated great respect and loyalty in some members of his expeditions, which, unfortunately were undone in others by his temper and other eccentricities. The more effective leaders at modern Antarctic stations express their concern for the welfare of personnel in a manner similar to Admiral Byrd's. A senior or master chief might pay an unexpected visit to a crew member for a chat and an informal inspection of the person's room for indications of maladjustment. Also, the station leader or the person tasked with the morale, welfare, and recreation (MWR) functions of the station might conduct more formal interviews and inspections during the winter months to ensure the safety and well-being of all personnel.

The most exceptional expedition leader was Sir Ernest Shackleton, who headed the Imperial Trans-Antarctic Expedition of 1914–15. His concern for the well-being of his personnel engendered motivation, teamwork, and extreme devotion. Frank Worsley, captain of the HMS *Endurance*, reflects on Shackleton's leadership style during their voyage of one thousand miles in a small sailboat:

> Looking back on this great boat journey, it seems certain that some of our men would have succumbed to the terrible protracted strain but for Shackleton. So great was his care of his people, that, to rough men, it seemed at times to have a touch of woman about it, even to the verge of fussiness. If a man shivered more than usual, he would plunge his hand into the heart of the spare clothes bag for the least sodden pair of socks for him. He seemed to keep a mental finger on each man's pulse. If he noted one with signs of the strain telling on him he would order hot milk and soon all would be swallowing the scalding, life-giving drink to the especial benefit of the man, all unaware, for whom it had been ordered. At all times he inspired men with a feeling, often illogical, that, even if things got worse, he would devise some means of easing their hardships. (Worsley, 1977, 169–70)

Ability to Participate in Group Activities and to Preserve Harmony

The traditional military approach to leadership is to prohibit fraternization among officers and enlisted personnel. The underlying assumption of this approach is that discipline would be eroded by the social contact and officers might be influenced by friendships to engage in differential treatment of subordinates. This approach makes a great deal of sense in a normal military organization, but the underlying structural relationships are quite different under conditions of isolation and confinement. The psychological distance between leaders and crew is reduced by the confined conditions, and the behavior of leaders should reflect the reduced distance. An effective way to define this relationship is for the leader to become involved in group activities. For example, a young officer of the *Erebus* commented on the leadership style of the sixty-year-old Sir John Franklin during their search for the Northwest Passage in 1845:

> He looks ten years younger and takes part in everything that goes on and with as much interest as if he had not grown older since the last expedition. We are all delighted to find how decided he is in all that he resolves on, and he has such

experience and judgment that we all look on his decisions with the greatest respect. I never felt the Captain was so much my companion with anyone I have sailed with before. He certainly made a friend of every person on board—not the slightest complaint. (Quoted in Mountfield 1974, 95)

Being interested and involved in the technical work of subordinates and contributing to the performance of routine chores are particularly important activities for leaders in isolated and confined environments. Nansen, for example, regularly worked alongside his crew when they performed physical tasks such as shoveling snow and carrying supplies. This tradition has persisted at modern Antarctic stations, where the more effective leaders participate in the normal rotation of housekeeping responsibilities. Leaders can also make special efforts to become involved in group activities and to maintain morale, such as occasionally organizing or playing a significant role in activities designed to increase group solidarity and team spirit. Dr. Frederick Cook provided an example of this kind of leadership behavior during the near-disastrous *Belgica* Expedition. On the occasion of Dr. Cook's birthday, amid the depths of the crew's midwinter depression, the ship's captain, Georges Lecointe, organized a celebration:

The captain has made the greatest endeavor to break the spell of "shivers" which hung over us. He fixed up in his full-dress suit, and induced the doctor to do the same. In this costume we came to the dining table, and took the cabin by surprise. (Cook [1900] 1980, 313)

At the conclusion of the meal, the captain presented Dr. Cook with a certificate thanking him for his friendship and promising to mend a pair of his knit stockings. A leader's attention to the affairs of crew members and personal involvement in them, as noted in this example, can make tolerable an otherwise unpleasant experience.

Emotional Control

Emotional control, one of the main leadership themes emerging from my review of conditions analogous to long-duration space missions, is reflected in many of the popular descriptions of desirable leadership traits (e.g., "calm judgment" and "remaining cool under all circumstances"). Often, when authors of secondary sources characterize explorers as exceptional leaders, they illustrate exceptional leadership abilities with examples of emotional control under stress. For instance, when Amundsen was forced to crash-land his two flying boats on the pack ice in 1925, he immediately organized the crews into work parties to level a runway on a large ice floe, so that the one undamaged aircraft might be used to reach safety. One of the party wrote that Amundsen enforced:

> An orderly routine—fixed hours for meals, for work and sleep, and for smoking and talking. He knew there was no quicker way to break men down under strain than to allow them to live haphazardly. An ordered existence, moreover, engendered confidence. This calm, unhurried way of doing things seemed to symbolize the ability of intelligence to overcome the inimical forces of nature. (Quoted in Huntford 1987, 197)

During three weeks of work with inadequate tools, the group managed to build a runway long enough to attempt a takeoff. Following several failures, the Dornier finally lifted into the cold polar air with all six members of the expedition onboard. Amundsen and his party, although they had been given up for lost, were back in Norway a few hours later. Amundsen's exceptional leadership and his calm deliberate actions under stress, in particular, contributed greatly to the group's survival. Many similar examples in the literature credit the emotional control of a leader with inspiring others to work in a coordinated fashion under conditions of confusion or crisis.

Another aspect of emotional control as an essential leadership trait involves a leader's ability to remain calm despite persistent interpersonal conflict with a member of the group. A leader who is quick to anger or who frequently resorts to punishment in order to maintain control loses the confidence and respect of the crew. The loss of confidence and respect usually contributes to further conflicts with the leader, in the manner of a positive feedback system.

Credibility

Credibility is extremely important to the leader in an isolated and confined environment, whether on an expedition, at a polar station, or onboard a spacecraft. All personnel recognize the risks involved in their special duty and know that emergencies require prompt and reasoned responses to avoid disaster. It is necessary for crew members to have confidence in their leader's abilities to take appropriate action when necessary and to be fair in discretionary decisions affecting the crew. That confidence is derived from the credibility of the leader, and credibility stems from the leader's qualifications and experience.

Generally, there is no substitute for experience in any endeavor, including leadership. When selecting a surgeon for oneself or a loved one, for example, it is comforting to know that the surgeon has performed many similar operations in the past; no one wants to provide his or her body for on-the-job training, even if the surgeon has been educated at the finest medical school. In any field, experience with comparable situations and contingency responses sets the expert apart from the most highly trained novice. Similarly, in the context of small-group leadership, there can be no substitute for experience when life-threatening risks abound. Crew members must have confidence in their leader's ability to respond in a crisis; experience with similar situations (preferably with successful outcomes) is the best way to engender that confidence and credibility. In this regard, the best examples of expedition leadership were exhibited by leaders who had previously demonstrated their exceptional capabilities. In particular, Fridtjof Nansen had crossed the Greenland ice cap in 1888 before organizing the Norwegian Polar Expedition; Roald Amundsen had served as mate onboard the *Belgica* and commanded the *Gjøa* during the first navigation of the Northwest Passage (1903–6) before making his successful bid for the South Pole in 1912; and Sir Ernest Shackleton had distinguished himself in the merchant navy and with Robert Falcon Scott's first Antarctic expedition before leading the men of the *Endurance* on their remarkable voyage.

Self-Confidence

Self-confidence emerged as a trait of effective leaders during the Navy's studies of leadership at Antarctic stations. A leader's confidence, or lack thereof, in his or her abilities becomes apparent to all members of a group who are living together in isolation and confinement. Crew perceptions of the leader's self-confidence clearly influence the crew's confidence in the leader's abilities and, ultimately, the credibility and effectiveness of the leader.

Flexibility and Adaptability

The ability of a leader to be flexible and accommodating to individual needs and preferences within the crew is important to group harmony and to the leader's effectiveness in influencing individual behavior. A leader must not be perceived as indecisive or hesitant in resolving an issue; however, the leader should remain open to others' opinions and be willing to modify a position, if appropriate, especially if there is little cost or penalty involved in the accommodation. An example of leadership flexibility and concern for group morale is provided by Shackleton, who believed that, if there was dissension in the group, the men might not provide their full effort when required. As a consequence of this belief, Shackleton was willing to go to great lengths to minimize the potential for conflict. For instance, he invited a "latent malcontent" to decision-making meetings and made him a part of the process, rather than a critic. Shackleton also assigned another disagreeable man to his tent; he was not at all fond of him, but he preferred putting up with his disagreeable nature to inflicting him on others in the group. Shackleton was by no means a weak leader, despite his efforts at accommodation. His nickname was "Boss," and his management style could be described as familiar but clearly in charge at all times. The effectiveness of Shackleton's style can be measured anecdotally by his success in leading his shipwrecked men to safety in one of the most amazing stories of endurance and survival ever recorded. In the introduction to Worsley's book about the boat journey, Sir Edmund Hillary remarks that Shackleton was the most admirable of all the polar explorers, despite the fact that all of his major expeditions failed to achieve their established goals (a "limited standard"):

> It was as a leader of men and an overcomer of appalling obstacles that Shackleton really excelled.... The enormous affection and respect he engendered in his expedition members (often mighty men themselves) shines through in their diaries and writings. (Worsley 1977, 12)

Shackleton exhibited his true leadership qualities when the *Endurance* became caught in the Antarctic pack ice, then sank, with all hands stranded on the floes. The twenty-eight members of the expedition camped on the ice for six more months, as the pack gradually broke up around them. Shackleton organized the men and led boat drills in preparation for their escape in three small cutters that had been saved when the *Endurance* sank. Rowing by day through the treacherous pack and camping on small floes during the night, the party finally made it to the desolate rock known as Elephant Island. Shackleton determined that they should not attempt to winter on the island because "[p]rivation and exposure had left their mark on the party, and the health and mental condition of several men were causing me serious anxiety" (quoted in Mountfield 1974). He and five others departed in the most seaworthy of their cutters on one of the most dangerous open-boat voyages in history. It was a terrible passage: freezing cold rain, nearly ceaseless gales, and a huge rogue wave that almost sank the stout little craft.

After sixteen days of enduring the worst that the sea could inflict, the 22-foot cutter and her crew landed on South Georgia Island, but they were on the side of the island opposite the location of the whaling station that they had hoped to reach. They could not risk launching the boat again, so Shackleton and two other men crossed the island, over sheer cliffs and down a glacier (a feat not accomplished again for another forty years), to reach the whaling station. There, Shackleton took an English whaler (without the owner's permission) and a volunteer crew of Norwegians in an attempt to rescue his party. They got within 70 miles of Elephant Island but were turned back by heavy ice. Shackleton then managed to acquire the assistance of a Uruguayan trawler and came within sight of Elephant Island, but the trawler had only three days of coal left in her bunkers and had to turn back.

Shackleton and his men on Elephant Island, 1916, enjoy a cup of hot tea following six months on an ice floe and a dangerous voyage in open boats. "Boss" Shackleton and five of his crew departed almost immediately for South Georgia Island to seek help. (Photo by Frank Hurley; courtesy of The Royal Geographical Society, London)

Shackleton then rode on a British mailboat to Punta Arenas, where he chartered a schooner, but he was again unsuccessful in reaching his stranded crew. Finally, he made his fourth attempt in a tug loaned by the government of Chile. Although extremely vulnerable to the ice, the tug navigated a clear passage to Elephant Island. There, Shackleton found the twenty-two members of the expedition living under the shelter of their upturned boats; after eighteen weeks on the island, they were eager to depart before the ice returned. Following brief celebrations in South America, the members of the expedition returned to Europe and to what later became known as World War I. Shackleton's courage and strong leadership qualities received credit for saving his crew from certain death.

On Shackleton's first trip south, he had been a member of Scott's famous *Discovery* Expedition of 1901–4. The expedition was composed of an unusual assortment of Royal Navy and merchant navy personnel and civilian scientists. Hillary relates a story told to him by Reginald Ford, a member of the expedition:

> He told me how difficult Scott had found his dealing with the merchant navy personnel, who were not accustomed to the rigid discipline of the Royal Navy. One merchant seaman in particular was most reluctant to accept orders and was regarded as a very bad influence on the rest of the crew. Scott decided that he would have to be sent back on the first relief vessel. Reginald Ford and Shackleton were present when Scott advised the seaman that he was being sent home. To Scott's absolute astonishment the seaman refused to be repatriated— he had a signed contract and knew his rights—he was staying on to the end of the expedition whatever Scott might think. Ford related how Scott simply didn't know how to handle the situation—the man after all was not subject to naval discipline.
>
> Then Shackleton, a merchant navy officer, asked permission to deal with the problem. Scott agreed and departed from the cabin—but Ford stayed on. Shackleton calmly informed the seaman that he was returning to Britain—the man insolently disagreed—so Shackleton, a powerful man, stepped forward and knocked him to the deck. The man rose slowly to his feet and Shackleton gave him his instructions once again. Somewhat more slowly and much less arrogantly the man refused. Once again the man was flattened by a mighty blow. When he got up this time and realized that Shackleton was prepared to carry on the procedure indefinitely he was happy to agree to an immediate departure.... No doubt it was a brutal answer to

a difficult problem but it was still a brutal age and Shackleton undoubtedly understood his men—he could be as gentle as a woman and incredibly considerate of his crew's welfare, or as tough as was required to deal with any problem. (Introduction to Worsley, 1977, 13–14)

Later during the expedition, Shackleton led the team that made an attempt to reach the South Pole. The party came close to their objective, but Shackleton realized that each additional day on the trail would reduce their chances of returning safely. He had the courage and good judgment to turn back before it was too late. Huntford (1986) reports that when Shackleton's wife asked him how he found the presence of mind to turn back, he replied, "I thought you would rather have a live donkey than a dead lion."

Team Approach

A team approach was found to be the factor that best discriminated between esteemed leaders (and followers), and lesser-liked leaders (and followers) at small Antarctic research stations. A team approach involves several of the specific traits described above, including a democratic or egalitarian orientation, concern for the well-being of crew members, active participation in the work and other activities of the group, and flexibility regarding policies and decisions. Modern explorer Thor Heyerdahl describes the leader's role in a team approach as being similar to that of an orchestra conductor. Each player has a different "instrument," or set of skills, and the leader's responsibility is to ensure that all members of the expedition are playing the same tune. Heyerdahl writes:

A successful expedition is the result of thoughtful planning and harmonious teamwork. Each person must feel that he or she is a necessary part of the team and that a successful outcome depends on them, but neither more nor less than on everyone else. There must be a feeling of friendship and equality where, nevertheless, everyone realizes why the leader is a leader among equals: because the leader is the one who knows best what it is all about. Thus I have always made it a point to sit down with the men, listening to everyone's opinions before important new decisions are made. Only when there is a lack of time, and a decision must be made immediately, have I given orders like a military officer. (Heyerdahl, personal communication, 1994)

NEGATIVE LEADERSHIP TRAITS

The introductory paragraph to this chapter indicates that most people become experts in negative leadership traits through personal experience with leaders. Two examples of negative leadership behavior can be illustrated by the actions of explorers Lt. Charles Wilkes, commander of the U.S. Exploring Expedition of 1838–42, and Lt. George Washington DeLong, captain of the *Jeannette* on her ill-fated voyage to the Arctic in search of the North Pole.

The U.S. Exploring Expedition got off to a bad start. Wilkes commanded a squadron of six small ships and a complement of 346 men; the expedition included nine civilian naturalists and artists, called "scientifics," whose primary responsibility was to collect examples of flora and fauna throughout the voyage. Friction between some sailors and the scientifics began as soon as the squadron sailed out of Norfolk; the seamen called the civilians clam diggers, bug catchers, and similar names because the seamen resented the extra work caused by their presence on the ships. Wilkes did nothing to mitigate this divisiveness, but that was one of the captain's lesser offenses. His biggest problem was his inflexibility in adjusting to the special conditions of an expeditionary voyage. For example, the junior officers of the *Vincennes* had converted the apartments of the deck officers into a lounge for off-duty hours. Wilkes believed that this would produce a familiarity prohibited by the regulations, so he ordered the practice stopped. The junior officers replied that the harmony of feeling between them and certain senior officers of the ship was highly commendable and transformed the ship into a home, but Wilkes was adamant. These and other examples of Wilkes's leadership style prompted young Midshipman William Reynolds to write the following in one of several long and informative letters to his family:

> [Wilkes has become] a false and malignant villain—no milder term will do. We have borne innumerable evils, the nature of the man has become changed, he is as one possessed by a demon; intoxicated with the power and rank of his situation.... Confidence in the Commander is destroyed; there is none where there should be all. Every man does his duty, but he keeps aloof from Captain Wilkes as if he were an adder.... Imagine a family where all are at variance with the father and you will know our state. (Quoted in Cleaver and Stann 1988, 117–18)

During their final night together, in San Francisco's Palace Hotel, Emma De Long wisely advised her young husband to secure the trust and respect of his crew as early as possible on their voyage north in the *Jeannette*. Apparently, De Long knew what he should do; in one of his last letters to Emma in 1879, he wrote with considerable insight regarding many of the most important leadership traits:

> I try to be pleasant and agreeable without being familiar, gentle but firm in correcting anything I see wrong, and always calm and self-possessed. I feel my responsibility and care and hope I appreciate the delicate position I am placed in of leading and directing so many people of my own age. (Quoted in Guttridge 1986, 78)

Knowing what to do and actually doing it, however, are two different things. De Long made significant errors in judgment almost as soon as the ship turned to follow the California coast north. Like Wilkes years before, he did nothing to stop the sailors' incessant scornful comments about the scientists in the party, some of whom were experiencing seasickness. Ignorant of the consequences that such divisive behavior might have on interpersonal relations, De Long even contributed to the teasing. Some of the scientists became increasingly withdrawn and estranged from the remainder of the crew. Later, De Long was quick to resort to punishment in enforcing his decisions and correcting what he perceived to be a lack of discipline. In all fairness, it must be noted that Lieutenant De Long did several things correctly and exhibited genuine concern for the welfare of his crew. He was handicapped by his relatively young age for command, however, and his handling of the unfortunate incidents early in the voyage eroded his credibility and the confidence that many in the party originally had in their leader. This lack of confidence would prove fatal when disaster struck the expedition in the pack ice.

RECOMMENDATIONS

Captain Mark Dembert, an Antarctic veteran and one of the Navy psychiatrists who screens personnel for Antarctic duty, mentioned that leaders always should be selected according to their individual capabilities relevant to specific mission requirements. This is even more important under conditions of isolation and confinement, where all issues tend to be magnified.

Good leadership can make the difference between success and failure, survival and disaster. It is always important under conditions of isolation and confinement, but good leadership is absolutely essential during critical situations. The crews of long-duration space missions deserve, and will require, exceptional leaders. The required leadership traits identified during my research are listed below.[1]

The leaders of future long-duration space missions must:

- be alert and motivated to perform well
- be self-confident, but not boastful
- be self-reliant and technically competent
- be flexible and adaptable, but firm when conditions demand firmness
- be neutral regarding controversial issues
- be able to tolerate intimacy and status leveling
- possess problem-solving abilities
- possess exceptional interpersonal skills
- operate with a democratic and egalitarian orientation and solicit the opinions of crew members in matters that affect them
- act decisively, when necessary
- operate with a team approach and foster teamwork among the crew
- exhibit concern for the well-being of crew members
- interact directly with each member of the small group
- become involved in group activities
- initiate and encourage efforts to maintain group harmony
- maintain emotional control in operational and interpersonal matters
- do what is necessary and take responsibility
- demonstrate credibility, that is, inspire confidence by demeanor and previous accomplishments

In addition, Nicholas and Penwell (1995) conducted an analysis of leadership issues in conditions characterized by isolation and confinement, including polar stations and a few expeditions. They categorize the traits of effective leaders as (1) personal traits, (2) task management style, (3) interpersonal style, and (4) group maintenance style. The researchers develop a general profile of effective leadership that is highly consistent with the previous recommendations. Nicholas and Penwell find that effective leaders tend to be individuals who work hard to achieve mission objectives, are optimistic, have the respect of the crew, ordinarily use participative decision making but take charge during crises, are sensitive to and make the crew feel valued, and expend effort to maintain group harmony and solidarity.

CHAPTER 8

MEDICAL AND PSYCHOLOGICAL SUPPORT

The curtain of blackness which has fallen over the outer world of icy desolation has also descended upon the inner world of our souls. Around the tables, in the laboratory, and in the forecastle, men are sitting about sad and dejected, lost in dreams of melancholy from which, now and then, one arouses with an empty attempt at enthusiasm. For brief moments some try to break the spell by jokes, told perhaps for the fiftieth time. Others grind out a cheerful philosophy; but all efforts to infuse bright hopes fail. Each man is intent on being left alone to take what comfort he can from memories of happier days, though such effort usually leaves him more hopelessly oppressed by the sense of utter desertion and loneliness.

—Frederick A. Cook, *Through the First Antarctic Night*

The first Belgian Antarctic Expedition of 1898–99, in many ways, was a precursor of things to come. It was the first expedition to camp, although briefly, on the Antarctic continent and the first to spend an entire year locked in its icy embrace. Despite the terrible experience of the crew, the return of the *Belgica* to Europe at the close of the nineteenth century demonstrated that it was possible to survive the austral winter, which immediately precipitated the expeditionary focus on the continent that continues to this day. A further precursive feature of the expedition relevant to this study was its international composition; during an era when expeditions were expressions of nationalistic tendencies, the Belgian Antarctic Expedition was cosmopolitan and, in this regard, truly modern. The crew of the *Belgica* consisted of nine Belgians, six Norwegians, two Poles, a Romanian, and an American, Dr. Frederick A. Cook.

Commandant Adrien de Gerlache, organizer of the expedition, secured an insufficient sum of $60,000 from the Belgian government to support the project. He purchased a Norwegian sealer which he re-christened *Belgica*, and assembled a crew. The physician selected for the expedition had backed out only a few days before the ship sailed, so de Gerlache placed an advertisement in the newspapers. Cook had made three trips to Greenland between 1891 and 1894 and jumped at the chance to be a member of the expedition. Chosen by de Gerlache on the basis of his Arctic experience, Cook joined the party in the roadstead of Rio de Janeiro, Brazil, in October 1897, two months after the *Belgica* had

Adrien de Gerlache, commandant of the Belgian Antarctic Expedition 1898–99. (From Cook, 1980)

departed Antwerp, Belgium, en route to Antarctica. The *Belgica* arrived in the Antarctic during January 1898, late in the season, but the crew was able to make several landings to collect geological specimens, lichens, moss, and insects. They conducted more scientific work than had any previous Antarctic expedition, but they probably spent too much time on shore. In March, the ship became trapped in the frozen Bellinghausen Sea and, locked in by pack ice, drifted there for more than a year. The crew was not fully prepared for the experience.

The medical officers of polar expeditions, and later at Antarctic research stations, usually experienced considerable frustration because they found few professional duties to perform. This was not to be the experience of Dr. Cook. The problem that occupied the thirty-two-year-old physician for the remainder of the expedition started when the ship became locked in the ice, but it became increasingly acute throughout the long winter night. Almost every member of the crew gradually became afflicted with a strange and persistent melancholy. The condition deepened into depression and then despair as the weeks blended one into another. Eventually, crew members lost almost total motivation and found it difficult to concentrate or even eat. One man weakened and died of a heart ailment that Cook believed was caused, at least in part, by his terror of the darkness. Another crewman became obsessed with the notion that others intended to kill him; when he slept, he squeezed himself into a small recess in the ship so that he could not be easily found. Yet another man succumbed to hysteria that rendered him temporarily deaf and unable to speak (Lansing [1959] 1994); additional members of the crew were disturbed in other ways.[1] It was to this dismal condition that Roald Amundsen referred when he later wrote, "Insanity and disease stalked the decks of the *Belgica* that winter."

Dr. Cook believed the malady to be caused more by the lack of light than the scurvy they were experiencing. Whatever the actual cause, it is clear that the problem was predominantly psychological. The dreaded polar night is not really that dreadful; it has been endured without ill effects by many explorers and countless indigenous inhabitants of the Arctic regions, but it took a terrible toll on the crew of the *Belgica*. The men suffered from poor circulation, heart troubles, and impaired digestion. Their diet was low in fiber and probably certain vitamins. Although vitamins had not been discovered yet, Dr. Cook believed that something might be lacking from the diet. He attempted to remedy the condition by encouraging the men to eat fresh penguin meat, but many found it unpalatable. He also prescribed an exercise program (see chapter 5) in an attempt to counter the growing symptoms of insanity among the crew, but walks on the ice devolved into a circular path around the ship that came to be known as the "madhouse promenade." Cook's journal entries reflect the depression into which this small society had fallen. The following is an example:

> The darkness grows daily a little deeper, and the night soaks hourly a little more color from our blood. Our gait is now careless, the step non-elastic, the foothold uncertain.... Most of us in the cabin have grown decidedly gray within two months, though few are over thirty. Our faces are drawn, and there is an absence of jest and cheer and hope in our make-up which, in itself, is one of the saddest incidents in our existence. There is no one willing to openly confess the force of the night upon himself, but the novelty of life has been worn out and the cold, dark outside world is incapable of introducing anything new. The moonlight comes and goes alike, during the hours of midday as at midnight. The stars glisten over the gloomy snows. We miss the usual poetry and adventure of home on winter nights. We miss the flushed maidens, the jingling bells, the spirited horses, the inns, the crackling blaze of the country fire. We miss much of life which makes it worth the trouble of existence. (Cook [1900] 1980, 319)

In desperation, Cook devised a method that he called the "baking treatment," in which the most seriously ill sat with their bodies exposed to the warm glow of the ship's stove for an hour each day. This therapy, combined with enforced portions of fresh penguin meat, seemed to help the men, but Cook observed that "surely one of the most important things was to raise the patients' hopes and instill a spirit of good humor" (Cook [1900] 1980). This he did consciously and persistently throughout the remainder of the expedition.

Cook described life onboard the *Belgica* as a "hellish existence," but he rose to the occasion and is credited with saving the expedition from psychological disaster, in the same manner that the Navy medical corpsman saved the remote-duty station (see Introduction). More than a decade later, Amundsen portrays the doctor's heroic actions:

> Cook's behavior at this time won the respect and devotion of all. It is not too much to say that Cook was the most popular man of the expedition. From morning to night he was occupied with his many patients, and when the sun returned it

> happened not infrequently that, after a strenuous day's work,
> the doctor sacrificed his night's sleep to go hunting seals and
> penguins, in order to provide the fresh meat that was greatly
> needed by all. (Amundsen [1912] 1976, 22–23)

The crew's spirits began to improve in the spring, but the ice floe that trapped the *Belgica* gave no indication that it would ever break up. It was necessary to escape the Antarctic because each man knew that to stay another year would be fatal. Laboring with large ice saws, axes, and explosives, the crew eventually blasted the ship free, but the *Belgica* did not reach open water for another month.

The *Belgica* arrived in Europe in November 1899, where the crew was greeted as if they had been to the moon and back. A few years later, in 1908, Cook was (arguably) the first man to reach the North Pole; in 1912, the *Belgica's* first mate, Roald Amundsen, was the first to reach the South Pole. It is unknown whether the improvements in the crew's mental and physical condition, which allowed their safe return (and further accomplishments), were the result of real or placebo effects of the baking treatment, better nutrition, supportive attention of Cook, or return of the sun. In any analysis, however, the *Belgica's* physician and photographer, Dr. Frederick Cook, played a significant role in saving the expedition from collapse.

The cause of the malady that affected the Belgica Expedition remains a mystery. The diet and lack of sunlight could have caused the anemia and depression, as Cook surmised, or perhaps the crew had suffered from a shared hysterical reaction or some other psychological group phenomenon. It might also have been simply a terribly boring and depressing experience that affected all members of the party and drove some beyond the limits of human endurance. Like most complex phenomena, it was probably caused by a combination of factors, but it was, most certainly, an experience of considerable relevance to the planners of future long-duration expeditions.

The following sections relate to medical support, psychological support, the role of the medical officer, and recommendations for future long-duration expeditions.

MEDICAL SUPPORT

The importance of an on-board medical support capability increases with mission duration. Longer missions increase the crew's exposure to risk, and the physics of interplanetary missions eliminate any opportunity for even a delayed medical evacuation, which might be possible from a lunar base. These conditions demand that long-duration missions be equipped with autonomous medical support capabilities. Several studies conducted during the past decade in support of space station development identify various equipment and design features necessary for medical care in space. Specific reports refer to radiation protection (Jordan 1983), space station medical science concepts (Mason and Johnson 1984), health care delivery systems (Logan, Shulman, and Johnson 1983), and the management of trauma and emergency surgery in space (Houtchens 1983; Rock 1984). Houtchens, in particular, provides a detailed inventory of most of the medical emergencies for which mission planners must be prepared. These include chest, abdominal, pelvic, genitourinary, and limb disorders; thermal and electrical burns; and trauma, among others. He emphasizes urological conditions and treatments because of increased risk of renal stone passage during space missions as a consequence of hypercalcuria, dehydration, and increased concentration of urine characteristic of weightlessness. Houtchens includes a protocol to assist the diagnosis of medical conditions in space and provides several designs for zero-gravity surgical facilities. A category of medical emergency usually overlooked, however, consists of complications occasionally associated with pregnancy.

Naturally, pregnancy was not a medical concern of the explorers or a consideration during the early years of routine Antarctic operations, but it has become a serious concern of Antarctic managers during the past several years. With the female portion of the U.S. Antarctic work force now approaching 40 percent, it is not surprising that between four and ten pregnancies have occurred each year at U.S. stations during the recent past. Most pregnancies occur during the summer months when the U.S. Antarctic population swells from three hundred or so to more than two thousand. Although pregnancy is discouraged in Antarctica, it is viewed as a treatable emergency when it occurs. A pregnant women is not evacuated if her condition is normal. Medical evacuation requires at least three days to perform, if all goes well, and risks the lives of fourteen air crew members.

Drs. Jean Rivolier and Claude Bachelard (1988) provide information about the incidence of medical problems at Dumont d'Urville, the French Antarctic station. With a station population of thirty personnel, the medical officer averages about twenty medical consultations per month. (Note: It is very easy to consult the physician, and medical services are available at all times, even for minor problems.) The most frequent reasons for visiting the doctor relate to work and recreation; 20 percent of all visits fall into this category. This is also the largest category of medical problems at U.S. Antarctic stations and has been responsible for as many as fifteen medical evacuations during the more accessible summer months. Many of the more serious examples of work-related injuries are severe traumas to the hands that require special skills to repair.

The second most frequent category of medical consultations at Dumont d'Urville is dental care (18 percent of visits), followed by digestive disorders (15 percent of visits). Skin problems and rheumatic complaints (e.g., lower back pain) each represent 10 percent; respiratory disorders, 8 percent; eye problems, 5 percent (most of the eye problems also could be categorized as work-related injuries); 5 percent of consultations relate to what the French categorize as neuropsychiatric disorders, mainly sleeping problems and headaches. Only 2 percent of medical visits concern infectious diseases, and almost all of these occur immediately following the relief of a team. The remaining 7 percent of medical problems are not categorized.

An estimated 10 to 20 percent of all medical consultations at Dumont d'Urville involve functional disorders, that is, disorders that might prevent a crew member from performing required tasks, at least temporarily. The functional disorders are primarily digestive, rheumatic, and neurological. Rivolier and Bachelard report that medical problems are much more frequent during the summer, when more work and active recreation occurs. Some types of medical consultations, however, increase during the winter; these are believed to be associated with difficulties of crew members in adapting to the isolated and confined conditions. Reportedly, serious medical problems are quite rare at Dumont d'Urville. Three or four patients require hospitalization each year, and one operation and one emergency evacuation are performed every four or five years. Similar to the U.S. experience, the most serious medical emergencies at Dumont d'Urville are the results of work-related accidents with equipment. There has been only one fatality in thirty-five years at the French station; a member of the crew disappeared in bad weather.

It is interesting to note that nearly half of the medical operations performed at the Dumont d'Urville station have been appendectomies.

Appendicitis is also the leading reason for U.S. Navy submarine mission aborts; it is followed by psychiatric problems, chest pain, and dental problems, in that order (Boeing Aerospace 1983). Dr. Desmond Lugg, head of Polar Medicine, Australian Antarctic Division, found a higher incidence of appendicitis at polar stations than in team members' home environments. He suggests the characteristic low-fiber diets as a possible cause (Lugg 1979). This risk formerly led to the practice of performing preventive appendectomies routinely on Australian expedition personnel prior to their departure for the ice. This practice has been largely abandoned, except for the physician in a remote-duty crew.[2]

Future long-duration space missions will require medical support capabilities that are similar to those of remote-duty stations, such as Navy ships and Antarctic research facilities. Important differences between facilities on Earth and in space derive from the considerably more confined compartments of spacecraft and the need to perform medical procedures in the absence of gravity. Special attention must be devoted to the design of equipment to contain and control blood and other body fluids as a result of traumatic injuries and operations. On-board decision aiding (i.e., expert systems) probably should be provided to assist the medical officer, but primary support to on-board medical personnel should be provided via radio by medical specialists at mission control. Further, gynecologic and obstetric capabilities likely will be necessary in the medical support facilities of long-duration spacecraft and space habitats.

PSYCHOLOGICAL SUPPORT

Isolation and confinement have been long recognized for their potentially devastating effects on the mental health of some individuals. Many of the earliest accounts of expeditions and voyages of discovery reflect the concern of ship captains for the mental state of their crews, during an era when concern for the well-being of sailors was extremely rare. Admiral Byrd's inventory of two coffins and twelve straitjackets demonstrates this recognition and concern. But, do isolated and confined conditions *really* cause a disproportionate incidence of psychological problems and aberrant behavior, compared with "normal" conditions? The materials reviewed as part of this research indicate that cases of psychosis and severe neurosis have been infrequent during expeditions and among the crews of Antarctic research stations. Minor emotional disturbances, however, are quite prevalent (Gunderson 1963, 1973a). In this regard, Shurley (1974) reports that "minor mental troubles are both common and temporary" at U.S. Antarctic stations.

For an early period of U.S. Navy psychological research at Antarctic stations (1961 to 1962), Gunderson (1968b) finds the incidence of diagnosed psychiatric disorders to be approximately 3 percent of total Navy Antarctic personnel, with most of the cases treated on an outpatient basis. This was compared to a 1 percent hospitalization rate for psychiatric disorders each year for the Navy as a whole. This early period is particularly relevant to the current analysis because the sizes of the groups and other characteristics of the early stations were more similar to what we might expect of future space expeditions than the larger, more modern Antarctic stations of the present. Rivolier and Bachelard (1988) report that about 12 percent of French Antarctic personnel exhibit various forms of inadaptation to the conditions, but only 1 percent of personnel are diagnosed as having actual psychiatric disorders. Lugg (1977) estimates psychiatric disorders at 1.8 percent among the Australians and Matusov (1968) reports 3.2 percent at Soviet Antarctic stations. Comparisons must be made cautiously, because of differences in the classification systems, but the values generally appear to be comparable, and all of the reported incidences of psychological problems are quite low despite Antarctica's reputation as a place that fosters insanity.

In a more recent personal communication, Ker Boyce, former medical officer for the Naval Support Force Antarctica, reported that only five of five thousand medical consultations at McMurdo Station involve prescriptions for controlled substances; these figures reflect a relatively young and healthy work force. During his tour of duty, Dr. Boyce handled between six and ten acute anxiety or situational depression episodes each season; usually a counseling session of about an hour's duration provided sufficient treatment. He saw no serious mental pathology among more than two thousand Antarctic personnel during his three years as force medical officer. "Serious," however, is a relative term in Antarctica.

Strange and Klein (1973) identify a set of psychiatric symptoms that occur regularly among the winter-over personnel at Antarctic research stations. Four of the symptoms, depression, hostility, sleep disturbance, and impaired cognition, are so common that they could be considered part of a typical and expected adjustment pattern. The pattern has been called the "winter-over-syndrome" for more than two decades. Normally, the syndrome does not interfere with an individual's task performance, but the symptoms occasionally become truly pathological, and normal functioning can be seriously impaired in extreme cases. The most common forms of psychopathology to develop among Antarctic personnel appear to be depression, alcohol abuse, paranoid reaction, and psychosomatic manifestation. It is extremely relevant to this discussion that symptoms were found to be more frequent at the smaller stations (e.g., eight persons) than at the larger stations, such as South Pole, with a crew of about twenty (Gunderson 1968c).

Similarly, neuropsychiatric disorders probably occur among submariners at a significantly greater rate than observed among the crews of surface ships. Tansey, Wilson, and Schaefer (1979) report the incidence of neuropsychiatric illness on submarines as nine cases per million person-days, compared with a rate of six cases per million person-days in the surface fleet. Onboard both submarines and surface ships, however, the rate of neuropsychiatric disorder was found to be very low when compared with eighteen cases per million person-days among individuals between twenty-five and thirty-four years of age in the general population. Further, Earls (1969) identifies a seven-state pattern of adjustment to the early Polaris submarine missions that is extremely similar to the winter-over syndrome:

1. premission—depression
2. first week—elation
3. quarter-way syndrome—increase in sick call visits, subjective symptoms
4. half-way syndrome—depression
5. three-quarter way syndrome—elevated mood
6. final week syndrome—apprehension and depression
7. final days of voyage—"channel fever" (hypomanic state)

Earls also finds that depression was the most common mode of adjustment to long-duration submarine patrols. He describes the phenomenon in remarkably understandable psychological terms:

> The crux of the various forces leading to this depressive position would appear to be the anger experienced by the various members of the crew. The anger is an outgrowth of the frustrations experienced by the submariner in dealing with his

> environment. However, there appears to be no personally or culturally acceptable means of discharging this anger. The paternalistic organization of the military system is one which does not permit the direct expression of anger and aggression toward the military system. In addition, there is the personal fear that the overt expression of anger may lead to a socially isolated position within an already isolated community. The individual has little opportunity to handle his hostile affect by sublimation, except through humor. The submariner is then forced to deal with his anger by denial, suppression, or turning against himself. The hostile affect becomes internalized, but it ultimately manifests itself as a depressive phenomenon. (Earls 1969, 122)

Although the seven-state pattern might be a characteristic adaptive mechanism of submariners in general, the stresses of long-duration submergence become too severe for some individuals and result in identifiable pathology. Weybrew (1979) summarizes the incidence of neuropsychiatric diagnoses onboard U.S. Navy submarines and finds that, of the 58 percent of the individuals labeled as neurotic, 54 percent were specifically described as anxiety neurotic, 22 percent as depressive, and 12 percent as phobic. (The remaining 22 percent of cases consisted of a variety of symptoms, including claustrophobia, eating disorders, headaches, and psychosomatic signs, among others.) Weybrew believes that this sustained and slowly developing anxiety, neurotic, depressive, and phobic symptomatology reflects a reactive pathology, "caused presumably by the emotion-evoking properties of the submarine environment itself," as opposed to acute stages of long-standing personality disorders that would have been detected during psychological screening and other selection procedures. Weybrew further believes that the submariners manifesting these neurotic symptoms must have developed relatively effective coping mechanisms for the elevated anxiety and depression because only 17 percent of those affected suffered significant performance decrements.

Gross pathology is identified during the screening procedures for prospective military and civilian volunteers for Antarctic duty. Individuals who would likely develop serious psychological problems in isolation and confinement are "de-selected" by the screening process. As is the case for submariners, there is also general agreement among members of the Antarctic medical community that the many minor psychological problems experienced by Antarctica personnel are reactions to the stressors associated with living and working conditions and that the reactions are usually exaggerations of adaptive mechanisms, probably developed by the individuals many years before their Antarctic duty. This is particularly true of obsessive behaviors, which cannot always be identified during screening procedures. Dr. Fred Glogower, who was responsible for Antarctic screening for nearly a decade, suggests that a relatively harmless obsession might be a more desirable, or at least more tolerable, pathology in an individual than the alternative (i.e., not coping).

Most of the psychological mechanisms that emerge as a means of coping with the stresses of isolation and confinement are relatively benign and tolerable—for example, a moodiness or depression that passes or a temporary withdrawal from group activities or social contact. Other coping mechanisms, however, are more serious. For example, cosmonaut Valery Ryumin (1980) describes an irrational and obsessive fear that he developed during his six-month mission onboard the *Salyut* space station. He feared that he might experience an attack of appendicitis or an abscessed tooth. Neither medical emergency occurred; however, for a few weeks, he was haunted by nightmares and preoccupied during waking hours with the frightening possibilities of an emergency appendectomy or deep dental pain. The clinical explanation is clear: the cosmonaut experienced a "binding" of diffuse anxiety (caused by fears of death or failure or, more likely, by the cumulative stress of his living and working conditions). In this regard, the obsession served as an effective coping mechanism that permitted him to endure the acutely stressful period. In other words, it was an unpleasant time for the cosmonaut, but the success of the coping mechanism must be measured by the outcome of the behavior: he survived to perform his mission with only minimal degradation of performance.

Antarctic managers have reported fears similar to those of Ryumin among winter-over personnel, but they are not really fears of illness or accident as much as concern about the capability of being cared for locally or being rescued. The fears are discussed openly during the brief summer but not during the winter months, when the stations are as isolated as if they were on the moon, and evacuation would be extremely dangerous and costly. Usually station managers can effectively counter the concerns with assurances that station personnel are able to handle most emergencies but that, if an emergency is serious enough, an individual can be rescued within four days, with concrete examples of rare midwinter evacuations provided for further assurance.

Although published acknowledgment of serious psychological disturbances in conditions of isolation and confinement are relatively rare, there is reason to believe that the actual incidence of all disturbances is underreported. For example, the phenomenon known as "screamin' seaman" onboard submarines and surface ships, actually an anxiety reaction, might be reported as other than psychiatric in nature or considered insufficient of note or undesirable on an individual's record. Weybrew reports from personal experience that more than a dozen acute anxiety reactions occurred among the crew on one of the initial long-duration submarine voyages during the early 1960s (personal communication). An anxiety reaction, also known as a "panic attack," is the most common pathological response to stress; it is typically characterized by screaming, hyperventilation, and chest pain. Because it is nearly impossible to abort a submarine mission, medical corpsmen on nuclear submarines have been trained in intervention techniques to counter anxiety reactions; the procedures involve anchoring the diffuse anxiety to a specific fear, then applying behavior modification to extinguish it. Although most of the therapy is performed on shore, submarine medical personnel must be prepared to respond to the emergencies as they occur under operational conditions.

Although extreme mental pathology is rare in the records of expeditions and Antarctic research stations, there have been serious incidents, such as the one summarized by Capt. Brian Shoemaker in the Introduction and the malady that affected the crew of the *Belgica*. In the latter example, Dr. Cook sadly describes the condition onboard the ship:

> For the past month we have not felt like writing. Our humor and our ambition are not such as to make us transfer ideas to paper easily. The long polar night lies heavily upon us. Our health has suffered considerably.... From day to day we all complain of a general enfeeblement of strength, of insufficient heart action, of a mental lethargy, and of a universal feeling of discomfort.... To sleep is our most difficult task, and to avoid work is the mission of everybody. Arctowski says "We are in a mad-house," and our humor points the way. (Cook [1900] 1980, 320, 330, 334)

Before.
After.

Frederick A. Cook.
Frederick A. Cook.

Roald Amundsen.
Roald Amundsen.

Emile Racovitza.
Emile Racovitza.

Before and after photographs of *Belgica* crew members, from top, Dr. Frederick A. Cook, Roald Amundsen, and Emile Racovitza. Cook wrote: "We were all reasonably good-looking when we embarked, but we were otherwise when we returned. The long night effected a radical transformation in our physiognomies." (From Cook [1900], 1980)

Fridtjof Nansen experienced a similar lethargy during the two years that he was locked in the north polar ice cap, as reflected in his journal[3]. The malaise onboard the *Fram* was short-lived and more effectively contained than that onboard the *Belgica*, however, because of better equipment, procedures, and leadership and most important, the extensive planning that preceded the Norwegian Polar Expedition. In his journal, Nansen describes his feelings:

> My mind is confused; the whole thing has got into a tangle; I am a riddle to myself. I am worn out, and yet I do not feel any special tiredness. Is it because I sat up reading last night? Everything around us is emptiness, and my brain is a blank. I look at the home pictures and I am moved by them in a curious, dull way; I look into the future, and feel as if it does not much matter to me whether I get home in the autumn of this year or next. So long as I get home in the end, a year or two seem almost nothing. I have never thought this before. I have no inclination to read, nor to draw, nor to do anything else whatever. The only thing that helps me is writing, trying to express myself on these pages, and then looking at myself, as it were, from the outside. (Nansen 1897, vol. 1, 372–73)

Admiral Byrd believed midwinter to be the most dangerous phase of a polar expedition. In 1929, Byrd wrote to his business manager and fund-raiser about his concerns:

> I wonder if you realize the personnel difficulties of a winter night not generally known by any but explorers who do not tell about them... Almost without exception, the veteran arctic explorers have told me many tales in order to warn me about this phase of the winter night. (Quoted in Rodgers, 1990, 135)

Byrd's party was indeed affected by the long period of isolation and confinement. Chronic depression overcame some of the men, so they spent much of their time in their bunks; others suffered from insomnia. Men became absentminded; they stared vacantly and had great difficulty concentrating on anything. This problem was reflected in their conversations, which did not remain long on one topic and often devolved into a salty banter. At least a few men felt persecuted by others and withdrew from the group.

Although extremely rare in the conditions that have been studied, a case of severe psychosis could be catastrophic on future expeditions. A severely disturbed member of a small crew would have significant effects on the group's ability to perform important tasks. Further, some psychological conditions are potentially infectious, thus precipitating similar or additional responses in others. In this regard, Gunderson (1963) found early in the Navy's psychological research program: "Appreciable increases in anxiety, depression, or irritability among even a few members of a small closed group become a serious threat to group solidarity and harmony." But, most important, there exists the danger of a manic or paranoid individual disabling key equipment or essential systems of a spacecraft or lunar or planetary outpost. The examples of psychosis and aberrant behavior that I have reviewed range from a few highly disruptive paranoid delusions (which required confinement and sedation) to the burning of the chapel at McMurdo station in 1978 (the arsonist was reported to have "gone a little screwy").[4]

Serious and mission-threatening psychological incidents will be unlikely during future space missions, largely as a result of effective personnel selection (rather than the well-intentioned and skillful, yet limited, screening performed for Antarctic duty). More important, the planners of future space missions will have the opportunity to observe the performance and adaptation of candidate crew members for several years as they prepare for their missions by enduring high-fidelity simulations. Despite these assurances, potential consequences of a psychological decompensation or serious pathology during a long-duration space mission strongly suggest that the medical support capabilities of spacecraft and planetary bases should include psychiatric intervention options. The intervention probably should come from psychological support personnel located at mission control. Although an elaborate complex, such as that supporting the Russian space program (Lenorovitz 1982; Ignatius 1992), might not be necessary, at least one clinician should be on call at all times to provide psychological intervention support and perhaps counseling or therapy in the event that aberrant behavior is reported or detected among space crews. To facilitate the process, the clinician should have a preestablished rapport with the crew.

In the highly unlikely event that extreme measures are required, the on-board medical supplies should include antipsychotic drugs to incapacitate a seriously disturbed crew member; Thorazine (chlorpromazine) is used most commonly in the modern analogues that I have studied. Special consideration is required to ensure the security of antipsychotic drugs and to define the necessity for drug intervention and the procedures for administration.

THE ROLE OF THE MEDICAL OFFICER

Baron Gaston de Gerlache, son of the leader of the Belgian Antarctic Expedition and an explorer in his own right, writes about expedition physicians in an introduction to the reprint of Dr. Cook's account of the *Belgica* Expedition:

> It is always difficult for the leader of a polar expedition to recruit a doctor who is well qualified for this kind of enterprise. For one thing, there are few candidates available because they hesitate to absent themselves from their practices for a long period. Secondly, a doctor is an individualist by nature and finds it hard to become the member of a team. Finally, and most important, the medical officer in a polar expedition must be interested in research and take part in the general scientific programme so as not to find himself with nothing to do when the expedition members are in good health and not in need of his services. Lack of occupation is not only frustrating for the man himself but it often has the effect of developing in him a critical attitude towards the way the expedition is being run, which then communicates itself to his colleagues. (Cook, 1980, I)

Indeed, Dr. Cook was critical of de Gerlache's decision to remain in the pack ice in 1898, a decision that sentenced the crew of the *Belgica* to a very difficult experience. It is to Cook's criticism that Baron de Gerlache responded in the above passage, but there is considerable truth to his observations, despite his defensive tone. From the earliest accounts to the present, it is recognized that the medical officer of a ship or expedition plays an important and difficult role, but if all goes well that role comes into play infrequently, if ever. Ross (1985) reports that the ships' surgeons of nineteenth century Arctic whaling and sealing vessels, usually medical students, had considerable free time, and many pursued natural history when on their northern voyages (i.e., collecting and describing the flora and fauna that they encountered). The most famous of these medical officers was Arthur Conan Doyle, who sailed to the Greenland whaling grounds onboard the *Hope* in 1880 and later created the Sherlock Holmes mysteries. Doyle wrote of his experience:

> I went in the capacity of surgeon, but as I was only twenty years of age when I started, and as my knowledge of medicine was that of an average third year's student, I have often thought that it was as well that there was no very serious call upon my services. (Quoted in Ross, 1985, 30)

Similarly, Nansen (1897) jokes about how little the *Fram*'s physician had to do:

> For the ship's doctor there was less occupation. He looked long and vainly for patients, and at last had to give it up and in despair take to doctoring the dogs. Once each month he too had to make his scientific observations, which consisted of weighing each man, and the counting of blood corpuscles, and estimating the amount of blood pigment. (Vol. 1, 244–45)

Submarine psychologist Ben Weybrew reported in a personal interview that Navy physicians were assigned to nuclear submarines until an unfortunate, and possibly anomalous, series of postmission suicides of physicians suggested a problem. Navy psychologists hypothesized that the physicians' services were required very infrequently, but, when a physician was needed, often the injury was so severe that the physician could do nothing to save the patient. This situation resulted in an absence of job satisfaction among most of the submarine physicians and serious depression in some. The Navy had similar experiences at Antarctic research stations, and, to a large extent, physicians have been replaced onboard submarines and at the smaller Antarctic stations by well-trained senior medical corps personnel who have ancillary duties. The crews appear to have as much confidence in the corpsmen as they do in the young Navy doctors. All participants are comforted by the knowledge that on-site medical personnel are supported by experienced medical specialists via satellite communications.

Dr. William K. Douglas, flight surgeon for Project Mercury, interviewed several former NASA astronauts concerning a variety of issues relevant to spacecraft design and procedures and reported the results to NASA (Douglas 1986a). In response to Douglas's questions about medical training for crew members of future space missions, the most common suggestion of the astronauts was that there should be either a flight surgeon on each crew or two crew members trained to the level of paramedics. Other astronauts believed that every member of the crew should have paramedic training and that a physician would not be necessary, unless he or she played another important role in the mission. Douglas concluded that at least two members of each space crew should have some degree of medical competence; if one were to become ill or disabled, the other would be available to provide care, in much the same way that reliability is increased by the redundancy of key mechanical and electronic systems on spacecraft.

Douglas suggested a reasonable compromise: select to serve as medical officer a physician who is also trained to perform the tasks required for a separate position within the crew and, from among the other members of the crew, select an individual to receive medical training equivalent to that of a paramedic. In any case, physicians would be welcome members of future long-duration space crews, but it is essential to the physicians' personal well-being and to overall mission success that they be assigned collateral duties to occupy their time meaningfully, in addition to their medical responsibilities. Just as Frederick Cook was eager to join the *Belgica* Expedition, qualified physicians, who are either already trained or willing to be trained in other mission-critical specialties should not be difficult to attract to long-duration space missions.

RECOMMENDATIONS

The following recommendations concerning medical and psychological issues relate to future long-duration space expeditions:

- Provide on-board medical support capabilities (facilities, instruments, decision aids, and remote diagnosis equipment) for *all* foreseeable, potential emergencies.

- Monitor premission health status closely, for example, to avoid dental problems, kidney stones, and other medical emergencies to the extent possible.

- Provide technically accurate information to crew personnel regarding emergency medical capabilities and limitations.

- Consider preventive appendectomies for the physician and/or medical corpsman candidates.

- Routinely monitor the adjustment and mental health of the crew.

- Provide psychological support personnel at mission control for remote monitoring of crew communications and behavior and to assist with intervention, if necessary.

- Provide on-board capability to restrain and sedate a seriously disturbed member of the crew, if necessary.

- Ensure that at least two members of the crew are sufficiently trained to provide emergency medical care, including responses to anxiety reactions.

- Ensure that medical personnel are fully engaged with meaningful technical work in addition to their medical responsibilities.

- Resist the temptation to assign the medical officer a formal leadership role in the crew. The medical officer can perform his or her medical responsibilities far better when independent of the command structure. This arrangement also permits the medical officer to serve as an informal adviser to the crew leader, with the capability of providing an alternative opinion or perspective on issues. A senior medical officer (who wishes to remain anonymous) suggests that the most appropriate role for the medical officers of remote-duty stations was described in the characters and screenplays of the original *Star Trek* television series. The physician of the fictional *Enterprise* was outside the ship's main chain of command, which facilitated confidential consultations with crew members, yet the physician was close enough to the captain, professionally and socially, to offer a dissenting opinion (often several in each episode) without appearing as a direct threat to the captain's judgment. According to this anonymous source, the fictional role provides an appropriate model for the medical officers of actual spacecraft.

CHAPTER 9

PERSONAL HYGIENE

24 December 1895: Now the candles are being lighted on the Christmas trees, the children are let in and dance round in joyous delight. I must have a Christmas party for children when I get home. This is the time of rejoicing, and there is feasting in every cottage at home. And we are keeping the festival in our little way. Johansen has turned his shirt and put the outside shirt next him; I have done the same, and then I have changed my drawers, and put on the others that I had wrung out in warm water. And I have washed myself, too, in a quarter of a cup of warm water, with the discarded drawers as sponge and towel. Now I feel quite another being; my clothes do not stick to my body as much as they did. . . .

Ugh, the clothes we lived in were horrible! And when we wanted to enjoy a really delightful hour we would set to work imagining a great, bright, clean shop, where the walls were hung with nothing but new, clean, soft woolen clothes, from which we could pick out everything we wanted. Only to think of shirts, vests, drawers, soft and warm woolen trousers, deliciously comfortable jerseys, and then clean woolen stockings and warm felt slippers—could anything more delightful be imagined? And then a Turkish bath! We would sit up side by side in our sleeping bag for hours at a time and talk of these things. They seemed almost unimaginable. Fancy being able to throw away all the heavy, oily rags we had to live in, glued as they were to our bodies! Our legs suffered most; for there our trousers stuck fast to our knees, so that when we moved they abraded and tore the skin inside our thighs till it was all raw and bleeding. I had the greatest difficulty in keeping these sores from becoming altogether too ingrained with fat and dirt, and had to be perpetually washing them with moss, or a rag from one of the bandages in our medicine bag, and a little water, which I warmed in a cup over the lamp. I have never before understood what a magnificent invention soap really is. We made all sorts of attempts to wash the worst of the dirt away; but they were all equally unsuccessful. Water had no effect upon all this grease; it was better to scour one's self with moss and sand. We could find plenty of sand in the walls of the hut, when we hacked the ice off them. The best method, however, was to get our hands thoroughly lubricated with warm bear's blood and train-oil, and then scrub it off again with moss. They thus became as white and soft as the hands of the most delicate lady, and we could scarcely believe that they belonged to our own bodies. When there was none of this toilet preparation to be had, we found the next best plan was to scrape our skin with a knife.

—From Nansen's diary, in *Farthest North*

Fridtjof Nansen and Hjalmar Johansen spent the nine-month Arctic winter of 1895–96 on the frozen shores of Franz Josef Land in a small hut built from stones and walrus hides. Their life in the hut was unpleasant in many ways, not the least of which was the decline in personal hygiene, which they were forced to endure because of lack of fuel for melting snow and the absence of other supplies. They cooked their food and illuminated their world with the small flame of a blubber lamp, which coated the inside of the hut and its inhabitants with soot and grease. Most readers will probably agree that the hygiene conditions described by Nansen are about as bad as humans can reasonably endure—but Nansen and Johansen survived the experience. Bursting from their den early in the spring of 1896, they expertly performed all of the technical tasks necessary to fight their way through pack ice before they reached the safety and comforts of civilization. They suffered much but went on to perform exceptionally well, despite the austere conditions of their months in isolation and confinement.

The two explorers lived together in a manner similar to Neolithic hunters who might have ventured too far and become stranded by an early winter storm. Although Nansen and Johansen survived, they suffered from the mind-numbing sameness of their days and the health-threatening condition of their personal hygiene. It would be unwise to expect future space explorers to endure the conditions that Nansen and Johansen experienced, but it might be comforting to mission planners to know that humans are capable of enduring the most austere living conditions, when they must, and of performing well afterwards.

The hygiene standards of long-duration space missions are likely to differ substantially from what has been acceptable during short forays into space. "Camping-out" conditions, such as those of the Apollo and space shuttle programs, pose little threat to crew adjustment and productivity during short-duration missions or during emergencies, even prolonged emergencies. Austere conditions, however, could seriously degrade human performance on routine missions, such as those planned for orbital space stations, and on longer duration missions,

Fridtjof Nansen at the camp of a British expedition after spending nine months in his Arctic hut. (From Nansen, 1897)

during which the crew would be required to remain alert and active and perform difficult mental and physical tasks. Personal hygiene is distinguished from sanitation in this context. Sanitation refers to measures designed to maintain an uncontaminated environment, whereas personal hygiene concerns the maintenance of body and clothing cleanliness. This chapter addresses two subissues associated with personal hygiene: (1) the need to provide adequate hygiene facilities, and (2) the need to ensure that the facilities are used by the crew.

HYGIENE FACILITIES

Fraser (1968a) summarizes, in excruciating detail, the results of several studies concerning the effects of minimal personal hygiene. From those reports, it can be concluded that human subjects in scientific studies are capable of endurance nearly as great as that of Nansen and Johansen; however, under routine conditions in operational environments, reduced standards of personal hygiene can significantly lower overall habitability and performance. There is a definite cultural component to concepts of cleanliness, and perhaps many Americans, compared with people in other societies, appear to be extreme in their concern for personal hygiene. Most Americans believe that they are "entitled" to at least one shower each day, whereas daily bathing is considered unusual in many countries. Americans are not alone in this concern for cleanliness and inoffensiveness, but the important point to understand is that the standard is external to the individual. It is a cultural standard; that is, it is learned.

Fraser and others maintain that it is possible to train people to accept reduced standards, and to a certain extent this occurs already. It probably would be unwise, however, to expect optimal performance unless certain minimal conditions of personal hygiene are provided. In particular, accommodations for personal hygiene are necessary in the following areas:

- shaving
- body bathing
- hand and face washing
- hair and nail trimming
- hair and scalp cleansing
- dental and oral hygiene
- clothing disposal or laundering

Most of these requirements have been adequately addressed for previous space systems, such as *Skylab*, the space shuttle, and the international space station. The question of whether to provide the capability for full-body showering probably will be debated by the designers of future long-duration spacecraft and is the focus of the remainder of this section.

In Antarctica and on ships and submarines, showers are appreciated luxuries; in underwater habitats and in the deck chambers of saturation divers, hot showers are considered a necessity to counter the effects of working in debilitatingly cold water. A collapsible shower was also included onboard *Skylab*. Although some of the *Skylab* crew truly appreciated the shower device, others considered the time required to set up, clean, and secure it to be excessive. Showers invigorated the crew, but the inordinate time requirement might have significantly eroded the positive effect on productivity. *Skylab* astronaut Alan Bean reported:

> After you finished the shower, instead of being able to dry off you had to stand around inside the shower for an additional ten minutes and halfway freeze (while using the vacuum hose to remove the water). So it turned out to be easier just to forget the whole thing, although it gets you nice and clean. (Quoted in NASA 1974, A-28)

The *Skylab* crew members varied in the time they devoted to personal hygiene. Most took a sponge bath each day and a shower each week. Col. Gerald Carr, commander of the third crew, commented:

> I think we kept ourselves extremely clean. It was one of the more pleasant aspects of the day. When we did our exercises, we worked hard, we sweated hard, and the opportunity to clean ourselves afterwards was welcome. It took a lot of time because all we had to clean ourselves with was a washcloth and a water squeezer, and that's a time-consuming process.
>
> Let me just at least say that the drive to keep yourself clean is still with you up there. We found it's easier to stay clean up there because we didn't sweat as much. We found that one full body wash per day was quite adequate, and that one shower per week was adequate. In fact, you could get along without the shower, if you kept up with the body wash and did a good job with that. But there's no substitute for running water all over your body and getting it in your hair and a shower is a very refreshing thing, but again it's very time consuming. (Quoted in NASA 1974, A-43)

Analysis of the *Skylab* debriefing reports indicates that sponge baths probably would be satisfactory for cleaning the skin on long-duration missions, but they are generally considered inadequate for cleaning the hair and scalp. At least two of the *Skylab* astronauts reported that their heads developed offensive odors between their infrequent showers. In addition to inadequate cleaning, sponge baths lack the psychologically refreshing value of full-body showering. Antarctic managers report that showers are important morale boosters at remote stations, especially on the occasions when brief "Navy showers" (water is turned off while lathering) are replaced by longer "Hollywood showers" (water is kept on during entire showering process). In 1989, the reverse effect occurred during a simulation of a military remote-duty system; there was a precipitous decline in crew morale when the allowable frequency of showers was reduced from daily showering to showers on alternate days in order to conserve water.

A shower facility is strongly recommended for future long-duration spacecraft and habitats. The shower onboard a space station or at a lunar base should occupy a compartment dedicated to that function so as to minimize setup and cleanup time for the busy crew; a compact facility similar to those developed for recreational motor homes has been recommended for orbital space stations (Stuster 1986). On a mission to Mars, however, there will be little room onboard the spacecraft to accommodate a permanent shower facility but probably an abundance of time for the crew. Deploying and stowing a *Skylab*-type shower might be an interesting diversion from the weekly routine, at least during the cruise phases of the voyage.

USE OF HYGIENE FACILITIES

Personal hygiene standards were constrained by the availability of water during the early polar expeditions, at the early Antarctic research stations, and onboard diesel submarines. The following passage from Rodgers' (1990) insightful history of Byrd's first expedition to Antarctica describes the hygiene conditions on the continent in 1928:

> The men did not bathe or do laundry often, although they did not have to in the cold, relatively clean snow desert. . . . In a practice they called dry washing, the explorers put clothes away without laundering them until the clothes the men were wearing were even dirtier. Then they put on the stored clothes, which seemed clean by comparison. The men tended to go too long before filling up the small round tub to take baths, which

were neither comfortable or convenient, and so suffered frequent boils and rashes. Byrd followed an unusual bathing
routine, washing a different third of his body every night.. . . .
Many did not shave, taking advantage of the opportunity to
see what kind of beard they could grow. Some, trying to make
hair care easier, followed a shipboard custom of shaving off all
the hair on their heads. Byrd did not grow a beard, but he and
many others cut their hair to the scalp. (P. 124)

There are fewer hygiene problems now, with more effective ice
melters at the modern Antarctic stations and unlimited capacity for
making fresh water onboard nuclear submarines. Where both groups
considered one shower every ten days a luxury in the "old days" of the
1960s, the crews of U.S. Navy submarines and Antarctic stations are
now encouraged to take a two-minute shower twice each week. A
Navy psychologist refers to these showers as "baptisms of cleanliness"
in a society that has practically made a religion of personal hygiene.

The capability for daily sponge baths and a full-body shower each
week or so would appear adequate to achieve an objective level of
cleanliness and to derive at least occasional subjective value from the
refreshing effects of a shower. The frequency of crew showering on
long-duration missions will be determined by the availability of water
produced by the closed-loop recycling system for that purpose. Water
might become available for relatively frequent showers at lunar and
martian bases if efforts to locate and convert subsurface ice are successful. But, even with significant advances in closed-loop technology,
water probably will remain a precious commodity onboard spacecraft.

Whatever hygiene schedule is ultimately determined, it is important
that individual crew members not be permitted to slip into patterns of
substandard hygiene. That some individuals allow themselves to
become slovenly and offensive to their comrades has been a regular
occurrence, from the earliest polar expeditions to modern Antarctic
research stations. This issue is important because it is a highly predictable source of interpersonal conflict. Navy Antarctic managers can
enforce standards on Navy personnel by requiring them to shower, if
necessary, but they lack that authority with the civilian support and
scientific personnel. Invariably, those who have permitted their
hygiene standards to slip have been civilians, from the "absentminded
professor" of the early stations to the construction workers of the present. Many conflicts within these small remote-duty groups have been
caused by this factor and many conflicts have been avoided only

because others in a group wished to avoid a confrontation that could seriously degrade group solidarity. The phenomenon always causes friction within a crew, especially between military and civilian personnel. Trivial issues are exaggerated in the "pressure cooker" environment of an isolated and confined group. A confrontation over personal hygiene is just the kind of issue that could precipitate a major problem for an individual, which quickly becomes a problem for the entire crew.

Ben Weybrew (personal communication) offered an explanation for the tendency in some individuals to allow standards of personal hygiene to change under conditions of isolation and confinement. He suggested that it is a function of Weber's law (see Welford 1968, 1976), the same principle by which we understand desensitization to any base constant or stimulus. In simple terms, the more grubby or odiferous one is, the more grubby or odiferous one needs to become before the change is noticed by the individual. For this reason, it will be necessary for crew leaders to monitor the hygiene of long-duration crews, at least informally, and to be assertive, when necessary, to enforce established hygiene standards. The main purpose of these actions would be to eliminate a potential source of conflict among crew members and to facilitate group harmony.

RECOMMENDATIONS

The following recommendations concerning personal hygiene issues relate to future long-duration space expeditions.

- Provide personal hygiene facilities for dental and oral hygiene, hand and face washing, body bathing, hair and scalp cleaning, hair and nail trimming, shaving, and clothing disposal or laundering.

- Provide facilities for daily sponge baths (e.g., following the exercise period).

- Provide the equipment to permit weekly full-body showering. More frequent showers would be better; less frequent showers would be tolerable.

- Develop and implement a personal hygiene schedule to allow for variations in thresholds of subjective hygiene.

- Provide at least one full-length mirror to reinforce the crew members' concepts of self-image.

Chapter 10

Food Preparation

We had tried the meat of penguins, but to the majority its flavor was still too "fishy." We entered the long night somewhat underfed, not because there was a scarcity of food, but because of our unconquerable dislike for such as we had. It is possible to support life for seven or eight months upon a diet of canned food; but after this period there is something in the human system which makes it refuse to utilise the elements of nutrition contained in tins. Against such foods, even for a short period, the stomach protests; confined to it for a long period, it simply refuses to exercise its functions. Articles which in the canning retain a natural appearance usually remain, especially if cooked a little, friendly to the palate. This is particularly true of meat retaining hard fibers, such as ham, bacon, dried meats, and corned beef. It is also true of fruits preserved in juices; and vegetables, such as peas, corn, tomatoes; and other dried things. Unfortunately this class of food formed a small part of our store. We were weighed down with the supposed finer delicacies of the Belgian, French, and Norwegian markets. We had laboratory mixtures in neat cans, combined in such a manner as to make them look tempting—hashes under various catchy names; sausage stuffs in deceptive forms, meat and fishballs said to contain cream, mysterious soups, and all the latest inventions in condensed foods. But they one and all proved failures, as a steady diet. The stomach demands things with a natural fiber, or some tough, gritty substances. At this time, as a relief, we would have taken kindly to something containing pebbles or sand. How we longed to use our teeth!

—Frederick A. Cook, *Through the First Antarctic Night*

Food is the quintessential habitability issue, whether onboard a wooden ship locked in the polar ice, a commercial airliner, or a spacecraft. Food assumes added importance under all conditions of isolation and confinement because normal sources of gratification are denied; usually, the longer the confinement, the more important food becomes to those confined. Lacking access to friends, family, normal leisure pursuits, and other customary sources of personal gratification, people naturally tend to focus on food as a substitute. The elevated importance of food under long-duration isolation and confinement has several predictable effects, including increased eating by some, increased complaining about the food by others, and increased time spent in conversation during and following meals; all three responses are often observed in the same individual. People who might eat only two meals each day when at home show up for all three meals at a remote-duty station just for the social contact. They might not be hungry but eat to be sociable, or because there is little else to do. Significant weight gains are not uncommon during isolation and confinement as a consequence of food's elevated importance.

The managers of many remote-duty environments recognize the importance of food in maintaining group morale and productivity and regularly provide sumptuous meals to their personnel. Supertankers, research vessels, commercial fishing boats, long-distance racing yachts, offshore oil platforms, and similar operations provide copious quantities of high-quality food to their crews. In particular, food has become such an important element onboard fleet ballistic missile submarines that, for years, meals have been served at cloth-covered tables in pleasant paneled dining rooms; three seatings are usually required for each meal and the food, served cafeteria style, is considered to be excellent. Also, open ice cream lockers are provided, and soft drinks and snacks are always available. At modern Antarctic research stations, food is equally important to the maintenance of both mind and body. The Antarctic managers and psychologists whom I have interviewed were unanimous in their concern not only for the nutritional value and variety of the food offered but for the manner in which the food is displayed and served. In the experience of these managers, good meals can be made more, or less, appealing by the combinations of foods offered and by the manner of serving, carefully or just plopped onto a plate. Dr. Fred Glogower is convinced that the dining facilities of a remote-duty station should have a pleasant and positive atmosphere;

he commented on how the occasional use of tablecloths has an enormous effect on Antarctic personnel. Clearly, individuals in isolation and confinement are nourished more than physically by their meals.

Mullin and Connery (1959) describe their experience regarding food at an Antarctic station during the IGY:

> As might be expected, "oral needs" were enhanced because of the absence of other basic gratifications. Appetite and consumption were enormous. Weight gains of up to 20 and 30 pounds were not unusual and slight pot bellies on otherwise slender young men were notable. Fortunately, the cook was competent, imaginative, and very anxious to please. His prestige was enormous. (P. 294)

The importance of food and mealtimes are so great in isolation and confinement that some observers believe that the cook at an Antarctic station can even determine the success or failure of the group's winter-over experience. At times, disasters have been narrowly averted when cooks temporarily refused to perform their duties. Gunderson (1966a) writes of the role played by cooks in the early years of routine Antarctic operations,

> [The person selected to be cook] is likely to encounter a range of comments about his proficiency as a cook, but generally cooks are held in higher esteem than any other occupational group in the Antarctic. (P. 5)

Similarly, Cook ([1900] 1980) writes of the role of Michotte, the ship's cook, and the concern shared by the members of the *Belgica* Expedition that he not be offended in any way that could affect his professional duties:

> Next to the Captain the cook is the most important personage on the ship; there are short instances when he even rises above the Captain. . . . We can afford to dispute with the naturalist somewhat, we can even doubt the Captain's eyesight, but we cannot even dream of endangering the good will of Michotte. (P. 182)

Behavioral issues that relate to food include self-selection and variety, requirements for meal preparation, special dinners, eating together, and alcohol consumption.

SELF-SELECTION AND VARIETY OF FOOD

A major change has occurred in eating habits in the United States during the past decade. Everywhere, people seem to be concerned about their weight, calories, the quality of the food they eat, and other health and fitness issues related to food. Consumption of fish and poultry has increased in recent years, as has the number of vegetarians. These social trends have been reflected in the changing preferences and eating patterns of the crews of nuclear submarines and the staffs of Antarctic research stations. Although copious quantities of food are still consumed onboard submarines and at Antarctica stations, there has been a demand for lower-calorie entrées at mealtime; people simply want the choice of eating a lighter meal, at least occasionally. The caloric content of food servings is now frequently listed on signs in the galleys of Antarctic stations, a service provided at the request of those who want to avoid the extraordinary weight gains experienced by previous winter-over personnel.

In addition to a general trend toward selection of "lite" foods, there is a tendency for food preferences of personnel to change within the course of a long tour in isolation and confinement. This sometimes occurs with pronounced effects onboard submarines. Commercial saturation divers and Antarctic winter-over personnel, among others, also report changes in food preferences. The cause of this apparent tendency is impossible to identify, but perhaps it is a physiological response to similar atmospheric conditions or to the monotony of available stimuli. It is possible, however, to anticipate preference changes in the design of food systems for future long-duration expeditions. For example, a pantry approach would permit self-selection, at least until the spacecraft's stores become depleted. A system in which meals are programmed for the duration of a mission could also accommodate shifts in preferences, perhaps identified during high-fidelity simulations on Earth, by the sequence of programmed meals.

The dislike for the *Belgica's* food, as expressed by Dr. Cook in the quotation at the beginning of this chapter, might also reflect a change in the taste preferences of the crew, but more likely it was a response to the monotonously soft texture of the prepared foods. Monotony of texture might also confront the crews of long-duration space missions because most foods prepared for space must be soft and gelatinous so that, in the absence of gravity, they remain in their containers until spooned out and stay in the spoon en route to the space diner's mouth. Loose food can float away, with the possibility of several negative consequences. Despite the challenges of designing food for zero gravity dining, variety in texture, in particular the provision of "crunchy" foods, will be essential on future long-duration expeditions.[1]

The best evidence to support at least the occasional self-selection of meals is provided by the results of Project Tektite, the underwater habitat experiment conducted in 1969–70 to study isolation and confinement similar to that of spacecraft. The *Tektite* crews were allowed self-selection of dinner items during three of the fourteen-day missions; to the extent possible, the crews' requests for food were satisfied by support personnel through trips to the closest supermarket, several hours away. Crews of the other seven missions were provided a preprogrammed selection of foods of good nutrition and quality. The initial response of the crews to the pre-programmed food was quite positive (Wortz and Nowlis 1974); the entrées were frozen prototypes of what later became a very successful retail product line. Despite the expense and care that went into the pre-programmed menus, thirty-nine of the forty debriefing complaints concerning food quality came from those eating the pre-programmed frozen food. Nowlis, Wortz, and Watters (1972) attribute this incredible difference in acceptability to the factor of self-selection:

> Our own observations would rate the frozen food higher in quality, both tastewise and nutritionally, than the meals the aquanauts chose for themselves. It is believed that totally independent judges would make similar ratings. Finally, 16 of the 20 complaints about food storage were from aquanauts in the preprogrammed food contingency, and 15 of the 19 complaints about too much waste were from the same group. Thus, it appears that the preprogrammed food not only ignored individual choices, but also was overpackaged for a small habitat. (Sec. 5, p. 7)

A food system that permits self-selection from a variety of meal options might reduce complaints and contribute to a solution to one of the fundamental problems of long-term habitability. Dr. Glogower, however, explained that some people complain about the food at remote-duty stations because they cannot easily complain about their decisions to volunteer for the special duty. It is more acceptable to displace the anger and frustration that they might feel by complaining about the conditions; food is usually first on the list. Dr. Cook candidly describes the phenomenon:

> There was a time when each man enjoyed some special dish and by distributing these favoured dishes at different times it was possible to have some one gastronomically happy every day. But now we are tired of everything. We despise all articles which come out of a tin, and a general dislike is the normal air of the *Belgica*. The cook is entitled, through his efforts to please us, to kind consideration, but the arrangement of the menu is condemned, and the entire food store is used as a subject for bitter sarcasm. Everybody having any connection with the selection or preparation of the food, past or present, is heaped with some criticism. Some of this is merited, but most of it is the natural outcome of our despairing isolation from accustomed comforts. (Cook [1900] 1980, 290)

REQUIREMENTS FOR MEAL PREPARATION

The problems encountered with food onboard *Skylab* have been or are being solved by the developers of food systems for the space shuttle and orbital space stations; for example, a pantry was installed on the shuttles in response to the astronauts' requests for variety and the capability to have an occasional between-meal snack. Although the *Skylab* crew complained about their food, their primary concerns seemed to be with the time required to prepare meals. Some of the astronauts began the preparations for the next meal (rehydration, chilling, and so forth) at the conclusion of the previous meal; others felt pressed by mission schedules and immediately departed the galley after a meal and went to the next task.

The desire to keep preparation time to a minimum is not unique to spacecraft, but it might be magnified in space because time is even more precious there than it is on Earth. It would appear that the food system designed for space stations and lunar or planetary bases should involve minimal meal preparation times. Easy and quick meal preparation will facilitate productivity by minimizing crew workloads; it should also contribute to maintaining the crew's morale by reducing another demand on their time. Fast meal preparation during routine operations, however, does not preclude more time-consuming and elaborate preparations occasionally, as conditions warrant. That is, even a food system designed for fast delivery probably should be flexible enough to permit the preparation of special meals, even if they are prepackaged portions similar to the routine meals. The system should also permit flexibility regarding how crew members use the system, for example, by sharing meal preparation responsibilities, rotating responsibilities, or preparing individual meals.

As discussed earlier, the crew of a mission to Mars will not operate under heavy workloads and severe time constraints for most of the expedition. Thus, the food preparation system designed for a mission to Mars could permit longer preparation times, and perhaps more elaborate meals could be routinely provided than are appropriate for the fast-paced lives of a space station crew. For some individuals, preparing the crew's meals on a rotational basis might serve as a welcome source of diversion and pleasant activity during the relatively quiet phases of a planetary mission. Perhaps a food preparation system with two modes would be possible: one for the cruise phase in which personnel take turns preparing relatively labor-intensive "evening" meals, and the other for breakfasts, lunches, and dinners during high-tempo operations. A dual-mode food system would compare with having two restaurants on board, with one offering a variety of nutritious "fast food" and one providing a more satisfying meal experience when time and schedules permit the luxury.

SPECIAL DINNERS

Since the days of sail, special dinners have motivated crews and helped to mark the passage of time during long voyages. For example, Columbus authorized special feasts on holidays during his voyage of discovery, even though the role of ship's cook as a specialist among the crew was not invented until the sixteenth century (Sale 1990). Likewise, the journals and secondary accounts of nearly all of the polar expeditions report the preparation of special dinners, a well-entrenched and advisable shipboard and expeditionary institution. Cook ([1900] 1980) describes the approach to special dinners taken by the crew of the *Belgica* during their long winter night:

> April 9. It is the birthday of King Leopold, of the Belgians, to-day. The [C]ommandant has made it a holiday and ordered a special menu with a liberal supply of wine to the officers and crew. All are expected to celebrate the day in good form. We enjoy these days of rest, recreation, and change from the usual formula of regular work, and we conscientiously point out, far in advance, the legal holidays of all lands and the birthdays of each of the men of the *Belgica*. It is a slow week when we have not succeeded in having at least one day set aside as a period of special feeding, followed by a flow of champagne. (P. 249)

July 4. It is the day of the Declaration of Independence of the United States. With characteristic Belgian thoughtfulness the Commandant has ordered a special feast and has sent up the Stars and Stripes to float over the *Belgica* to be waved by the virgin Antarctic breezes. America and American affairs are the topics around which our ideas revolve to-day. (P. 327)

July 21. It is the time for the Belgian national feasts, and we are making, during this period, hard efforts to boom up the failing spirits of the men. Special foods have been prepared to please the palates; wines are sparingly served to infuse an air of good cheer, and we try to steer the topics of conversation in such manner that a new interest may be created, but it seems to me that all of our good intentions in this direction are wasted. Arctowski and Dobrowolski are in a bad way. Knudsen, Johansen and Melaerts are in the baking treatment, and altogether we are in a deplorable condition. If it now became necessary to throw suddenly a difficult physical task upon the men there would be few able to endure it. (P. 336)

Christmas dinner in the saloon of the *Belgica*, 1898. Cook ([1900] 1980) writes: "We have long since worn out all social enthusiasm, and can unearth nothing new to infuse fresh life into the desired good cheer of our Christmas dinner." (Pp. 385–86)

Elaborate meals were served each Sunday onboard the *Belgica,* in addition to the meals that celebrated special events. Special-occasion and Sunday dinners provide an isolated and confined crew something to which they can look forward, and they also help to convey that time is indeed passing, despite the mind-numbing routine of a monotonous existence. Cook ([1900] 1980) writes:

> May 29. To day is Sunday; the men look forward with some anticipation to this day because Sunday is set aside, not as a day of worship, for I have never seen a man on the Belgica with a Bible or prayer-book in his hands, but as a time of recreation and special feeding. The few eatables which are still relished are placed on the menu for Sunday. This serves to mark time and to divide, somewhat, the almost unceasing sameness of our life. (P. 296)

Special meals were also prepared onboard the *Fram,* locked within a gigantic block of ice, as she drifted north at the opposite pole of the Earth, five years before the Antarctic voyage of the *Belgica.* Nansen (1897) quotes from an entry in his journal:

> Friday, September 29th. Dr. Blessing's birthday, in honor of which we of course had a fete, our first great one on board. There was a double occasion for it. Our midday observation showed us to be in latitude 79° 5' north; so we had passed one more degree. We had no fewer than five courses at dinner, and a more than usually elaborate concert during the meal. Here follows a copy of the printed menu. . . . I hope my readers will admit this was quite a fine entertainment to be given in latitude 79° north; but of such we had many on board the *Fram* at still higher latitudes. . . . Coffee and sweets were served after dinner; and after a better supper than usual came strawberry and lemon ice and lime juice toddy, without alcohol.

FRAM
MENU. SEPTEMBER 29, 1893

―――――――――――

Soup à la julienne avec des macaroni-dumplings.
Potage de poison avec des pommes de terre.
Pudding de Nordahl.
Glacé du Greenland.
De la table bière de la Ringnæes.
Marmalade intacte.

MUSIC À DINÉ

1. Valse Myosotic.
2. Menuette de Don Juan de Mozart.
3. Les Troubadours.
4. College Hornpipe.
5. Die letze Rose de Martha.
6. Ein flotter Studio Marsch de Phil. Farbach."
7. Valse de Lagune de Strauss.
8. Le Chanson du Nord.
9. Hoch Habsburg Marsch Kral.
10. Josse Karads Polska.
11. Vårt Land, vårt Land.
12. Le Chanson de Chaseuse.
13. Les Roses, Valse de Métra
14. Fischers Hornpipe.
15. Traum-Valse de Millocher.
16. Hemlandssång. "A le misérable."
17. Diamanten und Perlen.
18. Marsch de "Det lustige Kriget."
19. Valse de "Det lustige Kriget."
20. Prière du Freischütz.

(Vol. 1, pp. 255–56)

Later in the year, Nansen recorded one of several entries in which he expressed a feeling of guilt for how good the life was onboard the *Fram*. He knew that his family and, indeed, all of Norway and much of the world were concerned for the well-being of the members of his expedition. Families of the crew and others who read of the expedition assumed that crew members were living a life of severe deprivation. That life would come later for Nansen and Johansen, after they departed the *Fram* to make their dash north, then south to their dismal winter in the hut on Franz Josef Land. But, life onboard the sturdy and cozy *Fram* was anything but deprived:

Monday, December 25th (Christmas-day). Thermometer at 36° Fahr. below zero (-38°C). . . . They will be thinking much of us just now at home and giving many a pitying sigh over all the hardships we are enduring in this cold, cheerless, icy region. But I am afraid their compassion would cool if they could look upon us, hear the merriment that goes on, and see all our comforts and good cheer. They can hardly be better off at home. I myself have certainly never lived a more sybaritic life, and have never had more reason to fear consequences it brings in its train. Just listen to to-day's dinner menu:

1. Ox-tail soup;

2. Fish-pudding, with potatoes and melted butter;

3. Roast of reindeer, with pease, French beans, potatoes, and cranberry jam;

4. Cloudberries with cream;

5. Cake and marchpane (a welcome present from the baker to the expedition; we blessed that man).

Every one had eaten so much that supper had to be skipped altogether. Later in the evening coffee was served, with pineapple preserve, gingerbread, vanilla-cakes, coconut macaroons, and various other cakes, all the work of our excellent cook, Juell; and we ended up with figs, almonds, and raisins. (Nansen 1897, Vol. 1, pp. 348–49)

The traditions established by the early explorers have been inherited by their modern counterparts in long-duration isolation and confinement. Onboard U.S. Navy submarines, Saturday is frequently designated as "steak night," and the crews anxiously await and discuss the impending occasion. Special theme dinners are also prepared several times during a voyage; a dinner's theme is usually selected to correspond with the area of the world in which the submarine is cruising at that time (e.g., when near Hawaii, the cooks might prepare a luau, complete with three finger poi). Managers of U.S. Antarctic research stations use celebrations and special dinners to maintain morale throughout the long winter night. Many holidays and birthdays are celebrated, in addition to the traditional midwinter party. Perhaps the most enjoyable occasions, however, are the theme dinners, such as those on submarines; in addition to providing novelty in cuisine, some surprises are usually involved. For example, Mao and Confucius customarily make appearances on Chinese night, and Don Corleone often pays a visit to the group on Italian night. Special meals are talked about for days before and after the event. This practice can have an enormous effect on group morale during long periods of isolation and confinement.

Special dinners provide intangible benefits in addition to the entertainment and temporary diversion from routine operations. In particular, they help to mark the passage of time. The benefits of special meals are obtained even when what is served is not very special; clearly, such words as "variety," and "special" are relative terms. Regarding special meals, Lionel Greenstreet, first officer of the Imperial Trans-Antarctic Expedition, wrote in his diary after camping on a small ice floe for several months:

Day passes day with very little or nothing to relieve the monotony. We take constitutionals round and round the floe but no one can go further as we are to all intents and purposes on an island. . . . I never know what day of the week it is except when it is Sunday as we have Adelie [penguin] liver and bacon for lunch and it is the great meal of the week and soon I shall not be able to know Sunday as our bacon will soon be finished. (Quoted in Lansing [1959] 1994, 117)

Dr. Alexander Macklin, one of the expedition's two surgeons, wrote similarly of his experience :

We have been over four months on the floe—a time of absolute and utter inutility to anyone. There is absolutely nothing to do but kill time as best one may. . . . One looks forward to meals, not for what one will get, but as definite breaks in the day. (Quoted in Lansing [1959] 1994, 120)

When one is isolated and physically confined to a routine existence, it is important to have tangible indicators that progress toward a goal is being made. Sunday dinners and the occasional special theme dinner or holiday celebration help isolated crew personnel to recognize that time is indeed passing and that progress is being made toward the established goals. For these reasons, I suggest that the food system designed for future space expeditions (from space stations to interplanetary spacecraft) include the capability to accommodate weekly special dinners and occasional celebrations. This capability probably will necessitate bulk storage and family-style preparation of food for these special meals. This represents a departure from the self-selection, cafeteria, or pantry approach recommended in the previous section, but the two approaches are not mutually exclusive.

EATING TOGETHER

Fridtjof Nansen credited much of his expedition's success to the careful research and testing that he conducted in preparation for his attempt to reach the North Pole. Although his systematic and scientific approach to mission planning clearly contributed to the success of the expedition, there were other components as well. Nansen's leadership style was one important ingredient; that style included an egalitarian approach that was reflected in the entire crew eating together daily. Nansen insisted on communal living and dining during an era that was characterized everywhere by social stratification; for example, the *Belgica* expedition was composed of the ship's crew, who occupied the forecastle, and the officers and scientists, who had sleeping cabins and dined in the saloon. Nansen (1897) writes about food planning for his Norwegian Polar Expedition:

> Special attention was, of course devoted to our commissariat with a view to obviating the danger of scurvy and other ailments. The principle on which I acted in the choice of provisions was to combine variety with wholesomeness. Every single article of food was chemically analyzed before being adopted, and great care was taken that it should be properly packed. . . . Truly the whole secret lies in arranging things sensibly, and especially in being careful about the food. A thing that I believe has a good effect upon us is this living together in the saloon, with everything in common. So far as I know it is the first time that such a thing has been tried; but it is quite to be recommended. (Vol. 1, pp. 72–73, 356)

Eating together as a group is, indeed, recommended for small groups living and working in isolation and confinement. There is a

At the supper table on the *Fram*. For his etching, John Nordhagen copied a photograph taken on 14 February 1895. All thirteen crew members are depicted. The cozy, homelike atmosphere helped them to endure their three years of isolation and confinement. (From Nansen, 1897)

tendency for subgroups to form, even in the smallest crews; this tendency increases in larger groups. Subgroup formation typically occurs along national or vocational lines. Although this is a natural phenomenon, there can be negative effects on overall group cohesiveness when subgroups become cliques. On the early expeditions, deep divisions developed between a ship's crew and the scientists on board; these divisions caused erosions of group solidarity that negatively affected crew performance, especially under emergency conditions. Similar divisions were common at the early Antarctic research stations between Navy and civilian personnel, and conflicts still occur despite an increased sensitivity to these issues. Also, subgroup formation is pronounced onboard U.S. Navy submarines, with crews of more than one hundred men (officers and enlisted personnel) representing many occupational specialties.

Several means are available to mitigate the negative effects of subgroup formation. (Chapter 11 addresses in detail the relevant issues relating to group interaction.) In the context of food preparation, however, it is important to note the value of eating together as a means of fostering communication between and among individuals and subgroups. In short, eating together regularly, as the crew of the *Fram* did for three years, reduces the possibility of divisiveness among the group and facilitates group solidarity.

The most effective way of ensuring that a crew eats together is to offer meals at scheduled times. Onboard *Skylab*, the constant pressure from mission control and a tendency to overload the schedule resulted in infrequent meals together; in a larger group or over a longer period of time, the practice of eating separately could contribute to the erosion of group cohesiveness and, ultimately, affect individual and group performance. Without question, flexibility in the food preparation system is required. Inevitably, meals will be missed because of mission-related obligations, but it is critical that both the system and the schedules be designed to encourage crews to eat together as frequently as possible. At least once each day is strongly recommended, and dinner is the most likely candidate.

ALCOHOL CONSUMPTION

Alcohol has been a part of seafaring and expeditions since the earliest days, but the evidence is mixed regarding the advisability of alcohol on future space missions. Historically, examples of alcohol use include the following.

- Columbus's flagship, the *Santa Maria,* became hopelessly grounded on Christmas Day 1492 as the result of excessive drinking by her crew the night before. Although the morning was exceptionally calm, the helm never should have been entrusted to a young cabin boy while the rest of the crew slept off the effects of the alcohol that they had consumed (Fuson 1987).

- The records indicate that when George Weymouth prepared for his search for the Northwest Passage in 1602, he spent more money on beer (£120) for his ship, the *Discovery,* than he did for navigation equipment (£100) (Mountfield 1974).

- Alcohol might have played a role in the mutiny onboard Henry Hudson's *Discovery* in 1611. Hudson and several of his favorites among the crew were set adrift because Hudson was caught "stealing victuals" from the ship's stores by means of a hatch cut between his cabin and the hold. Hudson and the others were never seen again (Mowat 1977).

- Jens Munk, commander of the Danish ships *Unicorn* and *Lamprey,* wrote of his expedition to Hudson's Bay in 1619:

  "On Christmas Eve I gave the men wine and strong beer, which they had to boil afresh, for it was frozen to the bottom. Nevertheless, they had quite as much as they could stand, and were very jolly, but no one offended another with as much as a word" (quoted in Mowat 1977, 103).

- When young George De Long headed north in an American attempt to reach the North Pole in 1879 (260 years—nearly ten generations—after Munk's voyage), the *Jeannette* carried in her hold three barrels of lime juice (to prevent scurvy) and 800 gallons of alcohol, including brandy and Budweiser beer, for medicinal purposes and refreshment. On Christmas Day, De Long attempted "to inject conviviality" into his crew, who had been plagued with divisiveness from the start of the voyage. He ordered that three quarts of whisky be sent forward to the men in the forecastle, so they might drink a toast to distant loved ones. It was clear that De Long's gesture had the intended effect when the crew came aft to wish the officers and scientists a Merry Christmas and to invite them topside for some impromptu entertainment. Later, when the ship's surgeon informed De Long of a possible mutiny plan, he ordered a weekly issue of rum for all hands and added that it "gives them something to look forward to" (Guttridge 1986).[2]

- In 1881, the twenty-five men of the Greely Expedition were safely encamped in their snug prefabricated house in the Arctic, a 60-by-70-foot structure named Fort Conger. Birthdays at Fort Conger were occasions for celebration and a break in the routine. The celebrant was relieved of all duty for the day and offered the opportunity to choose the dinner from among the entire list of stores and delicacies available; he also received a quart of rum from the expedition's supply. The first man offered this special treatment set a precedent that was maintained throughout their stay at Fort Conger—he passed the bottle around among his comrades until it was empty (Todd 1961).

- Fridtjof Nansen took only about twenty-five bottles of fine cognac onboard the *Fram* because he believed that brandy drinking could have serious consequences on such a difficult and dangerous voyage. The ship's stores included large quantities of bock beer, however, which was consumed daily by the crew until the supply ran out about a year into the three-year expedition ("a day of mourning," according to Nansen). Special concoctions were prepared for celebrations during the remainder of the *Fram*'s voyage. For example, a "Polar Champagne 83°" was served during the second Christmas onboard the

Fram (a home brew with cloudberries, "which made a sensation"), and a punch bowl filled with "Chateau la Fram" helped the crew to celebrate the return of the sun in the spring (Nansen 1897).

- Cherry-Garrard (1930) reports that Robert Falcon Scott included in his expedition supplies only a few cases of wine for special occasions and some "excellent brandy" to be carried as medicinal comforts on sledge journeys. Cherry-Garrard writes, "Any officer who allowed the distribution of this luxury on nearing the end of a journey became extremely popular."

- Alcohol played a significant role during Admiral Byrd's first expedition to the Antarctic in 1928. Several members of the forty-two-man expedition periodically broke into the 55-gallon drums of pure alcohol at Little America; rowdy parties became a nightly occurrence during the winter months. Byrd and his second in command, Larry Gould, attempted to contain the drinking, but its continuation forced Gould to establish a curfew. Byrd was concerned that the drinking would lead to fighting so he admonished his men: "Harmony on the expedition is the most important thing." Despite his words, the admiral seemed unconcerned about the drunkenness and even appeared, at times, to encourage it (Rodgers 1990).

- Although alcohol is not officially condoned on either American or Russian space missions, there is evidence that alcohol is regularly provided to cosmonauts by the support personnel who prepare their supplies. On at least one occasion, a well-known cosmonaut consumed most of a bottle of brandy as soon as it arrived at the space station.

Heavy drinking has been a recurrent problem at U.S. Antarctic stations since the earliest days. Dr. Glogower reports that alcohol remains a principal culprit in nearly all problems that occur there, despite official efforts to discourage alcohol abuse:

The "club" is almost always mentioned within the first three words used to describe an incident at an Antarctic station.

Alcohol is a "wild card" in any situation. Either eliminate it, or limit consumption to one glass of wine per week. (Personal interview)

Not all Antarctic experts agree. For example, Dr. Ker Boyce is among those who believe that alcohol serves an important function to some individuals at Antarctic stations and that the benefits outweigh the occasional negative consequences of alcohol abuse. An individual might increase his or her consumption of alcohol, but there are fewer ways to get into trouble at an Antarctic station than at home. Alcohol helps some people to adapt to the isolation, confinement, and social conditions of life in Antarctica. For others, alcohol serves as an effective motivator—a can of beer to which one looks forward at the end of a difficult shift. Dr. Boyce believes it would be reasonably safe to provide moderate amounts of alcohol for space crews; after all, pilots are accustomed to controlling their alcohol intake with respect to their flying schedules. Reportedly, most of the *Skylab* astronauts would have preferred a drink with dinner during their missions; they had once attended a wine tasting party at the Space Center to select the wines that they liked best, but the plan was abandoned.

The question of whether to provide alcohol to space crews has been a major topic of discussion among European Space Agency planners. Many ESA planners consider a space station, lunar base, or mission to Mars to be inconceivable without the availability of alcohol for the crew. Some of the European scientists and engineers consider this issue to be paramount among the habitability concerns. They seem to fear that, without wine accompanying the meals, it might be difficult to recruit European crews for space duty, and certainly the life there would not be worth living. Enormous cultural differences in European and American approaches to this subject are reflected in the debate over alcohol in space.

An American approach might be to apply one of the key principles of the field of human factors engineering. That is, one must consider the consequences of an error or inadvertent act when designing precautions, or safeguards, in a system; the more serious the possible consequences, the more conservative must be the precautions. Thus, while limited and responsible use of alcohol might not result in significant problems onboard spacecraft, the possibility exists that an interpersonal problem might be precipitated by alcohol consumption or an emergency could occur that requires unimpaired cognitive and psychomotor abilities. The simple answer to the question is to prohibit alcohol—to eliminate the "wild card"—but this might not be the most appropriate response for long-duration missions.

A more reasonable approach might be to provide wine and spirits to be consumed by space crews on special occasions. The supplies would be rationed to prevent individual overindulgence, while retaining sufficient quantities for commemorating holidays, birthdays, and important "milestones" in the mission. Under these conditions, it is unlikely that a crew member would achieve a blood alcohol concentration that even approaches the legal limit for adult drivers in the United States (i.e., .08 or .10). No one would be permitted to jeopardize the craft, as did Columbus's crew. Crew leaders, of course, would be responsible for monitoring the performance of their personnel and for ensuring that at least one member of the party is designated to refrain from even the small quantity of alcohol served on a special occasion.

RECOMMENDATIONS

The following recommendations concerning food preparation issues relate to future long-duration expeditions.

- Design the food system to allow self-selection.

- Design the food system to provide a variety of dietary options, including variety in tastes and textures of food.[3]

- Design the food system to require minimal meal preparation times for space stations, planetary bases, and high-tempo operations on interplanetary spacecraft.

- Design the food system to accommodate more elaborate meal preparation when schedules and workloads permit; a dual mode system is recommended for interplanetary spacecraft.

- Allow flexibility in the method of food preparation (e.g., one crew member prepares dinner for the group or each member prepares meals individually).

- Encourage special dinners by providing an appropriately designed food system and a management philosophy that recognizes the benefits of special meals.

- Encourage crew members to eat together by providing adequate preparation facilities and space in the galley and dining area and adhering to a regular schedule of meals.

- Expect complaints about the food regardless of how much attention is devoted to ensuring that it is the best possible under the circumstances.

- Consider providing wine and spirits onboard long-duration spacecraft to be consumed in small quantities on special occasions.

CHAPTER 11

GROUP INTERACTION

20 May 1898: I do not mean to say that we are more discontented than other men in similar conditions. This part of the life of polar explorers is usually suppressed in the narratives. An almost monotonous discontent occurs in every expedition through the polar night. It is natural that this should be so, for when men are compelled to see one another's faces, encounter the few good and the many bad traits of character for weeks, months, and years, without any outer influence to direct the mind, they are apt to remember only the rough edges which rub up against their own bumps of misconduct. If we could only get away from each other for a few hours at a time, we might learn to see a new side and take a fresh interest in our comrades; but this is not possible. The truth is, that we are at this moment as tired of each other's company as we are of the cold monotony of the black night and of the unpalatable sameness of our food. Now and then we experience affectionate moody spells and then we try to inspire each other with a sort of superficial effervescence of good cheer, but such moods are short-lived. Physically, mentally, and perhaps morally, then, we are depressed, and from my past experience in the Arctic I know that this depression will increase with the advance of the night, and far into the increasing dawn of next summer.

—Frederick A. Cook, *Through the First Antarctic Night*

Mark Twain said, "One sure way to learn whether you like someone or not is to travel with them." For future space travelers, it will be essential to know for certain that one is indeed traveling with friends long before the spacecraft departs. Crews will experience interpersonal problems, however, even when they are traveling with colleagues whose friendship and compatibility have been established by years of selection, simulation, and training together. This is because most of the interpersonal problems that occur among isolated and confined groups are not really caused by the individuals; rather, the problems are the inevitable results of fundamental forces and processes characteristic of the experience. Sustained, close personal contact with other individuals, in particular, can be extremely stressful; this condition is exacerbated by additional sources of stress, such as danger, time pressure, equipment malfunctions, and high workloads (or conversely, boredom). The stress is cumulative; behavioral consequences are to be expected if there is no way available to eliminate the source of stress, for example, by removing oneself from the group temporarily. But, it is impossible to get away from one's comrades when living in isolation and confinement.[1] Clearly, this is what cosmonaut Valery Ryumin meant when he wrote that "all the conditions necessary for murder are met if you shut two men in a cabin measuring 18 feet by 20 and leave them together for two months" (Ryumin 1980).

Most behavioral scientists probably would maintain that group interaction is the most important of the issues addressed in this book. The explorers, in their accounts of isolation and confinement, and the Antarctic personnel who were interviewed tend to agree with this assessment: the smooth functioning of the group contributes greatly to mission success and can be essential to survival under emergency conditions. These social issues have been considered by some researchers to be so important as to be limiting factors. For example, in a study concerning the design of a lunar laboratory, it was concluded that the primary limiting factor for all extraterrestrial activities is the "problem of interpersonal relationships" among the isolated crew (La Patra 1968). Similarly, Dr. Oleg Gazenko, medical director of the Soviet and Russian space programs, notes that "the limitations of life in space are not medical but psychological" (in Oberg and Oberg 1986).

If interpersonal problems among the members of isolated and confined groups are inevitable, what can be done in the way of habitat design, operating procedures, and informal practices to minimize the problems or to mitigate the effects of problems when they occur? Responses to these questions are provided in the following sections devoted to organizational structure, intracrew communications, and interpersonal relations. Chapter 13 addresses the issue of outside communications.

ORGANIZATIONAL STRUCTURE

One of the themes that emerged from my review of journals, diaries, and accounts of expeditions is the importance of establishing a "spirit of the expedition" that serves to unify and motivate a group of individuals who might have little else in common. The spirit of the expedition is reflected in individual productivity and effective teamwork by the group as its members labor toward a common goal and endure the same deprivations. In the past, the leader of an expedition created this intangible spirit by his general credibility, his statements regarding the purposes of the endeavor, and the manner in which he treated the members of the expedition. Many unfortunate expeditions were handicapped by the absence of a unifying spirit because of the inability of their leaders to inspire a sense of purpose and group solidarity. The expeditions that lacked a unifying spirit were not necessarily doomed to failure, but many did suffer catastrophes when divisiveness prevented an orchestrated response to an emergency. It is possible that other expeditions, despite well-developed spirits of group solidarity, suffered similar fates, but I discovered none during my research. Rather, the expeditions with the most salient group solidarity were also the ones that achieved the most spectacular successes, measured by either accomplishment or survival against all odds.

The traits and practices of effective leaders in isolation and confinement are discussed in chapter 7, which describes, in general terms, the features of the optimal organizational structure for living and working in isolation and confinement. That structure is characterized by a team approach, defined as a democratic or egalitarian orientation; concern for the well-being of each crew member; active participation by the leader in technical work and other activities of the group; and flexibility regarding policies and decisions. In short, the optimal organizational structure for a group living in isolation and confinement requires situation-specific expertise and decision making, with the activities of the team members coordinated by a clear and credible leader. The leader consults with others in the group before making decisions that specifically affect them and with the entire group on issues that affect the group as a whole. The most effective leaders accomplish their objectives through consensus and skillful persuasion, but it is essential that the leader's role and authority be unambiguous and that the leader makes decisions as promptly and autocratically as necessary under the circumstances. Many observers have reported a tendency within isolated and confined groups for formal authority structures to become less tolerated over time and for group structure to become less complex. Special leadership and interpersonal skills are required to maintain authority and control under the status-leveling conditions of isolated and confined living; this ability can be critical to mission success. The interviews conducted and materials reviewed support the notion that good leadership might contribute more to mission success than good habitability.[2]

It follows that the optimal organizational structure for future long-duration expeditions requires a clearly defined and respected leader and a relatively flat hierarchy, that is, the leader may be perceived as the "first among equals" but have the ability to exercise clear authority when necessary. This approach is similar to the system that evolved at U.S. Antarctic stations during the decades in which the management of the stations during the winter months was the responsibility of Naval Support Force Antarctica. Station leaders consulted with civilian scientists and enlisted personnel on matters that affected them and with the group as a whole on group issues, despite the firm naval tradition of a hierarchical chain of command; however, it was always clear to the members of a party that the station leader had the ultimate authority to make whatever decisions might be required. This structure serves as the model for future remote-duty operations.

In 1991, conditions began to change at U.S. Antarctic research stations. Responsibility for station management ceased to revert to the Navy for the nine-month austral winter. The National Science Foundation now has full responsibility for management of the programs; the Navy's role is limited to providing logistics support (aircraft and ships) and a few other services. Civilian contractors, hired by NSF, provide most of the support services formerly provided by the U.S. Navy. The combination of military, scientific, and contractor personnel has resulted in a confusing organizational structure and contributed to problems involving issues of group interaction.

During the transition period, rifts that might normally occur between the few remaining Navy personnel and relatively undisciplined civilian construction workers have been exacerbated by the civilians' perception that the Navy still "runs the show." The civilians frequently attribute unpopular policies and decisions to the Navy when, in fact, they originated with the sponsoring organization or the contractor. For example, individuals at U.S. Antarctic stations must file a "foot plan" (similar to a pilot's flight plan) when they intend to leave a station, even for a relatively brief excursion, so that a station manager can send a search party should the personnel not return as scheduled. According to a former master chief of the command and a former commanding officer of Naval Support Force Antarctica, a contractor fired two civilian support personnel when it discovered that they had departed a station without filing a foot plan. The two civilians, as well as others who believed that they were wrongfully terminated, blamed the Navy, although they had actually violated the contractor's work rule. Ambiguities regarding authority foster divisiveness among an isolated and confined group. Confusing responsibilities and unclear chains of command, as noted here, should be avoided on future expeditions because they contribute to the interpersonal problems that are inevitable under conditions of isolation and confinement.

I strongly recommend that future long-duration space missions be approached as expeditions, rather than test flights, engineering projects, scientific experiments, or research and development programs. Central to an expeditionary approach is a planning process in which the leaders rely heavily on the lessons learned from previous expeditions. Further, to minimize the negative effects of isolation and confinement on group interaction it is essential to have the benefits of the esteemed leadership style described in chapter 7, a clear and unambiguous organizational structure, and a well-developed expeditionary spirit to unify and motivate the individual members of the crew to work together as a team.

INTRACREW COMMUNICATIONS

Unequivocal communications are absolutely necessary when living and working in an environment where errors could have grave consequences. Special attention to intracrew communications in technical or dangerous situations is consistent with the principle of human factors engineering mentioned in a previous discussion; that is, the possible consequences of errors and inadvertent actions must be considered when determining appropriate safeguards. Extreme measures are necessary to ensure accurate communication among members of a spacecraft crew because the possible consequences of miscommunication include mission- and life-threatening conditions. Ambiguous commands and misunderstood messages cannot be tolerated during the operation of complex equipment and life support systems in the void of space.

Although certain speech patterns appear to be more or less effective in coordinating group activity, Kanki, Folk, and Irwin (1991) found that predictability is the key to enhancing intracrew communication and group task performance. The authors determined that air transport crews that communicated in highly standard ways (i.e., using established terms, syntax, and feedback) made fewer errors during simulated missions than crews that communicated in nonstandard ways. This principle has been recently incorporated into some commercial aviation training programs. "Cockpit discipline," as the adherence to operating procedures and communications protocols is called, seems to increase in importance with increasing levels of automation. In particular, mode awareness of automated systems is facilitated by clear and consistent communications (Scott 1995).

The importance of clear communications is evidenced by the many air and sea disasters attributed to equivocal messages, misunderstandings, and other impediments to accurate and timely communication. The need for clear communications has been addressed, with varying degrees of effectiveness, in the aviation, air traffic control, submarine, and surface ship environments. Most relevant to future space missions is the form of communication that has evolved in the U.S. Navy's Submarine Service to minimize the possibility of confusion or misunderstanding. When requests are made or orders issued, the communication is in a form that is direct, precise, and provides feedback to ensure that both parties share the same understanding of the communication. Comdr. K. A. Lee, an experienced submarine officer, provides an example:

> Suppose a technician wants to shut down his computer to do some maintenance on it. He wouldn't just announce, "I'm going to turn off my computer for a while." Instead, he would go to the officer in charge and say, "Mr. Smith, I intend to de-energize the XYZ computer for a period of two hours to perform some maintenance duties," and then he'd name them. The officer in charge would then reply, "Very well, permission granted to de-energize the XYZ computer for two hours." He never merely says, "OK" or "Go ahead." Everyone has to have a clear understanding of what's going on. (Quoted in Sullivan 1982, 92)

Some of those who will serve as leaders and crew members of future spacecraft will have had prior aviation and/or military experience that has prepared them for the kind of precision and clarity in communications necessary for long-duration space missions. Many future crew members, however, will have civilian scientific and engineering backgrounds, and they will lack the training and special discipline required for safe and effective intracrew communications. For these reasons, it will be necessary to develop formal communications protocols for all crew personnel to follow when making requests, responding to requests, and otherwise exchanging technical and procedural information within the spacecraft or planetary base. In addition, it would be advisable for all crew personnel to receive crew resource management (CRM) training. An appropriately designed CRM program would sensitize individuals to the issues; remove impediments to communications; and generally facilitate fluid, timely, and accurate exchange of important information within the group. The relative effectiveness of various communications protocols and CRM programs could be evaluated during the many high-fidelity simulations that must be performed prior to a long-duration mission.

Also, it will be necessary to communicate general information and to share messages that lack immediacy among the members of the crew. For example, the *Skylab* astronauts reported that they would have benefited from some form of on-board office or central repository for procedures, schedules, and the reams of teletype messages received from mission control. *Skylab* also lacked a bulletin board for posting schedules and sharing messages; the astronauts tucked papers and notes behind any convenient wiring and bungee cords. Future spacecraft and planetary habitats should include a small area or workstation, dedicated to the overall management of the facility, that could serve as the mission commander's office. A simple bulletin board for posting schedules, reminders, and other relevant messages probably should be located in the wardroom or galley. Central storage of paper documents and a "low-tech" bulletin board are required in addition to any electronic systems that are developed to serve similar functions.

INTERPERSONAL RELATIONS

The topic of interpersonal relations does not fit neatly into any single category. Certain aspects of interpersonal relations are discussed in the chapters on leadership, food preparation, recreation, and privacy and personal space (see chapters 7, 10, 14, and 16, respectively). The discussion in this chapter focuses on intracrew conflict, crew composition, and proposed countermeasures to interpersonal problems.

Intracrew Conflict

Imagine living in a medium-sized motor home locked in with five other adults, for a period of three years. Socially, this situation approximates a mission to Mars. The crew will be excited following departure from Earth orbit, and extremely busy with important technical tasks, contingency planning, and mission-abort rehearsal activities. But a change will occur as the excitement dissipates and the days begin to blend into weeks, then months, as the crew make the transition to the cruise phase of the voyage. Each crew member's repertoire of jokes, anecdotes, personal experiences, and opinions will become well known to the other members of the tiny, closed society, if this has not already occurred during the years of premission training and simulations. Nothing that anyone says or does will seem new, and the crew members will become increasingly weary of each other. Previously innocuous mannerisms of crew mates will be magnified into intolerable flaws as the result of proximity and duration. Crew members will be able to escape the presence of others only by retreating to the lavatory or to the small compartments that serve as private sleep chambers. Interpersonal friction and overt conflicts among crew members are the inevitable consequences of these conditions, as related by Dr. Cook in the quotation that introduces this chapter.

Rivolier and Bachelard (1988) provide an additional description of the phenomenon from their experience with the French polar program:

> Every moment of daily life is communal, from the most mundane to the most exceptional. There is no escape from the group, which holds everyone prisoner. This, together with the almost total absence of external stimuli and distractions, makes it easy to understand how readily interpersonal conflicts arise. These conflicts are aggravated by insignificant material nuisances which assume unreasonable proportions. They are seen as constraints which are as difficult to tolerate as the annoying presence of the other overwinterers. (P. 80)

The cause of most of the interpersonal conflict that occurs within isolated and confined groups is that trivial issues are exaggerated. The stresses associated with isolation and confinement consistently result in minor interpersonal problems; sometimes major conflicts occur, but they are rare. Typically, the problem or conflict is precipitated by an issue that, under normal conditions, would be considered trivial or even inconsequential. The most trivial of issues, however, are predictably exaggerated beyond reasonable proportions by the relentless proximity of one's comrades and the other stresses of isolated and confined living that accumulate over time. A highly experienced civilian supervisor at McMurdo Station commented that she would frequently leave a heated discussion and wonder why she had become so "worked up" over a relatively minor issue. The following description of the midwinter period of Byrd's first Antarctic expedition illustrates the phenomenon:

> The men got on one another's nerves and were literally driven to distraction by petty idiosyncracies. Owens, for example, related how maddening he found De Ganahl's panting way of breathing, his belief in dreams, and his frequent use of the phrase "I'm sorry." The cultural disparities that made the camp a melting pot—and which Byrd said had inspired him to call it Little America—contributed to the friction. Byrd, for instance, had to tell New York Irishman O'Brien how infuriating others found his wisecracks. As a result of the petty conflicts, Czegka became so morose he threatened to kill himself. Doubtlessly referring to the machinist, Byrd wrote that he "had walked for hours with a man who was on the verge of murder or suicide over imaginary persecutions by another man who had been his devoted friend." (Quoted in Rodgers 1990, 135–36)

Dozens of cases of interpersonal conflict could be cited to illustrate the phenomenon of isolated and confined groups exaggerating trivial issues. Examples of interpersonal problems that occurred during earlier expeditions are described throughout this book. Following are more recent examples, beginning with three excerpts from early Antarctic station leaders' logs:

- "One civilian's coffee cup had become so dirty that I threw it in the garbage can. We had soup for evening meal and he used his cup. After finishing his soup he hung his cup on the rack without cleaning it. About an hour later he found the cup and wanted to know why I had put it where I had. I told him why whereupon he lost his temper and started acting like a child." (Quoted in Gunderson, 1973b, 150)

- "Morale not very good. C—who has generally been in good spirits was antagonized by the scientific leader over an inconsequential matter. Later C—after drinking, finally departed for the summer camp because 'he couldn't stand anybody any longer.' " (Quoted in Gunderson, 1973b, 150)

- "Cook's at it again. He's moody, definitely emotionally immature. Threw a lemon pie and cookies all over the galley the other day, then went to his room for a couple of days and wouldn't come out." (Quoted in Gunderson, 1973b, 150)

- A civilian construction worker was confronted by a Navy enlisted man when the worker began to wolf down his meal in the station dining room without first removing his winter gear. The Navy man sitting nearby had been enjoying his meal "in the finest restaurant in town," according to Dr. Glogower, while the civilian was having "a refueling stop." The brief confrontation over appropriate dining room behavior could have exploded into a major conflict, but it was resolved amicably.

- A member of the winter-over crew disliked the outside work required at a small station so she avoided some of her cooperative responsibilities. The group responded by excluding her from its activities (e.g., special dinners, videos), which caused her to withdraw further from the group. The problem reached crisis proportions (involving senior managers and psychologists many thousands of miles away) before it was resolved by transferring the crew member to a larger station and indoor responsibilities.

- Interpersonal problems seemed to plague Valentin Lebedev during his 211-day mission onboard the *Salyut* space station. Lebedev (1988) describes a running feud that developed between himself and his partner, Anatoly Berezovoy. Inexplicably, the conflict seems to have emerged within only a few days of arriving at the station. Berezovoy became irritated with Lebedev, apparently over instruments (a sextant and a camera) that Lebedev permitted to float freely in the station. A week later, Lebedev records in his diary, "My relationship with Tolia has stabilized in the past few days to the extent that we don't bother each other. I can live with this." Two months later, he notes, "We don't understand what's going on with us. We silently walk by each other, feeling offended. We have to find some way to make things better." Lebedev's journal entries indicate that their relationship improved slightly at times, but it was punctuated by a series of perceived transgressions—trivial issues— that eroded their comradeship and degraded their individual and collective task performance.

Perhaps the most relevant examples of interpersonal problems can be found in the account of the International Biomedical Expedition to the Antarctic provided by Rivolier et al. (1988). The IBEA, composed of twelve scientists from a total of five countries, was conducted, in part, to obtain information about group interaction that might be useful to future space missions. This objective was achieved; the interpersonal problems experienced during the IBEA are extremely relevant to the planners of future expeditions. Rivolier and his colleagues (1988) describe the problems:

> There were times such as at the onset of the laboratory pro-gramme in Sydney and at the arrival of the group in Antarctica when the group worked with a will as a team to unpack and test their gear. But the harmony was short-lived. Individuals asserted themselves. They competed with each other for status and responsibility, and they drew apart in their national groups. Occasionally they re-grouped according to their antipathy to particular experimenters, and even less occasionally they forgot their differences to enjoy each other's company. (P. 91)

One member of the expedition had to be evacuated for psychological reasons on the twentieth day of the seventy-one-day motorized tra-verse that began near the Dumont d'Urville station. The others endured for the duration of the mission but returned from the traverse "humorless, tired, despondent, and resentful." None of the participants found their Antarctic experience enjoyable, not as a result of the climate or hardships, but because the expedition was made extremely unpleasant by the "inconsiderate and selfish behavior" of their colleagues. Most of the interpersonal problems were precipitated by disagreements over the performance of necessary communal work and camp chores; these trivial issues were aggravated by underlying rivalries and cultural and language differences among the members of the party. The group was fragmented and lacked a unifying spirit or sense of mission, despite the efforts of the organizers.

The near social disaster of the IBEA was measured by a comprehensive program of qualitative and quantitative psychological research that began thirty days prior to the traverse and continued throughout the expedition; debriefings and counseling sessions took place when the group returned to Australia. The results of the psychological studies confirmed the importance to mission success of personal stability and interpersonal compatibility, in addition to professional competence. It is important to note that no special personnel selection procedures were followed in planning the expedition because the organizers lacked a pool of qualified scientists from which to choose participants. The organizers made the reasonable and, in retrospect, naive assumption that the individuals invited to participate would behave in a mature and cooperative fashion and that they would possess sufficient insight to decline if they believed themselves to be unsuitable for the experience. This assumption was proved false by the immaturity, insensitivity, jealousies, scapegoating, and otherwise divisive behavior of some members of the group. Fortunately, no serious emergency occurred that would have required a coordinated response; the experiences of previous expeditions suggest that the members of the IBEA might not have survived.

Crew Composition

An experienced winter-over manager described some of the "clubs" at Antarctic stations as appearing to be similar to the bar scene in the film *Star Wars*. He was referring to the diversity of the clientele, as well as to the atmosphere of suspicion and hostility that sometimes fills a room. Small groups of Navy officers, enlisted personnel, scientists, and various categories of civilian support staff can be found in a club during a particularly busy evening, with little or no social interaction among the groups. Gunderson (1966a) comments on the conflicts between military and civilian personnel at the early U.S. Antarctic stations:

> There are probably as many interpersonal difficulties within each of these groups (military and civilians) as between them; however, the presence of the two different occupational groups, whose members come from different educational and social backgrounds, tends to increase the likelihood of significant differences in goals and value systems. One recurrent issue, for example, is the importance of cleanliness and neatness in living spaces. The presence of extreme or rigid points of view on any subject of general interest or concern at the station might well lead to tension and conflict. (P. 6)

In fairness, it must be added that very few actual fights, maybe one or two each year, occur at U.S. Antarctic stations, and most people consciously attempt to remain inoffensive and tolerant of others. It is also important to note that there appear to be *no* racial conflicts at U.S. Antarctic stations. The U.S. Navy has devoted considerable attention to this issue, in general, and, at Antarctic stations, all of the personnel realize that they must get along and work together effectively because of their remote location. A hostile outside environment can be a unifying force.

Interpersonal problems can be relatively common under conditions of isolation and confinement; most of them are precipitated by trivial issues among the members of a group. If trivial issues are inevitably, and sometimes dangerously, blown out of proportion, it seems clear that a way to minimize the potential for this phenomenon would be to eliminate the differences among the members of an expedition, to the extent possible. Chapter 15 addresses the topic of personnel selection, but, in the current context of group interaction, it is important to note that the most successful (i.e., remarkable) expeditions have been conducted by relatively homogeneous groups or groups that have been organized specifically on the basis of compatibility. The most salient examples are Nansen's group of thirteen Norwegians who sailed onboard the *Fram* (Norwegian Polar Expedition, 1893–96), and the twenty-seven men carefully selected by Shackleton to conduct an ambitious expedition to Antarctica onboard the *Endurance* (Imperial Trans-Antarctic Expedition, 1914–15). The *Fram*'s crew endured three years of isolation and confinement and, in the process, reached what was then the point farthest north achieved by humans, an accomplishment of such magnitude at the time that modern readers might find it difficult to comprehend. In contrast, the *Endurance* never even reached Antarctica, but the performance of Shackleton's crew in surviving the loss of their ship might have been an even greater achievement than that of the Norwegians. It is true that both of these exemplary expeditions experienced some interpersonal problems but not nearly to the extent of contemporary expeditions composed of heterogeneous crews.

Is it feasible to consider selecting homogeneous crews for future long-duration missions to minimize the potential for interpersonal conflict? If it were feasible, a crew composed of Norwegian males, most of them with extensive seafaring experience, would appear, from the materials reviewed, to offer the best prospects for harmony and cooperation during the long-duration isolation and confinement of a space expedition. But, it is not feasible to select a homogeneous crew for future space missions because of the social and economic realities of such large-scale endeavors. Undoubtedly, international cooperation will be necessary to finance large-scale expeditions, such as lunar bases and interplanetary voyages. Thus, many future space crews will be composed of individuals from different countries and cultures. Already, foreign visitors have conducted successful missions onboard the *Salyut* and *Mir* space stations and international crews have performed well on U.S. shuttle flights, but the durations of these missions have been relatively brief. In the near term, the international space station will be routinely staffed by multinational crews for tours of ninety days or more, and it is extremely likely that lunar and interplanetary missions also will be cooperative ventures with crews drawn from among the spacefaring nations. In short, it appears inevitable that cultural differences, such as those that contributed to divisiveness onboard the *Belgica* and during the IBEA, will be present on future space expeditions.

Gender differences could provide yet another source of interpersonal conflict during a long-duration space mission. Some observers of the space program have predicted that serious problems could result from the formation of mixed-gender crews. Gender-related problems have been reported in conditions somewhat analogous to spacecraft. On certain Antarctic stations, offshore oil rigs, drilling barges, merchant ships, and naval vessels, for example, interpersonal problems associated with mixed crews have seriously affected crew performance. Usually on closer inspection, however, the problems appear to have been not directly attributable to mixed crews, but rather to the behavioral consequences of immaturity, faulty personnel selection, and inadequate premission training for both male and female members of the crews.

U.S. Antarctic research stations offer useful insights into the relationships among male and female professionals living and working in isolation and confinement. Women were first permitted at U.S. Antarctic stations in 1969, when a group of four women spent a few weeks at a field camp near McMurdo Station; the event stimulated headlines, such as "Powderpuff Explorers Invade the South Pole" (quoted in Satchell 1983). The first women were included in a winter-over group in 1974 when a nun and a female biologist spent an entire year at McMurdo Station. Along with nineteen men, the first woman wintered at South Pole Station in 1979. Michele Raney writes eloquently of her experiences as station physician that year and contrasts the novelty of her presence in Antarctica to the current routine integration of women in all aspects of Antarctic service, including management roles (Raney 1994).

Since 1979, increasing numbers of women have played important roles at U.S. Antarctic stations as scientists, Navy support personnel, and civilian contractors. Although some conflicts have resulted from the presence of women on what had been a male-only continent, they have been rare and usually minor. Capt. Brian Shoemaker, a former commander of U.S. Naval Support Force Antarctica, provides an interesting observation (personal communication). He had been a winter-over leader early in his career (during the male-only days) and later commanded all U.S. naval and scientific personnel for more than six years (following the transition to an "integrated" work force). Based on his experiences before and after the introduction of women to Antarctic stations, Captain Shoemaker believes that women contribute a stabilizing influence to the isolated research stations, especially during the long Antarctic winters. In the old days, he reports, wintering over was frequently an eight- to- twelve-month "animal show," with occasional fights, loud and boisterous behavior, and frequent disruptions. Winter-over crews now tend to be less disruptive and more concerned about their behavior or, more accurately, how women in their groups perceive their behavior. More important, the groups are believed to be more productive now than they were in the male-only days of Antarctica. Several experienced Antarctic managers confirm this observation.

Promiscuity has had a rare but occasionally disruptive effect at Antarctic stations. Winter-over personnel have reported that if a woman chooses to have a relationship during her stay in Antarctica, it is usually with one man. Senior personnel are typically selected over junior staff, and clean-cut Navy men tend to be favored over the civilian construction workers, which can contribute to friction between the military and civilian members of a remote-duty crew. In most cases, the other men tend to respect the decision once a woman makes a choice or makes clear her unavailability. Persistent, unwanted attention has occurred, however, with negative consequence to individual adjustment and group solidarity. Particularly disruptive problems develop when a woman and the station leader are involved in a relationship. In these circumstances, others in the group tend to claim that the leader has an unfair advantage. Potentially disruptive involvements by leadership personnel should be avoided onboard spacecraft and at lunar outposts and other remote-duty sites. In most other respects, however, it might be unwise for mission managers to dictate how crew personnel conduct this aspect of their personal lives.

Writers on this subject have pointed to potential romantic involvement as a serious concern for the managers and personnel of space stations and other long-duration space missions. It is true that extremely disruptive and even dangerous relationships have developed among mixed-gender crews at both large and small Antarctic stations. Many relationships, including long-standing marriages, have dissolved while one or both parties were on the ice; other situations have been so bizarre that it is remarkable that the individuals were capable of coping with the experience. I believe, however, that most of the concerns about mixed-gender crews will dissipate if personnel are carefully selected (rather than screened) and provided special training regarding the many potential problems associated with life in isolation and confinement. A comprehensive training program could develop a sense of mission, professionalism, and esprit de corps in crew members; if the training program is effective, the crew will share the common values of their organization and perhaps place the solidarity of the group ahead of personal interests. It is a disservice to future crews to assume that their behavior will be anything but professional. If romance develops, that is part of life, whether on Earth or in space. Behavioral scientists and planners have the responsibility, however, to identify possible problems and to suggest solutions, even concerning such fundamental human behaviors as interpersonal relations among mixed-gender crews.

The topic of sexual behavior in space has been avoided by NASA, not because NASA scientists and managers are naive or prudish but because any mention of the subject is guaranteed to be distorted, sensationalized, and trivialized by others, usually news reporters. The subject of sexual behavior on future long-duration expeditions requires serious discussion, despite the risk of distracting attention from other, more crucial and substantive issues.

Sexual gratification was so important to some previous explorers that they insisted on taking their wives or mistresses with them on long voyages. Commanding officers of ships and expedition leaders were sometimes permitted this luxury; for example, Robert E. Peary's wife, Josephine, accompanied him to Greenland in 1891 and on a polar expedition in 1893. Peary's decisions to take his wife were widely criticized, but Mountfield (1974) reports that she was eager to go and Peary wanted her with him, despite the hardships. It was Peary's opinion that an expedition involved considerable deprivation and anything that could make a journey more comfortable was highly desirable. Previously, officers in Louis-Antoine de Bougainville's expeditions had started a custom in which mistresses, dressed as the officers' personal servants, traveled with them onboard ships.[3] These sustained relationships, of course, were restricted to expedition leaders; subordinate crew members were limited to other sources of gratification.

Many later explorers reported that they attempted to avoid the subject of sex for fear of increasing their longings for female affection. For example, Shackleton's approach to dealing with sexual deprivation during expeditions was to pretend that women did not exist. In this regard, it is important to note that Rivolier and Bachelard (1988) believe that the presence of members of the opposite gender in an isolated and confined group is a stimulus that makes sexual frustration even more difficult to endure; it seems noteworthy that French behavioral scientists recommend a homogeneous crew composition for long-duration missions in order to minimize the possible sources of conflict.[4]

Kanas and Federson (1971), with tongue in cheek, probably addressed the subject of sex in space the most objectively in their report concerning the behavioral, psychiatric, and sociological problems that are likely to be associated with a multiyear mission to Mars. These investigators offer the following discussion under the heading, "Tension Reduction":

The question of direct sexual release on a long-duration space mission must be considered. Practical considerations (such as weight and expense) preclude men taking their wives on the first space flights. It is possible that a woman, qualified from a scientific viewpoint, might be persuaded to donate her time and energies for the sake of improving crew morale; however, such a situation might create interpersonal tensions far more dynamic than the sexual tensions it would release. Other means of sexual release (masturbation, homosexuality) would be discouraged because of the confined quarters and the lack of privacy on such a mission. Thus, it appears that methods involving sublimation are more practical than these more direct alternatives. (P. 38)

Some experts with firsthand experience in isolation and confinement maintain that the issues of mixed-gender crews and sexual behavior on long-duration missions are not nearly as problematic as might be generally believed. In particular, Antarctic managers and medical officers, based on their experiences with isolated and confined groups, have predicted that there will be few, if any, problems of this type on future expeditions that are staffed by well-trained individuals who approach their responsibilities in a professional manner. Alas, it appears that future explorers will be doomed to the fate described by Cherry-Garrard:

Both sexually and socially the polar explorer must make up his mind to be starved. To what extent can hard work, or what might be called dramatic imagination, provide a substitute? (P. 576)

Countermeasures to Interpersonal Problems

It would be prudent to implement extensive countermeasures to minimize the possibility of conflict in crews composed of individuals of different genders, cultural and national backgrounds, technical specialties, and ages. Appropriate personnel selection procedures, training programs, formal policies, and informal practices and customs could greatly reduce the potential for serious interpersonal problems to emerge during long-duration isolation and confinement. The ideal personnel selection system would identify those candidates who are both willing and capable of working with others and would actually select crews, at least in part, on the basis of specific intracrew compatibilities.

Years of training will be required to prepare candidates to serve as crew personnel for a long-duration space expedition. In addition to the necessary technical training, crew members must receive instruction in the behavioral and psychological problems that can occur during the expedition and in techniques that would be instrumental in helping them adjust to and deal with the circumstances as they arise. The training program should include specific examples of the habitability and behavioral principles that have been identified in the analogue and experimental literature in order to illustrate these principles in concrete terms. Role-playing exercises and group discussions will help to sensitize all potential crew members to the likely pitfalls of isolated and confined living. Some civilian contractor personnel receive brief orientations regarding these issues prior to their arrival in Antarctica. The orientations appear to have been instrumental in preventing many interpersonal conflicts simply because people are forewarned of the increased interpersonal sensitivity characteristic of the conditions. For example, crew members receive instruction in communicating clearly to someone that they want to be left alone and in respecting the signals of others, as well as the importance of doing so.

The training program developed for future long-duration expeditions should include instruction regarding the relevant behavioral principles, in addition to offering fairly simple guidelines, such as the following, to potential crew members:

- Avoid controversial subjects.[5]
- Consider the possible consequences before you say or do something.
- Do more than your share of communal tasks.
- Be considerate; more than that, try to avoid being annoying in any way.[6]
- Consciously attempt to be cheerful and supportive of your teammates.
- Be polite and respectful.[7]

Some selectees for U.S. Antarctic duty attend special programs designed to teach teamwork skills and to inspire self-confidence. Many who have attended these programs found them to be quite useful, whereas others considered the experience to be a waste of time. Clearly, teams do not materialize by accident; they are built from a variety of components, including technical ability, motivation, interpersonal skills, and a spirit or sense of shared objective that unifies the group. The components are combined during training, at which time the team is forged by the successful outcomes of the team members' coordinated efforts. The program to prepare crews for future long-duration expeditions should include team-building exercises that are relevant and meaningful to all personnel; the CRM training suggested in the previous section, Intracrew Communications, might be combined with the team-building program because the two programs share the same objective. Also, the evidence suggests that the importance of good leadership is elevated in isolated and confined crews and among groups of international composition; special attention will be required to ensure that their leaders demonstrate exemplary interpersonal skills and abilities.[8]

A well-designed training program will incorporate all of these lessons and many more. A lengthy training program along can go a long way toward homogenizing the crew by eliminating some cultural differences present within any group, but significant interpersonal differences will remain despite the crew members' years of training and simulation together. It is expected, though, that all crew members will be required to speak a common language or languages; a common language is a fundamental necessity for effective communication among crew members and between the crew and mission control personnel. In addition to appropriate personnel selection and formal training programs, it will be necessary to develop policies and informal practices designed to minimize the potential for interpersonal problems among long-duration crews. Incorporating the guidelines listed above in a "crew culture" program would be an important start.

A particularly divisive source of interpersonal problems is present when the normal tendency for subgroups to form is permitted to escalate to the development of cliques. In a study to establish design guidelines for enhancing group stability, Bender and Fracchia (1971) suggest that, while the tendency for subgroups to form is unavoidable, the environment should be structured to encourage maximum communication between members of various subgroups to offset, to some extent, the increased communication between members within subgroups. Although they serve as coping mechanisms for some individuals, subgroups can be disruptive and dangerous because one person (or more) is inevitably excluded.

As suggested in chapter 10, meals offer an opportunity for the type of communication among the members of an isolated and confined crew that will help to mitigate the normal tendency for subgroup formation. In this regard, Eberhard (1967) finds that men in confinement spend twice as much time eating as men in the general population, and Natani and Shurley (1974) report that personnel at South Pole Station spent nearly twice as much time eating during the winter months as they did in the summer; more important, "the extra eating time noted is evidence that the men took advantage of mealtimes to linger over their coffee in conversation." Eating together as a group is a natural activity that most people seem to enjoy; the benefits to group solidarity of eating together are so well known as to be a behavioral cliché. The requirement for daily nutrition and the apparent human tendency to find some pleasure in dining together offer valuable opportunities to encourage interpersonal communication within an isolated group that will foster group solidarity and counter the potentially negative effects of subgroup formation. It is important, however, that group activities, such as meals, are encouraged, without appearing to be ordered, because some individuals probably would object to a mandate as a demonstration of independence, or perhaps for other reasons.

Although some crew members will find reasons to eat by themselves and withdraw from the group in other ways, it is important that the equipment and procedures be designed in such a manner as to encourage group cohesiveness. For example, food preparation capability should facilitate the crew's eating together, and the wardroom or galley should be available for meals only at specific times. The wardroom or galley of future spacecraft and planetary habitats will also serve as the location for crew meetings, briefings, and group leisure activities. Accordingly, this facility will need to be large enough to accommodate all members of the crew simultaneously for dining and other functions.

A Final Note

The point is made in the preceding discussion that interpersonal problems are inevitable among individuals living in isolation and confinement for long periods, and that the inordinate incidence of these problems is a normal consequence of living in close proximity to others with no opportunity for variety or escape. Interpersonal problems are certainly common, but serious problems might not be inevitable, especially if the individuals are particularly compatible or if their solidarity is essential to their survival. For example, Lansing ([1959] 1994) writes of Shackleton and the crew of the *Endurance* adrift on their ice floe:

It was remarkable that there were not more cases of friction among the men, especially after the Antarctic night set in. The gathering darkness and the unpredictable weather limited their activities to an ever-constricting area around the ship. There was very little to occupy them, and they were in closer contact with one another than ever. But instead of getting on each other's nerves, the entire party seemed to become more close knit. (P. 42)

Individual compatibility and recognition of the need to maintain solidarity are among the ingredients of a successful long-duration expedition. Perhaps it was one or both of these factors that permitted Nansen and Johansen to endure together their nine months of confinement in their crude Arctic hut *without a single argument*:[9]

Our spirits were good the whole time; we looked serenely towards the future, and rejoiced in the thought of all the delights it had in store for us. We did not even have recourse to quarrelling to while away the time. After our return, Johansen was once asked how we two got on during the winter, and whether we had managed not to fall out with each other; for it is said to be a severe test for two men to live so long together in perfect isolation. "Oh no," he answered, "we didn't quarrel; the only thing was that I had the bad habit of snoring in my sleep, and then Nansen used to kick me in the back." I cannot deny that this is the case; I gave him many a well-meant kick,

Life in Our Hut by Fridtjof Nansen. (From Nansen, 1897)

but fortunately he only shook himself a little and slept calmly on. (Nansen 1897, vol. 2, 464)

RECOMMENDATIONS

The following recommendations relate to group interaction during long-duration isolation and confinement.

- Take an expeditionary approach to the planning of future long-duration space missions:
  - Focus on lessons learned from previous and similar experiences.
  - Provide the esteemed leadership style described in chapter 7.
  - Provide an unambiguous and relatively flat organizational structure, with clear leadership authority.
  - Generate a "spirit of the expedition" to unify and motivate the crew.
- Develop formal protocols to guide intracrew communications regarding technical and operational matters.
- Develop, apply, and evaluate crew resource management techniques and training.
- Provide a commander's workstation or "office" for facilities management tasks and records and for the general coordination of crew activities.
- Provide a low-tech bulletin board in the wardroom/galley, in addition to any electronic messaging systems that might be provided.
- Minimize differences among crew members by selecting and training that might lead to interpersonal conflicts, to the extent possible.
- Sensitize candidate crew members to the principles of habitability, for example, to expect that trivial issues will be exaggerated.
- Provide training in team building, crew resource management, issues associated with multicultural crews, and conflict resolution.

- Facilitate intracrew communications (and mitigate subgroup formation) by encouraging crew members to eat together and to engage in other group activities and by providing appropriate equipment and procedures.

- Encourage the development of informal procedures and elements of crew culture that facilitate group solidarity.[10]

- Consider husband-and-wife teams for mixed-gender long-duration crews.

- Design sleep chambers with removable partitions to accommodate husband-and-wife teams and to facilitate reconfiguration of the habitat interior, if necessary.

CHAPTER 12

HABITAT AESTHETICS

Rendering of the interior of Jules Verne's projectile-vehicle from the 1872 edition of *From the Earth to the Moon*. The etching illustrates some of the functional and aesthetic features of the design. The fictional craft carried a crew of three men and two dogs, including a sponsor's Newfoundland retriever (the dog "won't be hard to look at in the crowded projectile"). Dehydrated food for a year and fifty gallons of brandy were stored on board, but only enough water for two months was taken because they expected to find sufficient supplies on the moon's surface; future lunar explorers might rely on subsurface lunar water. The padded leather interior of the craft was aesthetically pleasing, but the primary function was to cushion any bumps the crew might experience as the projectile was launched from a huge cannon (not far from what is now the Kennedy Space Center) or when it splashed down in the Pacific Ocean near where Apollo capsules were recovered following their voyages to the moon.

Much intuitive and some objective evidence supports the notion that the aesthetics of an environment can affect human well-being and productivity. Conditions analogous to spacecraft and space habitats that I reviewed during a previous study of space station analogues range from the comfortably appointed suites of supertankers to the spartan confines of the saturation diver's deck chamber. The conditions described in this book range from cozy shipboard cabins to crowded tents pitched on storm-swept ice floes. In the full range of conditions studied, regardless of the aesthetic quality of the habitat, the people involved performed adequately—even admirably. But would they have performed even more effectively, or at the same level, without experiencing as much stress or as many negative feelings if the habitat had been designed to be both functional *and* aesthetically pleasing?

Although the "pleasingness" of a built environment might not be directly related to crew effectiveness, interior features certainly contribute to overall habitability, and, in indirect ways, the presence or absence of particular features probably affects individual adjustment and productivity. This question has been explored experimentally by Jon Rogers (reported in Connors, Harrison, and Akins 1985), who investigated the importance of decor to crews that were confined for ten-day periods under various conditions. He found that members of all-male crews, who were involved in meaningful work, considered the "plush" decor to be relatively unimportant; however, he reports that attractive surroundings were more important in mixed-gender crews and in situations where all-male crews had little work to perform. The importance of decor was at its highest level among mixed-gender crews that lacked meaningful work. These results suggest that habitat aesthetics might be an important factor during future expeditions and other remote duty involving long-duration isolation and confinement.

This chapter presents four key issues of habitat aesthetics: personalized decor, decoration of common areas, variation of stimuli, and designs to facilitate orientation to a local vertical.

PERSONALIZED DECOR

Crews had posted items of personal decor in all conditions of isolation and confinement that I have studied. The tradition was practiced by nineteenth century ships' officers who were permitted to decorate their cabins; many took the opportunity to give their quarters a personal touch, even a homelike atmosphere. For example, the small cabin shared by Midshipmen William Reynolds and William May on the *Vincennes* during the U.S. Exploring Expedition (1838–42) featured curtains, rugs, and other nonregulation furnishings; the conversion of the mid-deck to a comfortable officers' "lounge" prompted Lieutenant Wilkes to object to the fraternization (status leveling) among junior and senior officers (Cleaver and Stann 1988). In modern times, the most common items of personal decor displayed by isolated and confined personnel are photographs of family and friends, but their photographs also depict houses, automobiles, and other favored images. Photographs of the interior of *Skylab* reveal that even astronauts are subject to this proclivity; several *Skylab* crew members posted small pictures of loved ones.

The posting of personal photographs, in particular, appears to be a common and gratifying coping mechanism of crews in isolation and confinement. The display of personal items and the personalization of decor should not be discouraged onboard future space stations and spacecraft and at lunar and planetary habitats. The practice offers confined personnel an opportunity to live among important reminders of home and to exhibit creativity in defining a space or territory as their own. In fact, the interiors of personal sleep chambers should be designed to accommodate the tastes of occupants with a minimum of effort. Although personal preference and self-selection in sleep chamber decor items should be allowed, those items must be subject to the same restrictions that apply to all onboard materials (i.e., to minimize potential hazards from fire to outgassing). Constraints might limit conventional decor items to a few small photographs; however, they do not preclude the development of graphic materials that meet established safety standards.

DECORATION OF COMMON AREAS

Although the personalization of private quarters is acceptable, even to be encouraged, the posting of individually selected images in common areas is strongly discouraged. Displaying favored images in common areas is practiced in some of the space analogues that I have studied, but it has become less common during recent years, largely in response to social factors, particularly the increased presence of women in what had been traditionally all-male environments. During Project Tektite, for example, each crew decorated their habitat differently with pictures, pinups, and photographs. In recent years, however, policies concerning the posting of pinups in common areas have been established by individual submarine commanders and Antarctic station leaders; policies developed for the general Navy are applied, even though no women are currently among the crews of U.S. submarines. For the most part, pinup-type images are now officially discouraged in common areas on submarines, surface ships, and at Antarctic stations and are restricted to personal quarters, where provocative photos and posters of members of the opposite sex are frequently displayed.

The appreciation of form and artistic merit is very much a matter of personal preference. For this reason, it is important that any formal graphic art used to decorate common areas of isolated and confined habitats be either quite temporary or acceptable to all users of those areas. For example, many people appreciate the works of Jackson Pollack, Norman Rockwell, or the photographers of *Playboy*, but it would be unfair to inflict those tastes on others on a regular basis unless it were mutually agreeable. Differences of opinion concerning images and art posted in common areas could be a source of conflict during an expedition or at a remote-duty station but one that can be easily avoided. Because trivial issues are typically exaggerated beyond reasonable proportions among isolated and confined groups, individually selected graphic material is just the kind of issue that might precipitate interpersonal conflict. Photographs and other graphic art are important in common areas to increase visual variety, but the items should be selected by group consensus or scientific evaluation.

For many years, submariners and Antarctic winter-over personnel have claimed strong preferences for nature scenes, particularly seascapes and scenes involving wide-open spaces. A preference for westerns among all film genres also has been attributed by submariners and Antarctic personnel to a desire to view landscape-type scenes and simulate the exercise of distant vision. Nature prints, posters, and wall-size murals are favored items of decor at U.S. Antarctic stations. Cornelius (1991) reports that the bar at South Pole Station was decorated with a huge mural of a birch forest, on which crew members occasionally placed small cutout figures for amusement. More recently, false windows have been installed in personal quarters and common areas to display various types of dioramas, including a Miami skyline; reportedly, some individuals enjoy staring at the dioramas for long periods of time.

A few researchers have taken a sociobiological approach to explaining what appear to be common human preferences and aversions in graphic art. For example, Coss and Towers (1988) find that pictures of animals, especially birds, can enhance the aesthetic appeal of confined technical environments, but that images of nearby and staring animals (not just predators) can make people uncomfortable and are considered too threatening. Along these lines, Coss and Moore (1990) argue convincingly that there is an evolutionary foundation for the common human preference for sweeping views from an elevated perspective, especially for views involving bodies of water. They maintain that natural selection has predisposed members of the human species to favor views and scenes that in many ways replicate optimal living conditions during the millions of years of human evolution: an unobstructed view of a plain and a nearby pond, lake, or seashore from a safely elevated vantage point. Images such as these were found, through research among Australian Antarctic personnel, to be the most soothing and favored (Clearwater and Coss 1991). The universal appreciation for these scenes is confirmed by their similarities to the views from some of the most expensive modern real estate.

Recreation area in a small Antarctic research station. Photo illustrates a library, pooltable, and an outdoor scene (at right). (Courtesy of Capt. Fred Glogower)

Clearwater and Coss (1991) also found that landscape themes of vistas, highlighted by bodies of water, engendered greater relaxation throughout a year of isolation and confinement than human and animal themes; however, the relaxing effect of specific pictures declined over time. The implications of these results are clear. Landscape scenes, especially those overlooking bonds, lakes, and oceans, should be included in the graphic art used for posting or projection during future long-duration spacecraft and habitat missions. Habituation to the positive effects of the scenes can be minimized by the rotational display of many different images. In this way, the interior decor could be altered, for example, to reflect the changing seasons on Earth, thus providing an additional zeitgeber to the crew as well as a pleasant image. Also, the scenes could be changed more frequently, perhaps several times within a season, to add visual variety to an otherwise monotonous visual field; the images could be programmed to change automatically or selected by the crew from a number of options. Many techniques will be available to project or display the images, from beautiful, back-lighted transparencies to screen saver programs on computer displays.

Not much was written by the explorers concerning the aesthetic features of their ships and huts. A review of photographs taken during polar expeditions of the late nineteenth and early twentieth centuries, however, suggests that the preference for and possible utility of landscapes has been appreciated for at least one hundred years. For example, photographs and drawings of the interior of the *Fram* show several pieces of landscape and seascape art, probably oil paintings, adorning the walls of the ship's saloon, or wardroom. Nansen was an accomplished artist, and he favored outdoor scenes. Graphic art also decorated the interior of the *Belgica,* but the themes there appear to reflect a nautical preference.

VARIATION OF STIMULI

The need for variation in stimuli has been acknowledged in all of the design studies conducted during the past three decades on long-duration habitability. The desire for variety is also apparent in all of the conditions analogous to spacecraft that I have studied. It is not that spacecraft or spacecraft analogues are stimulus deprived, but that their crews experience a constant high level of stimulation because of the relentless proximity of other people. Although some of the tasks might be changeable and some will be quite exciting, much of the work of future explorers will have a routine sameness similar to Earth–bound laboratory and production work. The monotony experienced by those so engaged is exaggerated by the sameness of the confined environment. Only glimpses of Earth, the planets, and the stars and occasional leisure activities will be available to counter the monotony of routine long-duration operations. Reportedly, even conversations assume a monotonous tone among small isolated groups; following initial bursts of interpersonal exploration, there is a sameness to conversation as one becomes weary of repeated stories and mannerisms and the predictability of fellow crew members. Monotony of stimulation, even a high level of stimulation, can be a serious source of stress.

Variation in visual stimuli can be achieved through Earth and astronomical observation and leisure activities, as well as by the interior decor of the spacecraft or habitat. In addition to the display of specially selected graphic art, variation in visual stimulation can be accomplished by the use of colored surfaces and reflected lighting. Whereas variation in the color of surfaces would probably provide an adequate level of visual stimulation and be aesthetically pleasing, the use of colored indirect illumination of surfaces and objects offers greater possibilities for variation, or "perceptual richness," as defined by a spacecraft design study:

> Perceptual richness is the sensible variety offered by a given ambient. One method of providing perceptual richness is to vary the color, texture, and illumination of the surroundings. This can be done more easily if the basic interior color is white. White will pick up and reflect colors from the lights, act as a space expander, and provide a good background for bright color accents. (Righter et al. 1971, sec. 5, p. 1)

Color can serve more than one purpose in a designed environment. Color affects the reflectance of surfaces and objects, and many observers believe that color can influence the emotions or behavior of some individuals. In this regard, it has been found that some colors are perceived to be cool, tranquilizing, and restful; these are the blues, greens, and violets, which might be appropriate in sleep chambers and recreational areas. Red, orange, and yellow, considered to be warm or stimulating colors, perhaps can be useful in laboratories, workstations, and other task-oriented areas of a spacecraft or habitat. Generally, light colors are considered to be cooler than dark colors, but there is little agreement beyond these assumptions about the psychological effects of

interior color. For example, Fraser (1968a) summarizes a lengthy discussion of color and illumination with the following recommendations:

> A variety of colors can be selected for the interior of spacecraft
> and space dwellings. Cool, work-stimulating colors are rec-
> ommended for the work area, with bright contrasting accents
> on trim; warm, relaxing colors are recommended for public
> rest and recreation areas, again with contrasting accents and
> trim; while subdued, "homely" colors will be appropriate for
> personal areas. Generally, lightening of color values will assist
> in providing brighter interiors with a lower level of illu-
> mination. The latter, as much as feasible, should be indirect,
> diffuse and non-glaring. (P. 51)

Professor Munehira Akita of Japan's Kyoto Institute of Technology
suggests that colors can be used to help define working and living
spaces within a crowded remote-duty habitat. Dr. Akita further suggests changing colors periodically for variety; this could be achieved
more easily if colored lights were used (personal communication).

Guidelines have been established to help designers use interior
lighting to address the psychological considerations of illumination.
The *Lighting Handbook* of the Illuminating Engineering Society (IES) of
North America (Kaufman 1981) divides all environmental lighting systems into two basic types:

1. *Systems that flood a space somewhat indiscriminately with
   permissive illumination from general overhead luminaries.*
   These systems are behaviorally neutral in that they do
   not exert an intentional reinforcing or guiding influence
   on individual perceptions or behavior. Rather, they are
   designed to facilitate the performance of reading or
   manual tasks, random circulation and unguided attention, and flexible relocation of furniture, workstations,
   and objects without having to change the room lighting.

2. *Systems that develop specific patterns of light and shade to
   reinforce selected information or room cues.* These systems
   are designed to evoke behavioral responses by reinforcing a specific pattern of impressions.

The second category includes techniques that tend to influence personal orientation and user understanding of a room and its contents.
For example, the IES maintains that spotlighting and shelf lighting
affect user attention, whereas wall lighting and corner lighting affect
user understanding of room size and shape. Uniform peripheral light-

ing is used to create subjective impressions of spaciousness, and lighting also can be used to define an area within a larger space. There are many possibilities for using interior lighting to improve habitat aesthetics, as suggested by the IES:

> Lighting can be used in one way to produce a carnival-like atmosphere and in another way to produce a somber place for quiet meditation. Lighting can be used to produce a cold, impersonal public place or conversely, a warm, intimate place where one feels a greater sense of privacy. More than esthetic amenities are to be considered here, because these impressions or moods are often fundamental in satisfying some experience and activity requirements in a designed space. (Kaufman 1981, sec. 2, 2)

The preceding discussion concerns lighting as a source of visual variety and a way to help define areas in a confined space. The use of illumination as an aid in effective task performance is a separate issue, one supported by an enormous experimental literature and well-defined human engineering specifications; those specifications should be used to guide the design of systems for future spacecraft and similar habitats. In addition to this available guidance, mission planners should devote special attention to task-related lighting and other human engineering considerations, as suggested by the experiences of *Skylab* astronauts:

> Local lighting was marginally adequate. In several areas, illu-mination levels were much less than handbook values, and portable lights were necessary. In some instances, switches were located so inconveniently that the crewmen "made do" without proper light rather than take the time to go to the switch panel in another area. Lack of local control of lighting sometimes interfered with scheduled activities. When an experiment was conducted that required the operator and experiment station to be in darkness, the entire experiment area and living area had to be darkened. Lighting and compartmentation did not allow sufficient localized control of light. (Johnson, 1975, 21)

DESIGNS TO FACILITATE ORIENTATION TO A LOCAL VERTICAL

Space adaptation syndrome, a variation of motion sickness with exacerbated vestibular and perceptual components, has been the sub-ject of considerable research during the past decade. The onset of the illness, usually abrupt, is marked by sudden disorientation followed by vomiting. Generally, the condition lasts for a few days before the individual adapts; perhaps as many as 50 percent of all space personnel experience this unpleasant and disruptive phenomenon. Regular motion sickness was a frequent companion of the explorers and their crews during long voyages, but space adaptation syndrome is unique to space. Several comments made by *Skylab* crew members suggest that certain internal design features of a space habitat might either contribute to or mitigate the incidence of the syndrome.

Although the *Skylab* missions did not produce the first instances of space adaptation syndrome, they did provide the first opportunity for U.S. scientists to analyze the perceptual and physiological effects of living and working in a weightless environment. Previous spacecraft were too small to allow complete freedom of movement, and even shuttle astronauts do not experience the absence of restraint enjoyed by the *Skylab* astronauts. Indeed, it is unlikely that enclosed spaces comparable in size to *Skylab's* Orbital Workshop will be available again in space for human habitation for many years. *Skylab* was assembled from leftover components of the Apollo Program. The largest element was the Orbital Workshop, a cylinder 48 feet (15 meters) in length and 22 feet (6.5 meters) in diameter. The workshop was made from an unused third stage of a giant Saturn V rocket.

Each of the three *Skylab* crews included a "science pilot" (Owen Garriott, Edward Gibson, and Joseph Kerwin); the experiences of these men are largely responsible for our understanding of the behavioral issues associated with a weightless condition. Kerwin's comments and analyses are particularly perceptive:

> It turns out that you carry with you your own body-oriented world, independent of anything else, in which up is over your head, down is below your feet, right is this way, and left is that way; and you take this world around with you wherever you go. (Quoted in Cooper 1976, 23)

The concept of local vertical is alien to Earth-bound conditions because of the effects of gravity on the vestibular system. Kerwin's observation, however, explains the odd feelings, disorientation, and occasional nausea experienced by astronauts when they look up from a task and find themselves floating sideways or upside down in relation to the interior architecture. According to this interpretation, vestibular/perceptual confusion results when there are two conflicting sets of vertical cues, one's own local vertical (up is over the head, down is toward the feet) and the vertical cues provided by the interior space. The importance of local vertical to individual orientation in a weightless environment was particularly evident when Kerwin attempted to answer a radio call in the dark:

> "It was pitch black," he [Kerwin] said later. "When I scrambled out of bed, I had no way of determining up from down; I had no visual reference in the dark. I had to turn on the lights, but I just didn't know what direction to put my hand in. So I had to feel things to orient myself—I had to use touch instead of sight—and everything felt different because I didn't know my relationship to them. It took me a whole minute just to get the lights on." The confusion passed as soon as he had lined himself up visually with the room's local vertical; indeed, when an astronaut's own vertical was lined up with that of his surroundings, the two seemed to click into place, like a compass needle onto magnetic north. (Cooper 1976, 72)

Although all of the *Skylab* astronauts adapted to the weightless environment, the vestibular/perceptual phenomenon contributed to their marked preference for the low ceilings and more Earth-like rooms of *Skylab*'s lower deck. Reportedly, the astronauts felt most at home among the small rooms and enclosed spaces of their living quarters (sleep chambers, wardroom, experiments room, and hygiene area); there is apparently less risk of losing one's sense of local vertical when consistent orientation cues are readily available. These and other observations suggest that the interiors of spacecraft and space habitats should incorporate familiar Earth-like designs (e.g., low ceilings, horizontal layout) and provide abundant cues to reinforce perceptions of vertical orientation. In this regard, the color coding of ceilings, walls, and floors might help to mitigate the disorientation inevitably experienced in weightlessness. Some researchers suggest light blue ceilings and earth tones for the floors. It might also be wise to incorporate tactile cues, textures or shapes, to help crew members orient themselves in complete darkness, for example when lighting must be extinguished for special task performance or during an emergency.

Related to the problems experienced by *Skylab* astronauts regarding local vertical were their difficulties in adapting to uses of interior space that did not conform to Earth-bound practices. For example, the docking adapter, a long, narrow cylinder, included instruments, boxes, and workstations arranged radially around the interior of the structure. The docking adapter was so lacking in consistency that the two primary workstations, the solar console and the Earth resources experiment console, were about 90 degrees out of alignment. Reportedly, the docking adapter was built that way because the spacecraft designers wanted to see whether the crew could get along without a single vertical reference frame. The designers reasoned that if the astronauts liked the docking adapter, they could use the entire volume of a room in planning future space stations. Some designers believed that the use of a room might be increased sixfold by putting equipment not only on the floor but on the ceiling and the four walls, as well.

Eight of the nine *Skylab* astronauts disliked the use of space in the docking adapter. Probably no single issue received more negative comments from the crews than the configuration and design philosophy supporting this segment of the space station. Only Edward Gibson seemed to appreciate the apparent efficiencies achieved through maximum utilization of available space, but he too experienced difficulty when attempting to locate items within the cylinder.

The design of the docking adapter was a noble experiment, but the results should come as no real surprise. After all, humans are a terrestrial species that, until quite recently, has been confined to Earth's

Skylab. (Courtesy of NASA)

surface; throughout our evolution, we have been subjected to a consistent force of one gravity. Clearly, there are cultural (learned) components to our preferences and behavior, but there is something fundamentally different and truly alien about living in three-dimensional space. Even those species that occupy three-dimensional habitats, the fish and mammals swimming in the world's oceans and the birds flying through the oceans of air above Earth's surface, do not use their spaces randomly. They also adhere to a single orientation dictated by Earth's gravitational force. It seems reasonable to assume that, to ensure optimal habitability of spacecraft and to facilitate maximum productivity of crew personnel, it would be wise to provide interior configurations and uses of space consistent with a crew's biological and cultural preadaptation. It is possible that crew members could be selected, trained, and/or desensitized to perform adequately in spacecraft composed of docking adapter-type modules (i.e., without a consistent vertical orientation). Human behavior is truly pliable, but penalties accrue when individuals are routinely required to tax their capacities for adaptation.

RECOMMENDATIONS

The following recommendations relate to habitat aesthetics and configuration on future long-duration space expeditions.

- Design sleep station interiors to accommodate personalization of decor.

- Discourage personal decor in common areas.

- Encourage the display of carefully selected graphic art, especially scenes of the type found to be particularly pleasing and soothing (views overlooking plains and bodies of water); develop systems to project or display the images and to rotate the images displayed among several options (e.g., to reflect changing seasons on Earth).

- Provide variation of visual stimuli through color (either surface pigmentation or reflected illumination).

- Use different colors for ceiling, walls, and floors (overheads, bulkheads, and decks) to reinforce individual perceptions of local vertical.

- Incorporate shape or texture coding to help crew members orient themselves in darkness.

- Design interior architectures to incorporate familiar features of Earth structures (e.g., roomlike chambers, horizontal orientation).

- Design interior architectures to maintain a consistent interior orientation, to the extent possible.

CHAPTER 13

OUTSIDE COMMUNICATIONS

[The newspapers] were quite a blessing to me and I trust that next year I may receive a larger bundle with a few Lancaster papers in it. You say they have no news, but remember that even the old advertisements will be new to me and that the very sight of the old types... will be to me as grateful as the glimpse of the running stream is to the traveler in the Desert. Do not think me weak or childish in begging so earnestly and so repeatedly for long letters and every description of news from Home. Could you ever become a wanderer, you would soon learn the intense and yearning force with which our hearts turn to the Home we have left. Again and again let me entreat that all of you will write me such a letter as I have asked for in my long letter of a few days ago.

—Letter from Midshipman William Reynolds
USS *Vincennes*, to his sister, Lydia, 2 June 1839

A thirst for news from home is the most persistent theme of the letters written by Midshipman William Reynolds during the U.S. Exploring Expedition. In October 1840, he lamented that the letters he had recently received were ten months old and it would be more than a year before he received another. A period of a year and a half was the typical wait for a response to a letter mailed from the Pacific to Lancaster, Pennsylvania. Reynolds and his shipmates usually gave their mail to American vessels bound for the United States, with hopes that the ships would reach port safely and the letters would be deposited in the local post office; of the twenty-one letters that Reynolds wrote during four years at sea, only three failed to reach their destinations. Mail sent to the squadron, however, took even more circuitous routes, and many items went astray. Expecting that letters would be lost, Reynolds pleaded with his family to write frequently and to send mail by various routes so as to increase his chances of receiving precious information from home. Indeed, Reynolds' irritation with his commanding officer appears to have originated with Wilkes's secretiveness regarding destinations that prevented Reynolds from receiving his mail.

News of all types traveled slowly throughout the first half of the nineteenth century; for example, Reynolds was pleasantly surprised when he obtained American newspapers in Oahu that were fewer than eighty days old. His desire for timely news from home is typical of explorers and others who find themselves isolated from society. Although Sir Ernest Shackleton resisted pressure to equip the *Endurance* with a radio receiver in 1910, all subsequent polar expeditions have had some form of wireless communication available. In fact, radio played a major role in Byrd's first Antarctic expedition;

Radio entertainment at Little America, Antarctica, 1929. On Saturday nights everyone gathered around the radio to hear special broadcasts from the United States. (Courtesy of The Byrd Polar Research Center Archival Program, The Ohio State University)

the men gathered in the administration building and mess hall on Saturday afternoons to hear special programs broadcast to them on alternate weeks from General Electric Company's station WGY in Schenectady, New York, and Westinghouse Electric Corporation's station KDKA in Pittsburgh, Pennsylvania. The programs represent milestones in radio history in that they were the farthest that voice or music had been successfully transmitted at the time. Reception was poor, marred by the echo characteristic of long-distance radio communications (caused by signals taking paths of different lengths around Earth to reach the receiver). Rodgers (1990) reports that music never came through very well to Byrd's men at Little America, and nothing could be heard about a third of the time. Despite these problems, the men looked forward to the programs for entertainment and information.

Some of the programs involved the most famous celebrities of the day and must have been among the spectacular events of the pre-Depression era. Distinguished personalities and politicians spoke directly to the Antarctic explorers from the two radio stations; Harpo Marx even made one of his rare public utterances in one of these special national broadcasts. Letters were also read to the group over shortwave frequencies to supplement the limited personal communications permitted by code; sometimes friends and relatives even read the mail themselves. Occasionally, entire programs were devoted to an individual member of the party, as on "Paul Siple Day."[1] The special broadcasts were enjoyed by most members of the expedition; many reported in their diaries that they contributed a great deal to elevating the group's morale. The radio programs also helped to promote the privately funded expedition and gave a substantial boost to the young radio industry.

The special programs were not without problems. For example, some of the messages were rather personal and the public medium embarrassed the recipients. Others in the group were hurt because they rarely or never received radio mail. Tears welled in Siple's eyes when he heard his mother's voice. One man had the terrible experience during a program of being informed by his mother that his brother had died. Two men learned of the deaths of parents while onboard ship enroute to Antarctica. Rodgers (1990) accurately reflects, "While new technology eliminated some hardships, it added others."

The conditions analogous to spacecraft that I have studied vary considerably in all dimensions, including both physical and psychological isolation. For example, merchant, research, and fishing vessels are all separated from shore by several hours to several days of running time. Submarines are isolated for the durations of their missions, usually seventy to ninety days, and the personnel staffing Antarctic research stations are separated from the remainder of the world for nearly a year by geography and weather conditions. Saturation divers, such as the crews of *Sealab*, *Tektite*, and offshore oil operations, are similarly isolated by several hours to several days of decompression time, although they might be only a few feet away from their support personnel. All of these Earth-bound conditions share with spacecraft and planetary outposts a physical isolation from family, friends, and familiar environments; from support staff and distant managers; and from immediate rescue in an emergency. Conducting and coordinating communication with the outside world are major tasks for some individuals in remote-duty environments and require considerable time and skill. Outside communication is an extremely important issue in all isolated and confined conditions, from expeditions during the days of sail to modern space missions. The following sections address this issue in three categories: personal communications, mission-related communications, and communication lag times.

PERSONAL COMMUNICATIONS

Some form of personal communication is permitted in all of the isolated and confined conditions I have studied. For example, the Project Tektite undersea habitat had an intercom link with the surface, and *Sealab* was equipped with a direct telephone line (which, incidentally, allowed the aquanauts to speak directly to astronauts who were circling Earth in a Gemini space capsule). Antarctic station personnel were formerly limited to Ham radios for calls home, but they now have access to commercial satellite communication systems as well. Satellite communications can be expensive (two to ten dollars per minute, when available), so many people still rely on the Military Affiliate Radio System (MARS), which consists of Ham radio transmissions to the U.S. and telephone patches to the intended party. MARS communications are free, except for the collect telephone call from the stateside operator to the recipient, a call that must be arranged the day before the transmission from Antarctica; the conversations are also overheard by the two Ham operators who make the connection possible.

Submariners are now permitted to receive as many as eight "family grams," up to fifty words each, during a patrol; they cannot respond, however, because even a brief transmission could reveal the submarine's position. Reportedly, the family grams can be significant morale boosters during a long cruise, and the man who delivers the messages is a welcome visitor in all compartments of the boat. Commercial oil divers are prevented from directly communicating with the outside world because of their distorted voices (caused by breathing a mixture of helium and oxygen) and the prohibition against electronic devices in the explosive atmosphere of the deck chambers. A supervisor can convey personal messages to and from the divers in saturation through an air lock, however, and many divers become inveterate letter writers to pass the time and ultimately quench their thirst for information, much as young Midshipman Reynolds did more than 150 years ago.

Personal communications with family and friends are considered by most observers to be appropriate and necessary to maintain morale during long-duration isolation and confinement. Outside communications, however, can involve serious risks to personal adjustment and productivity. The two principal components of this risk are the potential for negative information to reach an isolated person and affect his or her performance, and the potential for one who is isolated to become preoccupied or even obsessed with outside communications.

Negative Information

Receiving negative information from home can have a catastrophic effect on the mental health of isolated and confined individuals. For example, receiving word that a child is ill or has been seriously injured can precipitate great remorse and guilt in a parent who has chosen a remote-duty assignment; the parent typically believes that the tragedy could have been prevented if he or she had been there. Pope and Rogers (1968) report that some Antarctic personnel developed psychopathology at the early U.S. stations in response to negative information received by radio and the midwinter mail drop. People who have wintered over have recently confirmed that negative news from home has a profoundly disturbing effect on some individuals. For this reason, it is the practice at U.S. and French Antarctic stations for a station leader to serve as a filter and prevent some information from reaching personnel who are determined to be at psychological risk. These decisions are made on an individual basis and only when it is clear that no purpose would be served by conveying the negative information. A Navy psychologist observed that "sometimes no news is good news, since we cannot evacuate someone with an existential dilemma."

Kelly and Kanas (1994) conducted a survey to which forty-six astronauts and eight cosmonauts responded about a variety of issues. The researchers found no consensus on the question of whether negative personal information should be withheld from crew members until the end of the mission.

I believe that most people who volunteer for expeditions involving long-duration isolation and confinement would want to be informed of negative news from home, for example, the premature death of a loved one. The potential consequences of such information to individual and group morale, as well as to task performance, however, could be severe or even threaten the mission if it led to deep remorse or depression. Personnel selection criteria can play a role in guarding against this possibility, but it also will be important for the planners and leaders of future long-duration missions to consider carefully the possible consequences of both providing and withholding information regarding death, serious injury, or illness of crew members' loved ones. Policies involving deception are inherently uncomfortable, and deceptions of the kind necessary to prevent negative news from reaching an individual would be difficult to maintain. There is the additional risk that the unraveling of such a deception might cause even more damage than it was intended to prevent. Further, a policy of screening out negative news from home might exacerbate the normal tendency among isolated and confined personnel to read things into messages that were not intended; in the extreme, an individual could become paranoid about the real or suspected withholding of personal information. Whether to provide or withhold negative information to isolated personnel is a difficult question; one that probably should be resolved before this inevitable issue arises, during full-mission simulations conducted in preparation for future long-duration expeditions.

Communications Obsession

The second component of the risk of personal communication involves the potential for isolated personnel to become preoccupied or, in the extreme, obsessed with personal calls home. Most U.S. Antarctic winter-over personnel find that a call home every one or two weeks provides sufficient personal contact with the outside world, but some individuals become preoccupied with outside communications. This preoccupation can be fueled from a variety of sources, including events and comments made prior to departure, ambiguities in letters and voice communications, humorous remarks that are misunderstood, and interpretations of comments that are made and those purposefully left unsaid. Antarctic personnel and submariners are aware that at least a few divorces occur during each winter expedition and submarine patrol. Sometimes, information about relationship problems is provided directly to an individual in letters and voice communications, but, in many cases, the message is conveyed indirectly by the tone rather than the content of the communication. Certain individuals in isolation and confinement, with plenty of time to think about things and limited opportunities to communicate, become highly sensitive and suspicious about the activities of their mates at home. Some Antarctic personnel have become so obsessed with calling home frequently and at all hours that they enter into a pathological and disruptive pattern; unsuccessful attempts to reach a loved one or unsatisfying conversations can lead to unnecessary worrying about both real and imagined events. Acute anxiety reactions have been associated with these obsessions among oil divers, submariners, and Antarctic personnel.

Rivolier and Bachelard maintain that some personnel (mostly single people lacking strong personal attachments) at French remote-duty stations do not manifest the need for frequent communication with home; other individuals, however, engage in frequent communication with the outside world, which can contribute to problems by reminding them of what they left behind. The authors make the radical suggestion of limiting outside communications to technical matters, and they support their suggestion with a cogent argument:

> Maintaining a (very artificial) link with "what is no more," i.e., the social and affective environment of the past, may serve not as a support but, on the contrary, as a negative stimulus. Some polar overwinterers feel that the rare telephone links with their friends and families, which are always very limited in terms of mutual comprehension and how much can be said, are stressful and leave them feeling depressed. The same applies to the wait for letters, which may arrive, for example, with the relief ship from the southern islands, but whose date of arrival is always unknown. Perhaps it would be better to sever all social and affective links, stop the waiting that may prolong the grief of separation, and stop sharing the agitation and

anxiety associated with political or international events. When contacts with the outside world are associated only with strictly technical matters, it becomes possible to find, within the microsociety of which one is a part and within oneself, a dynamism and reflection not to be found elsewhere. These views are doubtless not shared by everyone and in addition are applicable to varying degrees depending on the length of stays. (Rivolier and Bachelard 1988, 127)

Again, Rivolier and Bachelard make a courageous suggestion, but it is as unlikely to be followed by the planners of space expeditions as their recommendation for homogeneous crews. These suggestions of homogeneous crew composition and no personal communications home are both supported by the examples of expeditions that I have reviewed, especially the model expeditions. In particular, the exemplary Norwegian Polar Expedition was composed exclusively of Norwegian males who received no news from home for more than three years; they experienced a minimum of personal problems and performed their missions admirably. In contrast, most expeditions since the advent of wireless communications have been marred by disputes, misunderstandings, and other problems that were directly attributable to outside communications. As examples, Mountfield (1974) refers to the "heated airways" during the Fuchs-Hillary Expedition; many conflicts arose during Byrd's expeditions over communications, and the log of the U.S. Naval Mobile Construction Battalion (Special), the group that built McMurdo Station (a model for a lunar base construction project) between 1955 and 1957 in preparation for the IGY, reveals a pattern of communications problems, including frequent misunderstandings, hypersensitivity by the remote-duty personnel, and egregious insensitivity by distant managers. In many respects, Rivolier, Bachelard, and Shackleton are correct: If it were possible, no communications might be better than frequent communications with remote-duty personnel. Although both French recommendations are supported by the data, they are unrealistic. Social and political realities will not permit homogeneous crews, and modern expectations will not permit an absence of personal communication between Earth and distant voyagers. Regarding communication, therefore, it becomes necessary to strike a balance between too much and not enough.

Just as the realities of modern politics and economics will result in multinational crews composed of both men and women, modern expectations demand at least some access to outside communications for crew personnel. For example, the Russian space program permits cosmonauts to have weekly voice communications with their family members. The conversations are conducted in ten-minute segments, the period, during each orbit, when the *Mir* space station is in contact with ground controllers. In addition to conversations with family members, special interviews are conducted by scientific and political dignitaries, famous entertainers, and news reporters. In this respect, the Russian approach to outside communications is similar to that of Admiral Byrd; that is, communication is an opportunity for remote-duty personnel to reaffirm ties with home and to become informed, as well as an opportunity for both the remote-duty crew and people at home to be entertained. According to diaries of the cosmonauts, however, their favorite communications are the letters sent by schoolchildren and the notes slipped into newspapers and magazines by the support staff who prepare the spacecraft that periodically resupply the station.

The managers of modern U.S. Antarctic stations recognize the potential for problems resulting from contact by their personnel with the outside world. For this reason, individuals are advised to establish a regular schedule for calling home to minimize the possibility of unsuccessful attempts to reach a loved one, which can generate considerable worry. Also, failures to reach someone and, for that matter, delays of all types are frequently interpreted "on the ice" as serious problems and evidence of personal rejection; again, trivial issues are exaggerated beyond reasonable proportion. Antarctic personnel are further encouraged to ask questions that can be answered in a reasonable period of time and to attempt to resolve worrisome issues before concluding a conversation. Perhaps most important, those people planning to work in Antarctica, even for the brief summer period, are informed that any family problems they might have will become only worse as a consequence of the separation, and are advised to clear up any problems before departure.

The experiences of the key Navy psychologists who have been involved with the U.S. Antarctic program suggest that a certain amount of personal outside communication is morale enhancing, but the potential risks demand that policies be established to control voice communications. The general consensus is that personal calls during future long-duration expeditions should be moderately limited (e.g., biweekly or weekly transmissions of fifteen to thirty minutes each). At this time, Navy Antarctic personnel are limited to one weekly fifteen-minute telephone call and one weekly five-minute MARS call, but many of the calls are unsuccessful because of equipment problems, meteorological conditions, or no answer at the receiving end. Unlimited electronic mail, or typed messages transmitted at high speed to Earth stations, might serve as an acceptable supplement to limited personal voice communications on future expeditions. However, there could be problems. One of the Navy psychiatrists involved in Operation Deep Freeze (the name given to Naval Support Force Antarctica) reported that at least one crew member had to be relieved of duty because of an obsession with the new internet and e-mail capability at McMurdo Station. Regardless of the form and frequency of outside communication, it will be important to inform crew personnel and family members at home of the potential for problems to arise as a result of the misunderstandings and sensitivities characteristic of isolation and confinement, in addition to normal problems inherent in long-distance communication. Guidelines, such as those provided to Antarctic personnel, will be essential.

Personal communications should be conducted from crew members' private quarters rather than from a "public" on-board facility. Bender and Fracchia (1971) also offer this suggestion, which draws support from the experiences of personnel in all conditions of isolation and confinement, where privacy is a scarce commodity. The privacy of the personal transmissions must be maintained as well, through use of a scrambler or similar device. Because radio messages can be intercepted by anyone tuned to the frequency, many humorous and embarrassing anecdotes have been attributed to misunderstandings concerning the absence of privacy during radio transmissions. Privacy of personal communications should be ensured for the crew of future long-duration expeditions.

Arthur Violanti, an experienced Navy winter-over manager, was interviewed in 1991 while serving as Master Chief of the Command, Naval Support Force Antarctica. Violanti mentioned that an individual who has wintered-over in Antarctica can predict when the highs and lows of group morale will occur. In particular, the midwinter supply drop (made in June) is preceded by excitement and high morale and followed by individual depression and low morale. He attributes this shift in mood to the fact that the isolated personnel, who are extremely eager to receive mail from home, are almost always disappointed in the amount and contents of the mail that they receive. The worst possibility, however, is to receive no mail at all. For this reason, headquarters personnel thoughtfully prepare a "chiefs' package" addressed to the chief petty officers in the winter-over group so that they can fabricate a package of treats, as if it were sent from home, for anyone who fails to receive mail. Also, a practice on many expeditions has been for family members to prepare packages of small presents to be distributed to their relatives during the voyage, usually at Christmas. Nansen (1897) describes the response to this tradition during the crew's first Christmas onboard the *Fram*:

> All the lamps and lights we had on board were lit.... The bill of fare for the day, of course, surpassed any previous one—food was the chief thing we had to hold festivities with.... The culminating point of the festivities came when two boxes of Christmas presents were produced.... It was touching to see the childish pleasure with which each man received his gift.... He felt like it was a message from home. (Vol. 1, p. 344)

Individual diaries and accounts of many expeditions report the joy of the explorers in finding notes hidden in supplies by those who prepared the materials before shipment, sometimes several years before the cheerful messages were found and enjoyed.

MISSION-RELATED COMMUNICATIONS

When remote-duty personnel discuss their experiences, they nearly always mention the relationship between the isolated group of which they were a part and their headquarters personnel. In all of the conditions studied, this relationship becomes strained, at least periodically, and overt conflicts occasionally erupt. For example, Antarctic personnel and submariners often comment that their distant Navy managers never fully comprehend the constraints under which they operate. This perception was evident in the log maintained by Lt. Comdr. David Canham, Jr., while he and his men built the station that would house the IGY contingents. Canham's commanding officer and others further up the chain of command made decisions about equipment and supplies that were in direct contradiction to the requirements of the remote-duty personnel—it is clear from the record that they just did not understand. In addition, messages applying pressure to meet schedules and other perceived rebuffs were interpreted by the members of the struggling work force in the worst possible manner. Distant commanders often disregarded issues of tremendous, even life-threatening importance to the remote-duty crew and frequently subordinated the group's primary objectives (i.e., survival and construction) to tangential responsibilities (such as the posting of souvenir letters for the public). Rivolier and Bachelard (1988) cite similar examples from their experiences with French remote-duty stations:

> The home agency or laboratory is usually blamed for any difficulties encountered. People in the field and at home see things differently; even words have different meanings. An event considered insignificant at home takes on vital or dramatic importance in the field. The decisions taken and the terms applied no longer have the same meaning at the two ends of the chain. (P. 83)

Rivolier and Bachelard maintain that this phenomenon is common to all missions and all agencies, and that it is important to recognize that the isolated group represents a closed world with a unique frame of reference. Over time, the group has less and less in common with its managers and support personnel at home. In some cases, the rift becomes evident at a surprisingly early stage of a mission, and the differences and disputes accumulate rapidly. This phenomenon, unlike the occasional individual psychoses mentioned in chapter 8, is not a rare occurrence but, rather, a predictable and perhaps even natural response to the conditions of remote duty.

Communications problems between investigators on Earth and U.S. astronauts also have been reported, even during brief space shuttle missions. The problems have been minor and involved equipment malfunctions, unclear instructions, or last-minute changes for which the spacecraft crew were unable to prepare; irritability from sleep disturbances also might have been a factor. Lebedev's diary, however, provides many examples of mission-related communications problems during relatively long space missions; in fact, difficulties with ground control constitute the main theme that emerges from the cosmonaut's account of his 211-day mission onboard the *Salyut-7* space station:

> The hardest part of a prolonged flight is communication with Ground Control. Every minute we have to keep ourselves in complete control. Different people come online to talk to us and some of them have forgotten that a person in space is always busy working, even when he is asleep. Also when different people come online, they sometimes show their

emotions through the tones of their voices and things they say. Therefore, inappropriate words or jokes can put us off balance for an entire day. In general it is inappropriate for FCC [ground control] personnel to demonstrate their bad mood to the crew in space. (Lebedev [1983] 1988, 170)

Much later in his mission, Lebedev appeared to overreact to a question from a radio commentator, who asked whether his days seemed dull in comparison following an exciting and successful day working outside the space station during a "space walk." Lebedev reacted to this innocent question as if the reporter had suggested that he was no longer working on anything of importance. The exchange made the cosmonaut "feel tense again" and bothered him the next day when he was communicating with ground controllers about scientific experiments; ground control was slow to respond to a question about which cables to connect for an atmospheric measurement, then later there was another tardy response when Lebedev asked for guidance during a biological experiment. Lebedev writes of the incident that he raised his voice and gave the mission controllers a piece of his mind. He offended them and seriously strained their relationship.

Even on the *Sealab* and *Tektite* expeditions, which were relatively short-duration undersea experiments, there were problems between divers and "Earth people," as the topside staffs were called (Radloff and Helmreich 1968). Communications problems and strained relations between remote-duty staff and their support or headquarters personnel occur whether the relationship is between an Antarctic research station and program managers in the U.S., a field office of a corporation and company headquarters in another state, or a government research center and the agency headquarters in the nation's capital. As consequences of the structural relationship, hypersensitivities will exist, misunderstandings will occur, and delays of any type that affect the remote-duty group will be perceived as insults.

Conflict between headquarters and remote-duty, or field, personnel is a predictable, perhaps inevitable, phenomenon. For example, tensions between isolated crew members and researchers emerged early during recent simulator studies conducted for the European Space Agency. Sandal, Værnes, and Ursin (1995) report that all crew members mentioned conflict with simulation managers as the main source of frustration during their relatively brief simulated space missions. Several of the crew mentioned that they consciously used the managers as an "enemy" to provide an outlet for the aggression and interpersonal tension that developed within the isolated group.

Sells had accurately explained this phenomenon more than two decades previously:

> A mechanism of displacement of hostility frequently observed among isolated groups is the tendency to direct anger, scorn, even ridicule, with intensity often out of proportion to the focal issue, on external competitors and superior authorities. The naval literature, as well as reports of expeditions and military operations, reveals repeated instances of antagonism toward headquarters by field parties, and of complaints about "excessive demands" by outside persons who are said to be "unaware" of the ongoing realities. Some occurrences of this type have been suspected in the space program and may be expected with greater vehemence as time and distances increase. While the effects may be hygienic, insofar as they furnish a common target for the venting of repressed hostility, the positive values for group mental health may be more than offset by disruption of significant communications with base support groups. (Sells 1973, 294–95)

Psychiatrist Nick Kanas (1990) agrees that, in some cases, the anger expressed by isolated and confined crew personnel to headquarters personnel can be understood as "displacement of interpersonal tension to safer, more remote individuals outside." These events are usually distinguished from other conflicts by their abrupt onset and apparent lack of explanation, for example, a sudden outburst that takes everyone by surprise.

Although the "rift" phenomenon might be inevitable, certain measures can apparently mitigate the effects. For example, NASA's practice of using members of the astronaut corps as communicators must be beneficial in terms of establishing confidence and the appropriate rapport with spacecraft personnel. Also, during Project Tektite, the use of a two-way closed circuit television system seemed to eliminate much of the conflict characteristic of relationships between isolated crews and support personnel. The participants were able to observe each other, both at work and during leisure time, and they believed that this visual contact contributed to a better understanding of the conditions under which both groups operated. A two-way video capability between spacecraft or planetary bases and mission control might facilitate mission-related and personal communications. This is a question that might be answered during simulations conducted in preparation for future long-duration expeditions.

Similarly, onboard *Skylab*, NASA (1974) reports: "Frequent informal communications between scientist astronauts in orbit and the scientific ground-support personnel significantly enhanced the amount and quality of experiment data obtained." The value of this suggestion might have been confirmed on space shuttle missions, although communications problems between ground-based investigators and on-orbit personnel have not been eliminated.

The importance of good communications to technical performance and the clear potential for problems to occur as a consequence of communications problems strongly suggest that all of those using the communications network during future expeditions (scientists, mission controllers, and astronauts) receive guidance concerning proper network etiquette and the potentially explosive nature of the relationship between isolated individuals and their support personnel. Dr. Desmond Lugg provides specific guidance concerning this issue as his final recommendation in the week-long pre-departure orientation program for Australian Antarctic personnel. Lugg's advice, which he calls the "Rule of Ten," is to consider one's initial reaction to a message from family, friends, or headquarters, then divide it by ten before actually responding. This probably is good advice in many circumstances, but it is especially appropriate for remote-duty personnel.

COMMUNICATION LAG TIMES

One of Arthur C. Clarke's novels begins with the destruction of an enormous dirigible-like mother ship that was due to response lag in transmitting docking data to a robot craft. The data were transmitted from the mother ship to a distant satellite, then to the drone. A two-second delay in transmission, attributable more to busy transponders onboard the satellite than to the distances involved, and a sudden gust of wind affecting the dirigible resulted in an accident so expensive that it retarded the progress of space development for generations. Clarke, like Jules Verne before him, has a tendency to be strangely prophetic in his fiction.

There is a potential for serious problems to occur as a result of response lag times attributable to the enormous distances that messages must travel to control robotic vehicles and devices in space. Similarly, response lags in communications with a human crew will be increasingly troublesome as distances from Earth increase. It is believed that normal conversations with a Mars-bound spacecraft will cease at about two million miles from Earth, when the response lag time approaches a minute. Beyond that point, voice communications might give way to typed messages, similar to e-mail. Whatever the medium, communications protocols will be needed to facilitate the exchange of information. Protocols might include summaries of the previous message (to refresh the memories of the parties involved) and clear enumeration of requests for which responses are expected (i.e., a checklist-type memory aid for both parties). Increasing the autonomy of interplanetary spacecraft might also help by decreasing reliance on information provided from Earth and reducing exposure to problems caused by response lag. This was the policy pursued during the days preceding electronic communications. Ships were equipped to be as self-sufficient as possible. Although ship captains were provided with general orders and objectives, they were allowed considerable autonomy in activities and judgment. Communication lag times during the days of sail were measured in months and years, whereas the longest lag that will be experienced by a crew en route to Mars will be about ten minutes. Midshipman Reynolds and his shipmates on the *Vincennes* would have been delighted.

The issues associated with communication lags should be resolved during mission simulations conducted in preparation for future long-duration space expeditions. Simulations will also provide the crews and ground control personnel of future expeditions with opportunities to develop experience in communicating within the constraints imposed by the astronomical distances and response lag times of actual space missions.

A FINAL NOTE

When cosmonaut Sergei Krikalev boarded the *Mir* station in May 1991, he was a citizen of the Soviet Union and his hometown was called Leningrad; while in orbit he became a Russian from St. Petersburg. Ignatius (1992) reports that when Krikalev learned of the coup attempt against Mikhail Gorbachev, he refused to make contact with ground control for two consecutive orbits. "Finally, Mr. Krikalev spoke in a bitter, metallic tone. 'Yes,' he said. 'We've heard the news.'" But, the worst news that Krikalev heard was probably the message informing him that his return to Earth would be postponed several months because of the political and economic realities of the post-Soviet system. He was upset but at least partially placated by an additional EVA (extravehicular activity, or space walk) as part of an arrangement negotiated with ground control.

Isolated and confined personnel often take delays of all kinds badly, especially delays in their scheduled departures for home. An Antarctic manager mentioned in an interview that the greatest strain on individuals that he witnessed on the ice was caused by repeated delays in the arrival of an aircraft that would transport the crew on the first leg of their journey home. He observed some people break down and cry after five days of dragging their bags to the staging area in anticipation of a flight and repeated disappointment each day.

Explorers of all eras have desired news of current events at home, even if the news was not particularly encouraging. For example, Nowlis, Wortz, and Watters (1972) report that a lack of access to news was rated as the most disliked characteristic of the *Tektite* habitat, and Dr. Norman Thaggard's comments about feelings of cultural isolation onboard the *Mir* space station have dominated the accounts of that monumental mission. It seems natural that remote-duty personnel would be especially interested in news from home, especially about events that could affect their isolated condition. Despite the merit of Rivolier and Bachelard's recommendations presented above, I believe that news of the world and considerable access to personal communications with home probably should be provided to the crews of future long-duration expeditions, as it is to other remote-duty personnel, such as the crews of Antarctic stations and current spacecraft (i.e., space shuttles and *Mir*). Also, I believe that personal communications will enhance the morale of most individuals, even though they might stimulate nostalgic feelings and suppressed longings. Personal communications and news programming, at least occasionally from the hometowns of crew members, will help to affirm links with the crew's past and future. Cook ([1900] 1980), again speaks with relevance and provides the final comment on this subject:

> I have taken the trouble to make a personal canvass of every man of the *Belgica* to-day to find out the greatest complaints and the greatest longings of each. The result of this inquiry was certainly a lesson in curious human fancies. In the cabin the foremost wants are for home news and feminine society. We are hungry for letters from mothers, sisters, and other men's sisters, and what would we not give for a peep at a pretty woman? (P. 231)

RECOMMENDATIONS

The following recommendations relate to issues associated with outside communications on future long-duration expeditions.

- Consider the potential for receiving negative personal news as a possible personnel selection criterion (e.g., the number of close relatives that would be left at home).

- Consider likely reactions to negative news as a possible personnel selection criterion.

- Consider withholding negative news from a crew member if the individual is determined to be at severe psychological risk; otherwise, permit negative news rather than risk the likely consequences of censorship.

- Allow moderate amounts of personal voice communications (e.g., once or twice each week).

- Allow electronic mail.

- Ensure privacy of personal communications.

- Design communications systems to permit calls to be made from private quarters.

- Provide guidance to all communication network users concerning proper network etiquette and the potential for problems in their communications. Provide this guidance to regular network users, as well as to individuals, such as family members, who speak infrequently with the remote crew.

- Consider two-way video communications for technical messages and teleconferencing for group discussions, as lag times permit.

- Develop protocols to guide communications when lag times become a factor in interplanetary expeditions.

- Expect occasional strained relations between expedition personnel and mission control and other ground-based personnel, despite efforts to prevent the phenomenon.

- Provide news of current events to expedition personnel in each crew member's own language. Consider network, local news, and special programs prepared for the crew. Rather than stimulating longings for home, the tone and content of actual network news might make long-duration crew personnel quite happy that they are anywhere but on Earth!

CHAPTER 14

RECREATIONAL OPPORTUNITIES

January 1, 1899. At midnight we, of the cabin, went forward to surprise the crew. We took with us a liberal allowance of wine, also an abundance of cheese, ham, and biscuits for a lunch. The sailors received us with song and music, and then told us stories which were new to us, but had been told a hundred times in the forecastle. We in return did some speech-making, and a little story-telling, too. The meeting was certainly a success as an entertainment, and though the music was limited to accordions which, from the combined effects of cold, humidity, and rough usage, had many defects, we sat and listened to the discordant notes with real enjoyment.

—Frederick A. Cook, *Through the First Antarctic Night*

More attention has been devoted to the manner in which space travelers might occupy their leisure time than to any other habitability issue. Since the beginnings of human space flight, when the durations of missions were measured in minutes rather than days, more pages have been written on the subject of recreation and leisure than on any other behavioral topic related to space. The amount of effort devoted to recreation in space, primarily during the 1960s, reflects the belief of that period that long-duration missions would soon take place, perhaps immediately following a successful Apollo Program. The emphasis on recreation as a behavioral issue also reflects the widely held assumption that crew members would be at psychological risk during long interplanetary expeditions.

In one of the earliest studies concerning this topic, Eddowes (1961) conducted a survey of eighty male aerospace professionals to determine preferences in leisure activities; he believed that this sample would more closely resemble potential space crews than the general population. Eddowes found that reading was by far the highest-ranked leisure activity among the group.

A few years later, Eberhard (1967) produced a three-volume treatise for NASA on the subject titled, appropriately, *The Problem of Off-Duty Time in Long-Duration Space Missions*. In these volumes, he reviews nearly four hundred sources in an effort to identify solutions to what was believed to be one of the principal problems associated with a three-year mission to Mars. Questions concerning the meaningful use of off-duty time were considered to have great importance because mission planners assumed that there would be relatively little work for astronauts to perform while in deep space. It is now generally understood that there will be plenty of work and little leisure time for the crews of orbital space stations, lunar bases, and planetary outposts, and the workloads of interplanetary crews will not allow much free time for leisure pursuits except during the cruise phases of the missions. Eberhard makes two particularly valuable observations in his 1967 report, however, that are still relevant, even though current approaches to mission planning involve comparatively high workloads and few opportunities for scheduled recreation:

1. A distinction must be made between scheduled and unscheduled off-duty time. Eberhard defines scheduled off-duty time as that time allocated during a mission for crew members to engage in activities of their own choosing; all observers recognize that some time must be scheduled for leisure, even during the missions characterized by high workloads. Further, unscheduled off-duty time is the time available during the course of a mission as a consequence of allocating more time than required to perform scheduled tasks or as a result of other factors, such as equipment malfunctions or atmospheric conditions, that prevent scheduled tasks from being performed.

2. Often, more free time is available during a mission than had been planned. Eberhard finds that the actual amounts of off-duty time experienced in a range of remote-duty environments were greater than scheduled off-duty time because of unscheduled events, equipment breakdowns, and scheduled tasks performed faster than expected.

Eberhard also summarizes the results of studies concerning leisure activities that were conducted at the early Antarctic stations, when recreational opportunities were limited compared with leisure options available at modern stations. Eberhard concludes:

- The most likely off-duty activity is talking.

- Movies or a video equivalent would appear to be a good daily activity because time spent watching movies increases with length of time in confinement.

- There is a tendency for games to occupy less time as the mission progresses.

- Time spent reading might increase with mission duration.

- The importance of eating as an acceptable free-time activity should not be overlooked.

These observations appear to be as valid today as they were nearly three decades ago.

Fraser's (1968a) study of the intangibles of habitability also addresses the role of recreation and leisure during long-duration space voyages. Fraser suggests that space crews should be encouraged to use their leisure time for creative self-development; however, he concludes:

> Just as one cannot expect a man to divide his time between sleeping and working, one cannot expect him to devote all his leisure to self-development. Part of that time is reasonably spent in relatively passive amusement. (P. 55)

Doll and Gunderson's (1969) study of the hobby interests and leisure activities of Antarctic personnel reports differences in interests and activities between Navy and civilian staffs. Both groups, however, consistently rated movies, a passive amusement, as the favored leisure activity. The researchers also note the following:

- Study courses seemed to have less appeal for civilians than military personnel.

- Fiction was preferred to biographies and religious materials.

- Games (e.g., cards, chess) and graphic arts were not common pastimes.

- Musical preferences were sources of interpersonal conflict.

- Big changes in individual preferences for activities did not occur during the missions that were studied.

Two years later, Righter et al. (1971) identified eight requirements of crew leisure in a report concerning habitability guidelines for a space station with a twelve-member crew of mixed composition. These requirements represent the important reasons for allocating a portion of a crew's time to recreation and leisure:

1. Physical exercise for countering behavioral impairment

2. Physical exercise for countering physiological effects

3. Leisure time for development and maintenance of group morale and intragroup communication

4. Leisure time for countering feelings of deindividualization

5. Leisure time to increase daily variety

6. Leisure time for maintenance of social contact with the world and with one's home

7. Leisure time for constructive personal development and expanded educational repertoire

8. Leisure time for tension-induced autonomic arousal to return to basal levels

Concerning the last requirement, Weybrew (1963) hypothesizes in an earlier study that some individuals, when exposed to successive stressors, might fail to recover autonomic nervous system displacement induced by a stressor before a subsequent stressor is imposed. This could result in a "stair-stepping" response sequence to the stressors of an environment and ultimately contribute to chronic autonomic nervous system disequilibrium; in other words, the stress is cumulative and one can become "stressed out," with possible negative behavioral consequences. Weybrew believes that exercise, recreation, and leisure time allow tension-induced autonomic displacement to recover by insertion of a relatively tension-free time interval in the sequence. Essentially, this means that a schedule of all work and no play is not only dull but possibly risky to mental health. Weybrew's hypothesis encompasses the full range of human variation in attitudes regarding work. Even "workaholics" and "type A" personalities require tension-free time intervals to recover homeostasis. The principal problem associated with members of these groups, however, is that they typically fail to recognize the requirement.

Finally, Karnes, Thomas, and Loudis (1971) conducted a survey of test pilots, military pilots, aerospace engineers, and scientists to determine preferences in leisure-time pursuits. From the survey results, they concluded:

> The populations spend the greatest amount of leisure time in self-improvement, active recreation, and passive entertainment activities and the least amount of time in games and hobbies. Correspondingly, active recreational and passive entertainment equipment [was] most preferred and games and hobbies least preferred as leisure-time equipment for a space journey. (P. 57)

Recreation and leisure opportunities have increased at modern U.S. Antarctic stations in recent years. Navy and civilian managers have added many options to the books, films, lectures, limited crafts, and bars of the earlier days. At the larger stations, personnel can now choose from among many active recreational pursuits, such as bowling, volleyball, basketball, and indoor soccer; even golf is available for a few weeks each year at the Ice Hole Pines course near Williams Field. Science lectures are offered each Sunday night, as in the past; craft shops are available; and there are still bars or clubs at the stations (one during the winter and four during the summer months at McMurdo). In addition, radio and television stations are now operated by volunteers, and exercise classes, several organized sports leagues, and other competitions supplement the usual passive leisure activities.

Antarctic managers recognize the benefits of providing personnel with options to spending their off-duty time in the clubs. Further, Navy and civilian leaders believe that almost any activity that offers a "change of pace" to the routine of isolated and confined living is beneficial, especially if it requires creativity, such as special theme dinners that offer the additional benefit of involving the entire group. Most Navy managers view recreation as an important requirement for maintaining group morale and productivity. In fact, commanding officers have insisted that personnel receive Sunday off at least every other week during the busiest periods of the spring and summer. Time off from a busy schedule is considered a necessity to ensure individual adjustment and group productivity. When a day off must be canceled, the Navy managers try to announce this no later than the preceding Wednesday, but there is often a noticeable decline in performance despite the advance notification.

The explorers, whose accounts of expeditions were reviewed during this study, shared the concerns of Antarctic managers and earlier space mission planners regarding the use of scheduled and unscheduled free time during long-duration isolation and confinement. For example, Jens Munk recorded in 1619 that, during his search for the Northwest Passage: "The weather was rather mild, and in order that the time might not hang on hand the men practiced all kinds of games, and whoever could imagine the most amusement was the most popular" (quoted in Mowat 1977).

Two hundred years later, during the continuing search for the Northwest Passage, Lt. Edward Parry made the first planned Arctic wintering with his men of the *Hecla* and *Griper*. Although he was only twenty-eight years old (and, at that, the oldest member of the party), Parry recognized that boredom would be among the worst hazards for his men, especially for those in the group who possessed, as he put it, "little resource within themselves" (quoted in Mountfield 1974). Parry organized daily exercise for his crew, reading classes for the many sailors who could not read, and other more entertaining ways of

Amateur theater night onboard the *Alert*, in 1875. Boredom of the crew was one of the principal problems during Arctic naval expeditions of the eighteenth and nineteenth centuries. The tradition of staging plays, begun by Edward Parry, helped to break the monotony for the icebound crew. The costumes and footlights in this illustration suggest that the productions were considered important. (Courtesy of The Mansell Collection, London)

passing the long winter. Most notable among the entertainments were plays performed by and for the assembled crew every other week during the ten-month stay at their camp, called Winter Harbor. Parry wrote many of the plays himself, and acted in some, along with John Ross, who usually played the female roles; one of the plays had as many as seven characters, including five seamen, an Eskimo, and a polar bear. Parry also suggested a newspaper, which resulted in *The Winter Chronicle and North Georgia Gazette;* this started a tradition, continued to this day, of irreverent newsletters intended to inform and entertain the members of isolated and confined groups in the polar regions.

Parry's planning and attention to the welfare of his personnel were rewarded with a successful experience; he wrote, "I verily believe there never was a more merry and cheerful set of men than ours" (quoted in Mountfield 1974). Lt. Sherard Osborn, commanding officer of the HMS *Pioneer,* wrote similarly of his experiences during his search in 1850 for the survivors of the lost Franklin Expedition. The following delightful passages from Osborn's journal portray an entertaining and stimulating life for all crew members, despite the isolation and confinement of an Arctic winter:

> A theatre, a casino, a saloon, two Arctic newspapers (one of them illustrated), evening schools, and instructive lectures, gave no one an excuse for being idle. Vocalists and musicians practised and persevered until an instrumental band and glee-club were formed. Officers and men sung who never sang before, and maybe, except under similar circumstances, will never sing again; maskers had to construct their own masks, and sew their own dresses, the signal flags serving in lieu of a supply from the milliners; and, with wonderful ingenuity, a fancy dress ball was got up which, in variety and tastefulness of costume, would have borne comparison with any in Europe.

> Here, editors exhibited French ingenuity in saying their say without bringing themselves within the grasp of the censors; over here, rough contributors, whose hands, more accustomed to the tar-brush than the pen, turned flowing sentences by the aid of old and well-thumbed dictionaries. There, on wooden stools, leaning over long tables, were a row of serious and anxious faces which put one in mind of the days of cane and birch—an Arctic school. Tough old marines curving "pothooks and hangers" [practicing penmanship], as if their lives depended on their performances, with an occasional burst of petulance. (Quoted in Mowat 1977, 268–69)

Some expeditions seemed to suffer more from the enforced inactivity of the polar winter than others, despite the precautions taken by their leaders to forestall the advent of mind-numbing boredom. For example, Lt. George Washington De Long had provisioned the *Jeannette* with many items, including dominoes, chess, backgammon, cribbage, cards, and other games, to amuse his crew. The ship also carried several footballs and enough musical instruments to outfit a small orchestra. Although crew members used the recreation equipment at first, they seemed to lose interest by midwinter, and slipped into a melancholy passivity, perhaps exacerbated by the many interpersonal conflicts that were permitted to develop within the small group. Guttridge (1986) writes of the 1879 *Jeannette* expedition:

> A steady and emphatically reassuring routine was upheld even though every book had been read, all stories told, and games of cards, chess, and checkers long since abandoned.... Over breakfast the officers would relate dreams and theories, the wardroom complement smoking afterwards. (P. 145)

Similarly, Lt. Adolphus Washington Greely had made certain that the men of the Lady Franklin Bay Expedition of 1881 would have sufficient work and diversion to occupy their time during the Arctic winter. Greely knew that it was important to keep men busy in order to prevent adjustment problems, so he implemented "a mixture of necessary work, recreation, and make-work, subtly conceived" (Todd 1961). Meaningful work was created to fill the long days whenever possible. During their free time, the men played checkers, backgammon, Parcheesi, and cards by the light of kerosene lamps; gambling for money was prohibited, so they gambled for tobacco, their most precious commodity. In addition, the scientific staff and officers conducted a weekly lecture program (e.g., Greely on "the Arctic Problem"), and Fort Conger, as their hut was called, had a well-stocked library of more than one thousand volumes. Thus equipped, the twenty-five men of the expedition endured well their first winter in the Arctic, but their morale began to deteriorate when it became apparent that the *Neptune*, their resupply ship, had been unable to penetrate the pack ice. The expedition had food for three years, but the inner resources of the party were exhausted by the end of its first year in isolation and confinement. In December 1882, one of the men wrote in his journal how the confinement had increased the group's sensitivity to trivial issues, made them contentious, and eroded their abilities to enjoy the few diversions available to them:

> The monotonous routine of our life is felt more keenly every day.... Our time, after the usual hour's work in the morning, is spent in reading, writing or discussion.... Nothing seems to hurry the flight of time.... Everything annoys and aggravates us. We give way readily in any situation with a burst of unreasonableness, rather than bolster up our will-power.... The enthusiasm of the party for [holiday celebrations] has diminished considerably and a celebration, no matter how we strive to make it otherwise, becomes nothing more than a mockery. The men grow more captious daily. (Quoted in Todd 1961, 54)

The men were ready for rescue when their second Fourth of July at Fort Conger arrived, but the ship did not. Sgt. David Brainard, supply officer of the expedition, wrote in his journal:

> We no longer have the imagination necessary to provide entertainment for these holiday occasions. Our lone ceremony was the unfurling of the flag. Lieut. Kislingbury caused a little excitement when he presented the only cigars remaining in Grinnell Land to be contended for in a shooting match. Ellis won. We had a game of baseball afterward with Lieut. Kislingbury and Sergt. Gardiner the captains. Gardiner's team won by a run; score, 32–31. (Quoted in Todd 1961, 168)

Conversation is always a leading leisure activity of remote-duty personnel. A large portion of available free time is usually spent in conversation during the first several weeks of confinement as the members of a small group engage in a process of discovery about each other. Then, conversation typically gives way to other, often individual pursuits when members of the group grow weary of the sameness of the discussions and become annoyed by the mannerisms of their comrades. If the period of confinement is sufficiently long, the group might rediscover conversation, although the form of the exchange is often (but not always) sarcastic and unpleasant. In this regard, Cook ([1900] 1980) reports that the thoughts of the members of the *Belgica* Expedition "wheeled around the incidents of current events." For example, they held a beauty contest using nearly five hundred illustrations from the "Paris magazines" that were in the ship's library. Voting took place over a period of several days and the crew enjoyed the contest immensely. Then, according to Cook:

> The beauty contest in April was succeeded by heated discussions and sentimental philosophy for several weeks. This was followed by the serious sentiments caused by the last sight of the sun and the death of Danco. Then followed a lot of light talk about "Nansen," the cat and his future.... To-day [the Fourth of July] we are building up a United States of Europe, and are dreaming of annexing Canada and all of South America into one grand United States. (P. 327)

Cherry-Garrard (1930) describes the pattern of conversation that developed at Scott's hut on Cape Evans during the 1911–12 *Terra Nova* Expedition. Although some members of Scott's party were argumentative, it appears that the discussions, for the most part, were good-natured, and it was possible for a member of the group to control his level of participation in the discussions by careful seat selection at the dining table:

> One great danger threatened all of our meals in this hut, namely that of a Cag. A Cag is an argument, sometimes well-informed, and always heated upon any subject under the sun.... They began on the smallest excuses, they continued through the widest fields, they never ended; they were left in mid air, perhaps to be caught up again and twisted and tortured months after.... Scott sat at the head of the table . . . but otherwise we all took our places haphazard from meal to meal as our conversation, or want of it, merited, or as our arrival found a vacant chair. Thus if you felt talkative you might always find a listener in Debenham; if inclined to listen yourself it was only necessary to sit near Taylor or Nelson; if, on the other hand, you just wanted to be quiet, Atkinson or Oates would, probably, give you a congenial atmosphere. (Cherry-Garrard, 1930, 190)

Special dinners and celebrations (see chapter 10) are a means of making life in isolation and confinement more tolerable. Fridtjof Nansen recognized the benefits of special dinners and impromptu celebrations during the Norwegian Polar Expedition perhaps more than other expedition leaders. They regularly celebrated important milestones, such as the progress of the ship in her drift north in the ice pack. They also celebrated all birthdays on board, including the birthday of the *Fram*, and many other occasions of lesser importance to the crew. For example, the crew celebrated the occasion and toasted the health of the *Fram's* electrician when he set up the windmill that they had brought to the Arctic to generate electricity for their primitive electric lamps. Clearly, these celebrations contributed to the success of the expedition by promoting group solidarity, entertaining and motivating the men, and helping them to mark the passage of time during their three years together. Of the many celebrations held onboard the *Fram*, none was as noteworthy as Norwegian Constitution Day, 17 May 1894. Nansen described the event in his journal:

> Friday, May 18th. May 17th was celebrated yesterday with all possible festivity. In the morning we were awakened with organ music.... After this a splendid breakfast of smoked salmon, ox tongues, etc., etc. The whole ship's company wore bows of ribbon in honor of the day.... The wind whistled, and the Norwegian flag floated on high, fluttering bravely at the mast-head. About 11 o'clock the company assembled with their banners on the ice on the port side of the ship, and the procession arranged itself in order. First of all came the leader of the expedition with the "pure" Norwegian flag [without the mark of the union with Sweden]; after him [came] Sverdrup with the *Fram's* pennant, which, with its "FRAM" on a red ground, 3 fathoms long, looked splendid. Next came a dog-sledge, with

Norwegian Constitution Day, procession in the Arctic, 17 May 1894. (From Nansen, 1897)

the band (Johansen with the accordion), and Mogstad, as coachman; after them came the mate with rifles and harpoons, Henriksen carrying a long harpoon; then Amundsen and Nordahl, with a red banner. The doctor followed with a demonstration flag in favor of a normal working-day. It consisted of a woolen jersey, with the letters "N.A." [for normal arbeidsdage, or normal working day] embroidered on the breast, and at the top of a very long pole it looked most impressive. After him followed our chef, Juell, with "peik's" saucepan on his back [peik was the pet name for the cooking range in the *Fram*'s galley]; and then came the meteorologists, with a curious apparatus, consisting of a large tin scutcheon, across which was fastened a red band, with the letters "Al. St.," signifying "almindelig stemmeret," or "universal suffrage."[1] The stately cortège marched twice around the *Fram*, after which with great solemnity it moved off in the direction of the large hummock, and was photographed on the way by the photographer of the expedition. At the hummock a hearty cheer was given for the *Fram*, which had brought us hither so well, and which would, doubtless, take us equally well home again.... Meanwhile we went down into the cozy cabin, decorated with flags for the occasion in a right festive manner, where we partook of a splendid dinner, preluded by a lovely waltz.... After this a siesta; then coffee, currants, figs, cakes; and the photographer stood cigars. Great enthusiasm, then more siesta. After supper [yes, another meal later in the day], the violinist, Mogstad, gave a recital, then refreshments were served.... On the whole, a charming and very successful Seventeenth of May, especially considering that we had passed the 81st degree of latitude. (Nansen 1897, vol. 1, 483–86)

We should hope that the crews of future long-duration space expeditions will be permitted the luxuries of time and resources to engage in leisure and recreational activities; celebrations and special dinners, such as those recommended in chapter 10, would be particularly beneficial. Special meals and celebrations involve two important but separate behavioral issues: (1) the importance of eating together as a means of fostering group cohesiveness and communication and (2) recreation. The benefits to group cohesiveness and communication can be accomplished even if the crew members eat different foods, but they should eat at the same time and in proximity to each other, preferably while "sitting" around the wardroom table. The importance of special meals as a means to break the monotony of routine life and to help mark the passage of time is a separate issue. Although it is not necessary for the occasional special meals to be prepared from bulk supplies and served family style (i.e., from bowls in the center of the table), these meals would contribute to the shared experience if all crew members had the same food, even when individual meals must be prepackaged (similar to airline or space shuttle food). For example, on Italian night everyone eats lasagna; on French night, coq au vin; on Mexican night, enchiladas. The possibility of preparing meals from bulk supplies, rather than using prepackaged items, might have additional appeal to those who derive satisfaction from cooking. The possible benefits and difficulties associated with various forms of meal preparation could be studied during high-fidelity mission simulations.

In addition to religious, secular, and national holidays, the themes for special meals on long-duration expeditions are nearly limitless. A few possibilities, offered as suggestions to stimulate the thinking of those concerned with this subject, are birthdays of space pioneers (e.g., Kanstantin Tsiolkowsky, Hermann J. Oberth, Wernher von Braun, Yury Gagarin, Valentina Tereshkova, Aleksei Leonov, Neil Armstrong, Jules Verne, Arthur C. Clarke); anniversaries of significant space achievements (e.g., *Sputnik*, *Vostok 1*, *Apollo 11*, *Apollo-Soyuz* test project); and commemorations of fallen colleagues (e.g., those on *Soyuz 1*, *Apollo 1*, *Challenger*). Tributes to previous nonspace expeditions also might be considered (e.g., Cook, Shackleton, Dumont d'Urville, Amundsen), and a lighthearted celebration of the anniversary of the *Fram*'s reaching her farthest-north latitude would be particularly appropriate on the lunar or martian surface.

RECREATION AND LEISURE OPTIONS

The English word "recreation" is derived from the Latin for "restore to health." This is precisely the function that leisure time is intended to serve—to refresh and to restore capability. Recreation and leisure pursuits during long-duration expeditions can be active (e.g., card and board games, exercise) or passive (e.g., reading, sleeping, watching videos, listening to music). Passive recreation tends to be more relaxing than active recreation, but the concepts are not mutually exclusive.

Passive Recreation

In all of the conditions of isolation and confinement that I have studied, reading, listening to music, and watching films or television are among the favored leisure pastimes.[2]

Books played important roles in occupying the time of many previous explorers. For example, a French expedition to the Pacific, headed by Jean Francois de Pérouse in 1785, carried what was at the time a remarkable collection of 1,200 volumes onboard the ships *Boussole* and *Astrolabe*, and Greely had a library of about the same size at Fort Conger in 1881, including 1,000 novels, encyclopedias, and dozens of Arctic reference books. Nansen placed special emphasis on developing an extensive library for the *Fram* to sustain the crew, although he and Johansen were reduced to a few printed pages during their nine months in the hut on Franz Josef Land. Nansen wrote in his journal:

> It was a strange existence, lying thus in a hut underground the whole winter through, without a thing to turn one's hand to. How we longed for a book! How delightful our life on board the *Fram* appeared, when we had the whole library to fall back upon! We would often tell each other how beautiful this sort of life would have been, after all, if we had only had anything to read.... The little readable matter which was to be found in our navigationtable and almanac I had read so many times already that I knew it almost by heart—all about the Norwegian royal family, all about persons apparently drowned, and all about self-help for fishermen. Yet it was always a comfort to see these books; the sight of the printed letters gave one a feeling that there was, after all, a little bit of the civilized man left. (Nansen 1897, vol. 2, 456–57)

Paperback books are particularly well suited to confined and isolated conditions because they are compact, portable, and reusable. In fact, certain volumes receive so much use onboard submarines that new copies at the beginning of a cruise will be falling apart by the time the boat surfaces. In addition to satisfying cultivated interests in specific genres or authors, books also provide a relatively harmless mechanism for escape. This is particularly apparent in the intense confines of saturation chambers, where divers are forced to endure several days of inactivity during compression and decompression. Unable to escape one's fellows for even a moment causes some divers to turn inward; many who had never finished a book before have surprised themselves by becoming avid readers in saturation. Even onboard *Skylab*, reading was the only planned leisure activity conducted by the astronauts. Fiction seems to be preferred under conditions of isolation and confinement, but reference books always have been valued, especially during the *Terra Nova* Expedition when they were frequently used to settle one of the ongoing discussions described above by Cherry-Garrard (1930) as Cags.

Music is a uniquely human form of entertainment and expression; making and listening to music have been favored pastimes of explorers since the earliest days. Nearly all expeditions have included some form of music, from the songs of Columbus's crew to the player-organ on-board the *Fram*. Cherry-Garrard (1930) describes the importance of music to the members of Scott's last expedition:

> It was usual to start the gramophone after dinner, and its value may be imagined. It is necessary to be cut off from civilization and all that it means to enable you to realize fully the power music has to recall the past, or the depths of meaning in it to soothe the present and give hope for the future. (P. 198)

Listening to recorded music is also a common and highly appreciated leisure activity on submarines and at Antarctic research stations. Significantly, it is an activity that can be incorporated into routine tasks as well as into other leisure pursuits. Differences in personal preferences for musical styles, however, were reported as sources of

Card games during Byrd's first expedition to Antarctica helped the men to pass the long winter night. (Courtesy of the National Archives)

interpersonal conflict at the early Antarctic stations; fairly notorious disputes occurred between Seabees and scientists concerning preferences for country-western and classical music. Obviously, conflicts over music predate the advent of small portable stereos with lightweight headphones, available since the 1980s; these ubiquitous devices seem perfectly preadapted to confined conditions, such as those that will be found onboard space craft and at planetary bases. There will be no need to inflict musical preferences on one's comrades on future long-duration expeditions.

Onboard nuclear submarines and at Antarctic research stations, daily viewing of feature films is an overwhelming favorite leisure activity. In a recent habitability study of a military system, the crew preferred videotaped films and commercial television programs (i.e., sports events and news) to all other leisure activities (Stuster 1989). Gunderson and Weybrew (personal communications) both reported preferences among Antarctic and submarine crews for films depicting broad vistas and wide-open spaces, the kind of scenery found in old westerns. It is believed that this preference might reflect a desire of confined personnel to exercise simulated distant vision. Before videotapes replaced films in Antarctica, a station's limited collection might have been viewed dozens of times during a winter; dialogue was frequently memorized and chanted in unison by the audience. Occasionally, particularly bad films were creatively respliced, resulting in humor that the original film editors had not intended. Fraser (1968a) writes of this practice at the early Antarctic stations:

> Kinsey (1959) makes the interesting, but dubiously validated, suggestion that the selection of a few poor quality movies is desirable, not only to make the good quality appear better by contrast, but to mobilize, activate, and release anxiety, particularly that occurring from a more or less repressed feeling of hostility. (P. 64)

The final passive form of leisure activity identified as relevant to future expeditions is unstructured relaxation—an opportunity simply to contemplate preceding and impending events and activities. The following exchange recorded onboard *Skylab* illustrates this requirement:

> Question: Aside from your families, what do you miss most about being away from Earth?
>
> Science pilot: . . . The ability to recoup at the end of the day and to be able to analyze where you are going the next day. And to be able to take a really fresh, creative approach to the things you are doing.

Commander: I miss the opportunity to just sit down and—and relax. (NASA 1976, 7)

As mentioned above, humans require *recreation* to regain psychological homeostasis during periods of cumulative stress. Confined crews probably obtain a sufficient amount of *relaxation* during meals and sleep periods; however, to hasten the onset of sleep, it is wise to schedule an hour or so of quiet (relaxing) leisure time prior to the sleep period. Sleep is an important factor in isolation and confinement. It can be reasonably expected that crews of future long-duration expeditions will experience high workloads, enormous responsibilities, and frequent deadlines, all of which can contribute to sleep problems. For this reason, equipment designs and procedures must be developed to optimize the sleep quality of expedition personnel. Quiet leisure time prior to the sleep period is an example of what is required. For example, during the early phases of the *Skylab* missions, astronauts complained that they were frequently scheduled to perform operational tasks right up to the beginning of their sleep period. Some found it difficult to relax immediately; consequently, the onset of sleep was delayed. A program of sleep hygiene, to hasten the onset of sleep, is suggested in chapter 3. In addition, the following recommendation from the *Skylab* crew is endorsed: "A presleep period of one hour of mentally nondemanding activity should be planned in the crew's time line" (NASA 1974).

Future long-duration expeditions should be equipped with extensive libraries that include a broad range of literature and references. Large numbers of volumes can be stored on magnetic or optical media, but at least a few actual paperbacks should be included in the collection. Recreation equipment also should include prerecorded video programming and the capability to record commercial and special broadcasts for viewing at convenient times. A broad range of programming that includes educational and cultural materials, as well as serious drama and comedy, should be available. Previously, I had recommended that certain items be restricted from the film libraries of remote-duty personnel (i.e., films about confined groups in positions of extreme jeopardy). I was recently informed, however, that both versions of *The Thing* (about an alien at a polar station) have been viewed by hundreds of Antarctic personnel in recent years with no apparent ill effects. Perhaps more research is required to determine if films viewed by future expedition personnel should be censored in any way.

I firmly believe that, during future expeditions, video and television viewing should be a group activity that is conducted in a common area, rather than in private quarters. When videotape players replaced projected film at Antarctic research stations, the personnel tended to watch the tapes in their rooms; for some individuals, the video technology contributed to serious withdrawal from the group. Although some degree of withdrawal is a healthy coping mechanism, excessive withdrawal can be dangerous—in the extreme, it is called "cocooning." When Capt. Brian Shoemaker commanded the U.S. Naval Support Force Antarctica, he moved the tape machines from private quarters to common areas in an attempt to recapture some of the good-natured fun and camaraderie of the days before videotape players. The situation has changed; although nearly half of all private quarters at U.S. Antarctic stations now have televisions, station management encourages TV viewing in common areas. Station personnel reported in interviews that they greatly appreciated recorded commercial television programming from home. Holiday programs are especially treasured.

Active Recreation

Conversation is the leisure pastime in which isolated and confined crews engage most frequently. This is particularly true during the early phases of missions when the crew members are learning about each other and sharing the excitement of their mutual adventure. In the analogues studied, conversations, frequently called "bull sessions," encompass a wide range of topics. Most conversations among isolated groups can be classified as either work related or "sea stories"; group members generally avoid politics and religion as topics of conversation. Also, later in missions, there is a tendency for conversation to include sexual matters; many observers interpret this as evidence of underlying sexual tension handled largely through joking behavior. Conversation is a leisure activity requiring no equipment and involving no power consumption or weight penalty. Considerate and thoughtful conversation should be encouraged during future expeditions because pleasant social exchanges can facilitate adjustment to isolation and confinement. It will also be necessary to advise future crew personnel to respect their comrades' willingness to be engaged in conversation or their desire to be left alone; special attention, however, must be devoted to the tendency for some individuals to withdraw from the intense social contact of isolated and confined living. Habitat designers can encourage conversation by providing areas for interpersonal exchange (e.g., wardroom, galley, table design, insulated partitions forming quiet areas).

A common pattern that has been reported among Antarctic personnel involves making ambitious plans prior to departure to use their leisure time in Antarctica in a highly constructive manner, such as studying a language, reading worthy literature or technical volumes, listening to scientific lectures, and the like. Rather quickly, however, many of these good intentions are abandoned in favor of more passive activities, such as reminiscing, telling stories, and watching films. Conversely, early studies onboard nuclear submarines found an increasing desire for complexity of reading material and a significant interest in college and technical courses as the mission progressed. Course work is frequently pursued by Navy personnel as a means to advance in rank or grade, but interest in course work also might reflect the high morale onboard submarines.

Crew members should be permitted to pursue formal studies during long-duration expeditions, even though it is unlikely that many will be so inclined or enjoy sufficient free time. A more reasonable approach would be to organize a weekly lecture series, similar to those of previous expeditions, during which crew members make informative presentations in their areas of expertise. A lecture program would continue a tradition, established by the early explorers, of providing entertainment and education; perhaps more important, the lectures would have the added benefit of being group activities. Sunday night science lectures are among the only remaining group activities at modern U.S. Antarctic stations, aside from the special dinners and the competitions that involve segments of the group. The lectures are informative and include topics of local interest and instruction concerning valuable skills, such as cardiopulmonary resuscitation (CPR), but their primary attraction for those who attend is the group experience.

The making of music is another active leisure pursuit appropriate for future expeditions. Participatory musical activities have been enjoyed by many explorers and are especially appreciated by some Antarctic personnel. In particular, the log of the Seabee group that established McMurdo Station revealed that choir practice might have provided an effective coping mechanism for the commanding officer of the unit. Some musical instruments (e.g., guitars, electronic keyboards) could be sources of personal gratification and group enjoyment if played with consideration for fellow crew members during future expeditions.

Since the earliest days at Antarctic research stations, there has been an abiding interest in growing plants. Ryumin (1980) also describes the pleasure that he derived from tending the experimental garden onboard the Soviet *Salyut 6* space station, and Lebedev ([1983] 1988) reports similar experiences during a later mission. Anatoli Berezovoy, who shared the *Salyut 7* space station with Lebedev in 1982, told a reporter that Lebedev had never before grown plants, but on *Salyut*, he would rush to their "Oaziz" installation every morning as soon as he awakened to tend the peas and oats growing there. The agricultural activities apparently transcended the experimental requirements, and the cosmonauts found themselves devoting much of their leisure time to gardening. Gardening provides substantial gratification to many people in both isolated and nonisolated environments. Botanical experiments and larger-scale efforts to grow fresh vegetables for crew consumption should be included on future long-duration space expeditions; the integration of leisure and task-related activities would be one of the results.

The integration of activities is proposed in chapter 5 as a principle to be applied whenever possible in designing equipment and procedures for long-duration expeditions. In this regard, many potential crew members derive pleasure from writing letters, maintaining personal journals, and preparing scientific papers. These activities are suggested as particularly appropriate to future expeditions because they involve little in the way of equipment and materials and also represent opportunities for at least some individuals to combine required task performance with leisure. Also, as suggested before, this principle could be extended to the integration of recreation with exercise. The development by crew members of zero-gravity physical games and contests should be encouraged, and some individuals, for whom exercise is already recreational, will find that the video-bicycle ergometer tours (see chapter 5) might satisfy both recreation and exercise requirements. Similarly, any crew members who enjoy preparing food would be obvious candidates for "chef duty" for the special or theme dinners suggested in chapters 10 and 11. Applying the principal of integration of activities could improve overall habitability by providing a mix of work-related tasks and leisure options that optimally satisfy each individual crew member's requirements.

Windows

The favored leisure activity onboard *Skylab* was viewing Earth from the wardroom window. The astronauts were transfixed by the sights beneath them and amazed by the clarity with which features were visible. One *Skylab* astronaut even recommended that future space stations be equipped with clear, bubblelike observation domes to allow unobstructed views. When the *Skylab 4* crew finally took a day off at about the midpoint of their eighty-four-day mission, they spent much of that time gathered around the wardroom to watch the endless progression of sights below. Similarly, free time onboard *Mir*, the Russian space station, mainly consists of looking out of the window, according to Victor Blagov, deputy director of space flight for the program (Ignatius 1992). Earlier, the *Tektite* undersea habitat had a cupola that allowed 360 degrees of visibility, a feature similar to the suggested observation dome; *Tektite* was also equipped with smaller domed windows. Robert Helmreich reported that the windows served a very important function. Whenever crew members walked by one of the windows, they glanced outside, thereby experiencing short "packages" of leisure throughout the day.

Although windows were important sources of enjoyment for the crews of *Skylab* and *Tektite*, the evidence from submariners is somewhat disturbing. Dr. Ben Weybrew (personal communication) reported that submariners on patrol have a marked preference for movies that contain sweeping vistas and scenes of open country. He interpreted this preference as the expression of the submariners' needs to identify with the surface and to experience the illusion of long distance or infinite focus. Submarines offer little opportunity for focusing one's eyes on objects more than a few meters away. Scientists at the Naval Submarine Medical Research Laboratory discovered that submariners' eyesight is affected in specific ways by the absence of distant objects on which to focus. Kinney et al. (1979) found that submariners tend to develop temporary esophoria (cross-eye) during their seventy-day submerged missions, and distance vision might be permanently degraded over the course of a submariner's career. The researchers discovered this effect during a longitudinal study to determine the long-term consequences of exposure to the confined environments of nuclear submarines. They identified esophoria as a systematic problem and found that crew members were involved in an inordinate number of vehicular accidents after arrival at port. Submariners are now advised to avoid driving for three days following return from a cruise.

A related phenomenon onboard submarines is the importance of an occasional opportunity for a quick peek through the submarine's periscope. Ben Weybrew introduced this practice nearly thirty years ago, and it has become a tradition in the U.S. submarine fleet. In a history of submarine psychology, Weybrew (1979) reports:

> Significant peaks in the morale curve appeared during each of the 24-hour periods during which "periscope liberty" was granted for the crew. It was hypothesized that allowing men to line up for a few seconds of periscope viewing of the sea, a landfall, a cloud, or a bird in flight provided a "cognitive anchor"—reassurance that there was still a real world out there. (P. 11)

Weybrew further reports that when periscope liberty was allowed, a noticeable decrease in reported physiological symptoms occurred. If periscope liberty had been expected but was canceled, the crew experienced a precipitous increase in symptoms.

The evidence suggests that windows should be included in the design of future spacecraft and habitats, despite the engineering implications (primarily additional weight and maintenance requirements). At least one of the windows should be as large as *Skylab*'s window, and it should be free of nearby interior obstructions so that several crew members can gather for viewing. As a supplement to windows, the craft or habitat also could be equipped with video display terminals (VDTs) to display exterior scenes captured by the video cameras that will probably be necessary to monitor extra-vehicular activities (EVAs) and to conduct routine inspections of the exterior and immediate surroundings.

ROLE OF RELIGIOUS PRACTICES ON EXPEDITIONS

Religious practices, naturally, played a role in many of the earlier expeditions. By the end of the nineteenth century, however, religion was largely replaced by a scientific approach. Nansen, for example, did not hold beliefs in the supernatural, although he joked in his journal, "It would probably be well to have them," as he was preparing for his dangerous dash across the ice cap to reach the farthest north. A few years later, Cook ([1900] 1980) found that the *Belgica*'s library had no prayer books, and it contained only one Bible, which was kept under-cover. He writes:

> Religion is apparently not one of our missions. But then I must hasten to add that on an expedition of this kind land pilots are more necessary than "sky pilots." (P. 69)

Cherry-Garrard (1930) writes that, when the remaining members of Scott's party were preparing to depart Antarctica, they decided to erect a cross on Observation Hill as a monument to Scott and the other heroic members of the polar party who had all perished after reaching the South Pole the previous year. Some suggested a biblical passage because "the women think a lot of these things." Instead, the group agreed on the following appropriate line from Tennyson's *Ulysses*, "To strive, to seek, to find, and not to yield."

Religions, religious practices, and religious paraphernalia should be viewed as personal beliefs and personal equipment on future long-duration expeditions. Although a diversity of personal beliefs could be tolerated onboard a spacecraft or lunar base, it would be unfair to dedicate precious common areas for the practice of religious ceremonies. Religious ceremonies and practices performed by individuals should be conducted in their personal quarters. Multipurpose areas might be used occasionally for religious practices if those uses are agreed upon by all personnel who are inconvenienced by the gathering. Also, individual productivity lost as a result of religious practices (e.g., Moslem prayers that interrupt task performance five times each day) must be compensated from an individual's free-time allotment so as to ensure equanimity.

Religious practices are discouraged in order to minimize possible sources of conflict among crew members (trivial issues are exaggerated in isolation and confinement). It is unkind and unfair to inflict personal preferences in music and art on others who do not share those preferences, for example, by playing offensive music over a speaker system or displaying pinup pictures in a habitat occupied by a mixed-gender crew. For the same reason, it would be unwise to dedicate, and possibly use, common areas of a spacecraft or habitat for religious practices (i.e., for daily or weekly services).

Although religious *practices* are discouraged, celebrations of religious holidays are strongly encouraged. Christmas, Easter, Hanukkah, and several other religious and secular holidays are perceived by most people as milestones to the passage of time. For this reason, holidays provide excellent opportunities to provide the crew with the zeitgebers necessary to counter the blurring of time characteristic of isolated and confined living. Christmas and Hanukkah decorations displayed in the wardroom, even with explicitly religious motifs, would provide permissible, indeed welcome, visual variety and stimulation while reinforcing the notion that time is passing measurably and progress is being made toward the established goal. Special dinners to celebrate important holidays would further reinforce these concepts and provide opportunities to enhance group solidarity and cohesiveness, even if the crew is composed of different cultural or religious backgrounds. The latter statement assumes that the important holidays of all cultural backgrounds represented in the crew would be celebrated equally. This should not be a problem because it will be important to have frequent special dinners; holidays, from New Year's to Christmas, provide ready opportunities and themes for the special dinners.

RECOMMENDATIONS

The following recommendations relate to issues associated with recreation and leisure activities on future long-duration expeditions.

- Provide an extensive library of literature, including novels, biographies, poetry, and reference works. The library could be stored on magnetic or optical media, but some hard-copy volumes also should be provided because of their convenience and familiarity.

- Provide space for both personal and common storage of volumes.

- Provide personal compact tape players with lightweight earphones for leisure, exercise, and selected work-time music appreciation. Permit crew personnel to select prerecorded music for the voyage; provide additional selections (e.g., popular, classical, country, rock, jazz, seasonal) in a common music library.

- Provide capability for group music listening in wardroom/galley area.

- Provide on board capacity for tape player battery recharging.

- Provide capability for on board videotape or optical disc viewing as a group activity.

- Provide capacity for storage of videotapes or optical discs. Obtain a wide variety of titles, including classic movies, comedies, and westerns and adventures with outdoor scenes; "letterbox" format and appropriate display devices are recommended to obtain the film-makers' original wide-screen cinematography, especially for films with outdoor scenes. Also, provide documentaries and other educational programming, as well as seasonal programs and movies. Emphasize quality material, but also include items that are not particularly good (in case the psychoanalytic interpretation of responses to bad films at early Antarctic stations is correct).

- Include a selection of card and board games (e.g., cribbage, chess); identify any inappropriate games during premission simulations.[3]

- Schedule at least one hour of uninterrupted leisure time prior to each sleep period.

- Encourage conversation among the crew by designing areas and equipment (e.g., tables, workstations) that are conducive to communication.

- Provide constructive leisure opportunities, such as formal courses of study and experiments to be conducted and reported, etc.[4]

- Organize a weekly lecture series conducted by and for crew personnel.

- Permit or facilitate the development of an expedition newspaper to inform and entertain the crew. The newspaper could be prepared in electronic form with the assistance of mission control and might include information about the activities of spacecraft and mission control staffs.[5]

- Allow musical instruments on board, but require consideration when crew members play them. For example, an electronic keyboard or guitar could be equipped alternatively with headphones or a speaker, depending on the conditions or the musical proficiency of the crew members.[6]

- Apply the principle of integration of activities:
  - Include botanical experiments in operations as early as possible to incorporate leisure gardening with task-related activity.

  - Encourage the development of zero-gravity physical games.

  - Design ergometer/exercise devices to render exercise more recreational (e.g., incorporate video programming) and/or to have other functions (e.g., recharging batteries for the tape players).

  - Allow special dinners, and perhaps special preparation, to provide recreation as well as nourishment.

- Design the spacecraft or habitat to include as many windows as possible in order to reduce feelings of isolation and provide opportunities to exercise distant vision, as well as for leisure-time viewing.

- Allow leisure-time viewing of spacecraft or habitat exterior and surroundings via a system of exterior-mounted video cameras.

CHAPTER 15

PERSONNEL SELECTION CRITERIA

Men wanted for hazardous journey. Small wages, bitter cold, long months of complete darkness, constant danger, safe return doubtful. Honour and recognition in case of success.
—Shackleton's recruiting notice in London newspapers

Sir Ernest Shackleton's recruiting notice was both accurate and prophetic. The salaries offered to the volunteers were indeed small— only token payments for services (from $240 a year for an able seaman to $750 a year for the most experienced scientist); Shackleton, like many explorers, believed that the privilege of the experience should provide sufficient compensation. The Antarctic is always bitter cold, but it was particularly cold during the winter of 1914–15; the unusually heavy pack ice prevented the expedition from reaching the continent, then it held the *Endurance* and her crew in a relentless embrace. As for the long periods of darkness and constant danger, the twenty-eight men of the Imperial Trans-Antarctic Expedition continued to live onboard their trapped ship for five months but were forced to establish a series of camps on the pack ice when the *Endurance* was finally crushed by the pressure of the ice. The crew lived in constant danger on the floating ice for another five months, with only some supplies and three small open boats salvaged from the ship before she went down. As the men listened in the darkness, killer whales cruised the edges of the floes and bumped them from beneath in attempts to knock their prey into the frigid sea. Safe return was truly doubtful.

The floe on which the party was encamped became smaller and smaller with each storm. Shackleton led the men in boat drills so they would be prepared to evacuate the ice on a moment's notice, an action that became necessary when the ice began to break up beneath their camp. For the next six days they groped their way through the pack ice. They sailed, when possible, and then laboriously hauled their boats onto the floes to avoid being crushed when the narrow leads closed about them. The men nearly succumbed to dehydration and exposure during their escape. They had not touched land for 497 days when they finally crashed through the surf surrounding Elephant Island. But the adventure was not over.

Shackleton selected five members of the crew for a desperate mission: Frank Worsley, captain of the *Endurance*; Thomas Crean, second officer; Harry McNeish, ship's carpenter; and Timothy McCarthy and John Vincent, both able seamen. Along with Shackleton, they soon departed for help in the most seaworthy of their small craft, a 22-foot cutter named for one of the expedition's sponsors, James Caird. After nearly a year and a half at sea, icebound and adrift, the cutter and her crew made a voyage across one thousand miles of the stormiest ocean on the planet to reach South Georgia Island, one of the most remarkable passages in the history of seafaring. Lansing ([1959] 1994) writes that the sight of the *James Caird* would have seemed strangely incongruous had there been an observer:

> Here was a patched and battered 22-foot boat, daring to sail alone across the world's most tempestuous sea, her rigging festooned with a threadbare collection of clothing and half rotten sleeping bags. Her crew consisted of six men whose faces were black with caked soot and half-hidden by matted beards, whose bodies were dead white from constant soaking in salt water. In addition, their faces, and particularly their fingers were marked with ugly round patches of missing skin where frostbites had eaten into their flesh. Their legs from the knees down were chafed and raw from the countless punishing trips crawling across the rocks in the bottom. And all of them were afflicted with salt water boils on their wrists, ankles, and buttocks. But had someone unexpectedly come upon this bizarre scene, undoubtedly the most striking thing would have been the attitude of the men... relaxed, even faintly jovial—almost as if they were on an outing of some sort. (P. 236)

Worsley, the most experienced seaman in the group, was the natural choice to skipper the *Caird*. Worsley's diary, maintained with great difficulty during the voyage, contains several references to the social compatibility, indeed cheerfulness, of the *Caird*'s crew. For example, Worsley (1977) writes that the boat was covered with ice, all clothing and sleeping bags were soaked by the constant intrusion of heavy seas, and all six of the crew were suffering from frostbite and intermittent seasickness. The little boat took a wave that poured frigid water down their necks just as Worsley was relieving McCarthy at the helm on the tenth day of the voyage. Worsley felt like swearing but was shamed into good humor by McCarthy's greeting, "Its a foine day, sorr." The cheerfulness of individual members of the crew, Worsley reports, always brightened the spirits of others when conditions were at their worst. The cheerfulness was the result of Shackleton's selection of men on the basis of their social compatibility, as well as their experience and technical qualifications. Shackleton believed that keeping tempers in check and maintaining good cheer help a crew to endure hardships and to respond cooperatively during emergencies. Captain Worsley wrote in his diary that all members of the expedition attempted to live up to these goals as best they could. Cooperation and good cheer were the central themes of the spirit of this remarkable expedition.

After enduring sixteen days of hurricane conditions, the *Caird* and her worn-out crew landed on South Georgia Island, on the opposite side from Stromness Whaling Station, which was their destination. They had lost their rudder and had nearly lost their lives, as well, during their landing, so they dared not attempt to sail around the island for fear of being swept away. Later, they found their rudder in the surf, but two of the men were too weak to attempt even a short voyage. The only choice was for some of the others to cross the island on foot, which had never been done before, to get help. They knew that it was only 29 miles to the other side of the island, but glaciers and a snow-covered mountain range more than 9,000 feet high stood in their way. After a few days' rest, Shackleton and two others gathered a few supplies, binoculars, two compasses, a chart that only showed the island's coastline (the interior was blank), about 50 feet of worn-out rope knotted together, a pot and small one-burner stove for cooking, food for three days, and the carpenter's adz to use as an ice ax; the only superfluous item that Shackleton permitted was Worsley's diary. They left their heavy reindeer-hide sleeping bags behind because they planned to continue to the whaling station without stopping for sleep.

The traverse of South Georgia Island by Shackleton, Crean, and Worsley was a fantastic adventure in itself, one that was not accomplished again for another forty years. The three men climbed steep cliffs, crossed ice fields made treacherous by countless crevasses, endured freezing cold, and descended a glacier on a "sled" made by coiling their small length of rope beneath them. Thirty-seven hours after setting out, the tattered, exhausted, yet cheerful group was warmly greeted by the surprised whalers, who had assumed that all hands onboard the *Endurance* had been lost months before in the Weddell Sea; even more surprising was the direction from which the survivors had reached the safety of the whaling station. The whalers provided them with baths, clean clothes, and food, and a whaling ship retrieved the remaining crew of the *Caird* that night. Shackleton then coordinated four successive rescue attempts before he finally succeeded in reaching Elephant Island on 30 August 1916, eighteen weeks after his departure in the cutter. All members of the expedition soon returned safely to England and to a raging war that limited the honor and recognition that Shackleton had advertised and that the members of the expedition deserved. It is extremely relevant to note that *not a single member of the expedition was lost*, despite the danger and deprivation experienced by the men as castaways for nearly two years in the most inhospitable environment on Earth.

Shackleton's leadership abilities are cited earlier (see chapter 7) as a primary factor in the survival of the Imperial Trans-Antarctic Expedition. Leaders of the great polar expeditions conducted during simpler times were responsible for all aspects of an expedition, from fund-raising and personnel selection to actual execution of the established

Launching the *James Caird* at Elephant Island, 24 April 1916. (Photo by Frank Hurley; courtesy of The Royal Geographical Society, London)

plan. Like most of the leaders of successful (or remarkable) expeditions, Shackleton placed a heavy emphasis on personally assembling a team that provided the correct mix of intellectual, technical, and social skills. He built his crew around a nucleus of well-tested veterans with whom he had served during previous expeditions. In this regard, Shackleton subscribed to the fundamental principle of applied psychology: The best predictor of future performance is past performance. But, when it came to selecting the twenty or so newcomers his methods were less systematic and seen by some observers as even capricious. He interviewed each volunteer, usually very briefly, before making a decision to accept or reject the applicant. For example, he signed on a man as meteorologist who had practically no technical qualifications for the position, but whose manner, humor, and previous experience as an expedition anthropologist were appealing to Shackleton. The man immediately began a course of study in his new field and became quite proficient.

Shackleton selected other members of the party on the basis of their answers to his sometimes odd questions (e.g., "Why are you wearing glasses?" "Can you sing?"). A humorous, witty, or thoughtful response caused Shackleton to favor an applicant; defensiveness usually resulted in immediate disqualification. What Shackleton was apparently looking for in these brief interviews were indications that a volunteer was the type of man who could get along with others under difficult conditions. Although he lacked the tools of modern personnel selection and his decisions were made quickly, it is clear from a review of the crew's diaries and accounts of the expedition that "Shackleton's intuition for selecting compatible men rarely failed" (Lansing [1959] 1994). The exemplary manner in which the members of the expedition performed their tasks, cooperated, and remained in remarkably good spirits under the most austere and dangerous conditions imaginable validates both Shackleton's leadership *and* his personnel selection abilities.

Other explorers were not so skillful or fortunate. For example, the mutiny that resulted in the abandonment of Henry Hudson in what is now Canada in 1611 was led by Henry Greene, who had been a leader of a nonviolent mutiny four years earlier against Hudson. Why Hudson consented to take Greene onboard the *Discovery*, Hudson's fourth voyage to the Arctic (Smythe-Digges-Wolstenholm Expedition), is not known. The mutineers set Hudson, his young son, and several crewmen adrift in an open boat in the middle of the bay that now bears Hudson's name. They were never heard from again.

Similarly, before departure for the Arctic, Lt. George Washington De Long learned that one of his crew had spent time in an asylum following a "mental breakdown." He tried to have the man removed from the crew list, but political pressure forced De Long to retain him. The man's terminal medical condition (diagnosed as advanced stages of syphilis) emerged during the voyage north and required the constant attention of the *Jeannette's* physician. His illness also deprived the expedition of its primary navigator. More recent examples of poor personnel selection include the highly disruptive psychoses experienced at U.S. Antarctic stations during the International Geophysical Year of 1957–58 and during the preceding year and the behavioral problems of personnel attached to the International Biomedical Expedition to the Antarctic of 1980–81.

PERSONNEL SELECTION RESEARCH AT EARLY ANTARCTIC STATIONS

The Navy-sponsored program of psychological research at U.S. Antarctic stations (see chapters 8 and 11) was precipitated by a severe psychosis that emerged among the Navy crew preparing a base for the IGY. The early studies, conducted by Capt. C. S. Mullin, identified several psychological effects of the conditions at Antarctic stations; they included absentmindedness, fugue states, and sleep disturbances. The studies also determined the three main sources of stress experienced by station personnel to be (1) adjustment to the isolated group, (2) sameness of the milieu, and (3) absence of customary sources of gratification (Mullin 1960). These three categories continue to encompass the primary stressors for all remote-duty personnel.

Most of the research after 1961, conducted by Eric Gunderson and his colleagues at the Navy Medical Neuropsychiatric Research Unit (now known as the Naval Health Research Center), constitutes a valuable resource. In many ways, the conditions studied by Gunderson, Nelson, and the others at the earlier Antarctic stations more closely resemble what might be expected of future expeditions and remote-duty outposts than conditions at the modern stations. Similar research opportunities might never again occur on Earth.

The Navy's initial studies focused on the factors that affected individual adjustment to the austere and isolated conditions of the early stations and on the development of techniques for measuring crew adaptation and performance. By 1962, however, the emphasis of the research had shifted to the identification of individual characteristics that might be used to help select personnel for Antarctic duty. The research found that older, more experienced Navy personnel who had a background of accomplishment and conforming behavior were more likely to adjust and perform well at Antarctic stations than individuals who lacked these characteristics. The researchers found positive indicators for individual adjustment to be the personality qualities of emotional control, tact, self-sufficiency, conformity, low achievement needs, and mild pessimism. Negative indicators included a history of truancy or delinquency, strong hobby interests, and high expressed motivation; negative personality traits included aggressiveness, impulsivity, excitability, hostility, and high achievement needs. Neither past delinquent behavior nor need for avocational activity was systematically related to performance among the civilian personnel studied (Nelson and Gunderson 1963a; Nelson and Ovick 1964). In fact, civilian scientists tended to adapt better to the restricted environment than either military or meteorological personnel, as indicated by peer and supervisor ratings and motivation measures (Gunderson and Nelson 1964). Further, Nelson (1965) finds the three most important aspects of adjustment to the conditions of the early Antarctic stations, as judged by the personnel themselves, to be an individual's (1) enthusiasm to perform the work, as well as to help comrades; (2) consideration and friendliness when among others; and (3) capacity to control emotions so as not to be disruptive in either work-related or social situations.

The extensive Navy research program, involving several hundreds of winter-over personnel, permitted Gunderson (1966a) to refine the previous analyses and identify three clusters of behavioral traits that were highly correlated with effective performance at Antarctic stations. He labels the clusters (1) emotional stability, (2) task performance, and (3) social compatibility. *Emotional stability* involves an individual's ability to maintain control of his or her emotions, despite the stresses of isolated and confined living; "calm" and "even-tempered" are the ideal characteristics. *Task performance* refers to both task motivation and proficiency; "industrious" and "hard-working" describe the ideal traits in this category. *Social compatibility* includes a number of personal characteristics, such as likability, cheerfulness, and consideration for others; "friendly" and "popular" are the ideal characteristics. These categories have been used by Navy psychologists and psychiatrists for the past three decades to guide the screening of volunteers for Antarctic duty.

Researchers have estimated the relative importance of the three behavioral clusters to overall performance at U.S. Antarctic stations, as perceived by Navy and civilian winter-over personnel (Doll and Gunderson 1970; Gunderson 1973b). Crew ratings of their colleagues on the three behavioral traits were correlated with responses to a criterion item: "If you were given the task of selecting men to winter over at a small station, which men from this station would you choose first?" A fourth variable, friendship, was included in the analysis to serve as a control. Table 2 presents the three behavioral clusters and the control variable in rank order of importance, as indicated by the magnitudes of the correlations with the criterion. Social compatibility was judged as the most important cluster of traits by the civilians, whereas emotional stability was judged to be the most important by the military personnel. It is essential to note that both groups found personality traits, rather than task performance, to be the most important factors in determining the kind of individual with whom experienced personnel would want to share another year in isolation and confinement. These results are as statistically and intuitively valid today as they were when the studies were conducted, and they could be applied to the development of personnel selection criteria for other remote-duty environments, such as future long-duration space expeditions.

Table 2. Relative Importance of Behavioral Traits
to Successful Performance at U.S. Antarctic Stations

Order	Navy Personnel	Civilian Personnel
1	Emotional stability	Social compatibility
2	Task performance	Emotional stability
3	Social compatibility	Task performance
4	Friendship	Friendship

A further contribution of the Navy program was research concerning the concept of selecting individuals on the basis of interpersonal compatibility in order to facilitate group performance. Gunderson and Ryman (1967) and Gunderson (1968a) report several studies of group compatibility at extremely remote Antarctic stations. Some investigators believed that the research might eventually lead to useful approaches to what was then called the group assembly problem. More than a decade later, the concept reemerged in the field of aviation psychology when Robert Helmreich and others began selecting the crews of commercial airlines on the basis of interpersonal compatibility, as well as technical skill (Foushee and Helmreich 1988). Selecting for compatibility was linked to the emerging field of cockpit (now crew) resource management. Helmreich and other early CRM researchers demonstrated that many critical incidents in aviation, including several major disasters, were attributable to breakdowns in communication and coordination among the flight deck crew, and that many of the problems were caused by the personality traits and associated interpersonal behaviors of the individuals involved (Jensen and Biegelski 1989).

Selecting individuals on the basis of interpersonal compatibility is a good idea. This approach to personnel selection is supported by the fundamental assumptions of modern crew resource management, the results of extensive psychological research at U.S. Antarctic stations, and the accomplishments of the most successful expedition leaders of the past. Shackleton, Nansen, and Amundsen, in particular, placed special emphasis on the manner in which prospective crew would get along with each other during prolonged periods of isolation and confinement. It would be wise for the planners of future long-duration expeditions to do the same.

PERSONNEL SELECTION PROCEDURES FOR ANTARCTIC DUTY

Dr. Fred Glogower, a senior Navy psychologist, has been responsible for coordinating the psychiatric evaluations of prospective U.S. Antarctic personnel since 1985. These considerable responsibilities are ancillary duties for Dr. Glogower and the other Navy psychologists and psychiatrists who participate in the annual Navy support program called Operation Deep Freeze (e.g., Dr. Glogower headed the psychology department at Naval Hospital San Diego during most of the period in which he has been responsible for Antarctic screening). The psychiatric evaluations of Antarctic candidates consist of four parts: (1) a questionnaire, (2) a psychological test, the widely-used Minnesota Multiphasic Personality Inventory (MMPI), (3) an interview by a psychologist, and (4) an interview by a psychiatrist. The objectives of the evaluation are to determine if the applicant has a major psychiatric disorder that would render the individual unfit for assignment and to identify any significant character pathology or traits that would make the person unsuitable for the special conditions of isolated and confined living at a remote-duty station. Comdr. Nancy Bakalar, a Navy psychiatrist, has identified key interview questions that can reveal valuable insights about a candidate's suitability for remote duty. Dr. Bakalar encourages screeners to ask applicants about their employment history, the circumstances of significant others and their opinions about the applicant's decision to volunteer for the duty, and if the applicant is fully aware of the conditions at Antarctic stations. The screeners are also encouraged to ask the candidate about any financial or marital problems, previous psychological conditions, alcohol and drug use, and special personal requirements (e.g., hobbies, religion). Dr. Bakalar has found it particularly useful to ask applicants to describe the most distressing events in their lives and how they got through the difficult times. She also recommends asking applicants to describe how they might respond to hypothetical situations in Antarctica, such as having to live with an extremely unpleasant roommate. Much like Shackleton did many years ago, the evaluators use the responses to their questions to determine if an applicant's defenses or coping mechanisms are suitable for the special conditions of long-duration isolation and confinement. There is general agreement that mature coping mechanisms include sublimation, anticipation, suppression, humor, and altruism; other defenses, such as projection, hypochondriasis, passive-aggressive behavior, displacement, reaction formation, and psychotic denial, are considered to be immature, neurotic, or psychotic, depending on the severity of the maladaptive mechanism.

The evaluators review the MMPI results for each applicant and note any elevated subscales. They base the applicant's score on the combination of questionnaire, test, and interview data. In this process, the evaluators are instructed to place an emphasis on their "countertransference" to the applicant (Bakalar 1991). Countertransference is a psychiatrist's way of describing if he or she liked the applicant. Although this might be considered an excessively subjective measure, it must be recalled that the Navy research, discussed above, clearly indicates that success at remote-duty stations is linked to an individual's "likability." Applicants' scores range from a high of 6, reserved for well-adjusted, mature individuals, to a low of 1 for applicants determined to have severe pathology; the latter score is rarely assigned. Many applicants who receive a score of 4 or 5 are selected for Antarctic duty, along with those who receive the highest score. Dr. Glogower (personal communication) explained that the evaluators would like to restrict selection to applicants scoring a 5 or 6, but must accept some candidates who score

4 in order to fill staffing requirements. Table 3 provides a summary of the scoring system used by the Navy psychiatrists and psychologists.

The psychiatric evaluations performed by the Navy are essentially screening procedures, rather than personnel selection. The procedures successfully screen out candidates afflicted with gross pathology and others who have behavioral traits and personal problems that render them unsuitable for remote-duty. Whether or not an individual possesses the technical skills required for a particular job at an Antarctic station can be determined objectively, but technical performance is only a small portion of the minimum requirements for remote duty. For example, it can be assumed from objective criteria that a candidate has the skills and knowledge necessary to build a wall, but whether he or she can get along with others in isolation is a separate, and perhaps more important, question, and one that requires the subjective judgments of the evaluators to answer.

Logo of Operation Deep Freeze.

Table 3. Scoring System Used in Psychiatric Evaluations of
Candidates for the U.S. Antarctic Program

Score	Description of Applicant Based on Psychiatric Evaluation
6	Well-adjusted, mature individuals who give clear indication that they employ mature defenses effectively. They lack obvious psychopathology, and are likable or very likable during the interview.
5	Well-adjusted individuals with no major psychopathology who use mature or neurotic defenses. Countertransference is neutral to mildly positive.
4	Marginal applicants who are technically competent, perhaps have wintered over previously, who are marginally well adjusted and who have no significant social factors indicating that they should not be selected. Counter-transference is neutral to mildly negative.
3	An ambiguous score that is discouraged.
2	The individual is unfit or unsuitable because of psychopathology or severely negative behavioral traits.
1	Severe psychopathology.

Source: N. L. Bakalar, *Deep Freeze Evaluations*. Bethesda, Md.: Department of Psychiatry, National Naval Medical Center, 1991.

Dr. Glogower is convinced that most people, even many who are involved in the management and selection of remote-duty personnel, lack an appreciation for the psychological issues associated with small, heterogeneous groups living and working in isolation and confinement. Naturally, as a psychologist, Glogower might be expected to emphasize the importance of psychological factors, but his argument is convincing: Whenever debriefing accounts indicate that a remote group suffered a particularly bad year or when a crisis occurs at a station, the underlying cause is always attributable to social compatibility or emotional stability problems (i.e., psychological problems); bad winter-over experiences and crises at the stations are never caused by a lack of technical competence.

Glogower made the important suggestion that it would be far better to select individuals for remote-duty assignments who possess interpersonal skills and who get along with each other, rather than to focus on technical competence as the primary selection criterion. He offered a metaphor to explain his position: A baseball player might be a terrific hitter, batting .350 or so, but he is not very useful to his team if he is a poor fielder or has personality problems that annoy his teammates or get him into trouble. Further, the ideal team is composed of .270 hitters who can also field and run, who foster group solidarity, get along with each other, and function as a team. It is important to note in this regard that, under most circumstances, when an individual is found to be incompatible or disruptive to a group, he or she can be removed from the assignment (e.g., transferred, traded, fired, promoted). The managers of remote-duty posts, such as Antarctic stations, however, are denied this common remedy. The inability to remove a disruptive member of a remote-duty crew distinguishes personnel selection for this type of operation from all other personnel selection efforts. For future long-duration expeditions, this unique limitation requires that the interpersonal compatibility of candidate crew members be unequivocally established prior to the mission.

The candidates who are found acceptable for Antarctic duty, and tend to perform well "on the ice" are usually a little older than the average age of the crew, have had prior Antarctic or overseas work experience, possess at least normal socially adaptive skills and mature or minimally neurotic defenses, and have their personal lives in order (i.e., families will accept the separation). Glogower listed what he considers to be the minimum personal requirements for selection for remote duty. The candidate must

- be technically competent
- maintain motivation and productivity
- be healthy—no medical condition that would compromise effectiveness
- be free of psychological problems that would affect performance
- develop harmonious working relationships
- possess a sense of teamwork
- possess a sense of community
- possess effective conflict resolution skills
- be flexible

To this list might be added the adaptive personal characteristics identified by other Antarctic psychologists, such as emotional control, tact, self-sufficiency, and a sense of humor. Also, to be successful in isolation and confinement one should be easily entertained.

The personal quality of being easily entertained concerns a major paradox involved in the selection of personnel for remote-duty assignments, and it requires an explanation. "Action-oriented" people tend to volunteer for special work, such as staffing an Antarctic research station, going on an expedition, or serving as crew of a spacecraft, but the conditions of long-duration isolation and confinement favor just the opposite type of person from those who are normally attracted to these forms of special duty. Dr. Sidney Blair, the Navy psychiatrist who coordinated personnel selection for Operation Deep Freeze during the decade prior to Dr. Glogower's tenure, described this paradox at a U.S. Air Force Academy symposium:

> When I am asked, "If you want to be 100 percent sure that a person will adjust [to Antarctic duty], what do you look for?" My usual answer is that I look for somebody who loves their work. That is probably the most important thing on the list of positive factors. They have to love their work. It is almost all right if they love their work to the exclusion of everything else. However, it is not quite all right, because you do not get to work all of the time down there. There are other times that you have to fill. There are *a lot* of other times that you must fill. And, that leads to the kind of personality that I would look for if I were going to be 100 percent certain that the person would adjust. That person would be dull. Boring, to me. People who are very interested in art and music, who are highly interactive, who need a lot of supplies from outside in the way of things that interest them and excite them, simply have a low probability of doing well down there. Behavioral scientists like these people. They are, themselves, interested in art and music and all those things, and when a volunteer comes to an interview and says, "I want to go to Antarctica and I'm interested and excited about all this," the evaluator is likely to say, "Yes, you should go." But many of our misselects are selected on that basis. The inexperienced interviewer believes that these volunteers are marvelously interesting people, but actually what is required [in remote duty] is to be able to watch the same movie six, or eight, or ten times in a row and not feel the least bit uncomfortable about it. If they can talk to the same people day after day and really not have much new to talk about, they are probably going to adjust very well. It is true that we do send down a lot of interesting people because interesting people tend to want to go to Antarctica, and they can and do adjust well. But, if you wanted to be 100 percent sure that they would adjust well, you would choose people who were very dull. (Blair, 1986, 12–13)

Dr. Blair has identified one of the most important issues concerning the selection of personnel for remote duty. In this regard, Fridtjof Nansen found the inactivity of his confinement onboard the *Fram* to be the most difficult aspect of his entire expedition. Naturally, one who conceives, plans, then leads dangerous expeditions is likely to be action oriented and unaccustomed to forced inactivity. Nansen frequently wrote in his journal that, to survive isolation and confinement, one must learn to be idle without feeling guilty. He again reflected on the topic when he read the motto for the day in his English almanac on 10 December 1893: "He is happy whose circumstances suit his temper; but he is more excellent who can suit his temper to any circumstances." This brief passage from the philosopher, Hume, essentially conveys the key to effective personnel selection for remote-duty assignments.

The Navy reviewers are responsible for evaluating both civilian and military personnel for Antarctic duty; the psychiatric evaluation is the final step in the selection process. Dr. Glogower reported that the rejection rate declined from about 20 percent in 1985 to about 10 percent in 1994. He attributes this decline to guidance provided by the Navy psychologists to the contractor responsible for hiring the civilian support personnel and to the fact that there are now more candidates with previous winter-over experience (i.e., applicants who have demonstrated their abilities to perform well under the conditions). Despite use of the MMPI and the 6-point scale, however, the Navy's procedures are not very different from Shackleton's methods. They share the same objective and focus—to select individuals, by personal interview, who possess the personality characteristics that facilitate adaptation to the special conditions of remote duty. This is as it should be; the personal interview is the ideal method for evaluating individuals for assignments that involve long-duration isolation and confinement. An experienced evaluator can readily detect most disqualifying conditions during an interview by referring to an applicant's questionnaire responses and asking general and specific questions. In contrast, personality tests designed to identify pathology can be faked because the socially desirable responses are usually apparent to job applicants (Dolgin and Gibb 1989). For this reason, personality tests have limited value in personnel selection of this kind. If an applicant's pathology is apparent from MMPI results, it would also be obvious to a human evaluator, who has the added benefits of additional skills, probing questions, and an opportunity for firsthand observation of the applicant in an actual interpersonal exchange .

The personal interview is particularly appropriate for psychological evaluations for remote duty because the interview provides an opportunity to apply informally the highly reliable "job-sample" approach to personnel selection. The job-sample approach requires an applicant to perform a task or tasks abstracted from the actual work required on the job. Job-sample personnel selection tests typically provide the most valid predictions of job performance of all selection methods because the test is directly linked to on-the-job requirements. Examples of job-sample personnel measures are typing tests for clerical jobs, tests involving the interpretation of diagrams and schematics for troubleshooting jobs, and physical fitness tests for certain military specialties. Because interpersonal relations are a fundamental component of the "job" of isolated and confined crews, a well-conducted personal interview represents a sample of that "work" (even though the reviewers do not label the interviews as job sample tests). Shackleton recognized the relationship between a volunteer's performance during an interview and his likely performance later when confined with others for long periods under extremely austere conditions; so do Navy psychiatrists and psychologists. The Navy reviewers for Operation Deep Freeze have applied this approach with the result of effectively screening gross pathology from Antarctic duty for more than three decades. The reviewers also attempt to screen out applicants who are otherwise inappropriate for the special duty and to identify candidates who are particularly well suited. Navy psychologists and psychiatrists believe that their methods could achieve actual selection, rather than screening, if larger numbers of candidates were available.

It is important to consider the potential consequences of misselecting personnel for remote duty or accepting marginal individuals. It is extremely rare for gross pathology to go undetected during the Navy evaluations, and, according to Dr. Glogower (personal communication), "If you are not crazy before you go to Antarctica, the experience will not make you crazy." The reviewers, however, are frequently required to accept personnel who are not optimal candidates, and all personnel tend to suffer as a consequence. For example, a "crisis" occurred at one of the stations when a crewman complained to his superiors, 10,000 miles away, that he was being ignored and excluded from station activities by other members of the small group. The reviewers found this reaction to be understandable, even expected, because the applicant was identified as a "loner" during the evaluation interviews and for that reason was considered not to be an optimal candidate for the special duty, but he was selected anyway. Apparently, the crewman's loner activities were interpreted as rejection by the other members of the group, so they responded by rejecting him. The pattern of withdrawal, rejection, and further withdrawal reached crisis proportions even before the midpoint of the mission.

SELECTION OF PERSONNEL FOR FUTURE LONG-DURATION EXPEDITIONS

Santy (1993) and Santy and Jones (1994) review the various selection procedures currently used by NASA and by the space agencies of Europe, Russia, and Japan to select space crew. The NASA approach to psychological evaluation appears to be consistent with at least part of the expeditionary and Antarctic approaches described above; that is, the procedures focus on identifying pathological psychiatric conditions, in the past or present, that would disqualify an applicant from further consideration. Santy and Jones (1994) describe this "select-out" procedure as similar to the process by which other disqualifying medical disorders, such as cardiovascular disease, are diagnosed by the physician; NASA appropriately includes the psychiatric evaluation as part of the overall medical examination of an astronaut candidate.

In contrast, the European and Japanese approaches to space crew selection have emphasized psychological, or "select-in" criteria, rather than psychiatric screening. The European Space Agency's measures include psychological tests, but more emphasis is placed on psychomotor and cognitive performance than on an assessment of personality traits and behaviors. More important, the ESA selection program is heavily influenced by the northern European emphasis on looking to blood chemistry for indicators of an individual's likely future performance, especially under stress. Researchers in this field of psychoneuroendocrinology believe that they have found at least three endocrine factors with specific relations to psychological traits. Værnes et al. (1988) report that a catecholamine factor relates to ambition and time urgency; a cortisol factor relates to a high-defense mechanism (individuals with high-defense strategies, they believe, tend to perform inadequately in threatening situations); and the relation between an "androgen and estrogen factor" and personality is believed to be less stable. The researchers assert that these factors might be activated and sustained when an individual is confronted with unsolved problems, which could lead to pathology.

Japanese selection procedures include the process of interviewing an applicant's family and fellow workers to determine whether they approve of the candidate's application. Unfortunately, the European and Japanese measures applied to selection of space crew personnel have been based on assumptions about what personal qualities are appropriate for the work; the measures have not been scientifically validated. In fact, Santy and Jones (1994) report that little in the way of data exists to justify the validity of the measures, even in the field of European aviation selection from which the measures were derived.

Much has been written in recent years about the methodological problems and limited predictive validities of personality tests for selecting aviators in the United States (Dolgin and Gibb 1989). Also, the lack of validity for selection tests used by space agencies, and the emphasis on blood chemistry in some programs are reasons to be concerned about the efficacy of the personnel selection criteria and procedures that would be applied if a long-duration space expedition were to be organized in the near future. The problem is that the overwhelming need of personnel psychologists to quantify might have distorted their perception of the issues. It is a circumstance described by the cliché, "If your only tool is a hammer, all of your problems look like nails."

It is possible that some psychologists and neuroendocrinologists have been blinded to the most reliable measure of future performance by focusing on their traditional secondary measures, or indicators of likely behavior. That is, the developers of selection criteria have administered paper-and-pencil psychological tests, and even measured the levels of certain enzymes associated with nerve function, in order to infer how a candidate might perform in the future. For a variety of reasons, many selection experts have failed to recognize that the best measure of behavior is behavior, not a candidate's blood chemistry or responses to a psychological test, regardless of how well designed or culturally unbiased the test might be. In short, the fundamental lesson of applied psychology—the most valid predictor of future performance is past performance—seems to have been excluded from the process; but, how can an individual's past performance be used in a process designed to select the most appropriate candidates for future long-duration expeditions?

During World War II, U.S. military forces devoted substantial effort in identifying individual capabilities and characteristics that contribute to success as an aviator. Many types of testing methods were used, and new ones were developed specifically to assist in the selection of pilots and other specialists. The various methods included measures of psychomotor and cognitive function; personality tests; and questionnaires designed to elicit background (biographical) information about applicants. Following assignment, the test responses and biographical data (biodata) of applicants were compared with measures of actual technical performance to identify any correlations. An affirmative response to one particular question on the biodata form was a better predictor of success as a pilot than any personality measure or combination of measures attempted during the war. The question was, "Have you ever built a model airplane that flew?" Similarly, a biographical question administered to Navy personnel provided the best predictor of success as a marine mammal handler during the Vietnam War: "Have you ever maintained a saltwater aquarium?" In most applications of this technique, responses to more than one biodata question, and usually several, are found to correlate with successful performance in a job.

Radloff and Helmréich (1968) address the issue of biodata in their seminal work concerning adaptation to the isolation, confinement, and other stressors of life in the underwater habitat *Sealab*. They find that personality tests, what the authors call "psychologists' most cherished tools," failed to predict adjustment to *Sealab*, whereas biodata, such as an individual's age, birth order, and the size of his hometown, did correlate significantly with adjustment (i.e., older, later-born divers from small towns adjusted better than younger firstborns from larger communities).

There have been several dramatically effective applications of the biodata approach to personnel selection, but the technique has not been widely adopted by selection managers and researchers (Owens 1983). Biodata do not conform to traditional psychometric approaches to selection, which might be the primary impediment to full development of the method. The biodata approach to selection, however, is particularly appropriate for identifying promising candidates to serve as crew in remote-duty environments. Indications of technical competence could be obtained from objective information (e.g., resumes, accomplishments), as is the current practice, but indications of likely interpersonal performance obtained from biodata could be used both to screen candidates and to select the most appropriate individuals for the special duty.

Biodata are currently used to screen, or select out, astronaut applicants in the same manner as used by the psychiatric evaluators for Antarctic duty (e.g., history of mental illness, financial problems). Using biodata to select in, however, is another matter. From the published information, it would appear that NASA has used flight experience of a pilot as a select-in, biodata criterion.[1] Emphasizing aviation experience is presumably based on the similarities between operating an aircraft and operating a spacecraft. Although test pilot experience was clearly relevant to requirements for the early astronauts, it is reasonable to question the relevance of aviation, especially single-seat aircraft experience, to the requirements of future long-duration space expeditions, which will resemble sea voyages much more than aircraft flights. Aviator-type skills and abilities, of course, will be handy on space missions, especially under emergency conditions caused by the failure of automated guidance or propulsion systems, but social skills and certain personal traits will be required on a daily basis and will increase in importance with mission duration. Most important, certain social traits and behavioral traits have been clearly linked to mission success. Experience as a member of a successful team or crew would appear to be far more important to future astronaut effectiveness than experience as the pilot of an aircraft.

The question remains: What are the life experiences that might correlate with successful adjustment to and performance in the isolated and confined conditions of future spacecraft and lunar bases? For answers to this question, it is helpful to recall that Gunderson found the behavioral traits of emotional control, social compatibility, and technical performance to correlate with success in Antarctic duty, as measured by peer and supervisor ratings. In a similar fashion, Rose et al. (1994) have investigated the psychological predictors of astronaut effectiveness. The study involved sixty-five of the eighty-four members of the Astronaut Corps (in 1990) and completion of five separate personality batteries; peer and supervisor ratings were again used as dependent measures of individual effectiveness. Of the twenty-eight personality subscales studied, Rose and colleagues find five to be related to astronaut effectiveness:

1. high negative expressivity–negative communion (subordinate)
2. low impatience and irritability
3. low openness (to new ideas, approaches, and experiences)
4. low negative instrumentality (arrogance, greed, egotism)
5. high agreeableness

The investigators find that high levels of the undesirable personality characteristics (e.g., impatience/irritability, negative instrumentality) are present in both "more effective" and "less effective" astronauts. Low levels of the undesirable characteristics, however, are found only among the "most effective" astronauts, as rated by their supervisors and peers. In other words, many of the "less effective" and some of the "more effective" astronauts have high levels of the negative personality traits, but only "more effective" astronauts are characterized by low levels of the negative traits. In particular, only "more effective" astronauts are rated as "low" in impatience and irritability and "low" in the characteristics associated with negative instrumentality (e.g., egotistic, boastful, hostile, arrogant).

Two of the subscales, negative expressivity and low openness, require some elaboration. Four scales were used to assess negative expressivity-negative communion; individuals were rated in terms of being spineless, subordinate, servile, and gullible. Although there are clearly negative connotations to these descriptors, the investigators interpreted this result to mean that individuals who rate themselves as more servile or subordinate may be more other-directed (i.e., concerned with the needs and desires of their colleagues) than those who are rated lower on these scales. Low openness was the only indicator that seemed implausible to the investigators. High openness is affirmed by high scores on items such as "I often enjoy playing with theories or abstract ideas." In contrast, low openness is affirmed by high scores on items such as "I don't like to waste my time daydreaming," and "Once I find the right way to do something, I stick to it." Low openness was not expected to be a predictor of effectiveness. This result probably reflects a theme of pragmatism and industriousness in astronaut culture, rather than the narrow-mindedness implied by the label assigned to the subscale.

With the exception of low openness, the five variables that Rose et al. find to have significant correlations with astronaut effectiveness are related to an individual's interpersonal sensitivity and concern for others. The importance of other-directed qualities to ratings of effectiveness is consistent with the results of the earlier Navy research concerning Antarctic winter-over personnel (i.e., social compatibility, emotional control). Together, the results of these studies suggest that other-directed personality traits and interpersonal skills should be included as personnel selection criteria in choosing candidates for future space missions. It also appears that these behavioral factors will assume additional importance as space expeditions increase in duration.

Based on the results of the Navy research and more recent studies of astronaut effectiveness, it is possible to specify the behavioral traits and interpersonal skills necessary to perform well as a member of the crew on a long-duration expedition. Those traits are social compatibility or likability, emotional control, patience, tolerance of others, self-confidence without egotism, the capacity to subordinate routinely one's own interests to work harmoniously as member of a team, a sense of humor, and the ability to be easily entertained. Each of these characteristics might be shaped, or at least reflected, by life experiences. For example, the number of close friends that a candidate possesses might provide indications of his or her likability, or employment and marital history might provide information about an individual's emotional control, patience, and ability to work effectively with others. A properly conducted research program would lead to the identification of biographical information that reliably predicts successful performance in remote-duty environments. Biodata could be used as screening criteria, as is the current practice, and as select-in criteria when the measures have been validated, but even validated criteria based on biodata will be insufficient to ensure that the most appropriate personnel are selected for future long-duration expeditions.

High-fidelity simulations of expeditions, staffed by candidate crew members, should be performed as the final step in the selection and assignment process. High-fidelity simulations will provide crew candidates with opportunities to demonstrate to themselves and to mission managers that they can adapt to the many unique stressors associated with living and working in close proximity to others in isolation and confinement for long-durations. Like arduous special operations training in the military, the recommended space simulations will help to identify and disqualify those individuals who would be likely to fail under operational conditions. Ideally, the simulations should be as long as the planned expeditions; realistically, simulations of at least six months' duration should be conducted for formal evaluation of candidate performance in preparation for a two- or three-year expedition to Mars. Any personal traits and behaviors that would render an individual unsuitable for long-duration missions probably would emerge within six months of isolation and confinement. At least two simulations should be conducted concurrently, with the most appropriate candidates for an actual expedition selected from among the crews of the simulated missions. The long-duration simulations will result in individuals removing themselves from candidacy, as well as in the identification of candidates who would be both more and less effective under operational conditions.

The approach to personnel selection described in this section and outlined below can ensure that actual performance of candidate crew members will be evaluated. This approach avoids reliance on questionable secondary indicators of likely performance by focusing on the relevant and actual behavior of candidates. In this regard, the approach is consistent with the procedures followed by the most successful expedition leaders of the past and with the fundamental lesson of applied psychology.

RECOMMENDATIONS

The following recommendations relate to issues associated with personnel selection criteria for future long-duration expeditions.

- Develop a personnel selection program that is based on the behavioral principle that the best predictor of future performance is past performance.

- Avoid over-reliance on psychological tests of personality and evaluations of blood chemistry; personality tests can provide unreliable indicators of performance, and differential blood chemistry might not result in differential behavior.

- Emphasize actual performance of relevant behavior:
  - technical competence and task motivation
  - biodata indicators of relevant skills and traits

- interview responses
- peer and supervisor ratings
- performance and adjustment during high fidelity simulations

- Identify technically competent candidates, but select individuals who exhibit the following appropriate social skills and behavioral traits:
  - social compatibility, or likability
  - emotional control
  - patience
  - tolerance (i.e., low irritability)
  - self-confidence (without being egotistic, arrogant, or boastful)
  - subordination of one's own interests to the goals of the team
  - agreeable and flexible
  - practical and hard-working

To the above scientifically established traits might be added the following items identified anecdotally:
  - tactfulness in interpersonal relations
  - effective conflict resolution skills
  - sense of humor
  - the ability to be easily entertained

- Conduct high-fidelity simulations of planned expeditions, as the final step in the selection process, for formal evaluation of the relevant performance of candidate crew members before final assignments are made.

CHAPTER 16

PRIVACY AND PERSONAL SPACE

The bunks were each individual's private chamber in the close confines of the winter burrow. Most of the men decorated their spaces with wall hangings. Some built elaborate shelves and arrayed privacy curtains. The beds were sometimes refuges during free time in the always-dark hours the clock said was day. After lights-out at night, men lit candles on shelves over their bunks and for an hour or two read or wrote entries in pocket-sized, leather-covered diaries that had been provided.

—Rodgers's (1990) description of
Little America, Antarctica, 1929

The most frequently asked question regarding the habitability of remote-duty environments concerns spatial requirements; that is, how much privacy and personal space are necessary to support human adjustment and sustained performance? The answer to this question is of critical importance to designers because more space means higher costs for both equipment and transportation. The spatial requirements of functional areas can be defined objectively by conducting task analyses and applying anthropometric standards and ergonomic design principles. In other words, knowledge of reach envelopes, crew traffic patterns, and the like can be used to specify, with precision, the volumetric requirements for task performance and the associated interior architecture. At the heart of this question, however, is the assumption that *additional* space is required to satisfy the crew's subjective requirements for privacy and personal space in a confined habitat.

Most designers and behavioral scientists have assumed that a relationship exists between mission duration and spatial requirements in isolation and confinement. Spacecraft design studies and conditions analogous to spacecraft and planetary bases have shown a nearly linear relationship between duration of tour and sleep chamber or bunk volume; values ranged from a low of about 30 cubic feet for submarine bunks to a high of about 250 cubic feet for a 1972 design of a lunar habitability system. It is reasonable to question the assumptions about the subjective requirements of privacy and personal space and the relationship between duration of confinement and spatial requirements because the implications of the assumptions directly influence the estimated costs of planned expeditions. Certain expeditions might be considered unfeasible if the costs are believed to be too great. It would be unfortunate if the estimates were based on inaccurate assumptions about how much privacy and personal space are required to support a human crew.

Perhaps the uncertainties about crew privacy and personal space requirements are attributable to the fact that privacy and personal space are really two distinct concepts, with separate sets of behavioral implications, yet the terms are almost always combined in discussions of the issues. It is important to recognize that privacy is the quality of being apart from the company or observation of others, whereas personal space implies a human need for territoriality. This chapter discusses these two related yet distinct sets of concepts and requirements in separate sections.

IMPORTANCE OF PRIVACY

Evidence for the need to remove oneself occasionally from the company of others is found in all conditions of isolation and confinement. For example, onboard all vessels, from the humblest fishing boat to the grandest supertanker or aircraft carrier, crew members periodically seek the solitude of the stern, bow, flying bridge, or favorite compartment below decks to be apart from their shipmates. The constant interpersonal contact in a confined environment is highly stimulating; this effect is compounded in small crews, which can result in tedium and fixations on the annoying traits of one's comrades. The occasional withdrawal from the high stimulation of constant interpersonal contact is a normal and healthy coping mechanism that helps individuals to adjust to the many stressors of isolated and confined living. Cook ([1900] 1980) describes his desire to withdraw, therapeutically, from the company of his crew mates onboard the *Belgica*:

> If we could only get away from each other for a few hours at a time, we might learn to see a new side and take fresh interest in our comrades; but this is not possible. The truth is, that we are as tired of each other's company as we are of the cold monotony of the black night and of the unpalatable sameness of our food. (Pp. 290–91)

The crew of the *Belgica* was modern in its international composition, but the crew was organized in the traditional fashion, with the sailors berthed together in the forecastle (located in the bow) and the officers and scientists occupying compartments adjacent to the saloon, the all-purpose dining room and communal area, located in the main cabin toward the stern of the ship.[1]

In contrast to the *Belgica*, Fridtjof Nansen designed the *Fram* with the crew's quarters surrounding the saloon so that all members of the crew could live and eat together in the main cabin. This egalitarian approach contributed to the success of the Norwegian Polar Expedition, but even the humanist Nansen, who wrote frequently in his journal of the pleasant company and comradeship onboard the *Fram*, found it necessary to get away from the constant social contact among the ship's small society. In fact, there is an abrupt change in the tone of Nansen's journal entries and an improvement in his spirits when he reports that he converted a small deck cabin from storage space into a personal study and laboratory while the ship was locked in the polar ice cap. Although he worked long hours in the deck cabin, he also enjoyed it as a refuge:

> At least double the amount of work will be done if this cabin can be used in winter, and I can sit up here instead of in the midst of the racket below. I have such comfortable times of it now, in peace and quietness, letting my thoughts take their way unchecked. (Nansen 1897, vol. 1, 532)

Other members of the crew found various means of getting away. The engineer spent time in his engine room every day of the three-year expedition, as he meticulously disassembled, lubricated, and reassembled the *Fram's* machinery. Other crew members devised tasks that would require their occasional separation from shipmates; Captain Sverdrup even took long solitary walks on the ice in subzero temperatures.

This apparent need to get away from constant close contact with others is also observed at Antarctic stations. Nearly all personnel at U.S. stations are housed in two- and four-person rooms; two people to a room is the objective. This arrangement is viewed as a reasonable trade-off between maximum privacy and personal safety; if something were to go wrong with an individual in a private room it might not be discovered until too late. The assignment of two people to a room is a form of enforced buddy system to help ensure physical and psychological survival in a hostile environment. The roommates are expected to look after each other to ensure that no one slips unnoticed into illness or depression.

Some Antarctic personnel find sufficient private time in their shared quarters; for others, a laboratory or work area provides the solitude they need. Still others find truly creative ways to transport themselves, at least mentally, from the mind-numbing sameness of isolated and confined living. For example, an experienced Seabee described turning the heater in his room on high, occasionally, then looking at photographs and imagining he was with his family at the beach in California. The master chief called this a "low-tech holodeck experience," a reference to a facility onboard the fictional starship *Enterprise* that is used by crew members for entertainment and mental escape.

All of the experienced Antarctic personnel whom I interviewed agreed that it is important for individuals to be able to get away from others from time to time. The Navy physicians, psychologists, and psychiatrists who work with remote-duty personnel consider this to be a normal coping mechanism that can help an individual to regain "psychological homeostasis" by being understimulated for a while. Some people seem to require solitude more than others, but, for some individuals, withdrawal from social contact can become pathological. The buddy system helps, but station leaders, medical officers, and MWR specialists must remain vigilant throughout the year to ensure that no member of a station crew slips into a pattern of extreme withdrawal, called "cocooning."

Antarctic experts recommend that provisions should be made to permit isolated and confined personnel opportunities to get away from their fellow crew members. The experts strongly urge that a compartment be provided for personnel to obtain the privacy needed for occasional periods of quiet contemplation, reflection, or examination of their own adjustments to the conditions, or simply to make journal entries or compose letters without interruption. The compartment does not need to be large, perhaps just large enough for two individuals to hold a relatively private conversation or to play a game of chess. The compartment should be separate from the wardroom/galley and sleeping chambers. It might be viewed as a reading room or study to be used for task preparation, and it would be the logical repository for the habitat's library of digital and paper volumes. Although the crew would appreciate a window in the compartment, probably it would be viewed by designers as an unacceptable luxury.

It is important to understand that if a special compartment for privacy is not provided onboard spacecraft or at other remote-duty habitats, crew members will find their own areas to get away from their comrades. Some will retreat to work areas or reconfigure equipment and structures to obtain the moments of privacy required to maintain their adjustment to the stressors of isolated and confined living. Other crew members will probably locate and use other areas for this purpose, even when a special library compartment or something similar is provided. The point must be emphasized, however, that negative behavioral consequences are likely to accrue if there are no opportunities for individual privacy.

The sharing or rotational use of sleep chambers, known as "hot bunking," is considered by all observers to be the option of last resort. In any situation where it is employed, hot bunking is thoroughly despised for a variety of reasons. The primary reasons relate to the importance of privacy and a sense of personal space. The exclusive territory of one's bunk assumes added significance under conditions of isolation and confinement. That territory is a refuge from the cumulative stresses of the mission and near-constant interpersonal exchange.

Negative consequences to an absence of privacy were observed during a full-mission simulation of military remote-duty environments. One participating crew member found it necessary to withdraw from the simulation after only seven days because he could not tolerate the absence of privacy within the small habitat, where he lived with four other men. He shared a bunk on a rotational basis with another member of the crew, which meant that, for twelve hours each day, he had no place to get away from his comrades for more than a brief visit to the lavatory. Although his normal work prior to the simulation involved regular periods of isolation and confinement, he had never been confined for more than a few days at a time. He discovered much about himself by participating in the simulation; in particular, he found that he requires time alone to recover from the cumulative stresses of close interpersonal contact. Many otherwise qualified candidates for long-duration expeditions would experience similar reactions to extremely confined conditions. This is another reason for conducting high-fidelity simulations of planned long-duration expeditions, with participation of candidate crew members. The simulations can help to determine appropriate crew assignments for the mission.

Another aspect of isolation and confinement concerns the difficulty that individuals have in maintaining the security of private information. Winter-over personnel reported in interviews that everyone knows everyone else's business at an Antarctic station and that it is nearly impossible to maintain a secret. Perhaps most important, because of the proximity in which the crew members live, raised voices, especially during arguments, are often heard by the entire crew. People new to Antarctica are advised of this condition before they arrive, and efforts are made to sensitize individuals to the privacy requirements of others. In particular, they are instructed to provide clear cues when they wish to be left alone and to respect the cues exhibited by others.

NEED FOR PERSONAL SPACE

Nearly a quarter of a century ago, the National Academy of Sciences (1972) published a volume titled *Human Factors in Long-Duration Space-flight*, in which the authors report, "Needs for privacy, solitude, and territoriality become accentuated, even in short-term confined living and tend to intensify over time." In an earlier work, Fraser (1968a) addresses the issue of territoriality by referring to the sailor in his bunk and the soldier in his barracks room as having little privacy, but the individual's bunk, duffel bag, and foot locker are recognized by others in those environments as personal property and personal territory that can be invaded only with permission. This view of personal space is clearly evident onboard submarines, where a man's bunk, cramped though it is, serves as a place for sleep, reading, letter writing, and conversation. "Privacy" curtains are frequently drawn to shut out the light and to avoid visual inspection by others, but more fundamental is the perception among submariners that one's bunk is a "home" and personal territory.

Roger Dunham (1996) describes the importance of his "rack" (bunk) on board a special-purpose submarine in 1968:

> My rack was far more than just a place to sleep. When we left dry dock, it would become my sanctuary from the rest of the submarine world. I was assigned the middle rack; by lifting myself up and squeezing sideways into the coffinlike opening

and then reaching out and pulling my curtain shut, I was suddenly enclosed in a world of privacy that was unavailable anywhere else on the boat. (P. 24)

The importance of the bunk as personal space is reflected in the fact that one of the most disruptive events possible onboard a submarine is the theft of an item from a bunk, where many personal belongings are usually stored in and under the mattress. Reportedly, the entire crew is offended by such an egregious violation of individual personal space.

Although violations of personal territory can have serious consequences in isolation and confinement, some behavioral scientists have pointed to the positive aspects of territorial behavior; they believe that territoriality can facilitate group harmony essentially by the establishment of "rules" that help to govern interpersonal behaviors. For example, Altman (1973) writes, "One major function of territorial behavior is to set boundaries among group members, to facilitate and establish bases of interaction, and to smooth out functioning in a way analogous to social norms and conventions."

Providing personal space for crew members of space expeditions has been a part of every serious design study. Nearly all of the designs have included private sleep chambers for crew members, but there has been considerable variation in the volumes assumed to be appropriate for the conditions. Fraser (1968a) suggests that it would seem reasonable for private quarters to be provided for crew members on long-duration missions, but he laments that no studies had been performed to support the suggestion, nor was it clear how much territory an individual might require. That condition has not changed.

A few of the space analogues that I have studied are characterized by relatively small bunks or sleeping areas. For example, U.S. nuclear submarines provide only about 30 cubic feet of space per bunk, barely enough room for a tall person to stretch out. Also, the *Tektite* and *Sealab II* habitats and the *Ben Franklin* submersible all offered bunk volumes of fewer than 40 cubic feet, which is about the same size as the bunk areas in which commercial saturation divers routinely live for up to thirty days at a time. These "real-world" sleeping spaces are extremely small compared with the sleeping areas included in eighteen spacecraft designs prepared between 1961 and 1984; most of these designs offered sleep chamber volumes of 100–250 cubic feet.[2] The sleeping compartments onboard *Skylab*, another operational system, were of two sizes, 48 cubic feet and 63 cubic feet, which the astronauts reported were adequate for sleeping, but not for use during the day, for example, to read because the only restraint system available was the sleeping bag that hung from the wall. Consequently, if an astronaut wanted to be alone for a while in his quarters, he had to climb into bed. Based on the review of the space station analogues and soft-mockup experiments involving zero-gravity anthropometry, I estimate that a sleep chamber of approximately 84 cubic feet (i.e., 3 x 4 x 7 feet) would be appropriate for an orbital station with tours of duty between 90 and 120 days (Stuster 1986).

The review of voyages of discovery and expeditions, however, offers a new perspective on the issue of personal space requirements. Personal space is always limited onboard ships. For example, the whaling and sealing ships that ventured into the polar regions were mostly utilitarian craft, with few provisions for crew habitability. A young medical student, Stewart Lithgow, described his quarters while serving as ship's surgeon onboard the Dundee whaler *Alexander* in 1853. He had no place to store his clothes and equipment in the small compartment he had been assigned. When he retired for the first evening, he found that his bunk was 12 inches shorter than he was, with vertical dimensions no more generous; he hit his head every time he attempted to sit up. To make matters worse, his cabin mate snored "a dozen trumpets from nasal organs" (quoted in Ross 1985).

Although always at a premium, personal space onboard ships becomes even more scarce when the ship is outfitted for exploration or research purposes. Such was the case onboard the HMS *Beagle* during her famous voyage. The primary purposes of the expedition were to chart the coast of South America and to establish longitude more accurately by performing a series of chronological reckonings around the world. At twenty-two years of age, Charles Darwin was selected to be the ship's naturalist, a decision that greatly influenced the history of science.

The *Beagle* was only 90 feet in length, into which the seventy-four members of the expedition were crowded. The *Beagle*'s crew was indeed cramped when compared, for example, with the *Fram*'s 128-foot length and crew of thirteen, and the *Belgica*'s 110-foot length and crew of eighteen (The *Beagle* sailed in 1831, the *Fram* in 1893, and the *Belgica* in 1898.) Because of the limited space onboard the *Beagle*, Capt. Robert FitzRoy had placed twenty-two chronometers, in beds of sawdust, around the small cabin that he shared with Charles Darwin. As a result, Darwin found his sleeping space so confined that he had to remove a drawer from a locker to accommodate his feet. FitzRoy commented favorably on the naturalist's ability to adapt to the ways of a ship, but Darwin wrote to his former professor, "The absolute want of room is an evil that nothing can surmount" (quoted in Moorehead 1969). Although Charles Darwin seemed to adapt to the conditions during the five-year voyage, he never again left England for the remainder of his seventy-three years.

The *Fram* and the *Belgica* were also crowded, but with fewer people and more supplies than the *Beagle* had carried more than sixty years earlier. Whereas the *Beagle* was reprovisioned during her many stops, the *Fram* and *Belgica* carried all of the supplies that would be needed until each returned to civilization from their polar winters. In his diary, Dr. Frederick Cook wrote of the conditions onboard the *Belgica* as the ship was passing through the Straits of Magellan on 2 December 1897. He described the ship's library, which contained extensive collections of scientific and technical references, fine literature, and volumes on the polar regions, navigation, and other topics. Because of her cosmopolitan crew, the *Belgica*'s library reflected many languages.

Cook ([1900] 1980) also describes the living accommodations onboard the converted Norwegian sealer:

> The quarters for officers and men are fairly good—palatial, as comfort is measured on a sealer. The Commandant has a neat little room behind the mizzenmast, opposite to the kitchen. It is carpeted, nicely furnished, and the walls are artistically bedecked by old Dutch sketches, some paintings, and many photographs of polar scenes. We are so pressed for space, that we are told even this room will be partially filled with coal at Punta Arenas. The cabin is well aft; like the laboratory, the Commandant's room, and the kitchen, it is on deck. As we enter, to the right of the engines are the berths of the Captain and the mates, where they have the soot, steam, and smoke of the engine-room to impress upon them the importance of their work, while the noise is such that prolonged sleep is impossible. The [main] cabin is small, but full of comfort. It is as if eight men stood up around a small table, and a box were built around them, the corners and walls and ceiling being lined with books and instruments. It is not a very joyful place in the tropics, but when an endless sea surrounds us, and the wind is blowing, and the decks are covered with snow, then, with steaming food on the table, we shall find its true value. A door through the left of the cabin opens into an aisle, to the side of

which are the four berths where the devotees of science sleep. The sides are thoughtfully lined with lockers, but every nook, the beds, the ceiling, and at times even the floor, is covered with clothing, instruments and books. After a storm it is a sad rivalry in hopeless entanglement. The forecastle occupies the space between decks from the foremast to the stem. It is large, light, and, compared with the officers' quarters, extremely comfortable. We speak French in the cabin, German and French in the laboratory, and a mixture of English, Norwegian, and German in the forecastle. The life and order on board the *Belgica* is that of a well-regulated family. (Pp. 56–58)

Conditions onboard ships are crowded, but even at their worst ships are spacious compared with conditions endured by explorers on land. The experience of Nansen and Johansen living together for nine months in a 6 x 10–foot hut of stones and walrus hides is described in chapters 3, 6, and 9. Cramped as that hut must have seemed, it was roomy compared with what they experienced on the trail when they shared a small tent just large enough for their sleeping bags. Crowding

Camping on the trail in Antarctica. (Sketch by Dr. Edward A. Wilson, in Cherry-Garrard 1930)

together to eat and sleep in a small tent is the customary practice in polar regions at the end of a long day on the trail; the warmth of others' bodies is appreciated in freezing temperatures. The crowding becomes increasingly tiresome, however, when bad weather prevents the party from breaking camp; and all activities must be conducted within the limited protection of the small tent. The storms can last for several days, and some explorers have found themselves confined for much longer periods. For example, Dr. Alexander Macklin, one of the two physicians in Shackleton's Imperial Trans-Antarctic Expedition, described life in tent no. 5 on the ice floe in the Weddell Sea:

> There are eight of us living in it, packed like sardines.... Clark has an almost intolerable sniff—he sniffs the whole day long and almost drives one mad when one has to remain inside with him. Lees and Worsley do nothing but argue and chatter about trivial matters, and the rest of us can do nothing to escape from it. Lees at night snores abominably, and also Clark and Blackboro, but not so badly.... At times like this, with Clark sniff-sniffing into my ear, my only relief is to take up my diary and write. (Quoted in Lansing [1959] 1994, 118)

Shackleton and his men lived in the ice-beset *Endurance* for more than five months before their ship sank. They then camped on the floes for another five months until the ice began to break up around them, which forced them to take to their open boats. After a terrible week among the ice floes, they finally reached Elephant Island. Living conditions for the eighteen men who remained on the island when the *Caird* departed for help were not much of an improvement over conditions on the ice floes, but, at least, the island was not breaking up beneath their feet. As the members of the Greely Expedition had done years before, Shackleton's men constructed a shelter from one of their boats, and all eighteen lived under the protection of the upturned 22-foot hull for nearly five more months. Macklin wrote of their living conditions:

> It is hard to realize one's position here, living in a smoky, dirty, ramshackle little hut with only just sufficient room to cram us all in; drinking out of a common pot... and laying in close proximity to a man with a large discharging abscess–a horrible existence, but yet we are pretty happy. (Quoted in Lansing [1959] 1994, 212)

Even under routine, rather than emergency, conditions, life on land has been extremely confined for polar explorers. For example, Robert Falcon Scott's hut was a relatively spacious facility by expedition standards; it measured 50 x 25 feet, with 9 feet to the eaves. The two rooms, a wardroom and a bunk area, were defined by stacks of cases of supplies and materials. About twenty-five men of the expedition lived in the hut for more than two years between 1910 and 1913. The hut, especially the bunk area, was extremely crowded, but the men adjusted to the conditions and endured the restricted personal space quite well, just as Nansen and Johansen and Shackleton's men survived, and they performed admirably when required, despite their abominable living conditions.

The many examples of humans enduring extremely austere living conditions that are provided in these pages illustrate the adaptability of our species. Humans have lived crowded together in caves, huts, overturned boats, tents, and ships. They have survived these conditions despite hunger, exposure to the elements, and extreme boredom, among other sources of stress. When necessary, men living under these austere conditions have performed technical tasks with proficiency and have also adjusted to the intensified social environment. Further, at

The bunk area of Scott's hut, McMurdo Sound, Antarctica, 1911. (Photo by Herbert Pointing; courtesy of The Royal Geographical Society, London)

least as many expeditions have been characterized by interpersonal sensitivity and group harmony as by divisiveness. The elasticity of human behavior, demonstrated so clearly by these examples, should give considerable encouragement to the planners and designers of future expeditions. Humans have successfully endured austere conditions for long periods during previous expeditions, and their modern counterparts are likely to do the same, if required. The central question regarding all habitability issues, especially that of personal space, is: Would the crew have performed better had there been a greater provision for the intangibles of habitability? For example, would Nansen and Johansen have performed better in the spring of 1896 if they had been able to build a larger hut the previous year? Or, did the crowded conditions on Elephant Island negatively affect the behavior of Shackleton's crew? These questions cannot be answered, of course, but we do know that the individuals living in these austere conditions adapted to them and performed adequately, even admirably, when required. Many even maintained good humor during the worst of their experiences.

The above discussion must not be interpreted as recommending crowded and austere conditions for future space expeditions. Rather, it is clear that crowding and the absence of personal space impose unfortunate limits on an individual's freedom of movement and privacy and contribute to frustration and irritation in commonplace activities. The absence of private space into which one can retreat, as needed, can exacerbate the friction that normally occurs over trivial issues in isolation and confinement. Knowing that many individuals have endured austere conditions provides encouragement regarding the behavioral issues involved, but that knowledge of human adaptability does not mean that austere conditions are acceptable if optimal human performance is the objective. The unanswerable question remains: What is adequate or optimal?

Most behavioral experts and winter-over personnel agree that individual adjustment to isolation and confinement benefits from the availability of private space. Even though the rooms at Antarctic stations are shared with another person, the bed is one's own, and each person has a place to store belongings and an area to personalize with pictures and other special items. In this personal territory, one can even enjoy quiet moments alone when the roommate is elsewhere. This personal space is greatly appreciated by Antarctic personnel, as are the small bunks on submarines and ships appreciated by the crew members of those vessels.

Private sleep chambers of about 84 cubic feet were recommended for the international space station nearly ten years ago; private chambers are still recommended and the dimension of 84 cubic feet is still believed to be an appropriate size for a zero-gravity facility in which crews routinely serve rotational tours of duty. The English word *routine* is derived from the French for well-traveled path. Optimal conditions (e.g., a relatively spacious private sleep chamber) will be necessary habitability features of a space station when low Earth orbit becomes a well-traveled path. It might be necessary to devote more attention to the habitability of orbital space stations, and perhaps lunar bases, than to longer missions of a more expeditionary nature. Future explorers, for example, the first several crews to make the voyage to Mars, probably would not require the same amenities as their colleagues who are engaged in routine operations. Individuals who will repeatedly occupy a station on a rotational basis likely would soon regard austere conditions as unacceptable. Previous explorers, on the other hand, were willing to accept less than optimal conditions as part of the price they had to pay for being among the first.

Following this line of reasoning, it might be suggested that private crew quarters would be unnecessary on a mission to Mars. Perhaps crew members could simply sling their hammocklike sleep restraints between the exposed plumbing of the spacecraft's interior. This has been the practice onboard Russian space stations, according to French spationaute Jean-Loup Chretien's description of the haphazard sleeping arrangements that he encountered during his visits to *Soyuz-7* and *Mir*. The absence of private quarters was not a problem for pioneer General Chretien during his relatively brief tours in space. In truth, private quarters *are* unnecessary, as demonstrated by the many examples of explorers who have lived in crowded, communal arrangements, such as those in Scott's hut. Humans would indeed survive a mission to Mars without private quarters, but the probability of the crew's adjusting to the conditions and performing well during the mission would be increased if personal space were provided. Perhaps if the Soviet designers of *Mir* had devoted more attention to habitability features, such as private sleep chambers, the cosmonauts might not have experienced the fatigue and motivational problems that have apparently reduced their productive periods to a few hours out of each twenty-four-hour cycle during long missions (Covault 1988).

All of the available evidence suggests that private sleep chambers should be provided for all spacecraft and space habitat crews. Further, although the 84-cubic-foot sleep chambers for space stations, as suggested above, would be greatly appreciated by the crews of interplanetary spacecraft and habitats, the sleep chambers need not be that large to provide substantial benefits to habitability and individual adjustment. Privatized bunks, somewhat larger than those onboard U.S. submarines, might be considered as the absolute minimum size for a long-duration expedition, but a small bunklike chamber might result in serious problems, such as the inability of an individual to dress in private. Slightly larger chambers, measuring 3 x 3 x 7 feet (63 cubic feet), however, would be adequate to accommodate the objective anthropometric requirements of the crew, as well as most of the subjective requirements for privacy and personal space. A 63-cubic-foot volume would not provide much interior storage space, but it would allow for a small computer terminal, reading light, and limited storage for personal items; a 7-foot height or length would accommodate a 95th-percentile male astronaut. Although there is no up or down in the

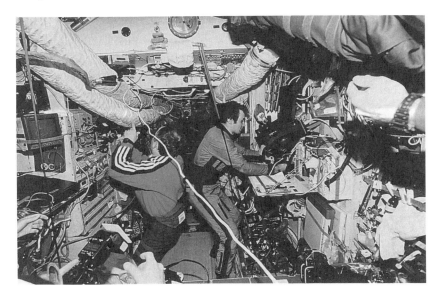

Interior of the Russian *Mir* space station. (Courtesy of NASA)

weightlessness of space, the possibility of disorientation cn awakening would be minimized if sleep chambers were oriented horizontally to the floor of the spacecraft; vertical orientation, with feet toward the floor and the sleep restraint attached to one bulkhead, also would be appropriate for an interplanetary spacecraft. The presence of gravity would require a horizontal orientation, resembling a conventional bunk, at lunar or martian bases.

Others who have considered these issues seriously have different opinions. Some designers believe that the sleep chambers on spacecraft should be designed to accommodate a variety of activities in addition to sleep and other quiet, individual pursuits. For example, it has been suggested that sleep chambers should be large enough to hold more than one person so they can be used for private conversations or group leisure activities. Although relatively large private quarters are an attractive objective, there is a more cost-effective approach to satisfy the subjective habitability requirements. In particular, most potential group activities can be accommodated by providing common areas, such as a wardroom/galley and library, as described in the previous section. Further, reconfigurable sleep chamber designs using collapsible, soundproof partitions would provide the flexibility that some crew members might find necessary, for example, if conjugal couples were to be selected as crew. Providing each crew member with a personal space large enough to accommodate group activities would result in much underused space and intolerable inefficiency.

Also, some designers maintain that a 7-foot ceiling in a vertical sleep chamber would not permit certain activities, particularly donning and doffing garments. Preliminary analyses using zero-gravity anthropometrics indicate that the suggested sleep chamber size would allow relatively easy changing of clothes. Only a few exceptionally tall crew members might be inconvenienced when dealing with pullover garments, and they would have to remove their sweaters and similar apparel before entering their sleep chambers to avoid striking their hands on the ceiling. Sleep chambers smaller than 84 cubic feet, such as the conventional bunk design, would require most dressing and undressing to take place in common areas.

It is important to emphasize that sleep chambers of moderate or small size, such as those recommended in the preceding paragraphs, are appropriate only if there are other areas in the spacecraft or habitat where individuals can occasionally find moments of privacy or opportunities for quiet conversation. In short, it is critical that sleep chamber design be linked to the design of other areas, such as the wardroom/galley and library/task-preparation area. The volume requirements for individual sleep chambers would increase substantially if adequate common areas were not provided for the crew.

RECOMMENDATIONS

Together, privacy and personal space represent one of the most important habitability issues. Design and procedural attention to habitability issues, such as privacy and personal space, significantly increases the likelihood of individual adjustment, accurate and timely task performance, and group productivity in a remote-duty environment. Perhaps more important, procedures and equipment that are designed to accommodate habitability issues reduce the potential for interpersonal problems and aberrant behavior during long-duration isolation and confinement. The following recommendations for future long-duration expeditions are based on the preceding discussion of issues associated with privacy and personal space:

- Include a "library" compartment in habitat designs to permit opportunities for the isolated and confined crew to obtain occasional moments of privacy and quiet reflection. The library could also serve other functions, such as a place for task preparation, confidential communications, and storage of the facility's collection of literature and reference materials.

- Include a privatized sleep chamber for each member of the crew. Sleep chambers of about 84 cubic feet are recommended. Smaller chambers could be tolerated, if necessary, with possible accompanying penalties to individual adjustment and performance. For example, smaller chambers would require that dressing be performed in passageways or other common areas, which would be problematic for mixed-gender crews.

- Avoid "hot bunking," or the sharing of sleep chambers on a shift basis.

- Expect crew members to withdraw periodically from social contact with other members of the crew. Moderate withdrawal is a healthy coping mechanism, but it can develop into a pathological response to isolated and confined conditions. Crew leaders and medical personnel must remain alert to ensure that individuals are not permitted to slip into a pattern of extreme withdrawal.

- Expect territorial behavior, such as attempts by crew members to usurp a workstation or storage area for personal space, if adequate personal space is not provided.

- Instruct crew members in the importance of clearly indicating one's wishes regarding interpersonal contact and the importance of respecting the wishes of others without taking offense. Premission training in interpersonal relations and participation in high-fidelity simulations of planned missions will engender sensitivities in candidate crew members that will prepare them to behave appropriately in the isolation and confinement of actual long-duration expeditions.

CHAPTER 17

REMOTE MONITORING OF
HUMAN PERFORMANCE AND ADJUSTMENT

As a psychiatrist, you have to develop a sensitivity to sound and intonation. Normally you see people and you get information from their body language and appearance. We have to compensate, like blind people do. It's an art form, really.
—Dr. Alexander Slyed, Russian
Spaceflight Control Center 1992

Dr. Alexander Slyed, a Russian psychiatrist, helps to monitor the mental state of cosmonauts onboard the *Mir* space station from the psychological support facility of the Russian Spaceflight Center, located in Star City near Moscow. The Russians have devoted considerable attention to monitoring and evaluating the adjustment of space crews, and mission managers routinely act on those evaluations when considered necessary. Intervention has ranged from providing surprise messages to crew members and special wake-up music, as is the traditional practice of NASA mission control, to more intrusive actions, such as workload reductions and the premature termination of missions (Newkirk 1990). Dr. Slyed told a reporter from the *Wall Street Journal* that the importance of psychological monitoring was made clear to mission managers when a pair of cosmonauts had to be brought home earlier than planned during the 1970s. "They fought like a cat and a dog," he reported, and finally one of them demanded, "If you don't bring us down to earth now, I am not going to work with this corpse any more" (quoted in Ignatius 1992). Apparently, greater attention has been paid to the remote evaluations since that incident, as a means to anticipate and perhaps mitigate similar problems before they become acute.

As Dr. Slyed listens to the communications from the *Mir* space station, he makes judgments concerning the cosmonauts' mental states and capacities for technical work. The psychiatrist even advises mission managers about what experiments and other tasks the crew members likely will be able to handle on a given day. He uses a soundproof room to speak privately with the cosmonauts. Dr. Slyed reported that he limits his private conversations with crew members to twice each week because other people in the space center have a tendency to become worried if they observe the psychiatrist talking with the cosmonauts. He has found that the cosmonauts are often resistant to direct questions about their adjustment or motivation, so he takes an indirect approach in these private sessions. For example, he might mention problems in Moscow in the hope of stimulating a cosmonaut's discussion of problems that he is experiencing in orbit.

Although the close scrutiny of crew adjustment by remote monitors might be justified by the number of interpersonal problems encountered on the *Soyuz* and *Mir* stations, it would appear that the monitoring could also contribute in important ways to the stress experienced by the cosmonauts. During his 211 days in space, Valentin Lebedev was concerned that he would be punished on his return to Earth if he showed any signs of the friction and dissatisfaction that he was experiencing. He complains in his diary of having to wear a mask of civility because, as soon as the mission controllers noticed any evidence of anger or conflict, they became worried and began speculating about the cosmonaut's behavior. For example, he received a call from the crew's ground-based physician one evening in which he was informed that irritation with ground control personnel had been evident during his previous communications; he was advised to be more careful in the future. Lebedev was unhappy about the ongoing friction with his crew mate and upset by his inability to express the frustration that he was experiencing with the ground control personnel, whom he considered to be responsible for procedural errors and delays. Despite his fears of punishment, Lebedev reports that he always felt better after speaking with the crew's physician, Dr. Eugeny Kobzevhe. The private chats seemed to help him a great deal in coping with the interpersonal problems that he had with his partner and with the frustration that he felt as a result of his conflicts with mission controllers (Lebedev [1983] 1988).

A psychological support service similar to the Russian facility probably should be developed to help monitor the medical and psychological well-being of crew personnel on future long-duration expeditions. Remote monitoring of crew behavior would be useful, even if the crew included a medical officer. The ground-based monitor might be viewed as an additional member of the crew who remains behind to represent the crew's interests and to provide a confidential, outside opinion regarding the behavior of distant crew members, when necessary. Counseling, words of encouragement and guidance, and other interventions should be available to the monitor. Presented below are some of the behaviors or cues that might be used by ground-based monitors to detect the need for various levels of intervention.[1]

POSSIBLE CREW PERFORMANCE AND ADJUSTMENT CUES

Several medical officers and psychologists who have been involved with Naval Support Force Antarctica were asked during interviews about the behaviors that they find indicative of crew performance and adjustment problems. Those interviews led to identification of the following thirteen cues:

1. sick calls
2. accidents
3. sleep problems
4. errors
5. delinquent behavior
6. interpersonal conflict
7. withdrawal into personal quarters
8. self-reports
9. complaints to crew leader or headquarters personnel
10. changes in communication tone or language
11. changes in frequency of outside communication
12. decline of participation in voluntary group activities
13. significant weight changes (losses or increases of more than 10 pounds)

The first three cues are the behaviors that the medical officer is most likely to observe. Patterns of sick calls, accidents, and sleep disturbances are often found by physicians in remote-duty environments to be attributable to an individual's preoccupation with a personal matter, such as a problem at home. To illustrate, an experienced Antarctic manager related the example of a galley worker who suffered two cuts and a burn during the same week. When the medical officer inquired if anything was bothering him, the galley worker explained that he had some financial problems at home that required his attention, but there was a two-week wait for an appointment to call home. The medical officer contacted the chaplain, who arranged the call, and the man was able to solve his financial problems and arrest his pattern of accidents. Similarly, frequent sick calls or visits to the physician for trivial or nonexistent medical reasons can also indicate an underlying adjustment problem. This behavior is rarely sinister or serious; usually, it is an expression of an individual's need for attention or to talk to someone about a personal matter.

Frequent errors; delinquent behavior, such as a pattern of showing up late for assignments or failing to perform as instructed; interpersonal conflict; and withdrawal into personal quarters are all behaviors interpreted by station managers and medical personnel as obvious indications of possible serious problems. A problem is even more clearly indicated when an individual actually reports a mental or adjustment problem to a medical officer or complains about a problem to a crew leader or headquarters personnel.

The final four cues involve more subtle behaviors that might or might not be indicative of a performance or adjustment problem. Antarctic managers and medical officers, however, are usually concerned when they notice that an individual has significantly increased or decreased his or her frequency of communication with home; a change in the frequency that a person calls home is often a response to a troubling message that has been received from the outside. Similarly, a decline in an individual's participation in group activities might indicate a normal tendency to withdraw occasionally from social contact, or it might be the beginning of a behavioral pattern that could lead to extreme withdrawal; station managers and medical personnel attempt to be particularly sensitive to this cue. Medical officers find that significant weight losses and gains can also indicate that a crew member is experiencing a personal problem.

Finally, Seabee managers of the naval support force who routinely communicate with remote station leaders usually develop interpretation skills similar to those described by Dr. Slyed in his statement introducing this chapter. The managers learn to interpret the tone and language of the remote-duty leaders as indications of their overall stress levels. The words that are used, the tone of the speaker's voice, and even the pauses and the presence or absence of laughter are used by sensitive managers to evaluate how a leader is coping with his or her considerable responsibilities. Familiarity with the leader's personal remote-duty leadership experience help with these subtle interpretations. The manager often uses these interpretations to guide the approach taken with the station leader, in the same manner that might be expected of skilled mission managers for future long-duration expeditions.

SPEECH ANALYSIS TECHNIQUES FOR DETECTING STRESS AND IMPAIRMENT

The vocal-auditory modality is the most important means by which several animal species communicate information about motivational states. Vocalization is produced by pulses of air that are generated by vibrations of the vocal folds and modified by the supralaryngeal vocal tract, which acts as an acoustic filter. The primary determinants of human vocalization are the respiration pattern and the changing tension of the muscle groups that are involved in phonation and articulation. Respiration and muscle tone have been long recognized as correlates of emotional tension; thus, it is likely that human speech reflects changes in the individual's underlying emotional state. Those changes in emotional state might be detectable in the sound waves produced by the vocalizations (Scherer 1986).

This is not a new concept. Since antiquity, the voice has been considered one of the most powerful indicators of emotional state. Interpreting speech tone and inflection is a skill learned at an early age and used throughout life to help understand the meaning of conversations and observations. Psychological interest in voice as an indicator of emotion has fluctuated during the past century. This subject is currently experiencing considerable research activity fueled by two separate areas of technological development: (1) voice recognition and activation of controls, and (2) remote monitoring of stress and workload of pilots. The developers of voice recognition and control systems must determine the limits of variation for key speech parameters in order to recognize accurately the words of individual speakers. Similarly, psychologists concerned with flight crew performance are interested in using measures of speech to determine the workload and stress levels of pilots. The appeal of speech as an indicator of stress or mental state is attributable to four factors: (1) a signal can be obtained from a crew located elsewhere with relative ease (e.g., acquiring acoustic signals with a microphone is easier than obtaining physiological measures); (2) the speech signals are acquired in a noninvasive, even unobtrusive, fashion without the need for additional equipment or sensors; (3) speech is produced naturally and frequently by flight crews; and (4) speech measures can be applied both in "real time" and after the fact to recorded communications (e.g., during an investigation of a critical incident) (Doherty 1991; Brenner, Doherty, and Shipp 1994).

Dr. Sam Schiflett of the U.S. Air Force's Armstrong Laboratory organized a symposium on the topic of vocal indicators of stress at the annual meeting of the Human Factors Society in 1991. Participants described several speech analysis techniques and presented the results of studies that evaluated the effects of situational stress, psychomotor workload, and alcohol consumption on a set of key acoustical parameters of the voice (Schiflett 1991). The most promising of the speech variables appear to be speech fundamental frequency, or pitch, and vocal jitter, which is the cycle-to-cycle variation in the period of the signal. Doherty (1991) reports that speech fundamental frequency exhibits a positive correlation with stress, whereas vocal jitter exhibits a negative, and statistically weaker, correlation with workload. This important symposium demonstrated that attempts to determine the level of stress of an individual by analyzing his or her speech have met with considerable success. The sensitivity of the techniques, however, is currently limited to identifying when an individual is exposed to either minimum or maximum levels of situational stress; neither fundamental frequency nor vocal jitter has yet to be found capable of distinguishing any intermediate stress levels. The research appears to be promising, despite the present insensitivity of the measures to gradations of stress level.

One particularly interesting paper presented in the symposium concerns the identification of alcohol impairment by analyzing in detail an individual's vocalizations. Pisoni, Johnson, and Bernacki (1991) describes the highly predictable manner in which speech is affected by alcohol impairment. They illustrate the diagnostic value of the technique by describing their analysis of taped messages from the captain of the *Exxon Valdez*, the supertanker that foundered and spilled her cargo in Prince William Sound, Alaska, in 1989. The researchers found gross errors and standard misarticulations that are typical of alcohol impairment. Most compelling, the duration of certain often-repeated words provided a clear indication of the captain's blood alcohol level at several intervals before and after the grounding. For example, the duration of the captain's vocalization of the name of his ship immediately preceding and immediately following the incident was nearly 50 percent longer than when he spoke the name thirty-three hours prior to the incident or several days later during a televised interview (i.e., about 650 msec versus 450 msec). The data actually portray the natural rise and fall of blood alcohol level, with the peak level reflected in the captain's transmission immediately following the grounding.

The research concerning detection of alcohol impairment by speech analysis is intriguing because of its implications and possible applications. For the remote monitoring of isolated and confined crew, a measure or multiple measures of speech might be used to detect any evidence of malaise, loss of mental focus, and lethargy that have been attributed to the mind-numbing sameness of isolation and confinement. Evidence of these symptoms might be detectable by voice analysis if the conditions have an effect analogous to the central nervous system-depressing effects of alcohol. Further, a fully mature and automated voice analysis system could be a quicker, less expensive, and less intrusive substitute for the mandatory chemical testing for alcohol and drugs in the transportation industry. A voice analysis technique would have the additional advantage of focusing on actual behavior and relevant performance, rather than relying on blood chemistry. Perhaps more important, it would be possible to evaluate key personnel before each shift with such a simple technique as speaking a few words into a microphone, in lieu of periodic random tests.

Ultimately, it might be possible to develop workstations and larger control systems that incorporate software with voice analysis algorithms. The software would recognize each individual speaker's voice and might automatically analyze the vocalizations for cues indicating situational workload stress or even a general impairment of cognition similar to alcohol effects. The system might provide feedback to the individual members of the crew for their personal information, or it might suggest or perhaps impose interventions (e.g., slowing down or speeding up a process to match the operator's current capabilities). The possibilities are nearly unlimited for applications of validated techniques for assessing emotional state by voice analysis.

RECOMMENDATIONS

The following recommendations relate to issues associated with the remote monitoring of crew performance and adjustment during long-duration expeditions.

- Instruct crew leaders, medical personnel, and mission controllers in the behaviors that could indicate underlying personal or adjustment problems.

- Continue the practice, begun during Project Mercury, of assigning a ground-based flight surgeon to a crew. The flight surgeon, supported by additional monitoring personnel with psychological training, would routinely evaluate the adjustment and performance of the crew and provide psychological support services as necessary. Also, the flight surgeon might be called upon to serve as the crew's unofficial ombudsman in representing their interests to expedition managers.

- Continue exploring the possibilities of developing reliable vocal indicators of stress, workload, and cognitive impairment.

PART III
THE IMPLICATIONS FOR THE FUTURE

The human factor is three quarters of any expedition.
—Roald Amundsen

Roald Amundsen is considered by many to be the greatest of the polar explorers. Inspired by accounts of Sir John Franklin, he abandoned plans for a career in medicine for a life of exploration and adventure. He served as mate onboard the *Belgica* and thus was among the first to survive an Antarctic winter. Later, in the converted herring boat *Gjøa*, he was the first to navigate the Northwest Passage, which had been the objective of many expeditions during the previous three centuries. Amundsen's greatest triumph, of course, occurred after he borrowed the *Fram* from Fridtjof Nansen for an Arctic expedition but instead sailed to the opposite end of Earth and with the appropriate planning and equipment, was the first person to reach the South Pole; he beat Robert Falcon Scott by thirty days. Amundsen is considered to be the greatest of the polar explorers because of his smoothly functioning, efficient, and successful expeditions. He was clever and methodical and, unlike other expedition leaders, he made a point to become a genuine expert in the techniques of travel and survival in hostile environments. Also, despite his focus on technical matters, Amundsen recognized the importance of human factors. He chose his men wisely, made certain that their workloads were adequate, and inspired confidence by his personal experience, accomplishments, and emotional control.

Historians favor Amundsen for his successes, and Sir Ernest Shackleton is frequently praised for his leadership. Still other writers commend Scott for his emphasis on scientific inquiries and for his compassion and courage in the face of death. The (seemingly) natural tendency to compare human abilities and accomplishments is reflected in the following tribute:

> For scientific leadership give me Scott; for swift and efficient travel, Amundsen; but when you are in a hopeless situation, when there seems no way out, get down on your knees and pray for Shackleton. (Quoted in Lansing [1959] 1994, 14)

It is true that Amundsen was remarkably successful in his endeavors and that Shackleton exhibited the highest quality of leadership, but it is also true that Scott emphasized science and was both courageous and unlucky.[1] It is instructive to make comparisons such as these. Much in the experiences of these and other explorers is relevant to future expeditions, but one stands apart in his significance to future explorers.

Modern exploration really began with Fridtjof Nansen and his Norwegian Polar Expedition. All who came after him benefited immensely from his experience. A zoologist and oceanographer, Nansen received his doctorate with a dissertation titled *The Structure and Combination of Histological Elements of the Central Nervous System*. The primary characteristic that distinguished Nansen from previous explorers was that he approached all aspects of expedition planning with scientific precision. He started by reading accounts of previous expeditions in order to learn from the experiences of his predecessors. Nansen remarked in his diary that, to his surprise, most of the problems confronting him had already been addressed and, in many instances, solved by previous explorers: wear appropriate clothing, pay special attention to nutrition, select crew members who can get along, then keep them busy and entertained. Nansen developed special high-calorie rations and systematically tested every item of food; he developed and evaluated sledges, harnesses, protective clothing, and other equipment; and he invented solutions to equipment problems, such as the Nansen cooker, that were used by generations of polar travelers. He even equipped his ship with wind-powered electric lights to illuminate the winter darkness at a time when electricity was still a novelty, and he fostered solidarity with an egalitarian approach to his crew during an era when expeditions were managed autocratically.

Of all of his accomplishments, however, Nansen is probably known best for the *Fram*. He conceived her design in response to his theory about the movement of polar ice. At the end of the nineteenth century, the Arctic was still among the world's biggest mysteries. It was unknown whether land, sea, or ice covered the pole. All attempts to reach the far north had ended in failure when the explorers' ships became trapped in frozen seas; most vessels were eventually crushed by the pressure. Nansen hypothesized that the ice cap moved in a westerly direction across the Arctic. He based his theory largely on a bit of the *Jeannette*'s wreckage discovered on the southwest coast of Greenland three years after De Long and his party had abandoned the *Jeannette* and thousands of miles away from her position when she was crushed by the ice in 1881.

The genius of Nansen's plan was to build a special ship for the expedition, rather than to convert an existing vessel; the ship would be designed to rise up out of the ice as the floes pressed against her hull, rather than to resist the full force of the pressure. The *Fram* was heavily built but constructed with no edges below the water line that might give ice a purchase on the ship; the keel was even recessed and all fittings were designed to be removed for a smooth and rounded profile. Critics scoffed at Nansen for his theory and predicted that his planned expedition would end in failure, but he persevered. He obtained an initial grant from the Norwegian government and additional funds later, when cost overruns resulted from an increase in the ship's capacity and margin for crew safety.

The *Fram*, which means "onward" in Norwegian, departed the beautiful Hanseatic port of Bergen on 1 July 1893. Sailing north and east, she crossed the Barents and Kara seas and skirted the northern coast of Siberia. Three months later, at a point closer to Alaska than Norway, the *Fram* headed into the ice pack, where she was purposely locked in the ice just north of 78° latitude. As the floes encroached and the forces on the *Fram's* hull increased, the sturdy little ship rose out of the ice and remained cradled above the pressure ridges for nearly three years, as she drifted with the ice pack across the top of the world. Nansen's design worked according to plan, and his theory of polar drift was confirmed. When it appeared that the *Fram's* course would take her no farther north across the polar ice cap, Nansen selected Hjalmar Johansen to accompany him on a dash to the pole with kayaks, sledges, and dogs. Cherry-Garrard (1930) describes Nansen's plan:

> This was one of the bravest decisions a polar explorer has ever taken. It meant leaving a drifting ship which could not be regained; it meant a journey over drifting ice to land; the nearest known land was nearly five hundred miles south of the point from which he started northwards; and the journey would include traveling both by sea and by ice. (P. 30)

By 7 April 1895, they were making only a mile headway over rough ice each day, so they turned back at 86°13' north latitude, which was 160 miles farther north than any explorer had previously achieved. Navigating with erroneous charts and caught by an early winter, Nansen and Johansen made it to Franz Josef Land, where they built a small hut in which they lived in complete isolation and confinement for nine months. They survived the extreme austerity of their life together with no apparent ill effects and pressed on eagerly in their kayaks in the spring of 1896. Then, on the same day that Nansen encountered the

English explorer Frederick Jackson in one of the most remarkable chance meetings in history,[2] the *Fram* broke free from the ice and headed for Spitzbergen and then Tromsö, Norway, where her crew was reunited after seventeen months of separation. The *Fram* steamed up Christiania Fjord on 9 September 1896, three years and three months following her departure. Nansen and his crew were greeted as if they had just returned from another planet.

The Norwegian Polar Expedition was the model for all subsequent polar explorers, and, in many ways, this expedition also provides an appropriate model for modern explorers. Nansen's systematic simulation, testing, and evaluation of every item of equipment and his meticulous attention to every detail and possible contingency set him apart from previous explorers. But, perhaps most important, Nansen recognized that the physical and psychological well-being of his crew could make the difference between success and failure. Accordingly, he provided a well-designed habitat, insightful procedures, and exceptional leadership to a qualified and compatible crew. Before Amundsen, Nansen knew that human factors were the critical components of any expedition; in Nansen's words, "It is the man that matters."

Nansen made several more expeditions to the Arctic and even contemplated an Antarctic expedition before he turned his attention to a career as statesman. There is much to learn from the experiences of remote-duty personnel and previous explorers, but Fridtjof Nansen provides a singularly instructive example. Historian David Mountfield (1975) writes of Nansen:

> His liberal conscience, profound intelligence and universally acknowledged integrity had lasting effects on Norway and on Europe. A powerful supporter of the League of Nations, he was appointed commissioner responsible for repatriation of prisoners of war after the First World War. The Russians would not recognize the League, but they would recognize Nansen, so he set up a private organization which repatriated about a half a million men in a very short time. He was later in charge of famine relief in Russia, Greece and Armenia. No man better deserved the Nobel Peace Prize, which he was awarded in 1922.... He died in May 1930 at the beginning of a decade in which he would have found little comfort. (P. 132)

CHAPTER 18

PRINCIPLES OF HABITABILITY AND OTHER LESSONS LEARNED

I identified several behavioral principles and lessons of relevance to future space missions during my review of previous expeditions, Antarctic experiences, and other examples of remote duty. Those principles and lessons are discussed in the preceding chapters, and nearly two hundred specific recommendations are presented in fifteen categories of behavioral issues.

The following key inferences emerged from my review:

- Humans can endure almost anything.
- Behavioral problems will occur.
- Trivial issues will be exaggerated.
- Relations between headquarters and remote-duty personnel will become strained.
- Zeitgebers are important.
- The larger the group, the greater is the tendency for subgroups to form.
- Self-selection is preferred to predetermination.
- Humans tend to thrive on variation.
- Most people like to be informed.
- Performance is facilitated when designs conform to human expectations.
- The longer the duration, the more important are privacy and personal space.
- Some individuals require tangible results.
- The integration of activities can improve productivity.
- Unplanned events will occur.
- There are paradoxes in designing for habitability.

HUMAN ENDURANCE

The primary lesson that can be learned from reviewing accounts of previous explorers is that humans are capable of enduring conditions far more austere and dangerous than ever would be considered for future long-duration expeditions. This is an important point, but not because a human crew would be purposely subjected to a spacecraft with the habitability of Nansen's hut. Rather, the importance of this information is in establishing that humans are extremely adaptable and capable of enduring and performing well under extremely austere conditions. For example, Shackleton's men adjusted quickly from their comfortable life onboard the *Endurance* to camping in tents on an Antarctic ice floe when their ship sank; the diaries reveal that members of the party remained cheerful and occasionally had to remind themselves of their desperate situation.

Forty years earlier, the *Polaris* had been similarly beset in the Arctic. Amid the confusion of rescuing supplies, the ship was swept away into the winter darkness. She carried half her crew to their deaths, and the remaining nineteen were stranded on an ice floe. Although the situation of the *Polaris* castaways seemed hopeless, none of them perished as the group drifted southward for nearly seven months and 1,700 miles with few supplies and minimal protection from the harsh environment. Ross (1985) writes: "Even the infant Charles Polaris, only two months old at the start of the voyage, had lived through the experience on an unorthodox baby diet of blubber, seal offal, pemmican, pulverized hardtack, and brackish water."

These examples demonstrate that humans can endure austere conditions when survival is at stake. Humans have also exhibited a remarkable capacity for adaptation to routine living at reduced standards. Descriptions of life on the trail and in Nansen's hut on Franz Josef Land illustrate the extremes of human mental and physical endurance. Even life at relatively comfortable base camps and winter quarters can be austere and unpleasant, yet the personnel usually adapt well and perform admirably when required. One member of Scott's *Terra Nova* Expedition writes under the heading "Life at Hut Point":

> Thursday 13 April 1911. Here we have an end to our sugar today. We have also finished our flour so we can't make patties. We have also finished our oatmeal, but we have lots of seal meat and biscuit and cocoa. Butter is running out, but we can't starve. And, we are a very happy party of bohemians.

> Our clothes are soaked in seal blubber and soot—black and greasy—and we are all bearded and very dirty. (Wilson 1972, 121)

The conditions endured by sealers and whalers were routinely far worse than the conditions onboard expedition ships. The crews of sealing and whaling vessels tolerated "crowded and unsanitary quarters, bad food, scurvy, harsh treatment, and long periods of boredom punctuated now and then by hard work and danger" (Ross 1985). Many voyages resulted in unintentional winters in the ice, yet crews returned year after year despite the unpleasant and unhealthy conditions. More than three thousand voyages were made to the Davis Strait whaling grounds alone during the nineteenth and early twentieth centuries. This portion of the polar whaling industry represents nearly 200,000 man-years under extremely austere conditions of isolation and confinement. Midshipman William Reynolds of the Wilkes Expedition described the adaptability of sailors in one of his letters home in 1839:

> As to bodily inconveniences, they are easily endured, and as long as the extreme of endurance is not called for, all are disposed to make light of the present and trust to better luck in future. Sailors are your true philosophers in these cases and never employ themselves in fancying their situation worse than it is. The curse of the Life is that we are separated so long from our homes and often removed from a knowledge of what is going on in the busy world of civilization. (Quoted in Cleaver and Stann 1988, 198)

The expeditionary conditions described thus far are related to the behavioral issues that are applicable to the design of equipment and procedures for future space expeditions; accordingly, previous chapters focus on sources of psychological stress. An additional issue, not yet addressed directly, is the physical stress, such as the physiological effects of weightlessness and increased exposure to radiation, that might be experienced by future space explorers. Detailed descriptions of the physical stressors experienced by polar travelers are excluded from the previous discussions because those stressors are unlike the physiological stressors of long-duration space missions. It might be instructive to note, however, that many polar explorers experienced extreme environmental and physiological stress in addition to the psychological stress associated with their isolated and confined conditions.

Nansen and Johansen used dogsleds in their dash north, as did Amundsen in reaching the South Pole. In contrast, Shackleton and

Scott experimented with ponies, dogs, and tractors, but they relied on "man-hauling," that is, pulling sledges, each loaded with 175 to 250 pounds of supplies and equipment, on their inland treks. It is difficult enough to travel over ice in the Arctic, whether assisted by dogs or on foot, but explorers can live "off the land" by shooting polar bears and seals for fuel and food. Explorers of the Antarctic are deprived of this possibility; there are no animals to hunt in Antarctica except at the edge of the ice. As a consequence, the early Antarctic explorers traveling over the ice had to carry with them all of the equipment and supplies needed during a traverse. They relieved some of the burden by positioning caches of supplies to be used on the return trip, but, in all instances, the difficult process of transporting such heavy loads was extremely difficult. In addition to suffering frostbite, hypothermia, altitude sickness, snow blindness, and painful injuries, most individuals on inland expeditions, according to one present-day analysis, did not consume nearly as many calories as they expended in hauling the heavy loads and maintaining body temperature. In short, the polar explorers' practice of hauling heavily loaded sledges usually led to their gradual starvation. Some of them made it to safety or to a cache of supplies before they expired, but others weakened on short rations and perished on the trail. For example, Scott and his polar party died when they were only 11 miles away from food and fuel.

Knowledge of the debilitating effects resulting from the practice of using human power to transport equipment and supplies in polar regions has not dissuaded modern adventurers from subjecting themselves to the same process. In fact, there exists a minor "expedition industry" composed of highly competitive adventurers who attempt extraordinary feats, such as unsupported treks through polar regions. Like many of the explorers of the past, the modern adventurers are financed by donations and proceeds from books and lectures. The most remarkable accomplishment in this category was the Pentland South Pole Expedition, the longest totally self-supported polar sledge journey ever made, when Sir Ranulph Fiennes and Dr. Michael Stroud crossed the Antarctic continent in 1992–92. Hauling sledges loaded initially with 485 pounds of supplies across the Antarctic landmass, they stopped for only a few minutes (and no food) at the Amundsen-Scott South Pole Station. The difficulties experienced by Fiennes and Stroud are impossible to convey in a brief description of their expedition. They consumed 5,200 calories per day, yet each lost nearly 25 percent in body weight during the ninety-five-day journey (Fiennes 1993). Three similar expeditions ended at the Amundsen-Scott South Pole Station that summer. These activities suggest that modern explorers are capable of achieving, if not surpassing, the physical and mental accomplishments of their predecessors during previous centuries.

If humans can endure and even adapt to such austere and difficult conditions as described in this book, it follows that providing the proper habitat, food, procedures, personnel, and leadership would increase the probability of a successful outcome to an expedition. Generally, expedition leaders who attended to these important issues have accomplished the most successful, or at least the most remarkable, missions. In short, the many examples of survival and endurance presented here strongly suggest that, in comparison, a one-year tour at a lunar base or a three-year expedition to Mars probably would be a "piece of cake" for a well-prepared crew.

BEHAVIORAL PROBLEMS

Providing appropriate habitats and procedures for carefully selected and well-led crews can reduce the stress experienced by isolated and confined personnel and thereby contribute to success of the mission. Some instances of behavioral, interpersonal, and what might be labeled "psychological" problems, however, will not be completely avoided during future long-duration expeditions, even if optimal conditions, procedures, and personnel are provided. The record of the past suggests that although serious problems will be unlikely, minor problems will be relatively common.

An important factor in dealing with problems is to understand that individuals respond to the cumulative stress of their experiences in different ways. Some crew members will develop constructive coping mechanisms for dealing with stress and inevitable adversity. For example, they will engage in physical exercise, seek out a comrade with whom to commiserate, or focus exclusively on their work. Others will become aggressive, slip into a depressive state, or exhibit other inappropriate behaviors. Most crew members, however, will adjust and perform well despite the isolated and confined conditions in which they live and work. In Dr. Fred Glogower's words, "The issue is not the feeling the crew person has, it's the manner in which the individual handles it. We all get angry. It is what we do about it that matters" (personal communication).

Time is the factor that can compound any problem. Even individuals who seem to adapt to the conditions during simulations might respond differently to the cumulative stress of an actual long-duration expedition. A high-fidelity simulation can create many of the anticipated mission conditions. Unless it is conducted in a remote environment, such as a specially built facility in Antarctica, however, it will lack a critical element for the participating crew: the realization that one cannot escape.

It is important to anticipate that some crew problems will occur on long-duration expeditions, despite the best efforts of designers and mission managers to prevent them, and these problems must be attended to when they occur. Concern for possible psychological problems should not be considered a reason to avoid a long-duration expedition with a human crew. Despite their frailties, humans rarely have been the limiting factor in previous expeditions. Rather, many of the explorers mentioned in this book endured much, adapted well to their environments, and performed admirably. All indications suggest that the same can be expected of future explorers.

TRIVIAL ISSUES

A primary reason why behavioral problems will occur on future long-duration expeditions is that trivial issues are exaggerated by people living and working under isolation and confinement. Minor annoyances, differences of opinion, or perceived transgressions that would be inconsequential under normal conditions can be magnified by isolated and confined personnel into issues of monumental importance. Evidence of this phenomenon was found in nearly all of the expeditions that I have reviewed, and it is a common occurrence at Antarctic stations. Biographer Roland Huntford, who probably has read more personal diaries of polar explorers than anyone else, noted:

> The particular risk of polar exploration is the strain of being cooped up for long in isolation. Friction is inevitable. The maddening proximity of a too-familiar face may be a torture in itself. The clash of personality has always been a danger more sinister than climate or terrain. (Quoted in Fiennes 1993, 99)

In *White Jacket*, Herman Melville ([1850] 1988) describes life onboard a U.S. ship of the line during the first half of the nineteenth century. The emphasis of Melville's story is an exposé of the strict discipline and corporal punishment practiced at the time, but he also describes conditions of life in a small, closed society that are relevant to analogous environments. In particular, he describes how the isolation and confinement of shipboard life contributed to the exaggerated drama of day-to-day existence. At one point, the title character says, "If ever there was a continual theatre in the world, playing by night and by day, and without intervals between the acts, a man-of-war is that theatre, and her planks are the *boards* indeed."

Rivolier and Bachelard (1988) describe life at French remote-duty stations in similar terms, as experiences that are lived in an intensely dramatic atmosphere. Their observations led them to conclude that a daily psychological drama, which is experienced with varying degrees of conscious comprehension, represents a compensation, or coping mechanism, for the frustrations and stresses of isolation and confinement. Excessive or permanent dramatization of daily life, however, can contribute to a crew member's exaggeration of trivial issues, which in turn can result in the erosion of group solidarity and the impairment of individual adjustment and performance.

The knowledge that trivial issues will be exaggerated and that conflict has a negative effect on group solidarity leads to the logical conclusion that mission planners must do whatever is practical to eliminate, or at least, to minimize the issues that could be seized upon and exaggerated by isolated and confined personnel. Many of the recommendations presented in this book are directed at eliminating sources of possible conflict among a crew (e.g., hygiene standards, communications protocols) and facilitating group harmony and solidarity (e.g., leadership style, eating together, group activities).

Many additional approaches to these suggestions are available. For example, Cherry-Garrard (1930) memorized several poems that he repeated to himself on the trail "during the blank hours of the daily march, when the idle mind is all too apt to think of food in times of hunger, or possibly of purely imaginary grievances, which may become distorted into real foundations of discord under the abnormal strain of living for months in the unrelieved company of three other men." Similarly, Dr. William K. Douglas reported that, during a stress test in an isolation chamber, astronaut John Glenn composed a poem, memorized it, and, on his release from isolation, wrote it down. Perhaps poetry, mantras, or similar autogenic techniques can be developed for use by expedition personnel to help them adjust to the conditions and to avoid conflict caused by the exaggeration of trivial issues. Humor is another method that can effectively limit the effects of this phenomenon.

Selecting homogeneous crews for future space expeditions has been suggested by some observers as a means to minimize the potential for conflict. This suggestion has the support of the experiences reviewed in this book; that is, homogeneous crews have been extremely effective in the past, compared with multinational crews and crews composed of distinct classes of personnel (e.g., scientific versus military). Differences among cultures represented in a crew were the sources of many trivial issues that have been exaggerated into conflicts; also, when multinational crews decompensate, they almost always fall apart into national groups. In addition to cultural differences, an unhealthy atmosphere of competition between national groups can emerge, which usually degrades the group's capacity for teamwork. Sometimes this competition is between members of the crew (e.g., relating to endurance, task performance, scientific accomplishment, or leadership), but, on other occasions, the competition is between equipment provided by the nations involved (e.g., Russian versus Canadian skis on a transpolar journey).

Although selecting homogeneous crews would minimize the possibility for conflict, it appears inevitable that future long-duration space expeditions will be performed by multinational crews. For this reason, it is extremely important to select compatible crew members, devote attention to the development of training programs for sensitizing candidate crew members to cultural differences, and develop procedures to minimize the possibilities for intercultural differences and other trivial issues that could be exaggerated into conflicts.

STRAINED RELATIONS

Many of the impediments to successful interactions between a remote-duty crew and the headquarters staff are expressions of the structural relationship (see chapter 13). The home agency, laboratory, or mission control is typically blamed for nearly all difficulties experienced in the field. For example, delays are interpreted by the remote-duty personnel as evidence that the crew is a low priority, and questions from headquarters about meeting deadlines or adhering to schedules are taken as criticism. In addition, actual criticism can be devastating to crew morale. The extreme hypersensitivity of remote-duty personnel in communications with headquarters can occur early in a mission and quickly degrade a previously effective relationship. From the crew's point of view, the managers located in the comfort and convenience of their facilities at home have failed to comprehend the constraints and stresses under which the remote-duty personnel must operate. Some crews come to believe that they have been ignored, if not abandoned.

Sells (1973) believes that a little of this phenomenon is probably a good thing, in that opposition to headquarters provides a unifying force for the remote crew. Although this effect is highly likely, the tendency for relations to become strained is a potentially dangerous phenomenon, and relations between the crew and their distant managers can become permanently damaged, if permitted. In extreme situations, groups that become highly unified in their opposition to headquarters sometimes cut themselves off completely and refuse any communication with the outside world. This would be an intolerable occurrence on future long-duration expeditions.

There are at least three causes of the hostility between remote-duty crews and headquarters personnel: (1) displacement of anger to outsiders, as described by Sells (1973) and labeled by Kanas (1990); (2) exaggeration of trivial issues; and (3) real and justifiable grievances resulting from the failure of headquarters personnel to understand the constraints imposed by the special conditions. To these causes could be added arrogance or other personality flaws, which some crew members might already possess and others might develop as a consequence of their unusual status.

There is a tendency for strained relations between remote-duty personnel and headquarters in all expeditions, missions, and agencies; it is not limited to remote-duty environments, such as polar research stations and spacecraft. The phenomenon occurs in all relationships between the headquarters of an organization and the personnel who live and work while physically separated from the personnel at headquarters. For example, the staff members of a corporation's field office or a government laboratory often feel estranged and unimportant when there is a delay in receiving information or materials from their headquarters located elsewhere. Headquarters personnel might consider the incident to be a trivial oversight, but the people in the field usually perceive it as part of a pattern of disregard. Hypersensitivity of remote, or field, personnel appears to be a normal, at least typical, human response that is predictably exaggerated by the special conditions of isolation and confinement. Knowledge of this phenomenon will permit the planners of future expeditions to develop training programs and procedures designed to contain the phenomenon and mitigate its negative effects on individual adjustment and overall mission performance.

ZEITGEBERS

Zeitgebers are the external cues that humans and other species use to regulate their internal biological rhythms. Maintenance of sleep schedules and overall task performance are facilitated by exposure to "normal" diurnal cues, such as the light-dark cycle and regular mealtimes. Conversely, the absence of diurnal cues can lead to sleep and performance problems; most future space expeditions will be conducted in the absence of normal cues. For these reasons, several suggestions for providing the crew with substitute zeitgebers are offered throughout this book. Chapter 3, for example, recommends that the internal lighting of spacecraft and planetary habitats be dimmed to correspond with nighttime at mission control and chapter 10 suggests that the capability for weekly special dinners be provided.

The importance of zeitgebers also applies to the passage of time on larger scales. In this regard, chapter 14 suggests that holidays, mission-milestones, and similar events be celebrated to help the crew mark the passage of time. Similarly, mission managers should structure long-duration expeditions with several intermediate goals to be achieved, rather than one large objective at the end. Intermediate goals will engender the feeling among the crew that they are making progress toward the ultimate goal. Days tend to blend one into another under conditions of isolation and confinement. External cues can help future explorers to adapt to their conditions.

SUBGROUP FORMATION

The formation of subgroups within a crew is a normal process, even within crews composed of only a few members; opportunities for subgroup formation increase with larger crews. Although some amount of subgroup formation might be a useful coping mechanism for certain individuals, subgroups can exert a distinctly negative influence on group dynamics. In particular, the formation of subgroups can erode crew solidarity and contribute to interpersonal conflict.

Several recommendations are offered in previous chapters to minimize the negative effects of subgroup formation. For example, dining together at least once each day, celebrations, and group recreational activities can facilitate communication among individuals and between subgroups (see chapters 11 and 12).

SELF-SELECTION

Evidence from previous expeditions, Antarctic winter-over experiences, and space analogue environments demonstrates that individuals generally prefer to make choices themselves, rather than have decisions made for them. For example, the Project Tektite crews exhibited strong preferences for meals that they were permitted to select versus the higher-quality meals that were provided in a predetermined fashion. Similarly, *Skylab* crew members were much more productive when they were allowed to select the order in which they performed tasks from a list of required activities than when mission control programmed all tasks.

The benefits of permitting crew members to make choices from among options results in several recommendations concerning exercise (chapter 5), workload (chapter 6), food preparation (chapter 10), and recreational opportunities (chapter 14) on future long-duration expeditions. The application of this habitability principle, of course, will be constrained by limited storage space and other engineering and logistical considerations, but crew members will benefit to the extent that this principle can be expressed in equipment and procedures.

VARIATION

If variety is the spice of life, variation in visual stimulation and activity can help to improve the palatability of life in isolation and confinement. The clear benefits of variety in a monotonous environment led to several design recommendations concerning task assignments (chapter 6), food preparation (chapter 10), habitat aesthetics (chapter 12), and recreational opportunities (chapter 14) for future long-duration expeditions.

INFORMATION

Humans, whether they are living "normal" lives or serving in a remote-duty environment, tend to be curious and particularly interested in information that pertains to themselves. As a consequence, most people like to remain informed. This principle applies to information of a general nature, such as current events or news, as well as to information about an individual's immediate interests or concerns. The latter category includes information about the mission, particularly any changes to the established plan; remote-duty crew members do not appreciate being among the last to learn of decisions that affect them.

This habitability principle also applies to personal information. Most remote-duty personnel are eager to remain in contact with distant friends and loved ones. Intense longings for news from home and sincere appreciation when information is received are described in chapter 13. The importance to some individuals of remaining informed leads to recommendations concerning outside communications for future long-duration expeditions. Chapter 13 also addresses the question of whether to withhold negative information from crew members.

DESIGN CONFORMANCE

Designing equipment to conform to user expectations is a basic principle of human factors engineering. The principle is derived from the fact that fewer errors are made and performance is facilitated when there is consistency to a design and when the design conforms to an established convention. Designing to conform to expectations is particularly important because humans tend to revert to expectations under emergency conditions or on other occasions characterized by high workloads and information overloading. The principle applies to the design of commonplace items, such as faucets and knobs (i.e., left and right turns, respectively, to turn on), as well as to the design of complex and exotic systems, such as spacecraft and planetary habitats.

It is recommended that designers avoid violations of expectations (i.e., established conventions) in designing controls and displays so as to minimize the potential for crew errors. Similarly, the interior architectures of space habitats should conform, to the extent possible, to expectations derived from Earth-bound experiences. For example, it is believed that a consistent orientation and consistent interior features would facilitate individual adaptations to zero gravity. Perhaps more important, designing to human expectations also would increase the probability of appropriate responses under emergency conditions (see chapters 6 and 12).

PRIVACY AND PERSONAL SPACE

This book describes many of the stresses experienced by remote-duty personnel and refers to stress as cumulative. Unrelieved stress accumulates whether one is living in a remote-duty station or a more conventional environment. Most individuals develop behaviors to cope effectively with the stress they experience. For actual relief of the accumulated stress, however, it is necessary periodically to experience relatively stress-free intervals. Under normal conditions, one can go for a walk or a short drive, or perhaps take a weekend outing or even an occasional vacation, in order to relieve accumulated stress. Obtaining stress-free intervals is often difficult under normal conditions, but it can be nearly impossible in remote-duty environments where fewer options are available. In fact, there is no escape from the close physical proximity of one's comrades when living in isolation and confinement; one can never really get away. For this reason, the personnel of remote-duty environments often withdraw from the high levels of social stimulation and other stressors as a way to relieve their accumulated stress. Some people even learn to be alone in the midst of a crowded room, but the process can be extremely difficult when there are no opportunities to remove oneself physically from social contact.

Periodic and temporary withdrawal from social contact is a common and healthy coping mechanism among isolated and confined personnel. This process should be facilitated by providing crew members with individual sleeping quarters (see chapter 3) and other common, or shared, areas where privacy can be obtained for an occasional quiet moment. Also, crew leaders and mission managers must remain alert to the possibility that a healthy and occasional coping mechanism can develop into a pathological pattern of extreme withdrawal, called "cocooning" (see chapter 17).

TANGIBLE RESULTS

Some individuals seem to respond better to tangible results for their efforts than others. This observation is the basis for several recommendations concerning motivational frameworks and equipment to encourage future space explorers to sustain the programs of vigorous exercise that will be required to counter the negative effects of zero-gravity on human physiology (see chapter 5). Further, mission managers should consider implementing means by which tangible results or similar reinforcers can be used to stimulate morale, enhance team-work, and motivate other desirable crew behaviors.

PRODUCTIVITY

The efficiency of a system is enhanced when multiple requirements are satisfied by the same action. For example, under high-workload conditions when free time is scarce, it might be useful to combine recreation or entertainment with the necessary exercise that must be performed by the crew or to integrate exercise with required task preparation and task performance. This principle is reflected in several recommendations concerning motivational frameworks to support required exercise and in the suggestion that certain equipment be designed for manual, rather than automatic, operation (see chapters 5 and 14).

UNPLANNED EVENTS

The expedition literature and accounts of Antarctic winter-over experiences contain countless examples of unplanned events that had significant negative effects. The violent and unpredictable storms and encroaching ice packs experienced by polar explorers will have paral-lels in solar storms, micro-meteoroids, and other dangers for future space explorers. In addition, even well-designed and heavily built equipment sometimes breaks, wears out, or simply fails to perform as expected under operational conditions. Equipment designed for use in space is not immune to this phenomenon, as evidenced by chronically malfunctioning space toilets and other serious equipment failures. As mentioned in the introduction to Part II, the same types of problems experienced by previous explorers will confront modern explorers. The details will be different, but the problems will be essentially the same.

The expectation that unplanned events will occur during future long-duration expeditions is not actually a principle, rather, it is an expression of probability. By definition, it is impossible to predict which of the many potential unplanned events will occur on a particu-lar mission. Therefore, planners must attempt to prepare for at least the most likely equipment failures and emergencies. Detailed contingency plans will be necessary to guide the crew's responses, but there are other implications as well.

Regarding unplanned events, the primary lessons from previous expeditions are twofold: (1) equipment and systems should be designed for maintainability, and (2) the crew probably will require the on-board capability to fabricate needed items from spare parts and materials. The customary practice of providing redundant systems on spacecraft will be insufficient to ensure the success of future long-duration expeditions. Triple redundancy (i.e., two backup systems) provides an additional safety margin, but there would be little confidence in a third unit if both the primary and secondary units had already failed. Important replacement parts for equipment usually can be obtained within a few days regardless of how remote a vessel or duty station is on Earth, but there will be absolutely no opportunity for recall or resupply during a long-duration space mission. The crew must take with them *all* of the materials and equipment they will need to effect repairs to their craft in order to fulfill mission objectives and, possibly, to survive. This means that even if redundancy is built into the systems, the crew will need spare components to repair the failed primary systems, as well as schematics, materials, and equipment to fabricate additional replacement components to serve as backups to the secondary units. Time will be the factor that compounds equipment reliability problems, as well as problems with the human components of the expedition.

Although the previous paragraphs might sound foreboding, it is important to recognize that responding to emergencies, making repairs, and fabricating equipment are activities to which humans are particularly well suited. Many earlier expeditions cited in this book involved clever on-site solutions to equipment problems and other unplanned events. Several of the expeditions were actually saved by the abilities of crew members to fabricate a patch, repair a pump, or modify an instrument or radio. Also, I have interviewed many Navy chief petty officers who confessed to making creative repairs to complex systems when standard replacement parts were unavailable. Roger Dunham's (1996) description of his use of a soft drink can to make an emergency repair to the propulsion system of a nuclear submarine is an extreme, but not particularly unusual, example of shipboard ingenuity that was inspired by necessity.

Even modern space missions have benefited greatly from human ingenuity and on-site fabrication of equipment solutions. Reportedly, an Apollo mission was saved by using the cap of a pen to activate a switch that had broken off, and satellites have been captured for repair by using devices fabricated from the materials at hand onboard the space shuttle. It is not only conceivable but likely that future explorers will require similar capabilities.

There is no digital, electronic, or mechanical substitute for an on-site human presence when an unplanned or unforeseen event occurs and a creative or unusual response is required. Humans possess levels of problem-solving ability, creativity, and dexterity that cannot be duplicated artificially for responding to equipment failures and other emergencies. Dr. Harry Wolbers (1984) studied the costs and benefits of the human role in space for NASA. Wolbers concludes that future space systems will rely heavily on the intellectual, sensory, and perceptual capabilities of human crews and on their fine manipulative skills. To exploit these capabilities fully, it will be necessary to provide future expeditions with compact equivalents of the machine and electronics shops carried onboard ships and maintained at remote-duty stations; materials also must be provided (including plenty of duct tape).

A final contingency planning lesson from previous expeditions concerns the development of appropriate storage strategies for remote-duty environments. The practice onboard many expedition ships, on traverses, and at polar base camps has been to store important items or materials in dispersed locations, rather than storing all of one type of supply together in one place. Dispersed storage increases the probability that necessary items would survive localized damage from fire or collision. Similar storage strategies seem appropriate for future long-duration space expeditions.

HABITABILITY PARADOXES

Part II presents many inferences, principles, and specific habitability recommendations derived from the study of conditions analogous to long-duration space missions. A few of the inferences, however, involve apparent contradictions. As examples, three common habitability paradoxes follow.

Paradox No. 1: Humans can endure almost anything, but good habitability enhances the possibility of their success. Many examples of human adaptability and endurance are presented in this book. These examples indicate clearly that properly selected and motivated individuals are capable of living and working under extremely austere conditions for relatively long periods of time. It is reasonable, therefore, to question why human factors engineers and other behavioral scientists consider it necessary to recommend habitability features, such as private sleep chambers, variety in exercise and recreation options, and other amenities that increase the size, weight, and expense of spacecraft. If Nansen and Johansen could endure nine months in their hut, why not build an extremely austere spacecraft to reduce the cost of an interplanetary expedition?

The answer to this question involves probabilities. Although the evidence from past experiences indicates that some humans could endure austere conditions for long durations and perform appropriately when required, the evidence also indicates that the probability of a successful outcome is increased if certain habitability features are provided. Just as a propulsion engineer might design a rocket component to withstand pressures greater than expected, it is prudent to incorporate habitability features to help contain or mitigate unexpected stress on the human crew.[1]

Paradox No. 2: Habitability is important, but work-related designs are more important. Evidence from expeditions, Antarctic winter-over experiences, and other spacecraft analogues indicates that "comfort" is one of the least important factors in the general habitability of a built environment. This point was made particularly clear during Project Tektite, the underwater habitat experiment conducted in 1969–70 to study spacecraft habitability issues. Because of the many constraints involved, *Tektite* was not well designed to support the work performed by the aquanauts. For example, all workstations and common areas of the habitat were designed for multiple purposes, which resulted in frequent interruptions of tasks and procedures. Further, the lack of readily available equipment and references were constant inconveniences that impeded crew performance and annoyed the participants. In contrast, *Tektite* was well designed for comfort. The facility contained many habitability features and amenities, including an abundance of windows and a delightful cupola used by the crews to make oceanographic observations and to obtain quiet moments away from the pressures of isolated and confined living. *Tektite*'s cupola was so appreciated by the crew that a similar feature was recommended for space station designs.

Interviews with crew members and observations conducted during the *Tektite* missions made it very clear that work support was of greater importance to the participating personnel than was the comfort of the habitat: "The single most important variable in the perceived habitability of this habitat was the degree to which aquanauts found the habitat supportive of their scientific and engineering tasks" (Nowlis, Wortz, and Watter 1972). The crews of future space expeditions will likewise require appropriately designed workstations and equipment to support their primary mission objectives, and they probably will perceive work support as more important than comfort or habitability. Although appropriate work support will be of considerable importance, evidence from the analogue environments suggests that the importance of the intangibles relating to habitability increases with the routinization of operations and with the duration of the voyage.

Paradox No. 3: Structure and consistency are keys to effective and productive group functioning, but self-selection and variety are keys to individual adjustment. Can both of these inferences be correct?

It appears from the materials reviewed that both inferences *are* correct, because they are not necessarily mutually exclusive in practice. For example, it will be essential for health maintenance that the crew members of future expeditions take regular nourishment. Also, to facilitate group harmony, it will be important for the crew to eat together as frequently as practical. Consequently, it would appear that mealtimes should be scheduled to achieve both requirements; however, self--election of food items might be permissible within the structure of the scheduled mealtimes. Similarly, daily exercise will be required to counter the muscle atrophy and cardiovascular deconditioning experienced in space, and leisure time will be required to forestall the onset of stress responses. Exercise and leisure time must be scheduled, and individual crew members must adhere, with some flexibility, to these schedules. Within the structured framework of the schedule, however, they could have considerable opportunity for personal selection among the available exercise and leisure options. Sleep is another issue that requires a structured approach to prevent sleep disturbances and free cycling and to facilitate individual and group performance, but individuals will differ in their sleep requirements. Although not everyone will feel the need to retire at the same time, all crew members should be ready for work when their watches, or shifts, begin. Flexibility concerning bedtime can be provided within the structure of a scheduled muster each morning.

Humans like to make choices for themselves, but a structured and organized approach to procedures helps to regulate behavior and facilitate individual performance and group interaction. Thus, self-selection and imposed structure can be viewed as complementary, rather than contradictory, components of habitability. Operationally, it might be desirable to honor the personal preferences of crew members when possible, if they fall within the structure provided by an established schedule or protocol.

CHAPTER 19

RECOMMENDATIONS FOR FUTURE RESEARCH

A book of this type cannot be considered complete unless it includes at least a few recommendations for additional research. Although much can be learned from the past regarding human behavior in isolation and confinement, much is yet to be done in preparation for future long-duration expeditions. The following items are offered as a partial list of research requirements. Satisfaction of these requirements would involve a variety of research methods, including analytical studies, laboratory experiments, and simulations, but mission planners are strongly urged to conduct high-fidelity mission simulations as the final step in evaluating all procedures and equipment developed for future space expeditions. Final simulations and crew exercises should be performed in an actual remote-duty environment to provide the force and fidelity of important conditions.

A FEW RESEARCH REQUIREMENTS

- Develop training programs to sensitize candidate crew personnel to the problems of isolated and confined living, including the cross-cultural issues associated with multinational crew composition.

- Develop and train crew personnel in techniques for facilitating communication and group harmony and for minimizing the incidence of interpersonal conflict.

- Develop techniques for routine and unobtrusive monitoring of mental health.

- Evaluate the applicability of the results of small-group dynamics research to the crews of spacecraft.

- Develop personnel selection criteria based on past performance and interpersonal skills, in addition to technical competence.

- Define leadership responsibilities and identify required leadership traits and capabilities.

- Define the most appropriate organizational structure for the various planned expeditions.

- Conduct a systematic task analysis of all proposed crew positions.

- Develop a cross-training plan, based on task analysis results, to permit the most efficient use of personnel and to prepare for contingencies.

- Identify appropriate equipment and motivational frameworks to encourage adherence to the schedule of regular physical exercise.

- Develop procedures and equipment for handling critical incidents, such as fatalities among the crew.

- Develop policies regarding outside communications, including negative personal news.

- Develop appropriate policies regarding recreational and leisure-time equipment, materials, programs, and policies.

- Develop meaningful tasks to occupy crew during the cruise phases of interplanetary transit, and for unplanned free time resulting from equipment malfunctions.

- Explore the advantages and disadvantages of different approaches to meal preparation.

IMPORTANCE OF LESSONS FROM THE PAST

On Thursday, 28 December 1893, Fridtjof Nansen was reading in his snug cabin onboard the *Fram*. The temperature outside was − 36 °F (− 38 °C), and all was shrouded in the perpetual darkness of the Arctic night. Nansen was reading the account of Elisha Kent Kane's 1852–55 expedition to search for Sir John Franklin and to reach the farthest north possible. Kane and the sixteen men under his command in the tiny *Advance* were unprepared for what awaited them in the Arctic. Their ship was beset. After two years in the ice, Kane and the fourteen surviving members of his party abandoned their vessel and began dragging their small open boats southward. The ragged group reached a Danish settlement ten months later, after a terrible journey over ice and water half the length of Greenland. The men would have perished had it not been for the Eskimos who provided them with food during their ordeal. Nansen interrupted his reading to record in his journal:

> I am reading the story of Kane's expedition just now. Unfortunate man, his preparations were miserably inadequate; it seems to me to have been a reckless, unjustifiable proceeding to set out with such equipment. Almost all the dogs died of bad food; all the men had scurvy from the same cause, with snow-blindness, frost-bites, and all kinds of miseries. He learned a wholesome awe of the Arctic night, and one can hardly wonder at it. He writes on page 173: "I feel that we are fighting the battle of life at disadvantage, and that an Arctic day and an Arctic night age a man more rapidly and harshly than a year anywhere else in this weary world." In another place he writes that it is impossible for civilized men not to suffer in such circumstances. These were sad but by no means unique experiences. (Nansen 1897, vol. 1, 353–54)

Nansen then wrote that he and his crew had experienced no aging or weakening influences; to the contrary, the quiet and regular life onboard the *Fram* made him feel younger and more refreshed than ever before. He sincerely recommended life under their conditions as a therapeutic experience. Nansen then recorded one of several notes in which he expressed feelings of guilt about the comfortable conditions onboard the *Fram*. He knew that loved ones at home would certainly be of the belief that the members of the expedition were suffering greatly from their isolation, confinement, and other deprivations. Instead, Nansen and his crew were comfortable and contented:

> I am almost ashamed of the life we lead, with none of those darkly painted sufferings of the long winter night which are indispensable to a properly exciting Arctic expedition. We shall have nothing to write about when we get home. I may say the same of my comrades as I have said for myself; they all look healthy, fat, in good condition; none of the traditional pale, hollow faces; no low spirits—any one hearing the laughter that goes on in the saloon, the fall of greasy cards, etc., would be in no doubt about this. But how, indeed, should there be any illness? With the best of food of every kind, as much of it as we

want, and constant variety, so that even the most fastidious cannot tire of it, good shelter, good clothing, good ventilation, exercise in the open air *ad libitum,* no over-exertion in the way of work, instructive and amusing books of every kind, relaxation in the shape of cards, chess, dominoes, halma, music, and story-telling—how should any one be ill? Every now and then I hear remarks expressive of perfect satisfaction with the life. (Nansen 1897, vol. 1, 354–56).

Nansen attributed the satisfaction onboard the *Fram* to proper preparation. "Truly the whole secret," Nansen wrote, "lies in arranging things sensibly, and especially in being careful about the food." He also believed that having the crew sit together for meals and use a common area for leisure hours helped to foster a spirit of cooperation and

The *Fram* locked in the polar ice. (Courtesy of artist William Gilkerson)

camaraderie that benefited the expedition. To Nansen's knowledge, it was the first time that all members of an expedition lived together in a relatively egalitarian atmosphere.

Perhaps the future explorers of space will benefit from the expeditionary and remote-duty experiences reported in this book. The likelihood of a successful expedition would be substantially increased if the lessons from the past were to be incorporated into the plans for the future. Possibly, the crew of a Mars-bound spacecraft will record for posterity in their journals how they feel guilty about their pleasant and comfortable life while others worry about them at home. And, when they return, they may reflect, as Nansen did, how their experiences, complete with real deprivations and yearnings, seem "like a far-off dream from another world."

EXPEDITIONS MENTIONED IN TEXT
(in chronological order)

Columbus's First Voyage of Discovery, 3 August 1492–15 March 1493
    Leader: Christopher Columbus (Italian sailing for Spain)
    Ships: Santa Maria, Pinta, and the Santa Clara (known as the *Niña*,
        the feminine form of the owner's name)

East India Company Expedition to the Davis Strait (Arctic), 1602
    Leader: George Weymouth (Dutch)
    Ship: *Discovery*

Muscovy Company Expeditions (Arctic), 1607 and 1608
    Leader: Henry Hudson (British)
    Ship: *Hopewell*

Hudson's Dutch East India Company Expedition (Arctic), 1609
    Leader: Henry Hudson (British, sailing for a Dutch company)
    Ship: *Half Moon*

Smythe-Digges-Wolstenholme Expedition (Arctic), 1610–11
    Leader: Henry Hudson (British)
    Ship: *Discovery*

Danish Expedition to the Northwest Passage, 1619–20
    Leader: Jens Munk (Danish)
    Ships: *Unicorn* and *Lamprey*

Cook's three voyages, 1768–71, 1772–75, and 1776–79
    Leader: James Cook (British)
    Ships: *Endeavour, Resolution, Adventure,* and *Discovery*

French Round-the-World Expedition, 1785–88
    Leader: Jean François de Galaup, Compte de la Pérouse (French)
    Ships: *Boussole* and *Astrolabe*

Royal Naval Expedition to the Arctic (also known as Winter Harbour Expedition and Parry's Expedition to Melville Island), 1819–20
    Leader: Edward Parry (British)
    Ships: *Hecla* and *Griper*

British Surveying Expedition (also known as the Voyage of the *Beagle*), 1831–36
    Leader: Robert FitzRoy (with Charles Darwin as the unpaid
        naturalist)
    Ships: *Beagle* and *Adventure*

U.S. Exploring Expedition (also known as the Wilkes Expedition), 1838–42
    Leader: Charles Wilkes (American)
    Ships: *Vincennes, Peacock, Relief, Porpoise, Sea Gull,* and *Flying Fish*

Franklin Expedition (Northwest Passage), 1845–47
    Leader: John Franklin
    Ships: *Erebus* and *Terror*

Search for Franklin Expedition, 1850–51
    Leaders: H. T. Austin (four-ship flotilla); Sherard Osborn in
        command of Pioneer (British)
    Ships: *Resolute, Assistance, Pioneer,* and *Intrepid* (the latter two
        were the first steam-powered ships to operate in the Arctic)

Weyprect and Payer Expedition to the Arctic, 1872–74
    Leaders: Karl Weyprect and Julius Payer (Austrian)
    Ship: *Tegetthoff*

Jeannette Arctic Expedition, 1879–81
    Leader: George Washington De Long (American)
    Ship: *Jeannette*

Lady Franklin Bay Expedition (also known as Greely Expedition) (Arctic), 1881–84
>   Leader: Adolphus Washington Greely (American)
>   Ships: *Proteus* (delivered the expedition) and *Thetis* (rescued the expedition)

Norwegian Polar Expedition, 1893–96
>   Leader: Fridtjof Nansen (Norwegian)
>   Ship: *Fram*

Belgian Antarctic Expedition (also known as *Belgica* Expedition), 1898–99
>   Leader: Adrien de Gerlache (Belgian)
>   Ship: *Belgica*

British Antarctic Expedition (also known as *Discovery* Expedition), 1901–4
>   Leader: Robert Falcon Scott (British)
>   Ship: *Discovery*

Amundsen's navigation of the Northwest Passage, 1903–6
>   Leader: Roald Amundsen (Norwegian)
>   Ship: *Gjøa*

British Antarctic Expedition (also known as *Terra Nova* Expedition and Scott's Last Expedition), 1910–13
>   Leader: Robert Falcon Scott (British)
>   Ship: *Terra Nova*

British Trans-Antarctic Expedition (also known as *Endurance* Expedition), 1914–16
>   Leader: Ernest Shackleton (British)
>   Ship: *Endurance*

Italia Expedition, 1926
>   Leader: Umberto Nobile (Italian)
>   Airship: *Italia*

Byrd Antarctic Expedition, 1928–30
      Leader: Richard E. Byrd (American)
      Ships: *New York* and *Eleanor Bolling*

Byrd's Expedition to Little America (also known as Byrd's Second
Antarctic Expedition, 1933–35)
      Leader: Richard E. Byrd (American)
      Ships: *Jacob Rupert* and *Bear of Oakland*

Kon-Tiki Expedition, 1947
      Leader: Thor Heyerdahl (Norwegian)
      Balsa raft: *Kon-Tiki*

Operation Hideout, 1953 (60 days)
      Leader: U.S. Navy
      Submarine: *Haddock*

U.S. Naval Construction Battalion (Special) Williams Air Operating
Facility (Antarctica), 1955–56
      Leader: David W. Canham, Jr.
      Ships: *Edisto*, *Areeb*, and *Nasperlin*

Sealab II, 1965 (three separate 15-day missions)
      Leaders: Various (U.S. Navy)
      Undersea habitat: *Sealab II*

Ra Expedition, 1969
      Leader: Thor Heyerdahl (Norwegian)
      Papyrus raft: *Ra*

Project Tektite, 1969–70 (*Tektite I*, 60 days; *Tektite II*, 14 and 20 days)
      Leaders: Various (National Aeronautics and Space
            Administration)
      Undersea habitat: *Tektite*

Skylab, 1973–74 (*Skylab I*, 28 days; *Skylab II*, 59 days; *Skylab III*, 84 days)
      Leaders: Charles Conrad, Jr.; Alan Bean; Gerald Carr (American)
      Space station: *Skylab*

International Biomedical Expedition to the Antarctic, 1980–81 (71-day traverse; five months total)

> Leaders: J. Rivolier, R. Goldsmith, D. J. Lugg, A.J.W. Taylor (international)
>
> Ship: *Thala Dan* (transport); motorized toboggans and tracked vehicles (traverse)

Soyuz T-5, 1982 (211 days)

> Leader: Anatoly Berezovoy (Soviet)
>
> Space station: *Salyut 7*

Soyuz TM-7, 1988 (25 days)

> Leader: Aleksandr Volkov (Soviet), with Sergei Krikalev (Soviet) and Jean-Loup Chretien (French)
>
> Space station: *Mir*

Rail Garrison Habitability Test, 1989 (32 days)

> Leader: Les Cooper (American)
>
> High-fidelity mockups of military rail-mobile habitats

Pentland South Pole Expedition, 1992–93 (95 days)

> Leader: Ranulph Fiennes (British)
>
> Aircraft (transport), skis, and sledges

NOTES

PREFACE

1. The previous study involved the systematic, comparative analysis of more
    than a dozen conditions that were considered to be similar in various ways
    to a low–Earth-orbit space station. Space station analogues were rated by
    seventy-six behavioral scientists and spacecraft designers in terms of four-
    teen dimensions to identify the conditions most similar to the anticipated
    low–Earth-orbit space station: duration of tour, amount of free time, size of
    group, physical isolation, psychological isolation, personal motivation,
    composition of group, social organization, hostility of environment,
    perceived risk, types of tasks, preparedness for mission, quality of life
    support conditions, and physical quality of habitat. That ranking exercise
    produced the following results.

Rank	Analogue	Combined Mean Value
1	*Skylab 4*	86.81
2	*Sealab II*	70.93
3	*Tektite I*	69.40
4	*Tektite II*	66.89
5	Submarines (FBM)	63.46
6	Antarctic research station (South Pole)	59.35
7	Commercial oil-field diving	57.12
8	Long-distance yacht racing	56.66
9	Commercial fishing vessels	54.10
10	Research vessels (coastal)	53.45
11	Ra expedition	52.99
12	Supertankers	49.21
13	Offshore oil platforms	41.52

2. Literate people in 1492 no longer believed that the world was flat; the Greeks had proved the sphericity of Earth nearly three centuries before Christ. In fact, that same year, Martin Behaim in Germany produced a terrestrial globe. The question under debate was the size of the planet, not its shape. During the third century BC, the Greek astronomer Eratosthenes accurately calculated the circumference of Earth with the use of a shadow-casting pole at the Tropic of Cancer and of geometry; five hundred years later, the geographer Ptolemy estimated the Earth to be one-fourth smaller than its actual dimensions; the Ptolemaic Earth is portrayed in the Behaim globe, and it played a part in Columbus's plans to sail to Cipango (i.e., Japan). He calculated a degree to be 56.66 miles when it is actually 69 statute miles at the Equator, one of the most fortunate mistakes in history. Had Columbus known that the distance was 10,000 miles, rather than 3,200 miles, he might not have embarked on the journey. He estimated the distance to his destination at 3,100 miles and was off by only 100 miles. He maintained the correct latitude for Japan, but a New World blocked his course and saved the admiral and his crew from an impossibly long voyage to the Orient.

3. When explorers of earlier times philosophized about the significance of their work, they frequently spoke in terms that sound odd to the modern ear. In particular, it was common and acceptable usage until fairly recently to refer to the human species as "man" or "mankind." Please overlook these and other archaisms in quotations presented in this book. They are simply the reflections of earlier ages and do not affect the merit of the information or opinions that are conveyed.

CHAPTER 1. SCIENTIFIC CONCERN ABOUT BEHAVIORAL EFFECTS OF ISOLATION AND CONFINEMENT

1. For additional reviews of research concerning isolation and confinement and related behavioral issues, see Burns, Chambers, and Hendler, 1963; Rasmussen, 1973; Edholm and Gunderson, 1973; Connors, Harrison, and Akins, 1985; Evans, Stokols, and Carrere, 1988; and Harrison, Clearwater, and McKay, 1991.

CHAPTER 2. DESCRIPTION OF THE RESEARCH

1. The inspiration for reviewing the accounts of expeditions came in 1986 following my presentation at the International Symposium on Psycho-Neuro Endocrinology in Bergen, Norway. The Norwegian Underwater Technology Center had invited me to present my "slide show" about space station habitability at the symposium. At that time, NUTEC was exploring the possibility of building a monobaric habitat on the North Sea floor to serve as a substitute for an oil platform in very deep water. Recognizing the similarity of a deep sea oil facility to spacecraft, NUTEC scientist Dr. Ragnar Værnes asked NASA about the behavioral issues associated with

space station design; NASA suggested that he call me, which led to the presentation, in Bergen. Immediately following the presentation I was approached by Dr. Carl Wilhelm Sem-Jacobsen, a Norwegian physician, who strongly suggested that I look into the expeditions of Fridtjof Nansen for additional lessons of relevance to the design and conduct of future space missions. I am grateful for the suggestion.

2.   Some of the earliest fictitious accounts of space missions are remarkably accurate in their descriptions or predictions. For example, the projectile in Jules Verne's *From the Earth to the Moon* (originally published in 1866) was about the same size as an *Apollo* capsule; carried three men, as did *Apollo*; and was launched from a site in Florida, as was *Apollo*, to achieve lunar orbit. Three years later (one hundred years before *Apollo 11*), Verne brought the spacecraft home in *Round the Moon*; it splashed down 250 miles off the California coast, only 2-1/2 miles from where certain *Apollo* spacecraft also splashed down.

3.   Nelson suggests site visits, or observation, as an indirect technique for the study of isolated and confined groups. "Participant observation" is the principal method in the tool kit of anthropologists. In participant observation, the observer becomes, to the extent possible, a member of the group that is the focus of the study. In time, the "subjects" become desensitized to the observer's special status and behave normally. This technique has been the basis of many illuminating ethnographies and focused studies on groups ranging from tribal societies to industrial work teams. The method would be particularly appropriate for the study of groups living under isolation and confinement, such as Antarctic winter-over teams and high-fidelity simulations of long-duration space missions.

4.   Fuson (1987) writes that Columbus's journal (known then as *diario de a bordo*, or *Diario de Colon*, and in English as *Journal of the First Voyage*) was the first log written for a wider audience than other mariners. The journal is actually addressed to the royal sponsor of the venture, Hernando and Isabel (known incorrectly as Ferdinand and Isabella). Accordingly, the diary is "remarkably detailed and wide-ranging, especially when compared to the accounts of many other voyages even in the centuries to follow." He continues:

> A sailor reading Columbus's log today will understand every entry; the sea is unchanging, and the rig of a modern sailing vessel, while more efficient, has not changed much from the caravels of the Discoverer. So it is not surprising—to a sailor—to find that (except for racing yachts and the clipper ships) a vessel propelled by sail, anywhere from something over 30 feet to fair-sized windships, will make on the average the same daily run—about 100 miles a day. (P. xv)

5. The irony of this quotation is that Scott failed to heed his own advice a few years later. His exotic equipment (by the standards of the day) was untested, and, in many ways, he was unprepared for the expedition when he sailed onboard the *Terra Nova* in 1910. Scott's attempt to be the first to the South Pole was a disaster, but he gave good advice.

CHAPTER 3. SLEEP

1. For humans, sleep and wakefulness, cognition and motor performance, body temperature, serum hormone levels, and urinary excretion vary rhythmically. Takahashi and Zatz (1982) explain:

> The susceptibility of animals to toxic agents varies dramatically with the time of day [for example], a standard dose of *Escherichia coli* endotoxin will kill about 80 percent of a group of mice when given early in the evening and will kill less than 20 percent in the middle of the night. Similarly, the sensitivity of many sensory and regulatory processes such as photoreception, synaptic excitability, and receptor mediated events vary with a circadian rhythm. Clearly, the physiological state of an organism varies throughout the day. Oscillatory systems permit organisms to anticipate periodic events in the environment and to initiate slow processes before they are required. Circadian systems thus provide a framework for the temporal organization of the animal; as Pittendrigh has emphasized, "they organize 'a day within,' that is, an evolved match to the periodicity of the external world." (P. 1105)

2. The researchers found that the quality of sleep was somewhat different in Antarctica. In particular, the time to onset of sleep was longer among Antarctic personnel (15.4 minutes) than among the same men in temperate zones (3.5 minutes), and there was a reduction in REM (rapid eye movement) sleep of about 20 percent. Neither difference was statistically significant. A major change was found, however, in the nearly complete loss of SWS (slow wave sleep, or stage 4) at the end of the polar winter. Also, the SWS had failed to return six months after the subjects returned home from Antarctica (from a baseline mean of 20 minutes of SWS per night, to 2.8 minutes during the winter, to 1 minute following return to the United States) (Shurley 1974; Natani and Shurley 1974).

3. Lieutenant Greely was the leader of the Lady Franklin Bay Expedition, later to become infamous as the Greely Expedition for its grizzly tale of survival, cannibalism, botched logistics support, and the relationship of politics to science. The expedition was one of two parties sent to the Arctic by the U.S. government in 1881 as part of the International Polar Year. For the first time in history, a dozen countries cooperated in a scientific venture.

4.   From *Lessons Learned from the* Skylab *Program* (NASA 1974, 86):

> In the early phases of the mission, *Skylab* crewmen complained
> that too often they were scheduled to perform operational or
> experimental activities right up until the beginning of their
> sleep period and that it was quite difficult to relax abruptly
> and go to sleep. The one hour of uninterrupted presleep
> activity was observed as a constraint during *Skylab 4*. (P. 86)

CHAPTER 5. EXERCISE

1.   Master Chief Violanti founded the Ice Hole Pines Golf Course in 1990. The
     nine-hole par 3 to 5 regulation course is located at Williams Field, near
     McMurdo Station, Antarctica. Green Kool-Aid is sprayed on the ice near
     the pins to make the greens the customary color, and used Christmas trees
     are placed on the largely flat course following the holiday to assist the
     players' depth perception. An annual tournament attracts about
     twenty-five players.

2.   The range of possible programming is limitless. Video recordings of great
     bicycle paths of the world is a favored suggestion, for example, ergometer
     "tours" of the Rhine Valley on Monday, the Swiss Alps on Tuesday, and
     Mount Haleakala on Wednesday; headphones; and a stereo audio track of
     the actual sounds (documentary style) might lend realism to the experi-
     ence and contribute to the diversion. The ergometer could even be pro-
     grammed to provide variable resistance to the operator to correspond with
     the terrain on the screen. I believed this to be an original concept when I
     suggested it in the space station report more than ten years ago. Since that
     time bicycle-video exercise devices have become commercially available.
     Many options for video programming are possible to make exercise more
     recreational. The key operating principles in this regard should be variety
     and self-selection.

CHAPTER 6. WORKLOAD

1.   Roald Amundsen ultimately died in the Arctic, more than twenty-five
     years and many adventures later. In 1928, he came out of retirement at age
     fifty-six to accompany a French rescue party searching for Umberto Nobile
     and his crew of the airship *Italia*. (Amundsen and Nobile had crossed the
     Arctic together two years earlier in the airship *Norge*.) *Italia* had crashed on
     the ice in an attempt to fly over the North Pole. The airship's gondola was
     ripped off by the impact with the ice. Ten men, including Nobile (and his
     dog), were spilled out onto the floes, along with many emergency supplies
     (including a radio); the *Italia* and the six crewmen who remained onboard
     were never seen again. Nobile and the others were on the ice for four
     weeks before a rescue plan was implemented. Amundsen and the French
     crew were lost somewhere over the Barents Sea during their search for
     survivors. A Swedish pilot located Nobile's camp, which became

established in popular lore as the "Red Tent." The pilot landed, but the small plane could carry only one additional man, so he took Nobile (and his dog). No further trips by air were possible. The Soviet icebreaker *Krassin* eventually rescued an additional survivor of the party. Nobile returned to Italy in disgrace.

This incident in the history of polar exploration was documented in the 1971 Russian-Italian film, *The Red Tent*. In the film, Nobile, played by Peter Finch, is haunted in his later years by the ghosts of some of those involved in the crash and rescue. Sean Connery, perfectly cast as Amundsen, advises an aging and sleepless Nobile to forgive himself for surviving while others perished.

2. Regarding the performance of housekeeping duties, Cook ([1900] 1980) writes, in a manner characteristic of his era:

> It contains a lesson. It teaches us how much of the drudgery of life is done uncomplainingly by mothers, sisters, wives, and other members of the family circle. It makes us feel the importance of feminine existence, causes us to see the ups and downs, the ponds and eddies, the rapids and cataracts of the humdrum side of life, which man ordinarily escapes. (P. 373)

CHAPTER 7. LEADERSHIP

1. Leadership skills must not be limited to the designated expedition or station leader. Others in the group also must be capable of assuming situation-specific leadership responsibilities and larger leadership roles, when necessary. In a recent study of Navy SEALs, small, lightly armed units that operate independently in denied territory, experienced SEALs were adamant that it is essential to mission success for all members of the team to be both good leaders *and* good followers, depending on the circumstances. Further, SEALs have developed calm decision making under stress as a core theme of SEAL culture. For example, when young Lt. (jg) Joseph Robert Kerrey and his platoon were engaged by a superior enemy force in 1969, he exhibited this core SEAL value by quickly comprehending the dynamic situation and directing an appropriate course of action, despite having been severely wounded early in the firefight. In addition to the tactical results of his leadership (e.g., directing counterfire, dividing the unit into two elements to obtain a crossfire, securing an extraction site), the Medal of Honor citation also refers to the young SEAL's "presence of mind" and his ability to "maintain calm, superlative control" (Stuster et al. 1994). These traits also will be required of future space crews.

CHAPTER 8. MEDICAL AND PSYCHOLOGICAL SUPPORT

1. Even the ship's cat behaved oddly, despite a diet of fresh meat. The cat had been named "Nansen," in backhanded honor of the Norwegian

explorer who had returned from his Norwegian Polar Expedition only a year before the *Belgica* sailed. Cook writes in his journal, 26 June 1898:

> Altogether "Nansen" seemed thoroughly disgusted with his surroundings and his associates, and lately he has sought exclusion in infrequented corners. His temperament has changed from a good and lively creature to one of frowning discontent. His mind has wandered and from his changed spiritual attitude we believe that his soul has wandered too. A day or two ago his life departed, we presume for more congenial regions. We are glad that his torture is ended, but we miss "Nansen" very much. He has been the attribute to our good fortune to the present, the only speck of sentimental life within reach. We have showered upon him our affections, but the long darkness has made him turn against us. In the future we shall be without a mascot and what will be our fate? (Cook [1900] 1980, p. 326)

2. Rivolier and Bachelard (1988) report that the risks involved in performing an appendectomy at a remote-duty station, if necessary, do not justify routine appendectomies as a preventive measure. Dr. William K. Douglas, flight surgeon for Project Mercury; Desmond Lugg, head of Polar Medicine, Australian Antarctic Division; and most other physicians agree with this assessment. It might be appropriate, however, to reconsider this approach concerning the crew of long-duration space missions. An operation in the weightlessness of space or at a lunar or planetary base might be considerably more problematic than in the medical facility of an Antarctic station. Further, the penalties for having a member of a small crew in space out of commission while being treated with drugs to forestall an acute attack or during recuperation from surgery probably would be far greater than the inconvenience of temporarily losing the services of an Antarctic crew member. Finally, sufficient time would be available prior to the launch of a long-duration space mission to perform operations on the crew members, perhaps years in advance, to avoid any possible postoperative complications, such as adhesions, that could affect mission performance.

3. Nansen (1897) also reports a classic anxiety-fixing dream, similar to one experienced by many college students, in which he returned home from the North Pole but had nothing to write about because he forgot to take measurements with his instruments.

4. Strange and Klein (1973) provide the following example of extreme psychological disturbance at an Antarctic research station:

> The most spectacular instance of emotional disorder occurring in these isolated stations during this recent three-year period was a case of paranoid psychosis. Although the final specific diagnosis might be debated by psychiatrists of different

backgrounds, there can be no doubt that this patient was overtly psychotic with paranoid delusions and assaultive behavior. It eventually became necessary to treat him with high doses of phenothiazine medications and isolate him from the other station personnel. It was later learned that he had ill-defined but probably similar, although less severe, problems in the past. It is significant that his delusions developed in a tense emotional milieu which was marked by conscious homosexual anxiety stimulated by a schizoid, effeminate and seductive member of the group. There was unusually heavy alcohol intake, chronic suspiciousness, and much hostility. It was a climate well designed to reinforce the unhealthy psychological defense mechanism of projection and thereby breed paranoia. The confined intimacy of these isolated groups enccurages tendencies to projection, and paranoid feelings can occur. As might be expected, alcohol use makes them worse. (P. 414)

CHAPTER 10. FOOD PREPARATION

1.   Cherry-Garrard (1930) observes that variety in meals is important, even when personnel operate on short rations, as were the depot parties on Scott's last expedition to Antarctica:

I moved into Scott's tent for the first time in the middle of the Depot Journey, and was enormously impressed by the comfort which a careful routine of this nature evoked. There was a homelike air about the tent at supper time, and, though a lunch camp in the middle of the night is always rather bleak, there was never anything slovenly. Another thing which struck me even more forcibly was the cooking. We were of course on just the same ration as the tent from which I had come. I was hungry and said so. "Bad cooking," said Wilson shortly; and so it was. For in two or three days the sharpest edge was off my hunger. Wilson and Scott had learned many a cooking tip in the past, and, instead of the same old meal day by day, the weekly ration was so manoeuvred by a clever cook that it was seldom quite the same meal. Sometimes pemmican plain, or thicker pemmican with some arrowroot mixed with it; at others we surrendered a biscuit and a half apiece and had a dry hoosh, i.e. biscuit fried in pemmican with a little water added, and a good big cup of cocoa to follow. Dry hooshes also saved oil. There were cocoa and tea upon which to ring the changes, or better still "teaco" which combined the stimulating qualities of tea with the food value of cocoa. Then much could be done with the dessert-spoonful of raisins which was our daily whack. They were good soaked in tea, but best perhaps in the biscuits and pemmican as a dry hoosh. "You are going far to earn my undying gratitude, Cherry," was a satisfied remark of Scott one evening when, having saved, unbeknownst to my companions, some of their daily ration of cocoa, arrowroot, sugar, and raisins, I made a "chocolate hoosh." But I am afraid he had indigestion the next morning. (Pp. 330–31)

2. The *Jeannette* Arctic Expedition was sponsored by James Gordon Bennett, publisher of the *New York Herald,* who had just previously sent Henry Morton Stanley to Africa in search of Dr. David Livingstone.

3. Gen. Jean-Loup Chretien, the French spationaute, has been a guest on both *Salyut 7* and *Mir* space stations. It was reported that, during his *Mir* mission, he carried many delicacies to the station. These included compote of pigeon with dates and dried raisins, duck with artichokes, oxtail fondue with tomatoes and pickles, beef bourguignonne, sautéed veal marengo, ham and fruite pâtés, cheeses, nuts, and chocolate bars. Sergei Kirkalev, one of the cosmonauts who spent twenty-five days with General Chretien, reported, "The food was OK, but a little heavy for space. It was good to get back to plain black bread after he left" (SF 1994).

CHAPTER 11. GROUP INTERACTION

1. The term "comrade" is particularly appropriate in the context of isolation and confinement. The modern version of the word is derived from the Middle French usage, which refers to a group of soldiers who sleep in the same room.

2. In an early study of isolation and confinement, Pinks (1949) found that the morale and efficiency of Air Force loran station technicians were maintained at higher levels in those situations where living conditions and habitability were described as "good," compared with those characterized as "poor." He found, however, that morale and efficiency were higher with poor conditions and good leadership than with good conditions and poor leadership.

3. Although these arrangements seemed to work well for the officers, Mountfield (1974) reports that, in the initial case, "the 'servant's' disguise was immediately penetrated by the sexually aware islanders of Tahiti."

4. Explorer Thor Heyerdahl, author of *Kon-Tiki* (1950) and *The Ra Expeditions* (1971), provides the following relevant observation:

> Sex is of course a bit of a problem when a team of men are away from women over long periods. On my trans-oceanic raft expeditions we have never been longer from women than two or three months at a time, and then we have made it a rule not to talk about women or sex, nor for that matter about anything else that may bring up longings and cause for someone to look for the end of the project. During longer periods, like

archaeological expeditions to isolated areas, I have seen some
of the best and friendliest men who had been faithful to their
wives at home, completely lose their own character and
personality, getting cranky, suspicious, and even quite evil.
Home again they return to themselves. This is what we have
termed, "expedition fever." It is, of course, the main duty of the
expedition leader to find means of preventing bad feelings
between the members of his crew when he notices that
something may be brewing, but he must put his words in such
a way that neither of the parties is aware of his efforts.
(Personal communication, 1994)

5.   Charles Darwin was appalled by the slavery and brutality that he and his
shipmates on the *Beagle* found during their stops in Brazil. He spoke of it
to Capt. Robert FitzRoy, who viewed slavery as an ancient institution with
much in its favor. A heated discussion ensued, at the conclusion of which
Darwin said he could no longer share a cabin, or a ship, with someone
who held such views, and walked out of the cabin. FitzRoy continued with
his rage, but he eventually realized that he had gone too far and had hurt
Darwin's feelings. He sent for Darwin, offered his apologies, and asked
him to stay. Darwin was eager to accept because he believed that "it was
the great adventure of the voyage that mattered … it was more important
than any private quarrel" (Moorehead 1969). Fortunately, the plan called
for FitzRoy to take the *Beagle* north for two months to continue the coastal
survey and for Darwin to remain ashore to make collections and
observations.

6.   Some individuals develop annoying mannerisms during their lives and
never realize the negative effects of these behaviors on others. Perhaps
special training, counseling, or postsimulation debriefing sessions can help
to rid prospective crew personnel of any mannerisms that might be exceptionally irritating during long-duration isolation and confinement. A
particularly annoying trait, under any circumstances, is a tendency to
complain about things, for example, to repeatedly complain about the difficulty of one's work, compared (explicitly or implicitly) with the work of
others. Dr. E. A. Wilson, chief of the scientific staff on Scott's last expedition, had a similar pet peeve:

There is nothing so irritating as the man who is always coming
in and informing all and sundry that he has repaired his
sledge, or built a wall [to protect a tent or pony], or filled the
cookers, or mended his socks. The best sledger is the man who
sees what has to be done, and does it—and says nothing about
it. (Quoted in Cherry-Garrard 1930, 330)

7.   Years after the expedition, Cherry-Garrard (1930) could recall pleasant
memories as well as the nightmares of "the worst journey in the world."
Maybe because the members of Scott's party were British, they tended to

remain particularly civil to each other, despite incredibly austere and dangerous conditions. For example:

> How good the memories of those days are... with ready words of sympathy for frost-bitten feet; with generous smiles for poor jests; with suggestions of happy beds to come. We did not forget the Please and Thank you, which means much in such circumstances, and all the little links with decent civilization which we could still keep going. I'll swear there was still a grace about us when we staggered in. And we kept our tempers—even to God. (P. 296)

The last few pages of Scott's diary contain probably the saddest story in the history of exploration. The five-man polar party, led by Scott, had endured nearly three months of "man-hauling" their supplies up a glacier and over uneven ice to reach the South Pole, only to find that Amundsen, using dogsleds, had beat them by about a month. The weather worsened on the trek back. Petty Officer Edgar Evans, the strongest member of Scott's party, weakened first, possibly because the equal rations could not sustain his larger body; he was frostbitten, then fell, probably sustaining a brain injury. Army Capt. Lawrence ("Titus") Oates, sensing that his weakness was jeopardizing the chances of the others, simply walked out of the tent to his death after he said, "I am just going outside and may be some time." The three remaining members of the polar party were within 11 miles of the supply cache that would have saved them, but the unrelenting storm prevented their reaching it. When the search party found Scott, Wilson, and Lt. Henry Bowers several months later, they were lying side by side in their tent, with Scott in the middle, one arm across the body of his friend Wilson. Scott's diary and the letters to his wife and the families of the other men describe a civility and grace in the face of death that is difficult to convey. Three weeks before the final journal entry, with one man dead, another in terrible shape, and the group running low on food and fuel, they must have expected the worst, yet they maintained good spirits when talking together. At that time, Scott wrote, "I don't know what I should do if Wilson and Bowers weren't so determinedly cheerful over things." His final journal entry was a plea to the supporters of the expedition, "For God's sake look after our people."

8. Walter Sullivan, *The New York Times*, 6 October 1970, reports on the analysis of group dynamics conducted by two Soviet members of Thor Heyerdahl's international crew of the papyrus raft *Ra*, which sailed from North Africa to the Caribbean in 1969:

> The two scientists reported that, in their view, an international crew, in a situation of confinement, prolonged isolation, and peril was beneficial. Confrontation with common problems and dangers soon broke down the barriers rooted in nationality, they said, as the raft began sinking and had to be

lashed together. The patterns of alliance and hostility fluctuated, they reported, although Mr. Heyerdahl always retained his position of leadership and good relations with all. A commanding personality, in such a situation, is "extremely important" they said, and Mr. Heyerdahl fulfilled that role.

9. There is considerable merit to Nansen's approach to living in isolation and confinement; he was especially concerned about maintaining group solidarity. While still onboard the *Fram*, locked in the polar ice cap, Nansen (1897) wrote of the experience:

> We lead a winter life... as if we had brought a bit of Norway, of Europe, with us. We are as well off as if we were home. All together in one saloon, with everything in common, we are a little part of the fatherland, and daily we draw closer and closer together. (Vol. 1, 367–68)

10. Supertanker voyages are the longest uninterrupted sea journeys since the days of sail. The enormous sizes of modern supertankers often prevent them from taking the most direct routes to or from points of loading and offloading. The two routes for which supertankers were principally designed are (1) the Persian Gulf to Europe via the Cape of Good Hope and (2) the Persian Gulf to Japan via the Straits of Malacca. The distance of each route is more than 11,000 miles, which means that a round-trip roughly equals a circumnavigation of the globe. At a speed of 14–15 knots, each journey, one way, takes about ten weeks and occasionally longer. The voyage between the Persian Gulf and North America takes about the same amount of time. Because loading and discharging of oil is conducted at offshore terminals, it is not uncommon for a crew member to spend a year or more without setting foot on dry land (much longer periods have been reported). The policy of most American carriers is to limit crew members to two consecutive voyages (five to six months), separated by six weeks to two months of leave. Thus, in duration of tour, at least, supertanker voyages are analogous to some future long-duration expeditions.

Mostert (1974) provides the following description of informal group activities that developed among the officers of the P and O Line's supertanker *Ardshiel*. The informal activities and characteristic British civility helped the men to endure their months and years away from home:

> After dinner the party moved to the coffee-table in the ward room. "Who is going to be mum?" someone invariably asked, and whoever was nearest to the coffee began pouring, while others handed around the cups, the milk and sugar. Thomson usually dominated the conversation, and recounted to the juniors tales of his past experience, to which they patiently

listened. These were stories they'd heard often enough, and would hear many times again before they left the ship. It was not however a lengthy ordeal. After half an hour or so, the master would suddenly announce, "Well, I suppose I'll go up and do my book of words," and vanished. As a rule, he was followed by the chief engineer.

The departure of the two most senior officers brought a distinct lightening of atmosphere to the room; but however much it lightened, the mood of the wardroom always remained somewhat formal and well-mannered. There was seldom any horseplay or ribaldry. One was again aware of the social lassitude of long confinement: the quality of desultory and inactive converse that is not listlessness but rather that emptiness of real mutual interest that settles upon men who have heard each other out too often. And one was aware not so much of the remoteness of the world at large but of most of the ship itself; it was the feeling of being inside a walled-in community upon one end of an otherwise uninhabited island whose opposite shore few ever bothered to visit and some scarcely knew, and which one actually had to wonder about from time to time.... They seemed to prefer gathering in each other's cabins, as if in retreat from the huge and impinging emptiness of the ship; and there, in a fog of smoke and a growing litter of beer cans, the hubbub, ribaldry, affectionate jeering, and repartee absent from the wardroom asserted itself. (P. 93)

CHAPTER 13. OUTSIDE COMMUNICATIONS

1. Paul Siple was a 20-year-old Boy Scout (actually an assistant scoutmaster) selected to accompany the expedition to Antarctica and return on the *New York,* one of the ships that transported the party. Larry Gould, Byrd's second in command, was impressed with Siple. He convinced Byrd to permit Siple to stay on as a zoologist and taxidermist, based on his merit-badge experience and college biology major; also, Gould needed help because he had taken over the administrative duties of the expedition's original executive officer. Siple later earned a Ph.D. in geography and worked with Byrd on all of his subsequent private and government expeditions. He returned to Antarctica six times. During and after World War II, Siple worked for the U.S. Army as a cold weather expert and science adviser, and he developed the concept of the "wind-chill factor" and the associated equation. He was a president of the American Association of Geographers and a science adviser to the U.S. embassies in Australia and New Zealand. He died in 1968 at the age of fifty-nine. A small U.S. research station was named for him and operated from 1969 through 1988.

CHAPTER 14. RECREATIONAL OPPORTUNITIES

1. Nansen (1897), with characteristic humor, writes in a footnote:

    > Up to this day I am not quite clear as to what these emblems were intended to signify. That the doctor, from want of practice, would have been glad [for] a normal day's work ("normal arbeidsdag") can readily be explained, but why the meteorologists should cry out for universal suffrage passes my comprehension. Did they want to overthrow despotism? (Vol. 1, p. 484)

2. For example, the table on the following page summarizes the free-time activities of the twenty-three participants in a full-mission simulation of a military remote-duty environment. Eighteen members of the crew occupied the security car (SC); the commander and four other officers occupied the launch control car (LCC).

3. The board game Risk was one of the few sources of interpersonal conflict during a thirty-two-day full mission simulation of a military remote-duty system. Several heated discussions were observed when crew members played the game. They recognized the potential for serious problems to develop as a consequence of playing this particular game, so the crew, on their own, decided to retire it for the duration of simulated the mission. The crew enjoyed other games without incident, including several stimulating games of chess played with two boards over a radio system between crew members confined to separate isolated habitats (Stuster 1989).

    Similar competitions might be considered for the crews of future long-duration expeditions. For example, games could be played between spacecraft personnel and mission controllers, the crews of other spacecraft, or members of a group at an Antarctic station.

4. The Navy has found that Antarctic personnel who participate in formal courses of study (i.e., through colleges or universities) have a high rate of completion. Personnel who attempt to pursue an individual study program (e.g., learn a language on their own), however, tend to be less likely to achieve their objectives because they fail to maintain their commitments.

5. The "publication" of newspapers, begun by Parry in 1818, is a long-standing practice on expeditions. The tradition continues at U.S. Antarctic stations, often with the emergence of an "underground" press. The publications are usually informative, sometimes critical, and always entertaining for those who prepare and read them. For example, a newspaper titled *Framsjaa* appeared onboard the *Fram* following her crew's first Christmas locked in the ice; it contained hand-drawn illustrations, descriptions of recent events (in verse!), and a humorous advertising section. The

Summary Analysis of Crew Free-Time Activities During the
Thirty-Two-Day Rail Garrison Habitability Exercise, December 1989

Activity	Weeks 1 and 2		Weeks 3 and 4	
	Number of Crew	Mean Ranking	Number of Crew	Mean Ranking
Watching videos	21	4.3	23	2.9
Watching television[a]	20	5.0	13	2.3
Reading periodicals	20	6.9	19	6.1
Reading books	19	3.4	19	3.5
Sleeping	19	3.9	20	3.1
Talking	19	6.5	19	5.8
Writing letters	18	6.9	8	7.9
Eating	16	7.8	18	7.0
Listening to radio	14	7.1	8	7.5
Listening to tapes	13	4.9	12	6.4
Running[b]	13	8.3	0	0.0
Playing ball	9	9.4	0	0.0
Lifting weights	8	8.6	4	6.3
Studying	7	6.3	6	4.3
Exercising (e.g., sit-ups, etc.)	6	9.0	4	7.0
Playing cards	6	9.3	5	8.6
Playing solitaire	6	9.7	9	6.6
Playing Trivial Pursuits	5	11.2	13	8.9
Exercising with skiing device	5	13.4	0	0.0
Working while off duty	5	14.6	1	16.0
Writing in journal	4	13.5	3	13.7
Playing Risk	3	5.7	6	8.5
Playing Monopoly	3	8.7	3	7.0
Solving crossword puzzles	3	11.3	1	8.0
Exercycling	2	12.5	3	9.7
Drawing or painting	2	19.5	3	7.3
Sitting and smoking[c]	1	4.0	0	0.0
Practicing with drumsticks	0	0.0	1	10.0
Playing Nintendo[d]	0	0.0	7	7.0

[a] Television was unavailable in LCC during weeks 3–4.

[b] Running was impossible during weeks 3–4 because all crew members were confined to the habitat.

[c] Smoking was impossible during weeks 3–4 because all crew members were confined to the habitat.

[d] Nintendo was unavailable to crew during weeks 1–2 and located in SC during weeks 3–4.

Framsjaa was read aloud as a group activity, but then almost every activity onboard the *Fram* was a group activity. Also, Mountfield (1974) writes the following about Robert Falcon Scott's *Discovery* Expedition in 1902:

> The winter passed very comfortably. The ship's company, seg-regated into officers and men, appears to have gotten on well. On occasion when voices were raised, the warning, "Girls, girls!" was often enough to break the tension. Shackleton edited the inevitable *South Polar Times* which is said by those who have courageously plodded through a large portion of numerous similar publications to have been one of the best explorers' newspapers. (P. 144)

6. Music has played a large role in the entertainment of many expeditions. For example, "sing-songs" were numerous on Scott's *Terra Nova* Expedition in 1911–12. During a sing-song, each man offered a verse in turn around the dinner table or contributed to the wine fund if creativity failed him. Cherry-Garrard (1930) notes:

> The expedition was very fond of singing, though there was hardly anybody in it who could sing.... All through the expedition the want of someone who could play the piano was felt, and such a man is certainly a great asset in a life so far removed from the pleasures of civilization. (Pp. 10, 38–39)

In *Voyage of the* Discovery, Scott (1905) tells about an officer who played the piano each evening during his first expedition to Antarctica in 1902. He described their hour of music each evening as an institution that none of them would willingly forego. Scott explored in simpler times, but group music (whether listening to it or actually making it through song or instrument) probably would still be a beneficial form of recreation on future long-duration expeditions. In this regard, MacDonald's *Polar Operations*, a 1969 handbook for polar explorers, includes the following caption to a photograph of Coast Guard men playing basketball on the ice: "Group recreation helps keep members of an expedition on an even keel." That advice applies to many forms of recreation, including music.

CHAPTER 15. PERSONNEL SELECTION CRITERIA

1. What was required to be an early astronaut? Sherrod (1975) reports on the process:

> In December 1958, plans had been made to post civil service notices inviting applications for astronaut service, GS-12 to GS-15, salary $8,330 to $12,770. President Eisenhower thought this ridiculous, and decided that the rolls of military test pilots would furnish all the astronauts necessary. "It was one of the best decisions he ever made," said Robert Gilruth sixteen years later. "It ruled out the matadors, mountain climbers, scuba

divers, and race drivers and gave us stable guys who had already been screened for security." From the records of 508 test pilots, 110 were found to meet the minimum standards (including the height and age limitations, 5 feet 11 inches and 40 years).

After further examination, the 110 were narrowed to 69, then to 32, who were put through strenuous physical tests: How much heat could the man stand? How much noise? How many balloons could he blow up before he collapsed? How long could he keep his feet in ice water? How long could he run on a treadmill?

Worst of all, the astronauts thought, were the 25 psychological tests that entailed minute and painful self-examination ("Write 20 answers to the question: 'Who am I?' ") From the 18 survivors, seven were chosen in April 1959, and they would remain the Nation's only astronauts for three and one-half years. Their IQs ranged from 130 to 145, with a mean of 136. Even before they had accomplished anything they became instant heroes to small boys and other hero-worshipers around the world.

Among those who flunked the first round were James Lovell and Charles Conrad, who were picked up in the Second Nine in 1962 and went on to make four spaceflights apiece—a record they shared only with John Young and Tom Stafford. The Second Nine proved even more stable than their predecessors. Excepting Ed White, killed in the spacecraft fire of January 1967, and Elliott See, who died in a place crash, all commanded Apollo flights.

The Second Nine were test pilots, too, but two of them were civilians: Neil Armstrong, who had flown the X–15 for NASA, and See a General Electric flier. By the time the third group of fourteen was selected in 1963 the test-pilot requirement had been dropped—as had most of the outlandish physical tests— but the educational level had risen to an average of 5.6 years of college, even though the IQ average fell a couple of points below the first two groups. Four of the fourteen would die in accidents without making a spaceflight.

The fourth group of six men wasn't even required to be pilots because they were scientists (doctors of geology, medicine, physics, and electrical engineering) who, after selection, had to take an extra year to learn to fly. Because three missions were cut from the program, only one, Harrison Schmitt, was to fly in *Apollo*. Three others flew in *Skylab*.

The fifth group was the biggest of all, nineteen pilots, of whom twelve would fly in *Apollo*, three in *Skylab*, and one in *Apollo-Soyuz*. The Sixth group, eleven more scientists, scored the highest mean IQ, 141, but they came too late to fly and six resigned before 1975. The final group of seven transferred from the Air Force's defunct Manned Orbital Laboratory in 1969 and their hope had to rest on the resumption of flight with the Space Shuttle about 1979. [The first shuttle was actually launched on 12 April 1981.]

What did it take to become an astronaut? Dr. Robert Voas, a psychologist who was the Mercury astronauts' training director, detailed the required characteristics as he saw them: intelligence without genius, knowledge without inflexibility, a high degree of skill without overtraining, fear but not cowardice, bravery without foolhardiness, self-confidence without egotism, physical fitness without being muscle-bound, a preference for participatory over spectator sports, frankness without blabbermouthing, enjoyment of life without excess, humor without disproportion, fast reflexes without panic in a crisis. These ideals were fulfilled to a high degree. (Pp. 146–47)

CHAPTER 16. PRIVACY AND PERSONAL SPACE

1. The title of Richard Henry Dana's ([1840] 1927) famous account of his voyage to the coast of California in 1834–36 refers to the traditional distinction between officers and sailors. The sailors' berths were always forward of the mizzen mast of a sailing ship, hence *Two Years Before the Mast*.

2. Following are sleeping compartment dimensions for some of the space analogue environments reviewed for this study:

Analogue Environment	Sleeping Compartment Dimensions
Submarines	75" x 28" x 24"= 30.4 cubic feet
Tektite I & II	72" x 28" x 30"= 35 cubic feet
Sealab II	78" x 28" x 30"= 37.9 cubic feet
Ben Franklin	78" x 29" x 30"= 39.3 cubic feet
Saturation chamber	76" x 30" x 31"= 40.9 cubic feet
Skylab 4, chamber 1	78" x 38" x 28"= 48 cubic feet
Skylab 4, chamber 2	78" x 48" x 29"= 62.8 cubic feet
Antarctic stations	6' x 12' x 7' = 504 cubic feet

Following are dimensions and explanations of some of the design studies reviewed:

Design Study	Durations/Dimensions
Davenport et al. (1963)	30 days minimum volume = 25 cubic feet; 180 days = 36.
Boeing (1966)	Earth orbiting space station; 180 days = 70 cubic feet.
Celentano et al. (1963)	200 days; tolerance = 40; performance = 75; optimal = 134 cubic feet.
Stuster (1986)	Systematic comparative analysis; 90 days = 84 cubic feet.
Righter et al. (1971)	Habitability guidelines; 180 days; four options: 103, 138, 234, and 244 cubic feet.
Fraser (1968a)	Lovelace intangibles study; "long duration" = 130 cubic feet.
Fraser (1966)	60 days = 150 cubic feet.
Loewy and Snaith (1972)	Earth orbital station = 169 cubic feet.
Showalter et al. (1972)	Lunar habitability system; 202 and 255 cubic feet.

CHAPTER 17. REMOTE MONITORING OF HUMAN PERFORMANCE AND ADJUSTMENT

1. *The Log of the U.S. Naval Mobile Construction Battalion (Special)* was maintained by Lt. Comdr. David Canham, Jr., from December 1955 through March 1957, while the Seabees were preparing the Williams Air Operating Facility at McMurdo Sound for the IGY. A highly disruptive schizophrenia emerged among the crew during their period of isolation (see chapter 1). The crewman's mental problem and the disruption that it caused prompted the recommendation, recorded in the Log, that a psychiatrist be made available for the "long range observation of wintering personnel."

PART III. THE IMPLICATIONS FOR THE FUTURE

1. Cherry-Garrard's version of this comparison, as stated in the preface to the second English edition (1930) of *The Worst Journey in the World*, differs little from the version related by Lansing:

   > For a joint scientific and geographic piece of organization, give me Scott; for a winter journey, Wilson; for a dash to the Pole and nothing else, Amundsen; and if I am in the devil of a hole and want to get out of it, give me Shackleton every time. (P. 6)

   Also, it has been said that Scott should have devoted more attention to planning and testing and to the development of procedures to guide emergency responses. Cherry-Garrard opens his book, *The Worst Journey in the World*, with the sentence: "Scott used to say that the worst part of an expedition was over when the preparation was finished." Apparently Scott was not fully prepared for either of his major expeditions. Cherry-Garrard describes the first several months of the British Antarctic Expedition of 1901–4 (known as Scott's first expedition, or the *Discovery* Expedition, from the name of the ship on which the party sailed) as a series of equipment failures and procedural mistakes. Scott (1905) acknowledged the condition when he wrote: "Not a single article of the outfit had been tested; and amid the general ignorance that prevailed the lack of system was painfully apparent in everything." Scott's lack of planning was apparent in the *Terra Nova* Expedition, as well. Neither the ponies nor the motorized tractors had been properly tested to evaluate their feasibility for the trip to the pole. But, most important, had Scott developed and clearly communicated appropriate procedures to the support teams, the polar party probably would have been rescued before they succumbed to starvation and the elements. Sitting with his comrades in their tent, while waiting for death to claim them, Scott wrote in his journal, "We took risks, we knew we took them; things have come out against us, and therefore we have no cause for complaint."

2.   Nansen and Johansen departed their winter lair on 19 May 1896. They made their way south alternating between pulling their small sleds over the ice and paddling or sailing their kayaks, as conditions permitted. The sleds carried the kayaks over ice floes and were then lashed to the walrus-hide decks of the kayaks for water travel. High winds frequently confined them to their small tent for days at a time, slowing their progress.

By 12 June, twenty-four days after departing their hut, they were short of provisions and confused about their location. They tied off their kayaks at the edge of a floe and began to climb to a high point on the ice to get a better perspective on their surroundings. A sudden change in the wind caused the kayaks to break free, carrying away all of the remaining supplies and equipment. The kayaks were lashed together and their high rigging caught the wind. The two explorers ran to the edge of the ice where Nansen tossed his watch to Johansen, took off a few outer garments, then jumped into the water and swam toward the drifting kayaks. Both men realized the danger involved, but they realized instantly that they would not survive without their equipment and boats.

Nansen was nearly exhausted when he finally caught up with the flimsy craft. He pulled himself onto the deck with great difficulty and lay there panting. In a condition that must have approached hypothermia, Nansen paddled the kayaks back to the ice floe and his waiting comrade. He changed into dry clothes, climbed into a sleeping bag for warmth, then slept. They took to the kayaks again the next day.

As they were making their way through the floes in separate kayaks on 15 June, a solitary walrus suddenly shot up out of the water next to Nansen, threw itself over the deck, and punctured the craft's hull with its tusks. Nansen hit the walrus as hard as he could with his paddle, but the creature attacked again, nearly capsizing the boat and spilling its contents into the sea. Nansen reached for his rifle, but when he turned back to shoot, the walrus was nowhere to be seen. Nansen made it safely to an ice floe where he patched his kayak as his clothes, sleeping bag, and photographic equipment dried in the Arctic air.

Two days later, Nansen arose to begin the daily routine of polar life. He started the fire, put a pot of fresh ice on to boil, cut up some of the remaining meat, then added it to the pot. He was nearly back into his sleeping bag to wait in warmth for their meager breakfast when he noticed the mist rising off the ice, revealing nearby land. He climbed to a high point for a better view. As he was staring in awe at the "Arctic majesty" Nansen thought he heard a dog bark. He roused Johansen from his sleep, dumped most of their remaining food into the pot, ate a quick meal, then set off over the ice toward the land from which he thought the sound must have come. As he approached he heard a shout—the first unknown human voice he had heard in three years, and the only voice other than his own and Johansen's in more than a year. His heart pounded with excitement as he ran closer and yelled with all of his strength. He heard another shout, then saw a dark figure in the distance. He waved his hat. The figure waved back. At a distance, Nansen heard the man speak to his dog in English; he concluded that this must be Frederick Jackson, the English explorer who he knew had been planning an expedition to Franz Josef Land.

The two men approached each other, then shook hands, but Jackson did not recognize Nansen even though they had met previously. They spoke for several minutes before Jackson stopped suddenly, peered into Nansen's face, then asked quickly, "Aren't you Nansen?" Nansen later wrote:

> On one side the civilized European in an English check suit and high rubber water-boots, well shaved, well groomed, bringing with him a perfume of scented soap, perceptible to the wild man's sharpened senses; on the other side the wild man clad in dirty rags, black with oil and soot, with long uncombed hair and a shaggy beard, black with smoke, with a face in which the natural fair complexion could not possibly be discerned through the thick layer of fat and soot which a winter's endeavors with warm water, moss, rags, and at last a knife, had sought in vain to remove. No one suspected who he was or whence he came. (1897, vol. 2, 529–30)

Nansen and Johansen spent the next several weeks in the relative comfort of Jackson's Russian-style log cabin at Cape Flora, Franz Joseph Land. They were grateful for the hospitality, but eager to return to their homes and concerned about their shipmates on the *Fram*. To everyone's delight, Jackson's resupply ship, *Windward*, made it through the ice pack on 26 July. Nansen and Johansen were on board when the ship departed for Norway on 7 August, under full sail and steam.

The *Windward* sailed into Vardö Haven six days later. Nansen reports that he and Johansen were in a small boat headed for shore even before the *Windward's* anchor was dropped. Their first stop was the telegraph office, where Nansen placed on the counter a bundle of nearly 100 telegrams to be sent. The manager of the office hesitated at first. It was an extraordinary order and the men looked like pirates despite their best efforts and the hospitality of the British expedition. His attitude changed abruptly, however, when his eyes fell on Nansen's distinctive signature. The man was delighted to be the person to inform the world that two members of the Norwegian Polar Expedition had returned safely from the farthest north, and they expected the *Fram* to be home soon. Nansen received the following telegram a week later, on 20 August 1896:

> Fram *arrived in good condition. All well on board. Shall start at once for Tromsö. Welcome home!*
>
> —Otto Sverdrup

CHAPTER 18. PRINCIPLES OF HABITABILITY AND OTHER LESSONS LEARNED

1. Creedon (1991) offers another reason for providing a well-designed habitat for future space explorers:

    > The Spartan life on the Soviet space station *Mir* will never quite do, and how could it? This country isn't Sparta, it is the modern Athens; and the American desire to bring a certain civility into space, to bring our values with us, is a noble one—at least in theory.

REFERENCES

Altman, I. 1973. An ecological approach to the functioning of socially isolated groups. In *Man In Isolation and Confinement*, edited by J. E. Rasmussen, 241–70. Chicago: Aldine Publishing Co.

Amundsen, R. [1912] 1976. *The South Pole: An Account of the Antarctic Expedition in the* Fram *1910–1912*. London: John Murray.

Bakalar, N. L. 1991. *Deep Freeze Evaluations*. Bethesda, Md.: Department of Psychiatry, National Naval Medical Center.

Barabaz, A. F. 1984. Antarctic isolation and imaginative involvement: Preliminary findings. *International Journal of Clinical and Experimental Hypnosis* 32:296–300.

Bender, H. E., and J. Fracchia. 1971. *Habitability System Environmental Requirements and Design Guidelines for Group Stability*. Washington, D.C.: National Aeronautics and Space Administration. Report No. CR 115179.

Binder, A. 1964. Statistical theory. *Annual Review of Psychology*, 15:277–310.

Blair, S. 1986. Untitled presentation. In Behavioral issues associated with isolation and confinement: A panel discussion conducted at the Tenth Psychology in the DoD Symposium, J. Stuster, chair and ed., U.S. Air Force Academy, Colorado Springs, Colo., 17 April.

Boeing Aerospace Company. 1983. *Space Station/Nuclear Submarine Analogs*. Granada Hills, Calif.: National Behavioral Systems.

Boeing Aircraft Company. 1966. Preliminary technical data for earth orbiting space station. In *Standards & Criteria*, Vol. II, Report No. MSC-EA-R-66-1.

Brenner, M., E. T. Doherty, and T. Shipp. 1994. Speech measures indicating workload demand. *Aviation, Space, and Environmental Medicine* 65 (January):21–26.

Burns, N. M., R. Chambers, and E. Hendler, eds. 1963. *Unusual Environments and Human Behavior*. London: Free Press of Glencoe.

Byrd, Richard E. 1935. Discovery: *The Story of the Second Byrd Expedition*. New York: G. P. Putnam and Sons.

———. 1938. *Alone*. New York: G. P. Putnam's Sons.

Cantrell, G. K., and B. O. Hartman. 1967. *Application of Time and Workload Analysis Techniques to Transport Flyers*. Brooks Air Force Base, Texas: School of Aerospace Medicine. Report No. SAM-TR-67-71.

Carr, G. 1986. Untitled presentation. In Behavioral issues associated with isolation and confinement: A panel discussion conducted at the Tenth Psychology in the DoD Symposium, J. Stuster, chair and ed. U.S. Air Force Academy, Colorado Springs, Colo., 17 April.

Celentano, J. T., D. Amorelli, and G. G. Freeman. 1963. Establishing a habitability index for space stations and planetary bases. *Proceedings of the American Institute of Aeronautics and Astronautics* 63:139.

Cherry-Garrard, Apsley. 1930. *The Worst Journey in the World*. New York: Dial Press.

Chiles, W. D. 1982. Workload, task, and situational factors as modifiers of complex human performance. Chap. 2 in Vol. 3 of *Stress and Performance Effectiveness. Human Performance and Productivity,* edited by E. A. Alluisi and E. A. Fleishman. Hillsdale, N.J.: Lawrence Erlbaum Associates.

Chiles, W. D., and O. S. Adams. 1961. *Human Performance and the Work-Rest Schedule*. Wright-Patterson Air Force Base, Ohio: Aeronautical Research Laboratory. Report No. ASD TR 61-270.

Clearwater, Y. A., and R. G. Coss. 1991. Functional aesthetics to enhance well-being in isolated and confined settings. In *From Antarctica to Outer Space: Life in Isolation and Confinement,* edited by A. Harrison, Y. Clearwater, and C. McKay. New York: Springer-Verlag.

Cleaver, A. H., and E. J. Stann. 1988. *Voyage to the Southern Ocean: The Letters of Lieutenant William Reynolds from the U.S. Exploring Expedition 1838–1842*. Annapolis, Md.: Naval Institute Press.

Collins, Michael. 1990. *Mission to Mars: An Astronaut's Vision of Our Future in Space*. New York: Grove Weidenfield.

Compton, W. D., and C.D. Benson. 1983. *Living and Working in Space: A History of* Skylab. Washington, D.C.: National Aeronautics and Space Administration.

Connors, M. M., A. A. Harrison, and F. R. Akins. 1985. *Living Aloft: Human Requirements for Extended Spaceflight*. Washington, D.C.: National Aeronautics and Space Administration.

Cook, Frederick A. [1900] 1980. *Through the First Antarctic Night 1898-1899: A Narrative of the Voyage of the* Belgica *among Newly Discovered Lands and over an Unknown Sea about the South Pole*. Montreal: McGill-Queen's University Press.

Cooper, G. E., and R. P. Harper, Jr. 1969. *The Use of Pilot Ratings in the Evaluation of Aircraft Handling Qualities*. Washington, D.C.: National Aeronautics and Space Administration.

Cooper, H. S. F., Jr. 1976. *A House In Space*. New York: Holt Rinehart, and Winston.

Cornelius, P. E. 1991. Life in Antarctica. In *From Antarctica to Outer Space: Life in Isolation and Confinement,* edited by A. Harrison, Y. Clearwater, and C. McKay. New York: Springer-Verlag.

Coss, R. G., and M. Moore. 1990. All that glistens: Water connotations in surface finishes. *Ecological Psychology* 2:367–80.

Coss, R. G., and S. R. Towers. 1988. Provocative aspects of pictures of animals in confined settings. *Anthrozoös* 3, no. 3.

Covault, C. 1988. Record Soviet manned space flight raises human endurance questions. *Aviation Week and Space Technology*, 4 January, 25.

Creedon, J. 1991. Editorial. *Final Frontier* 4, no. 5:63

Dana, Richard Henry. [1840] 1927. *Two Years before the Mast*. New York: Grosset & Dunlap.

Davenport, E. E., S. P. Congdon, and B. F. Pierce. 1963. The minimum volumetric requirements of man in space. *AIAA* 63:250.

David, L. 1990. Antarctica eyed for cheap Mars simulations. *Space News*, 2 July.

Doherty, E. T. 1991. Speech analysis techniques for detecting stress. In *Proceedings of the Human Factors Society 35th Annual Meeting*. Santa Monica, Calif.: The Human Factors Society 689–93.

Dolgin, D. L., and G. D. Gibb. 1989. Personality assessment in aviator selection. In *Aviation Psychology*, edited by R. S. Jensen. Brookfield, Vt.: Gower Publishing Co.

Doll, R. E., and E.K.E. Gunderson. 1969. *Hobby Interest and Leisure Activity Behavior among Station Members in Antarctica*. San Diego, Calif.: U.S. Navy Medical Neuropsychiatric Research Unit. Unit Report No. 69–34.

———. 1970. The relative importance of selected behavioral characteristics of group members in an extreme environment. *Journal of Psychology* 75:231–37.

Douglas, W. K. 1986a. *Human Performance Issues Arising from Manned Space Station Missions*. Moffett Field, Calif.: Ames Research Center. NASA Contractor Report 3942.

———. 1986b. Untitled presentation. Behavioral issues associated with isolation and confinement: A panel discussion conducted at the Tenth Psychology in the DoD Symposium, J. Stuster, chair and ed., U.S. Air Force Academy, Colorado Springs, Colo., 17 April.

Dunham, R. 1996. *Spy Sub: A Top Secret Mission to the Bottom of the Pacific*. Annapolis, Md.: Naval Institute Press.

Earls, J. H. 1969. Human adjustment to an exotic environment: The nuclear submarine. *Archives of General Psychiatry* 20:117–23.

Eberhard, J. W. 1967. *The Problem of Off-Duty Time in Long-Duration Space Missions*. 3 vols. NASA CR 96721. McLean, Va.: Serendipity Associates.

Eddowes, E. E. 1961. Survey of leisure time activity, implications for the design of a space vehicle. *Aerospace Medicine* 32:541–44.

Edholm, O. G., and E.K.E. Gunderson. 1973. *Polar Human Biology*. London: William Heinman Medical Books.

Evans, G. W., D. Stokols, and S. Carrere. 1988. *Human Adaptation to Isolated and Confined Environments: Preliminary Findings of a Seven Month Antarctic*

Winter-Over Human Factors Study. Washington, D.C.: National Aeronautics and Space Administration.

Fiennes, R. 1993. *Mind over Matter: The Epic Crossing of the Antarctic Continent.* New York: Delacorte Press.

Foley, T. 1995. NASA team modifies Mars Direct mission. *Space News* 30 January, 8.

Foushee, H. C., and R. L. Helmreich. 1988. Group interaction and flight crew performance. In *Human Factors in Aviation*, edited by E. L. Weiner and D. C. Nagel. New York: Academic Press, 189–228.

Fraser, T. M. 1966. *The Effects of Confinement as a Factor in Manned Space Flight.* Albuquerque, N. Mex.: Lovelace Foundation. NASA CR 511.

———. 1968a. *The Intangibles of Habitability during Long Duration Space Missions.* Albuquerque, N. Mex.: Lovelace Foundation. NASA CR 1084.

———. 1968b. Leisure and recreation in long duration space missions. *Human Factors* 10, 483–88.

Fuson, R. H., ed. and trans. 1987. *The Log of Christopher Columbus.* Camden, Maine: International Marine Publishing Co.

Gibson, E. G. 1975. *Skylab 4* crew observations. Chapter 3 of *Biomedical Results from* Skylab. Washington, D.C.: National Aeronautics and Space Administration.

Gunderson, E.K.E. 1963. Emotional symptoms in extremely isolated groups. *Archives of General Psychiatry* 9, 362–68.

———. 1966a. *Adaptation to Extreme Environments: Prediction of Performance.* San Diego, Calif.: U.S. Navy Medical Neuropsychiatric Research Unit. Unit Report No. 66-17.

———. 1966b. *Selection for Antarctic Service.* San Diego, Calif.: U.S. Navy Medical Neuropsychiatric Research Unit. Unit Report No. 66-15.

———. 1968a. *Interpersonal Compatibility in Restricted Environments.* San Diego, Calif.: U.S. Navy Medical Neuropsychiatric Research Unit. Unit Report No. 7-24.

———. 1968b. Mental health problems in Antarctica. *Archives of Environmental Health* 17:558–64.

———. 1968. *Psychiatric Problems in Polar Environments.* San Diego, Calif.: U.S. Navy Medical Neuropsychiatric Research Unit. Unit Report No. 68-4.

———. 1973a. Psychological studies in Antarctica: A review. In *Polar Human Biology*, edited by O. G. Edholm and E.K.E. Gunderson. 352–61.

———. 1973b. Individual behavior in confined or isolated groups. In *Man in Isolation and Confinement*, edited by J. E. Rasmussen. 145–66.

Gunderson, E.K.E., and P. D. Nelson. 1963. Adaptation of small groups to extreme environments. *Aerospace Medicine* 34, 1111–15.

———. 1964. *Adaptation of Scientists to the Antarctic.* San Diego, Calif.: U.S. Navy Medical Neuropsychiatric Research Unit. Unit Report No. 64-5.

Gunderson, E.K E., and D. Ryman. 1967. *Group Homogeneity, Compatibility, and Accomplishment*. San Diego, Calif.: U.S. Navy Medical Neuropsychiatric Research Unit. Unit Report No. 67-16.

Guttridge, L. F. 1986. *Icebound: The* Jeannette *Expedition's Quest for the North Pole*. Annapolis, Md.: Naval Institute Press.

Hackman, R. J., and R. E. Walton, R. E. 1986. Leading groups in organizations. In *Designing Effective Work Groups*, edited by P. S. Goodman & Associates. San Francisco: Jossey-Bass, 72–119.

Halberg, F. 1959. Physiologic 24-hour periodicity in human beings and mice, the lighting regimen and daily routine. In *Photoperiodism and Related Phenomena in Plants and Animals*, edited by R. B. Withrow. Washington, D.C.: American Association for the Advancement of Science, 803–78.

Harrison, A., Y. Clearwater, and C. McKay. 1991. *From Antarctica to Outer Space: Life in Isolation and Confinement*. New York: Springer-Verlag.

Heyerdahl, Thor. 1950. Kon-Tiki. New York: Rand McNally and Co.

———. 1971. *The* Ra *Expeditions*. New York: Doubleday and Co.

Hockey, G.R.J. 1986. Changes in operator efficiency as a function of environmental stress, fatigue, and circadian rhythms. In *Handbook of Perception and Human Performance*, edited by K. Boff and J. P. Thomas. New York: Wiley & Sons.

Houtchens, B. 1983. *System for the Management of Trauma and Emergency Surgery in Space*. Austin: University of Texas, Department of Surgery.

Huey, B., and C. D. Wickens, eds. 1993. *Workload Transition: Implications for Individual and Team Performance*. Washington, D.C.: National Academy Press.

Huntford, R. 1984. *Scott and Amundsen: The Race to the South Pole*. New York: Altheneum.

———. 1986. *The Last Place on Earth*. New York: Weidenfeld and Nicolson.

Huntford, R., ed. 1987. *The Amundsen Photographs*. New York: Atlantic Monthly Press.

Ignatius, A. 1992. Russian psychiatrist tries to make sure Russian cosmonaut stays up. *Wall Street Journal*, 5 February.

Jensen, R. S., and C. S. Biegelski. 1989. Cockpit resource management. In *Aviation Psychology*, edited by R. S. Jensen. Brookfield, Vt.: Gower Publishing Co., 176–209.

Johnson, C. C. 1975. Skylab *Experiment M487: Habitability/Crew Quarters*. Houston, Tex: Johnson Space Center.

Johnson, J., and B. Finney. 1986. Structural approaches to the study of groups in space: A look at two analogs. *Journal of Social Behavior and Personality* 1:325–47.

Kanas, N. 1990. Psychological, psychiatric, and interpersonal aspects of long-duration space missions. *Journal of Spacecraft* 27:457–63.

Kanas, N., and W. E. Federson. 1971. *Behavioral, Psychiatric, and Sociological Problems of Long-Duration Space Missions*. Houston, Tex.: Johnson Space Center. NASA TM X-58067.

Kanki, B. G., V. G. Folk, and C. M. Irwin. 1991. Communication variation and aircrew performance. *International Journal of Aviation Psychology* 1:149–62.

Karnes, E. W., J. K. Thomas, and L. A. Loudis. 1971. Recreational preferences in potential space crew populations. *Human Factors* 13:51–58.

Kaufman, J. E., ed. 1981. *IES Lighting Handbook: Application Volume*. New York: Illuminating Engineering Society of North America.

Kelly, A. D., and N. Kanas. 1994. Leisure time activities in space: A survey of astronauts and cosmonauts. *Acta Astronautica* 32: 451–57.

Kerwin, J. P. 1975. Skylab 2 crew observations and summary. Chap. 4 of *Biomedical Results from* Skylab. Houston, Tex.: Johnson Space Center.

Kinney, J.A.S., S. M. Luria, C. L. McKay, and A. P. Ryan. 1979. Vision of submariners. In *Undersea Biomedical Research* 6: Supplement, Preventive aspects of submarine medicine, S163–64.

Klein, T. J. 1970. A workload simulation model for predicting human performance requirements in the pilot-aircraft environment. *Proceedings of the 14th Annual Meeting of the Human Factors Society*, San Francisco: The Human Factors Society.

Kubis, J. F. 1965. Habitability: General Principles and applications to space vehicles. Paper presented at the Second International Symposium on Basic Environmental Problems of Man in Space, Paris. Quoted in *Development of the Lunar Habitability System*, edited by D. T. Showalter and T. B. Malone. Alexandria, VA: Matrix Research Company, 1972.

Labov, W., and J. Waletzky. 1967. Narrative analysis: Oral versions of personal experience. In *Essays on the Verbal and Visual Arts*, edited by J. Helm. Seattle, Wash: University of Seattle Press.

Lansing, A. [1959] 1994. *Endurance: Shackleton's Incredible Voyage*. New York: Carroll and Graf Publishers.

La Patra, J. W. 1968. *Moon Lab: Preliminary Design of a Manned Lunar Laboratory*. A Stanford–Ames Summer Faculty Workshop Study. Moffett Field, Calif.: National Aeronautics and Space Administration.

Lebedev, Valentin. [1983] 1988. *Diary of a Cosmonaut*. College Station, Tex.: Phytoresource Research, Inc. Originally published in Russian.

Lenorovitz, J. M. 1982. Control center supports Soviet *Salyut* spacecraft. *Aviation Week and Space Technology* 26 July, 94–96.

Loewy, R., and W. Snaith. 1972. *Habitability Study: Earth Orbital Space Stations*. New York: Loewy & Snaith, Inc. NASA CR 124276.

Logan, J. S., E. L. Shulman, and P. C. Johnson. 1983. *Health Care Delivery System for Long Duration Manned Space Operations*. Intersociety Conference on Environmental Systems, July 11–13, San Francisco, Calif. Houston, Tex.: Johnson Space Center.

Lugg, D. 1973. Anatomy of a group in Antarctica. M.D. thesis. Adelaide, Australia: University of Adelaide.

———. 1977. *Physiological Adaptation and Health of an Expedition in Antarctica with Comment on Behavioural Adaptation*. (Cited in Rivolier and Bachelard, 1988.) Australian National Antarctic Research Expedition (ANARE) Scientific Report, Series B (4), No. 126. Canberra, Australia: ANARE.

———. 1979. Appendicitis in polar regions. Diploma in Polar Studies. Scott Polar Research Institute, University of Cambridge.

———. 1991. Current international human factors research in Antarctica. In *From Antarctica to Outer Space: Life in Isolation and Confinement*, edited by A. Harrison, Y. Clearwater, and C. McKay. New York: Springer-Verlag.

MacDonald, E. A. 1969. *Polar Operations*. Annapolis, Md.: U.S. Naval Institute Press.

Mandler, G. 1979. Thought processes, consciousness, and stress. In *Human Stress and Cognition: An Information Processing Approach*, edited by V. Hamilton and D. M. Warburton. Chichester, England: Wiley and Sons.

Mark, H., and H. Smith. 1991. Fast track to Mars, *Aerospace America*, 36–41.

Mason, J. A., and P. C. Johnson, eds. 1984. *Space Station Medical Science Concept*. Houston, Tex.: Johnson Space Center. NASA TM-58255.

Matusov, A. L. 1968. Morbidity among members of the Tenth Soviet Antarctic Expedition. *Soviet Antarctic Expedition* 38–256. (Cited in Rivolier and Bachelard, 1988.)

McGuire, F., and S. Tolekin. 1961. Group adjustment at the South Pole. *Journal of Mental Science* 107:954–60.

Melville, Herman. [1850] 1988. *White-Jacket*. Annapolis, Md.: Naval Institute Press.

Mocellin, J., and P. Suedfeld. 1991. Voices from the ice: Diaries of polar explorers. *Environment and Behavior* 23:704–22.

Moore-Ede, M. C., F. M. Sulzman, and C. A. Fuller. 1982. *The Clocks That Time Us*. Cambridge, Mass.: Harvard University Press.

Moorehead, A. 1969. *Darwin and the* Beagle. New York: Harper and Row.

Mostert, N. 1974. *Supership*. New York: Alfred A. Knopf.

Mountfield, D. 1974. *A History of Polar Exploration*. New York: Dial Press.

Mowat, Farley. 1977. *Ordeal by Ice: The Search for the Northwest Passage*. Toronto: McClelland and Steward, Ltd.

Mullin, C. S., Jr. 1960. Some psychological aspects of isolated Antarctic living. *American Journal of Psychiatry* 117:323–27.

Mullin, C. S., Jr., and H. J. Connery. 1959. Psychological studies at an Antarctic IGY station. *U.S. Armed Forces Medical Journal* 10:290–96.

Mullin, C. S., H. J. Connery, and F. A. Wouters. 1958. *A Psychological-Psychiatric Study of a IGY Station in Antarctica*. Bethesda, Md.: U.S. Navy, Bureau of Medicine and Surgery, Neuropsychiatric Division.

Mumford, M. D., J. O'Connor, T. C. Clifton, M. S. Connelly, and S. J. Zaccaro. 1994. Background data constructs as predictors of leadership behavior. *Human Performance* 6, no. 2:151–95.

Nansen, Fridtjof. 1897. *Farthest North*. 2 vols. New York: Harper & Brothers.

Nardini, J. E., R. S. Herrmann, and J. E. Rasmussen. 1962. Navy psychiatric assessment in the Antarctic, *American Journal of Psychiatry* 119:97–105.

Natani, K., and J. T. Shurley. 1974. Sociopsychological aspects of a winter vigil at South Pole Station. In *Human Adaptability to Antarctic Conditions*, edited by E.K.E. Gunderson. Vol. 22. Washington, D.C.: Antarctic Research Service, American Geophysical Union, 89–114.

National Academy of Sciences (NAS). 1972. *Human Factors in Long-Duration Spaceflight*. Washington D.C.: National Academy of Sciences.

National Aeronautics and Space Administration (NASA). 1974. *Lessons Learned from the* Skylab *Program*. Houston, Tex.: Johnson Space Center.

———. 1976. *The Methods and Importance of Man–Machine Engineering Evaluation in Zero-G*. Houston, Tex.: Johnson Space Center. *Skylab* Experience Bulletin No. 26.

National Aeronautics and Space Administration/National Science Foundation (NASA/NSF). 1990. *Use of Antarctic Analogs to Support the Space Exploration Initiative*. Washington, D.C.: National Aeronautics and Space Administration and National Science Foundation.

Nelson, P. D. 1962. *Leadership in Small Isolated Groups*. San Diego, Calif.: U.S. Navy Medical Neuropsychiatric Research Unit. Unit Report No. 62-13.

———. 1964a. *An Evaluation of the Popular Leader*. San Diego, Calif.: U.S. Navy Medical Neuropsychiatric Research Unit. Unit Report No. 63-9.

———. 1964b. Similarities and differences among leaders and followers. *Journal of Applied Psychology* 63:161–67.

———. 1964c. Supervisor esteem and personnel evaluation. *Journal of Applied Psychology* 48:106–9.

———. 1965. *Psychological Aspects of Antarctic Living*. San Diego, Calif.: U.S. Navy Medical Neuropsychiatric Research Unit. Unit Report No. 64-28.

———. 1973. Indirect observation of groups. In *Man in Isolation and Confinement*, edited by J. E. Rasmussen. Chicago: Aldine Publishing Co.

Nelson, P. D., and E.K.E. Gunderson. 1963a. *Effective Individual Performance in Small Antarctic Stations: A Summary of Criterion Studies*. San Diego, Calif.: U.S. Navy Medical Neuropsychiatric Research Unit. Unit Report No. 63-8.

———. 1963b. *Personal History Correlates of Performance among Military Personnel*. San Diego, Calif.: U.S. Navy Medical Neuropsychiatric Research Unit. Unit Report No. 63-20.

Nelson, P. D., and J. M. Ovick. 1964. *Personnel History Correlates of Performance among Civilian Personnel in Small Antarctic Stations*. San Diego, Calif.: U.S. Navy Medical Neuropsychiatric Research Unit. Unit Report No. 64-4.

Newkirk, D. 1990. *Almanac of Soviet Manned Space Flight*. Houston, Tex.: Gulf Publishing Co.

Nicholas, J. M., and L. W. Penwell. 1995. A proposed profile of the effective leader in human spaceflight based on findings from analog environments. *Aviation, Space, and Environmental Medicine* 66, no. 1:63–72.

Nowlis, D. P., E. C. Wortz, and H. Watters. 1972. Tektite II *Habitability Research Program*. Huntsville, Ala.: Marshall Space Flight Center. NASA Contractor Report 123496.

Oberg, J. E. 1982. *Mission to Mars: Plans and Concepts for the First Manned Landing*. Harrisburg, Pa.: Stackpole Books.

Oberg, J. E., and A. R. Oberg. 1986. *Pioneering Space*. New York: McGraw-Hill.

O'Leary, B. 1987. *Mars 1999*. Harrisburg, Pa.: Stackpole Books.

Owens, A. G. 1966. The assessment of individual performance in small Antarctic groups. Part I: OIC's rating scales. Research Report 3/66. Melbourne: I Psychological Research Unit, Australian Military Forces.

———. 1968. Some biographical correlates of assessed performance in small Antarctic groups. Research Report 12/68. Melbourne: I Psychological Research Unit, Australian Military Forces.

Owens, W. A. 1983. Background data. In *Handbook of Industrial and Organizational Psychology*, edited by M.D. Dunnette. New York: John Wiley & Sons, 609–44.

Palinkas, L. A. 1987a. *Antarctica as a Model for the Human Exploration of Mars*. San Diego, Calif.: Naval Health Research Center. Report No. 87-16.

———. 1987b. *Group Adaptation and Individual Adjustment in Antarctica: A Summary of Recent Research*. San Diego, Calif.: Naval Health Research Center. Report No. 87-24.

Palmai, G. 1963. Psychological observations on an isolated group in Antarctica. *British Journal of Psychiatry* 109:363–70.

Pinks, R. R. 1949. *Report of Psychological Survey of Arctic Air Force Loran Stations*. Bolling Air Force Base: Human Resources Research Laboratory. HHRL Report 1.

Pisoni, D. B., K. Johnson, and R. H. Bernacki. 1991. Effects of alcohol on speech. In *Proceedings of the Human Factors Society 35th Annual Meeting*. Santa Monica, Calif.: The Human Factors Society, 694–98.

Pope, F. E., and T. A. Rogers. 1968. Some psychiatric aspects of an Antarctic survival experiment. *Journal of Nervous and Mental Disease* 146:433–45.

Radloff, R. W. 1973. Observing isolated groups in field settings. In *Man in Isolation and Confinement*, edited by J. E. Rasmussen. Chicago: Aldine Publishing Company, 195–218.

Radloff, R. W., and R. Helmreich. 1968. *Groups under Stress: Psychological Research in* Sealab II. New York: Appleton-Century-Crofts.

Raney, M. 1994. Woman in a man's world: A personal and management perspective. In *Gender on Ice: Proceedings of a Conference on Women in*

Antarctica (under the auspices of the Australian Antarctic Foundation at Hobart, Tasmania), edited by K. Edwards and R. Graham. Canberra: Australian Government Publishing Service, 39–47.

Rasmussen, J. E., ed. 1973. *Man in Isolation and Confinement*. Chicago: Aldine Publishing Co.

Reichhardt, T. 1990. Marathon men. *Final Frontier* 3, no. 1:42–44, 55–56.

Riessman, C. K. 1993. *Narrative Analysis*. Newbury Park, Calif.: Sage Publications.

Righter, C. E., D. P. Nowlis, V. B. Dunn, N. J. Beltan, and E. C. Wortz. 1971. *Habitability Guidelines and Criteria*. Huntsville, Ala.: Marshall Space Flight Center. NASA CR 103028.

Rivolier, J., and Claude Bachelard. 1988. Studies of analogies between living conditions at an Antarctic scientific base and on a space station. Unpublished manuscript.

Rivolier, J., R. Goldsmith, D. J. Lugg, and A.J.W. Taylor. 1988. *Man in the Antarctic: The Scientific Work of the International Biomedical Expedition to the Antarctic (IBEA)*. New York: Taylor & Francis.

Rock, J. A. 1984. An expandable surgical chamber for use in conditions of weightlessness. *Aviation Space and Environmental Medicine* 55:403–4.

Rodgers, E. 1990. *Beyond the Barrier: The Story of Byrd's First Expedition to Antarctica*. Annapolis, Md.: Naval Institute Press.

Rohrer, J. H. 1961. Interpersonal relationships in small isolated groups. In *Psychophysiological Aspects of Space Flight*, edited by B. E. Flaherty. New York: Columbia University Press.

Rose, R. M., L. F. Fogg, R. L. Helmreich, and T. J. McFadden. 1994. Psychological predictors of astronaut effectiveness. *Aviation Space and Environmental Medicine* 65:910–15.

Ross, W. Gilles. 1985. *Arctic Whalers, Icy Seas: Narratives of the Davis Strait Whale Fishery*. Toronto: Irwin Publishing Co.

Ryumin, V. 1980. 175 days in space: A Russian cosmonaut's private diary, edited and translated by H. Gris. Unpublished manuscript.

Sale, K. 1991. *The Conquest of Paradise: Christopher Columbus and the Columbian Legacy*. New York: Plume Books.

Sandal, G. M., R. Værnes, and H. Ursin. 1995. Interpersonal relations during simulated space missions. *Aviation Space and Environmental Medicine* 66:617–24.

Santy, P. A. 1993. *Choosing the Right Stuff: The Psychological Selection of Astronauts and Cosmonauts*. Westport, Conn.: Praeger Publishers.

Santy, P. A., and D. R. Jones. 1994. An overview of international issues in astronaut psychological selection. *Aviation Space and Environmental Medicine* 65:900–3.

Satchell, M. 1983. Women who conquer the South Pole. *Parade Magazine*, 5 June, 16–17.

Scherer, K. R. 1986. Voice, stress, and emotion. In *Dynamics of Stress: Physiological, Psychological, and Social Perspectives,* edited by M. H. Appley and R. Trumbull. New York: Plenum Press.

Schiflett, S. G. 1991. Vocal indicators of stress, workload, and intoxication: Speech analysis techniques. In *Proceedings of the Human Factors Society 35th Annual Meeting.* Santa Monica, Calif.: The Human Factors Society.

Scott, A. J. 1994. Chronobiological considerations in shiftworker sleep and performance and shiftwork scheduling. *Human Performance* 7:207–33.

Scott, Robert Falcon. 1905. *Voyage of the* Discovery. New York: Dodd, Mead & Co.

Scott, W. B. 1995. United training stresses cockpit discipline. *Aviation Week & Space Technology* 142, 50–51, 6 February.

Sells, S. B. 1962. *Military Small Crew Performance under Isolation and Stress. Critical Review: Selection, Indoctrination, and Training for Arctic Remote Duty.* Fort Wainwright, Alaska: Arctic Aeromedical Laboratory.

———. 1973. The taxonomy of man in enclosed space. In *Man in Isolation and Confinement,* edited by J. E. Rasmussen. Chicago: Aldine Publishing Co.

Serxner, J. L. 1968. An experience in submarine psychiatry. *American Journal of Psychiatry* 125:25–30.

Sherrod, R. 1975. Men for the moon: How they were chosen and trained. In *Apollo Expedition to the Moon,* edited by E. M. Cortright. Washington, D.C.: National Aeronautics and Space Administration.

Showalter, D. T., and T. Malone. 1972. *The Development of a Lunar Habitability System.* Houston, Tex.: Johnson Space Center. NASA Contractor Report 1676.

Shurley, J. T. 1974. Physiological research at U.S. stations in Antarctica. In *Human Adaptability to Antarctic Conditions,* edited by E.K.E. Gunderson. Vol. 22. Washington, D.C.: Antarctic Research Service, American Geophysical Union.

Smith, W. M. 1961. Scientific personnel in Antarctica: Their recruitment, selection, and performance. *Psychological Reports* 9:163–82.

———. 1966. Observations over the lifetime of a small isolated group: Structure, danger, boredom, vision. *Psychological Reports* 19:475–514.

Smith, W. M., and M. B. Jones. 1962. Astronauts, Antarctic scientists, and personal autonomy. *Journal of Aerospace Medicine* 33:162–66.

Stokes, A. F., A. Belger, and K. Zhang. 1990. *Investigation of Factors Comprising a Model of Pilot Decision Making, Part 2: Anxiety and Cognitive Strategies in Expert and Novice Aviators.* Savoy: University of Illinois, Aviation Research Laboratory. Report No. ARL-90-9/SCEEE-90-2.

Strange, R. E. N.d. Thoughts on psychiatric screening of Antarctic winter-over personnel. Unpublished paper by a Navy psychiatrist involved in personnel selection and debriefing.

Strange, R. E., and W. J. Klein. 1973. Emotional and social adjustment of recent U.S. winter-over parties in isolated Antarctic stations. In *Polar Human Biology*, edited by O. G. Edholm and E.K.E. Gunderson.

Stuster, J. W. 1983. *Biological, Psychological, and Sociological Issues with Design Implications for a NASA Space Station, and Dimensions to Describe Space Station and Analogous Conditions.* Santa Barbara, Calif.: Anacapa Sciences, Inc. Technical Report 553-1.

———. 1984. *Summaries of Alternative Analogues to a NASA Space Station and Description of a Evaluation Methodology.* Santa Barbara, Calif.: Anacapa Sciences, Inc. Technical Report 553-2.

———. 1986. *Space Station Habitability Recommendations Based on a Systematic Comparative Analysis of Analogous Conditions.* Moffett Field, Calif.: Ames Research Center. NASA Contractor Report 3943.

———. 1989. *Rail Garrison Phase III Habitability Test: Final Report.* Norton Air Force Base, Calif.: U.S. Air Force Ballistic Systems Division.

———. 1990a. *Space Craft Design Issues: A Report to ESA's HABEMSI Study Team.* Santa Barbara, Calif.: Anacapa Sciences, Inc.

———. 1990b. *Space Craft Design Issues: A Report to ESA's HABEMSI Study Team Part 2, Lunar Base and a Mission to Mars.* Santa Barbara, Calif.: Anacapa Sciences, Inc.

Stuster, J. W., H. Goforth, K. Prusaczyk, and L. Meyer. 1994. *Analysis of the Most Physically Demanding Missions and Tasks Performed by Navy SEALs.* Santa Barbara, Calif.: Anacapa Sciences, Inc.

Sullivan, G. 1982. *Inside Nuclear Submarines.* New York: Dodd, Mead & Co.

Takahashi, J. S., and M. Zatz. 1982. Regulation of circadian rhythmicity. *Science* 217:1104–11.

Tansey, W. A., J. N. Wilson, and K. E. Schaefer. 1979. Analysis of the health data from 10 years of Polaris submarine patrols. In *Undersea Biomedical Research* 6: Supplement, Preventive aspects of submarine medicine.

Taylor, A.J.W. 1978. Antarctica psychometrika unspectacular. *New Zealand Antarctic Record* 6:36–45.

———. N.d. The selection of people for work in polar regions. Unpublished background paper prepared for the Working Group of the World Health Organization.

Tierney, P. 1984. Test by fire and ice. *Omni* 7, no. 3:116–22, 168.

Toby, A. 1988. Who gets jetlag? *Washington Post*, 10 May, H-1.

Todd, A. L. 1961. *Abandoned: The Story of the Greely Arctic Expedition 1881–1884.* New York: McGraw-Hill.

Værnes, R. 1991. *Human Isolation Study 1990.* Bergen, Norway: Norwegian Underwater Technology Center.

———. 1993. *EXEMSI '92.* Bergen, Norway: Norwegian Underwater Technology Center.

Værnes, R., M. Warncke, T. Bergan, and H. Ursin. 1988. Selecting the right crew for future space stations: An analysis of selection research on offshore divers, aviation pilots and other high risk groups in Scandinavia. In *Proceedings of the Colloquium on Space and Sea*, European Space Agency.

Vernikos-Danellis, J., C. M. Winget, C. S. Leach, and P. C. Rambaut. 1974. *Circadian, Endocrine and Metabolic Effects of Prolonged Bedrest: Two 56-Day Bedrest Studies*. Moffett Field, Calif.: Ames Research Center. NASA TM X-3051.

Webb, E. J., D. T. Campbell, R. D. Schwartz, and L. Sechrest. 1966. *Unobtrusive Measures: Nonreactive Research in the Social Sciences*. Chicago: Rand McNally.

Welford, A. T. 1968. *Fundamentals of Skill*. London: Methuen & Co.

———. *Skilled Performance: Perceptual and Motor Skills*. Palo Alto, Calif.: Scott, Foresman & Co.

Weybrew, B. B. 1957. *Psychological and Psychophysiological Effects of Long Periods of Submergence: Analysis of Data Collected During a 265-Hour Completely Submerged, Habitability Cruise Made by the USS* Nautilus. New London, Conn.: U.S. Naval Medical Research Laboratory.

———. 1963. Psychological problems of prolonged marine submergence. In *Unusual Environments and Human Behavior*, edited by N. M. Burns, R. Chambers, and E. Hendler. London: The Free Press of Glencoe.

———. 1979. *History of Military Psychology at the U.S. Naval Submarine Medicine Research Laboratory*. Groton, Conn.: Naval Submarine Medical Research Laboratory. NSMRL Report No. 917.

White, S. C., and J. H. Reed. 1963. Habitability in space stations. *Proceedings of the American Institute of Aeronautics and Astronautics* 63:139.

Wickens, C. D., A. F. Stokes, B. Barnett, and F. Hyman. 1988. Stress and pilot judgment: An empirical study using MIDIS, a microcomputer-based simulation. Proceedings of the Human Factors Society 32nd Annual Meeting. Santa Monica, Calif.: Human Factors Society.

Wilson, E. 1972. *Diary of the* Terra Nova *Expedition to the Antarctic, 1910–1912*. London: Blanford Press.

Wolbers, H. 1984 *The Human Role in Space*. Huntington Beach, Calif.: McDonnell Douglas Astronautics Company. MDC Report H1295.

Worsley, F. A. 1977. *Shackleton's Boat Journey*. New York: W. W. Norton.

Wortz, E. C., and D. P. Nowlis. [1974?] The design of habitability environments. Unpublished paper.

Wright, M. W., J. Chylinski, G. G. Sister, and B. Quarrington. 1967. Personality factors in the selection of civilians for isolated northern stations. *Canadian Psychologist*, 8a:23–31.

Zubek, J. P. 1963. Counteracting effects of physical exercise performed during prolonged perceptual deprivation. *Science* 142:504.

———. 1973. Behavioral and physiological effects of prolonged sensory and perceptual deprivation: A review. In *Man in Isolation and Confinement*, edited by J. E. Rasmussen. Chicago: Aldine Publishing Co., 9–83.

Zubrin, R., and D. Baker. 1990. Humans to Mars in 1999. *Aerospace America*, August, 30–41.

INDEX

Wolbers, Harry, 318
workload, 4, 74–94, 165; and food
preparation, 149–50, 162; high, 76–
80, 237, 314, 316; and leadership,
299, 313; low, 81–89, 222; and
remote monitoring, 289, 293–96;
and sleep, 49; transition from low
to high, 89–92
Worsley, Capt. Frank, 104, 108, 111,
248–49, 281

zeitgebers, 45, 47, 54–55, 243–44, 303,
312

ABOUT THE AUTHOR

Jack Stuster is a principal scientist at Anacapa Sciences, Inc., a human factors and applied behavioral sciences research firm located in Santa Barbara, California. He received a bachelor's degree in experimental psychology from the University of California, Santa Barbara, and master's and Ph.D. degrees in anthropology from the same institution. A certified professional ergonomist (C.P.E.), Dr. Stuster specializes in the measurement and enhancement of human performance in extreme environments.

 In addition to his work for the National Aeronautics and Space Administration and the European Space Agency, Dr. Stuster has studied the work performed by U.S. Navy SEALs, explosive ordnance disposal technicians, the crews of high-speed hovercraft, maintenance personnel, and military leaders. Dr. Stuster also conducts traffic safety research and instructs law enforcement and national security personnel in the use of advanced techniques for the analysis of criminal intelligence.

The **Naval Institute Press** is the book-publishing arm of the U.S. Naval Institute, a private, nonprofit society for sea service professionals and others who share an interest in naval and maritime affairs. Established in 1873 at the U.S. Naval Academy in Annapolis, Maryland, where its offices remain today, the Naval Institute has members worldwide.

Members of the Naval Institute receive the influential monthly magazine *Proceedings* and discounts on fine nautical prints and on ship and aircraft photos. They also have access to the transcripts of the Institute's Oral History Program and get discounted admission to any of the Institute-sponsored seminars offered around the country. Discounts are also available to the colorful bimonthly magazine *Naval History*.

The Naval Institute's book-publishing program, begun in 1898 with basic guides to naval practices, has broadened in recent years to include books of more general interest. Now the Naval Institute Press publishes about 100 titles each year, ranging from how-to books on boating and navigation to battle histories, biographies, ship and aircraft guides, and novels. Institute members receive discounts of 20 to 50 percent on the Press's nearly 600 books in print.

Full-time students are eligible for special half-price membership rates. Life memberships are also available.

For a free catalog describing Naval Institute Press books currently available, and for further information about joining the U.S. Naval Institute, please write to:

Membership Department
U.S. Naval Institute
118 Maryland Avenue
Annapolis, Maryland 21402-5035
Telephone: (800) 233-8764
Fax: (410) 269-7940
Web address: www.usni.org